SOUTHERN
Water,
SOUTHERN
Power

SOUTHERN
Water,
SOUTHERN
Power

How the Politics of Cheap
Energy and Water Scarcity
Shaped a Region

CHRISTOPHER J. MANGANIELLO

The University of North Carolina Press
Chapel Hill

Designed and set in Miller and Serifa types by Rebecca Evans
Manufactured in the United States of America

Portions of Chapters 1 and 2 appeared previously in somewhat different
form in Christopher J. Manganiello, "Hitching the New South to 'White
Coal': Water and Power, 1890–1933," *Journal of Southern History* 78, no. 2
(May 2012): 255–92. Reprinted with permission.

Portions of Chapter 5 appeared previously in somewhat different form
in Chris Manganiello, "Georgia's Urban Drought History. Who Knew?"
Flagpole Magazine, May 6, 2007.

The paper in this book meets the guidelines for permanence and durability
of the Committee on Production Guidelines for Book Longevity of the
Council on Library Resources.

The University of North Carolina Press has been a member of the
Green Press Initiative since 2003.

Jacket illustration: Buford Dam (Lake Lanier), 2007. STAFF/REUTERS/
Newscom.

Library of Congress Cataloging-in-Publication Data
Manganiello, Christopher J., 1973–
Southern water, Southern power : how the politics of cheap energy and
water scarcity shaped a region / Christopher J. Manganiello.
pages cm
Includes bibliographical references and index.
ISBN 978-1-4696-2005-3 (cloth : alk. paper)
ISBN 978-1-4696-2006-0 (ebook)
1. Water resources development—Social aspects—Southern States.
2. River engineering—Southern States—History. 3. Dams—Southern
States—Design and construction—History. 4. Water-supply—Political
aspects—Southern States. 5. Southern States—Economic conditions.
I. Title.
HD1694.A5M235 2015   333.91′40975—dc23
2014037020

Contents

Illustrations and Maps

Acknowledgments

Writing a book is exhilarating and exhausting. But finishing a book might be harder than the writing, particularly without institutional resources. The process has taken me far longer than I anticipated due to some expected twists and unexpected turns. Computer crashes, fire alarms prompting library evacuations, unanticipated extra hours consumed by my day job, and unanticipated family obligations were just some of the curve balls in the final throes. So it is with deep satisfaction that I can move beyond this project after acknowledging those who helped along the way.

Mark Simpson-Vos at the University of North Carolina Press has stuck with me over the years. I am grateful for the time and energy Mark and his staff, particularly Brandon Proia and Stephanie Wenzel, have invested in the project.

At Western Carolina University, where I discovered the seed for this project as a graduate student, I am thankful for the training, wisdom, and inspiration from Rob Ferguson, Gael Graham, Libby McRae, Daniel Menestres, Scott Philyaw, Daniel Pierce, Richard Starnes, and Vicki Szabo.

The University of Georgia was a great place to labor alongside some of the most productive and creative graduate students, faculty, and friends I have ever encountered, including Stephen Berry, Jim Cobb, Brian Drake, Chase Hagood, Shane Hamilton, John Hayes, Jim Gigantino, Darren Grem, Ivy Holliman, Catherine Holmes, John Inscoe, Tim Johnson, Robby Luckett, the late Jason Manthorne, Barton Meyers, Bethany Moreton, Steve Nash, Kathi Nehls, Tom Okie, Tore Olsson, Bruce Stewart, Drew Swanson, Levi Van Sant, and the Georgia Workshop in the History of Agriculture and Environment participants. A very patient Amber Ignatius did the heavy lifting necessary to assemble the base maps. I'd like to think the long conversations with Christina Davis, my adjunct-carpool-copilot, improved my teaching. Bert Way in particular was a reliable sounding board and source of southern environmental and geographical knowledge. I will always value his two cents. Paul Sutter has been the most important influence on this project. His endless enthusiasm, perfectly packaged advice, and inspirational intellectual scope have affected every page of just about everything I have written. I cannot thank Paul enough for all of the advice, professional opportunities, and energy he provided during and after my academic career.

When working outside the University of Georgia but while still engaged there, I was grateful when Mark Hersey and Claire Strom asked the right questions at the 2009 Workshop for the History of Environment, Agriculture, Technology, and Science. I must credit Jim Giesen for helping me think through the South's "water problem." Jeffrey Stine, Pete Daniel, and the National Museum of American History colloquium fellows fostered a wonderful intellectual environment at the Smithsonian Institution. Scout Blum, Marty Reuss, and Mart Stewart provided critical and useful feedback on conference papers.

Many librarians, archivists, and a few lawyers helped with this project, including Eugene Futato (University of Alabama), Leanda Gahegan (National Anthropological Archives), Herb Hartsook (South Carolina Political Collections), Guy Howard (National Archives Southeast Region), and Jill Severn (Richard B. Russell Library for Research and Political Studies). While I am acknowledging library staff, I especially want to thank all the library administrators who trust patrons will use digital cameras as research tools appropriately and safely. If I had not been empowered to make my own digital versions of critical documents, then this book would have been a very different product.

In 2012, I took a timely career turn into environmental public policy. I have learned more than I could have ever anticipated from Sally Bethea, Tonya Bonitatibus, Chandra Brown, Juliet Cohen, Joe Cook, Ben Emanuel, Jennette Gayer, Laura Hart, Neill Herring, Jenny Hoffner, Todd Holbrook, April Ingle, Lauren Joy, Colleen Kiernan, Emily Markesteyn, Gil Rogers, Gina Rogers, Gordon Rogers, Stephanie Stuckey Benfield, and Mark Woodall. This is probably as good a time as any to explain that this book is not a Georgia River Network project. The arguments, interpretations and conclusions—as well as any mistakes—presented here are my own.

The family matters. My siblings, and their growing families, have been remarkable trailblazers and teachers in their own right. My parents have offered unending support and truly believe in education and intellectual curiosity. As a parent myself, I see why I will never be able to repay my parents for all of their sacrifices.

I can happily say that my wife has been a part of my life for longer than I have been working on this project. In the time it took me to finish my degree she completed two while tending the garden, monitoring the books, keeping an eye on the family, and following her own career path. She also put up with a lot—those lost months I spent reading for comps, my research trips, my long absence on fellowship, and keeping us all going in the final mile. For those reasons and a whole lot more, I dedicate this book to her.

SOUTHERN
Water,
SOUTHERN
Power

Southern Water, Southern Power

Over the course of three years beginning in 2006, the Southeast faced the worst drought in its history. As rain stopped falling from the sky from northern Alabama to central North Carolina, rivers dried up, and residents of the southeastern part of the United States nervously watched water levels in reservoirs drop dramatically. The lack of rain and diminished river flows so alarmed energy producers and regulators from seven states that representatives from five investor-owned energy companies, five public energy generators, and multiple federal agencies quietly convened at Atlanta's Hartsfield-Jackson International Airport to discuss how to keep the lights on and avoid rolling blackouts.[1] In the South, water and power were inextricably connected.

The drought also stressed municipal drinking water supplies in momentous ways in 2007. One small Tennessee community's water source—a deep well—went dry, forcing the town to truck in water. By November, other communities—including North Carolina's capital, Raleigh—reported having only a three-month or less supply of water on hand. Southeastern residents unaccustomed to urban drought were clearly anxious; at least one Atlanta homeowner stockpiled thirty-six five-gallon water jugs in his basement. But the most visible consequence of the drought in Georgia—and a persistent source of local anxiety, regional conflict, and national media attention—was the growing ring of red clay around a blue reservoir named Lake Lanier.[2]

Located in northern Georgia, Lake Lanier is responsible for meeting the water needs of upward of 3 million metro Atlanta residents plus millions of people and countless uses farther downstream. The U.S. Army Corps of Engineers (the Corps), the federal agency responsible for managing Buford Dam, which impounds Lake Lanier, was releasing water from the dam into the Chattahoochee River to meet downstream needs in Alabama, Florida, and Georgia and to comply with federal laws. Besides meeting Atlanta's water purposes, Lake Lanier's regulated releases from Buford Dam were crucial to wastewater assimilation for dozens of communities; golf course and agricultural irrigation; industrial consumers like Coca Cola and Pepsi Co.; electric generation at hydro, coal, and nuclear facilities owned and operated by the Atlanta-based Southern Company's subsidiaries; and commercial and endangered aquatic species in Florida's Apalachicola River and Bay.[3] If Lake Lanier or the Chattahoochee below Buford Dam dried up, then the consequences were real. Modern life in the booming Sun Belt would grind to a halt.

As the lake's water level steadily dropped, Georgia officials grappled with a cascade of possible consequences for Lake Lanier and downstream needs if the drought were to continue. In an effort to nudge ordinary Georgians to save water, Governor Sonny Perdue declared October 2007 "Take a Shorter Shower Month." The state's Environmental Protection Division prohibited all outdoor watering in 61 of the state's 159 counties as the region's worst drought in history got even worse.[4] These state mandates helped preserve the region's water supply and sparked a culture of conservation among Georgia's citizens, but by the end of 2007 Lake Lanier was still eighteen feet below "full pool." State requirements, federal agency decisions, and human behavior alone could not refill the region's streams, rivers, and working reservoirs.

After three dry years, the region rebounded vividly. In September 2009, a series of storms dropped fifteen to twenty inches of rain throughout metro Atlanta in one seventy-two-hour period. Lake Lanier—drained to its record low point in December 2007—gained three feet alone during the September 2009 rainstorms. Yet these gains came with significant costs. Multiple Atlanta suburbs—from the affluent homes in Buckhead to manufactured "mobile" homes in Cobb County—flooded when area creeks and streams poured out of their banks during the cloudbursts. Authorities closed multiple interstate highways when the flooding Chattahoochee River washed over and submerged bridges. Officials blamed at least ten deaths on flooding and more than $500 million in damages on what experts now considered one of metro Atlanta's worst floods on record. In what became one of the state's wettest years, the rest of 2009's record rainfalls refilled Lanier, and the massive artificial lake reached full pool and pre-drought levels by October.[5] As reliant as the water levels in rivers and artificial lakes were on the vagaries of the weather, southerners were also very much responsible for their own water choices.

While Georgians and their neighbors suffered through a major swing from drought to flooding, a U.S. district court judge issued a ruling that made the region's water insecurity even worse. In July 2009, Judge Paul Magnuson determined that Congress had never authorized Lake Lanier to store municipal drinking water and that some metro Atlanta communities were illegally tapping the federal reservoir. Judge Magnuson ordered the Corps' engineers to reduce municipal water withdrawals from Lake Lanier to 1970s levels by July 2012 unless Alabama, Florida, and Georgia approved an Apalachicola-Chattahoochee-Flint River compact to end a twenty-year-long conflict over allocation of water between the three states—popularly referred to as a tristate water war. Though this order has since been overturned (and was subsequently appealed to the U.S. Supreme Court, which declined to hear the case), at the time the judge's strict interpretation of legal and political history suggested Congress had only authorized construction of the Lake Lanier reservoir and Buford Dam project in the 1940s for flood control, to produce hydropower, and to regulate stream flows for downstream navigation and other benefits. Even Atlanta's well-known Mayor William B. Hartsfield clearly understood congressional and the Corps' intent for Lake Lanier. He quipped before a Senate subcommittee in 1948 that Atlanta needed a reliable water supply, but the city was "not in the same category" as cities "in arid places in the West."[6]

Within days of Magnuson's 2009 legal order, Georgia's power struggle over water intensified. Metro Atlanta, a region comprised of over a dozen counties and more than 5 million people, had already been short of its water needs before Judge Magnuson's ruling. Governor Sonny Perdue launched a multiple-front response that exacerbated long-standing intrastate tensions. First, Governor Perdue drafted Michael Garrett, then the Georgia Power Company's CEO, to "quarterback" the state's response. This selection was calculated to unify and mobilize Georgia's corporate and utility interests, the stakeholders with the most to lose from heightened water insecurity—and with the most leverage on the local, state, and national levels. Garrett had climbed corporate ladders in the Southern Company's subsidiaries, with management and executive tours of duty in the eighty-year-old Atlanta-based corporation's even older subsidiaries: Alabama Power (established 1912) and Mississippi Power (1924).[7] Second, Perdue also hastily assembled a Water Contingency Task Force. Cochaired by Coca-Cola Enterprises' CEO John Brock and loaded with eighty-eight individuals who primarily represented metro Atlanta's corporate interests (including Home Depot, Delta Air Lines, Sun Trust Bank, Georgia-Pacific, and UPS), the task force looked around the state for solutions to Atlanta's impending municipal water shortage. After holding a series of closed-door meetings that legally barred public participation, the powerful task force released an official report on water supply alternatives for the sprawling southern megalopolis that brought all of the state's working rivers and reservoirs into sharp focus.[8]

The Task Force's December 2009 report provided Governor Perdue with a lengthy list of options to resolve metro Atlanta's future water supply challenges. One element of the report also ignited a "two Georgias" rhetoric that has forever pitted metro Atlanta against the rest of the state.[9] Among water supply choices—including "no regret" conservation measures, new water supply reservoirs, and desalination—the task force also evaluated interbasin transfers that could pipe water from the numerous corporate and federal reservoirs found throughout the state's hinterlands to slake metro Atlanta's core thirst. Two of the task force's potential tools specifically targeted the Savannah River valley's water resources and raised eyebrows. One of the interbasin transfer options would have pumped 50 million gallons of raw water per day from the Georgia Power Company's Lake Burton—constructed in the 1920s to store Tallulah River water and generate hydroelectricity, and now surrounded by million-dollar homes—over a low ridge that divides the Savannah and Chattahoochee River basins. Pumps, pipes, and creeks would direct the Savannah River basin's raw water into the Chattahoochee River basin and metro Atlanta's municipal water treatment and distribution systems some seventy miles distant. Another task force idea included a 100-million-gallons-per-day water withdrawal from the Corps' Lake Hartwell and hydroelectric dam project in rural Elbert County, also in the Savannah River basin. After pulling water from Lake Hartwell, the pumps would transmit water over rolling hills and shallow valleys via an eighty-mile pipeline to suburban Gwinnett County in metro Atlanta.[10] When skeptical boosters, elected officials, and newspaper editors from downstream cities and rural parts of the state discovered the interbasin transfers would tap their local rivers and water sources, they reminded constituents and readers that "Metro Atlanta wants Augusta's water" and told Atlanta to keep its "hands off the Savannah River."[11] Atlantans' demands—like those discussed in the task force's report—have historically pulled, with the strength of a tractor beam, the surrounding hinterlands and their natural resources into the city's orbit.

The "two Georgias" oratory amounted to more than simple political theater. During the 2010 General Assembly session, the Georgia state legislature and environmental agencies never actually considered specific interbasin transfers to resolve metro Atlanta's then-critical water problem. But the governor's Water Contingency Task Force menu motivated hinterland legislators—including at least 24 state senators (of 54) and 68 representatives (of 180)—to support legislation that would have made it difficult to transfer large quantities of water over great distances to water lawns and fill swimming pools in Atlanta.[12] The interbasin transfer legislation, however, stalled and died when a Senate Natural Resources and Environment Committee chairman refused to allow the bill out of committee or onto the floor for a full Senate vote knowing the bill would pass by a wide margin.[13] Amidst the worst drought in history, a destructive bout of flooding, and the prospect of new legal restrictions on the use of water from Lake Lanier, legislators jousted over theoretical projects that would have increased water insecurity throughout the region.

This high level of anxiety in a water-rich region was perplexing to me. For all of my adult life I have driven across and flown over the southeastern United States, and for the last decade I have researched the history of the region's relationship with its waterways. It is hard to go anywhere in the Piedmont or Blue Ridge and not find a stream, river, or big pool of water. Early on I discovered that all of the Southeast's major lakes not only are artificial, but many are privately managed. This basic fact sets the Southeast's history of water and power—of water supply, users, and rights—apart from other regions of the United States. As I studied the history of the region's hydraulic waterscape, the drought intensified, and I wondered why the Piedmont—a place with an average of forty-five to fifty inches of rain and a long agricultural legacy, as well as a documented history of flooding—was suffering. Why was a place dotted with lakes and known for its cotton, peaches, peanuts, humidity, swamps, and malaria embroiled in intrastate and regional conflicts typically associated with Los Angeles and Las Vegas in the Colorado River basin, or with California's and Idaho's irrigated valleys?

For a long time, the primary southern response to water problems was to bend rivers to meet human demands. As such, water problems—not unlike many other southern problems—involved solutions that were typically resolved only to meet very specific ends and created new problems.[14] Fickle water supplies, multistate water wars, and interbasin transfer regulation, as my own inquiry revealed, are actually modern acts in the region's long-running environmental history.

Southern Water, Southern Power focuses on one region where Americans deployed political power to control conversations about water supplies and river manipulation. But this is also a national story about American individualism, equity, and the contest to define what constitutes the proper use of common natural resources. This environmental history of the Southeast illustrates the central role that water played in shaping human choices and physical landscapes. The parties and interests who drove many of these changes had three primary goals: to produce energy, to build a modern South, and to resolve water insecurity brought about by flooding and recurrent drought.

First and foremost, southerners made choices to control water resources in conjunction with their energy decisions. The region has historically lacked abundant coal, natural gas, and other forms of energy. Put another way, the Southeast's hydraulic waterscapes—the hydroelectric dams, transmission lines, and reservoirs with their associated leisure economies—have been inscribed with social and cultural meaning; the waterscapes tied together the demands for water and energy, and eventually flood control, drought management, and other environmental services.[15] But it all started with an energy-water nexus that has left an indelible footprint on the region's cultural and natural history.

When it comes to conversations about energy history and policy today, the fossil and mineral fuels—coal, petroleum, natural gas, and uranium— drive the discussion.[16] The energy-water nexus—or the direct relationship between water supplies and energy production—adds a new twist and has recently emerged as one of the nation's more vexing future challenges. According to the Department of Energy's Sandia National Laboratories, "The continued security and economic health of the United States depends on a sustainable supply of both energy and water. These two critical resources are inextricably and reciprocally linked; the production of energy requires large volumes of water while the treatment and distribution of water is equally dependent upon readily available, low-cost energy."[17] The energy-water nexus affects national energy producers, municipal water suppliers, agriculturalists, environmental health, and every American who turns on a faucet or flips a light switch. In the Southeast, water was always a critical ingredient in energy production for antebellum waterwheels, New South and New Deal hydroelectric dams, and Sun Belt coal burners and nuclear reactors. Waterwheels and hydroelectric facilities relied on falling water to turn turbines to generate organic energy for centuries, and fossil fuel and nuclear plants transform liquid water into steam to make electricity.

Without water, it would have been—and will be—nearly impossible to produce all the energy and products required by consumers and for economic development. Furthermore, the culturally defined and politically managed energy and water connection has been complicated by physical environmental conditions.

The second critical element to understanding southern environmental history is a reckoning of how people responded to water insecurity. The following narrative demonstrates why Georgia's dramatic 2007 drought and flooding events of 2009 were not isolated moments of water insecurity. The Southeast's rural and urban political economy has always contended with these issues. In 1912, for example, a northeast Georgia newspaper columnist sympathized with a movement to save the beautiful Tallulah River and the majestic Tallulah Falls that were slated for destruction. The Georgia Power Company was planning—and eventually completed—a hydroelectric dam to produce electricity "to turn Atlanta's wheels" ninety miles away.[18] During the response to the 2007 drought, the Georgians who worried about interbasin transfers taking water from Lakes Burton or Hartwell to benefit Atlanta understood—as those did in 1912—that energy, geography, and power connected water-rich hinterlands to millions of people in a resource-poor core dependent on unreliable water supplies in a humid region once assumed to have plenty of water. Until the last few decades when Georgia agriculture blossomed into a multibillion-dollar sector, the humid Southeast's water and power history has been primarily a story about urban and industrial power.

Finally, the example of Georgia's powerful shifts from record droughts to record floods illustrates how water insecurity has been manufactured and was only partly natural throughout southern environmental history. Twin risks—flooding and drought—have been present and persistent across the region for some time. There are many interpretations of flooding in the Southeast, yet there are surprisingly few published histories of agricultural and urban drought.[19] The political economy evolved to manage too much or too little water because these environmental conditions generated economic uncertainty and social conflict. But the risk management solutions for drought and flooding created a false sense of security. Drought, of course, is only partly a natural disaster. Meteorological drought is a normal climatic condition caused by a lack of rainfall over prolonged periods. This type of drought has occurred for millennia and only became a cultural problem when the lack of rainfall reduced the availability of water supplies and limited human choices.

Yet drought, like many other natural disasters identified by historian Ted Steinberg, can reveal "human complicity" in constructing a landscape subject to nature's whim and fury where the human victims in earthquakes, tropical storms, and flooding were often powerless and the beneficiaries were often economically powerful. On many occasions, Georgians had considered disasters like inland flooding, tropical storms, and punishing droughts to be localized natural disasters that wreaked unavoidable havoc, thereby threatening human life and economic progress. The solutions for weathering disasters—while couched as serving the public good—often produced future risk and benefited very specific constituencies. For example, levees historically solved local flooding issues but exacerbated problems for adjacent and unleveed communities in subsequent floods. Deeper water wells and more reservoirs also resolved local municipal water supply shortages during droughts for the short term, but problems reemerged in the future as population and demand outstripped supply. In both examples, risk management solutions generated by a small number of decision makers intent on avoiding future natural disasters created a false sense of security and manufactured future risk.[20]

Southeastern water problems—as creations and natural phenomena—cannot be separated from energy choices, the region's political economy, and mercurial environmental conditions. Water quantity and quality were always critical ingredients for energy production and political calculations but have always been changeable natural elements. *Southern Water, Southern Power* takes a long view of southern rivers and modernization, asking who altered the region's waterways and what environmental conditions inspired them to act.

The late journalist and environmental writer Marc Reisner observed that the "reasons behind the South's infatuation with dams was somewhat elusive." In his critical and much-admired history of water and power in the arid American West, *Cadillac Desert*, Reisner repeatedly demonstrated how boosters, engineers, and politicians made water flow over mountains to moneyed interests. He was just one of many writers to interpret the American West's complicated history of water and power.[21] In a brief detour to the American South, Reisner noted the different types of structures, from "water-supply reservoirs and small power dams" to "a handful of mammoth structures backing up twenty-mile artificial lakes." The Southeast had a high annual precipitation rate and a history of devastating floods and was well known in Mark Twain's Mississippi riverboat narratives. In describing the region's humidity, as well as the hydroelectric dams and channelized rivers that moved water and vessels efficiently, Reisner identified the complexity of the Southeast's water problems, economic past, and social relations.[22]

Much has been written about southern rivers from the perspective of river admirers, corporate historians, and nature writers.[23] Academic scholars have also explained the rise of the New South (1890–1930) from the perspectives of capital flows, branch offices, regional upstarts, industrial geography, local governments, planters, industrialists, and boosters in an effort to explain the region's industrial and urban growth as processes of change and continuity.[24] Pathbreaking research has revealed the degrees to which industrial managers and workers manipulated one another within one critical sector—the textile industry—to demonstrate the important social and political consequences of economic development.[25] Others have credited federal stimulus and liberal local incentives with the rise of the industrial New South and post-1945 Sun Belt eras.[26] Connected to this memory, which is as important as it is problematic, are histories centered around the Tennessee Valley Authority (TVA) that insinuate that only the federal government manipulated southeastern rivers with large hydroelectric dams to stimulate the southern economy and primarily did so only during the New Deal (1933–44). Focus on the TVA has obscured the New South activity before the Great Depression and the U.S. Army Corps of Engineers' critical role after World War II.[27] Nearly all observers have presented only casual links between cheap human power and cheap natural power to explain the region's growth. In an important exception, scholars observed the nexus of water and power in the coercive southern institution of slavery. Coastal Plain rice plantations had depended on southern tidal rivers and African American slave labor to supply the technical forces and environmental knowledge necessary for crop survival. However, after the American Civil War and without slave labor, the planters' "hydraulic machine" fell apart as emancipated laborers walked away from the rice fields, the rivers washed away protective dikes, and rice cultivation was no longer economically viable.[28]

Climate, topography, and environmental conditions have mattered in southeastern environmental history, but even here, the Mississippi River and the Deep South have received the lion's share of attention.[29] The other side of this climatic coin, drought, has equally influenced the region's history and is dismayingly absent from public memory.[30] In the first half of the twentieth century alone, droughts reduced agricultural production, limited industrial operations, required suburbanites to conserve water and energy at home, and affected urban centers far removed from water sources.[31] After these agricultural and urban droughts, energy executives diversified company generation technologies, local governments raised taxes to increase water supply capacity, and federal engineers replumbed the southeastern waterscape on a massive scale across the Piedmont South from Alabama to Virginia.

From an airplane flyover or a Google Earth screen shot, the American South looks not unlike the arid American West. Dense urban cores and cul-de-sac suburbs give way to a patchwork of agricultural communities, open space, and steeper terrain. From the sky, the South reveals a distinct similarity to parts of the arid West in the presence of artificial waterworks such as dams, ponds, and reservoirs. Large and small reservoirs now dot the landscape from Mississippi east to Georgia and north through the Carolinas. (Only within the last thirty years have circular green patches in southern Georgia begun to appear, indicating the presence of groundwater pumping and center-pivot irrigated farming once isolated to the Great Plains.) On the ground and zoomed in, the most prominent evidence of human alteration of the regional environment remains thousands of aging ponds, impoundments, and reservoirs of varying size and shape.[32] Corporate players and state actors manipulated the Southeast's river environments, and they engineered "Georgia's Great Lakes," small agricultural reservoirs, and rivers to overcome regional environmental conditions.[33] The humid South, as Marc Reisner intimated in *Cadillac Desert*, was no more monochromatic than the American West, where a diversity of social and environmental realities produced a range of water management solutions in the Colorado, Sacramento, and Columbia River basins. Reisner was on to something, but he had only scratched the surface. Given the history and prominence of the American West, one is left to wonder why southern scholars, journalists, and observers have been so slow to notice the compelling similarity that Reisner saw as early as the 1990s. Understanding where southern reservoirs and artificial water structures came from, the corporations and state institutions who built them, and what purposes this manufactured waterscape has served unlocks an untold story about southern waterways and urban-industrial power.

Southern Water, Southern Power moves beyond the well-known histories of flooding in the Mississippi Valley and irrigation in the American West and places cheap energy and water insecurity at the center of the region's political economy and transformation. In *Southern Water,*

Southern Power, the rise of the New South cannot be disconnected from the genesis of the regional hydraulic waterscape. Beginning in the New South era, private corporations and transnational actors manipulated environmental conditions to produce energy decades before the arrival of a New Deal big dam consensus of the 1930s. During the Great Depression, flood and energy politics influenced New Deal liberalism and remapped southern communities far removed from the Tennessee River valley. And water and cheap energy also rested at the core of post–World War II Sun Belt economic development, conservative politics, and recreation planning. Regardless of time and place, the people and institutions that put these changes in motion learned repeatedly how their power would be challenged by their competitors, customers, constituents, and nature. And above all, the floods and droughts—the slower, forgotten, but no less economically damaging regional water problem—considerably influenced New South, New Deal, and Sun Belt history.

When I started this project, I thought about specific rivers—the Tennessee, Catawba, Savannah, Chattahoochee, Coosa, Alabama, and Tombigbee—that had figured prominently in the region's history as transportation conduits or because of their capacity to flood and induce human suffering. Southern lakes and droughts, I soon learned, had received far less attention despite their direct connection to some of those same rivers and the region's political economy. Only one of the Southeast's three physiographic provinces hosts what one might call "lakes," though midwesterners and New Englanders might not recognize them. For example, the Southeast as a whole is home to alluvial "oxbow" and natural lakes cut off from river channels in the Coastal Plain. Furthermore, shallow "Carolina Bays" on the southeastern Coastal Plain can be considered lakes, but according to one scientist, "No clear consensus has been reached regarding the complex issue of the origin of" these bodies of water.[34] There is, however, consensus on the origin of the lakes in the Piedmont and Blue Ridge mountain physiographic provinces. New South capitalists, New Deal regional planners, and Sun Belt boosters coordinated the construction of large artificial reservoirs in these two physiographic provinces to spur industrial development, consolidate or challenge corporate power, and deliver a multitude of economic and social benefits to urban customers, rural citizens, leisure seekers, and shareholders. In the process of assembling this extensive hydraulic waterscape, corporate and state operatives attempted to conquer environmental conditions such as flooding, drought, and a lack of quality indigenous fossil and mineral fuel sources.

After I looked at the rivers, dams, and reservoirs, the deep and rich story about water and power in the U.S. South became more evident. Not only is this a history of waterways and environmental change; it is also a story about how private corporations, public institutions, and citizens challenged one another to manage natural resources equitably while stimulating and sustaining economic growth. As artifacts, the elements of the modern Southeast's hydraulic waterscape illustrate a complex flooding, drought, and energy history and demonstrate some of the ways that southerners have responded to the region's environmental and social struggles. Old water problems and energy choices consistently stirred up political friction and contributed to building new working, living, and leisure environments during the New South, New Deal, and Sun Belt eras.

The Savannah River, which forms the boundary between South Carolina and Georgia, perfectly illustrates how people negotiated regional water insecurity and attempted to bend rivers to meet human demands throughout the U.S. South. I focus primarily on the Piedmont Province and to a lesser degree the Blue Ridge physiographic regions because people shaped valleys in these sections on a more substantial scale than they did on the Coastal Plain.[35] No waterway—in the Southeast or elsewhere—has the same history. Some have important flood, navigational, or recreational stories. For other rivers, private and federal agents' singular focus was to turn river currents into useable energy. If each of these individual river stories represents a tributary, they all flow together in the Savannah's basin to tell multiple river stories in a single Piedmont space. As such, the Savannah River presents a case study in the broadest sense; other river valleys throughout the region witnessed or were subjected to individual private and public water management schemes. However, no other regional watershed can showcase all of those schemes in one geographic place like the Savannah.

People dramatically altered the Savannah River and other southeastern valleys after the mid-nineteenth century to solve the region's recurring water problems and meet culturally defined energy needs primarily for urban and industrial applications. In the first of three formative periods, a cast of influential characters from corporate institutions initiated a privately financed dam and reservoir building program to spur economic development and meet expanding energy demands during the critical New South moment (1890–1930). Corporate titans, free-market capitalists, and transnational engineers built an extensive network of hydroelectric dams, backup coal plants, and textile villages in the heart of the southern Piedmont, and they connected these nodes of production and consumption with an elaborate system of overhead transmission lines. Emergent energy companies and the textile industry attempted to control rivers and former agricultural workers, and in the process they blended the region's water, labor, and racial problems. These independent and often multi-state energy conglomerates operated above and beyond traditional political boundaries, deployed corporate and electrical power to build regional monopolies, and demarcated the New South's territory with high-tension electric power lines. At the beginning of the twentieth century, urban and industrial centers emerged as white and black southerners left fields for factories in Atlanta, Charlotte, and towns of varying sizes. Energy—human and hydroelectric—made the era's spectacular industrial growth possible. But within two decades, a multiyear regional drought brought this mushrooming hydraulic waterscape and the New South to its knees between 1925 and 1927. Additionally, the drought revealed the danger of technological plateaus where producers and consumers relied entirely on renewable and organic energy sources such as water. As the record drought ended, the region's energy brokers bridged a technological gap in the first of many electric generation upscalings. But even as they shifted from organic and hydroelectric generation to fossil fuels and thermoelectric generation in coal-burning plants, operators and clients could never distance themselves from southern rivers. Executives in boardrooms, residents in cities, and mill workers, it appeared, could not escape—without significant external assistance—water problems within a New South bound together by transmission lines and rivers like the Savannah and its tributaries.

During a second period, between 1930 and 1944, the legacies of New South capitalism shaped New Deal liberalism as Americans redesigned the nation's waterways during depression and war. A combination of economic and environmental factors altered the fate of southeastern rivers and highlighted the difficulty in determining who—corporate players or state agents—was better equipped to manage the region's water and energy future more equitably. For example, after the 1920s drought, disastrous floods swept the nation from the Mississippi to the Ohio and the Savannah. As the Great Mississippi Flood (1927) wreaked havoc and captivated media attention, the U.S. Army Corps of Engineers was undergoing an institutional transition the deluge cemented. At the time of the flood, Corps engineers were already evaluating the capacity of the nation's rivers to produce hydroelectric energy, to irrigate fields, and to meet other comprehensive needs. Soon after the Great Mississippi Flood, Congress conferred all river management activities—defense, navigation, and flood control—upon the Corps and asked the institution to continue surveying the nation's rivers. Along the Savannah River, two serious droughts bracketed a major flood while the Corps appraised the valley. On the tail of the 1920s record drought, record Savannah River flooding in October 1929 revealed the inequity of river management and ruptured communities while exposing one Georgia city's racial geography. Drought, flooding, and the global Great Depression dealt New South capitalism a collective blow and opened the door for a new alternative.

The federal initiative to control environmental conditions in the nation's river valleys dovetailed with liberal New Dealers' motivation to challenge the corporate and monopolistic models that had claimed these rivers decades earlier in the name of industrial development. The New Dealers' quest to anchor economic liberalism and decentralize industrial development began in Tennessee, where they launched the TVA (1933) to limit monopoly power in the energy sector and to improve southern social and environmental conditions. The TVA institutionalized a New Deal big dam consensus whereby large multiple-purpose dams joined flood control, energy production, and agricultural improvement. When this regional planning and New Deal big dam consensus encountered resistance, bipartisan conservatives blew new life into old agencies, namely the U.S. Army Corps of Engineers. With new power and New Deal experience, the Corps divorced TVA regional planning and the trio of dam benefits that improved navigation, generated electricity, and provided flood protection. Southern Democrats repackaged New Deal liberalism and turned the Savannah River valley's environmental manipulation over to the Corps after 1944. Corps engineers emerged—uncomfortably—as the new arbiters responsible for balancing the legacies of New South laissez-faire and New Deal liberalism to meet the Sun Belt's energy and water demands.

In the final and third, post-1945 river development period, Sun Belt corporate and state institutions sparred over how best to approach the water and energy challenges in the Savannah and other river valleys in order to serve urban and industrial consumers. Unlike the flurry of corporate projects completed during the critical New South period and the liberal New Dealers' unrepeated TVA model, the Corps burst upon the scene and became the Sun Belt's primary water and power broker. In the Savannah

River valley alone, the Corps completed three massive multiple purpose dam and reservoir projects in a publicly funded attempt to solve the region's water challenges and redefine regional power. Nearly all southern politicians, community leaders, and ever-present boosters initially invited and welcomed these injections of federal economic development dollars. The corporate energy producers, however, did not, and they challenged "public power."

Opposition to the Corps arose on many other fronts. Energy executives and their allies in Georgia, South Carolina, and North Carolina continued to build new projects. They also objected to federal energy programs that resembled retro–New Deal liberal initiatives or represented threats to Sun Belt free enterprise. Discussion of water rights emerged as a critical concern among conservatives after the 1950s drought and the Supreme Court's *Brown v. Board of Education* (1954) order to desegregate schools and public facilities, including recreational destinations. In this postwar climate, the Democratic Party's fracture lines widened and the New Deal big dam consensuses' once-formidable list of supporters shrank. Sun Belt boosters and Democrats worked tirelessly to wrangle federal dollars, but plans for public power and multiple-purpose dams began to crumble in the 1960s. The New Deal big dam consensus, however, was wounded by more than push-back from Sun Belt corporations and conservative critics.

After 1945, a cross section of Sun Belt citizens emerged from the grass roots. These southerners registered complaints in response to the Corps' real estate, reservoir management, water quality, economic, and environmental policies. Not all criticism was unfounded. In a refrain that would repeat itself throughout the Corps' existence, officers and engineers took on tasks to complete their dam and reservoir plans for which they were not entirely prepared. When corporate engineers and New Dealers built power projects before 1945, they treated *water quantity* as the primary environmental challenge. Water "conservation" was a risk management activity devoted to storing floods and producing additional water supplies to outlast future droughts. After 1945, the Corps' last Savannah River valley big dam demonstrated how the national conversation about waterways, urban-industrial energy, and pollution had shifted. By the 1970s, Congress was dismantling the multiple-purpose trio of benefits of the New Deal's big dam consensus, and the function of free-flowing water influenced the Corps' final Savannah River valley project. Countryside conservationists and environmentalists demanded a new environmental accounting from

Sun Belt commercial promoters, and they valued *water quality* in the shadows of hydroelectric dams and water storage reservoirs inspired by New South capitalism and New Deal liberalism.

Out of this New-South-to-Sun-Belt water and power history, one special river in the Savannah River basin was spared. As countryside conservationists and environmentalists around the nation and the Sun Belt mobilized in the 1960s, they looked at rivers such as the Chattooga as examples of undammed, wild, and scenic rivers worthy of federal protection. The Chattooga River—James Dickey's *Deliverance* river—encapsulates the American South's nearly century-long water and energy history. Whereas the Georgia Power Company had built a hydraulic system to expropriate energy from northeastern Georgia rivers in the 1920s, the company delivered the adjacent Chattooga River to the environmental and paddling community for safekeeping in the 1960s for a variety of reasons. By the 1960s the company had abandoned the hydroelectric dams it had first proposed during the New South era and favored Sun Belt nuclear-generated electricity to save the nation from an anticipated energy famine. Not all of the Sun Belt's water problems could be solved so easily, but the Chattooga River's history illustrates how water and power continued to cycle in the region with important consequences for southeastern rivers, energy, and environments.

The political economy of water and environmental conditions shaped the history of the Southeast's inland waterways. Recurrent floods and droughts challenged energy companies and dam builders in ways that made empire building impossible and controlling labor difficult in the southern Piedmont's hydraulic waterscape. A history of the material environment of the Savannah River and other river valleys reminds us that how people talked about and constructed ideas about "Nature" was as important as how they lived with, adapted to, and claimed the valley's physical water resources over time. Southeastern waterways—from the Catawba and Alabama to the Tennessee and Chattahoochee—have individual histories that are best embodied by the Savannah River's physical geography. Valley residents and investors certainly valued the river and its beauty, waterpower, flood control, and navigational utility, but they never fully commodified water or rationalized a system subject to intense flooding and cyclical drought. Rather, engineers responded to floods and droughts with reservoirs and other technologies to meet specific political and economic needs in exact historical moments. All too often, their solutions prompted new debates, incited social conflict, generated more demand, and manufactured future risk. Throughout the past and in today's contemporary context, these reservoirs and structures inflated expectations and oversold benefits while water challenges persisted. The U.S. South's working reservoirs are indeed human creations and technological artifacts and thus do not behave entirely like natural or static lakes. In these storied waters, hatchery-raised bass run for fishing tournaments, invasive aquatic grasses like hydrilla bloom, pollution-laden sediment settles, and water levels can fluctuate widely. In this framework, the artificial reservoirs perform cultural and environmental functions, but not necessarily functions for which the projects were originally designed. As the more recent droughts, floods, and Lake Lanier's fluctuating water level demonstrate, people's expectations of the region's reservoirs have shifted in a postindustrial society, while the insecurity induced by unpredictable drought or flooding remains basically the same. Today, as in the past, equitable distribution of a valuable natural resource once assumed to be plentiful remains at the center of the region's modern conflict.

This project has no intention of furthering a myth of "southern exceptionalism" or environmental determinism. A history of the Southeast's hydraulic waterscape demonstrates how this particular natural resource was a critical element in conversations and choices about how to build a modern, urban, and industrial society. As in other regions of the United States, people shaped the American South's historical experience through the selective application of technology and concentration of capital in the process of responding to shifting environmental realities. The existing water history has treated the American West's water insecurity as exceptional, and nonhistorians have been responsible for dismantling this myth. By historicizing the American South's water and energy past, I simultaneously hold the region apart to explain what makes southern water and power choices different while bringing the region into the larger discussion about the nation's energy-water nexus and water supply future.[36]

From the New South to the Sun Belt periods, water has been a critical part of the southeastern political economy. Community and regional leaders understood that power flowed from Piedmont and Blue Ridge rivers. Successful New South capitalists and political interests influenced the shape of New Deal liberalism and Sun Belt conservatism. Dams—as symbols of corporate monopoly or public works projects, or as providers

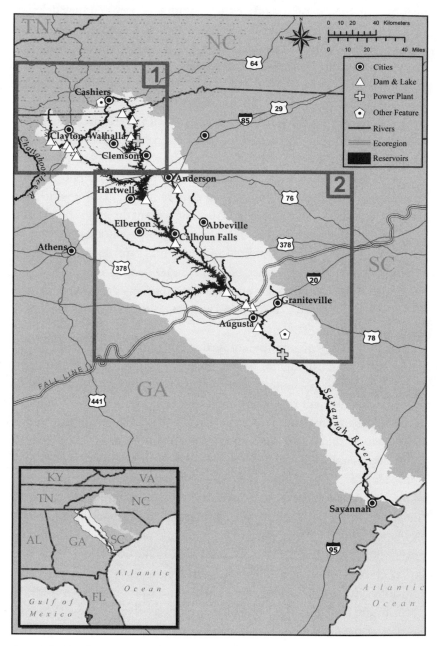

Savannah River basin, 2013 (map by Amber R. Ignatius)

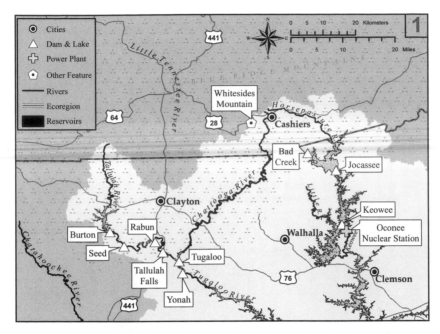

Upper Savannah River basin, 2013, showing selected Georgia Power and Duke Energy sites (map by Amber R. Ignatius)

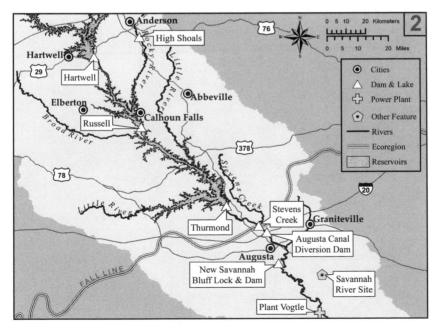

Middle Savannah River basin, 2013, showing selected sites (map by Amber R. Ignatius)

of environmental services—frame the picture of this narrative. Energy demands and environmental conditions, including droughts and floods, rest
in the heart of the historic and modern social conflict over urban-industrial
development, consumer markets, and recreation space. *Southern Water,
Southern Power* demonstrates how decisions informed by energy needs
and water insecurity influenced physical and political landscapes.

CHAPTER 1

Lowell of the South

There are no lakes in any part of the region under
consideration except a few near the coast, a position
which renders them of no value as regards water-power.
—George F. Swain (1885)

After months of planning and recovery from an industrial accident, John Muir began his southern walking tour in late 1867 at an unusual and critical turning point in the region's history. Well in advance of his better-known and published experiences of his first summer in California's Sierra Mountains, Muir passed through Georgia in the wake of the American Civil War on his "thousand mile walk" from the Midwest to the Gulf of Mexico. After arriving in Gainesville, Georgia, Muir spent September 24 "sailing on the Chattahoochee" with an old friend from Indiana. While cruising the "first truly southern stream" he had ever encountered, the two men set about "feasting" on ripe wild grapes that dropped into the unencumbered upper Chattahoochee River. Muir and his host followed the apparently free-flowing river's cue and currents and discovered masses of grapes floating effortlessly in slow churning "eddies along the bank." Other enterprising men working with the river from boats and the shore easily collected the grapes from these pools where the river's current slacked. Muir enjoyed some of the delicious grapes right out of the river, as well as the muscadine wine they produced. "Intoxicated with the beauty" of the river's banks and intrigued by what the banks farther down the river might look like, Muir briefly contemplated traveling the Chattahoochee by boat to the gulf. However, he opted to forgo the water route in favor of overland travel to really see the southern landscape, and eventually, he reached Augusta by foot.[1]

In deciding to walk and record his observations, Muir contributed to a set of social and economic assumptions about the American South. John

Muir wanted to disengage from an "entangling society," according to environmental historian and biographer Donald Worster, but he did not avoid journaling and judging the region as a rural and uncivilized backwater.[2] Furthermore, Muir encountered a postbellum South that remained—like the majority of the nation at the time—primarily an agricultural region with wild margins that lacked the pristine wilderness usually associated with the Sierra Club's first president.[3] In his travels across the Chattahoochee, Oconee, and Savannah River valleys, Muir "zigzagged . . . amid old plantations" and encountered former slaves working and harvesting low-hanging bolls in cotton fields for wages. Muir also encountered the "northern limit" of the longleaf pine (*Pinus palustris*) ecosystem. The trees fascinated Muir: "sixty to seventy feet in height, from twenty to thirty inches in diameter, with leaves ten to fifteen inches long, in dense radiant masses at the ends of the naked branches." The cotton fields, African American laborers, plantations, and timber all pointed to a real, antebellum past powered by human and animal muscles sustained by soil. Muir described these social and economic realities and perpetuated a historical narrative of life and labor in the American South that overlooked critical components of the region's environmental, industrial, and organic energy history.[4]

Before the Civil War, Piedmont southerners had already begun to move beyond agricultural production and muscle power, and they relied on southern rivers and renewable energy to do so. When Muir reached Augusta and the fall line—the point where the Coastal Plain and Piedmont merge and easy upstream navigation ends—he did not say anything about the Old South's antebellum textile mills or industrial artifacts. Nor did he describe the 1,000-foot-long rock dam that diverted the Savannah River's current from a series of rocky shoals into a maze of linear waterpower canals. Augusta's industrialists had re-created a version of the New England Waltham-Lowell system that Henry D. Thoreau described in *A Week on the Concord and Merrimack Rivers* (1849). Augusta's system never reached the scale Thoreau found during his New England paddling trip, and the New England factory system and mill towns were, of course, rare. Scattered grist- and sawmills in the Savannah River's creeks and tributaries—such as William Gregg's Horse Creek valley mills—were more common throughout early America, including the Southeast. Regardless of scale and technological diffusion, Augusta's system captured an organic and renewable energy source, reorganized modes of production, required external collaboration, and altered the river's environment. And from this perspective, Augusta looked a lot like a New England mill village in an agricultural nation.[5]

The upper Chattahoochee and Savannah Rivers did flow freely through Blue Ridge and Piedmont agricultural landscapes with "intoxicating banks" in the nineteenth century. Downstream at the fall line, however, Old South entrepreneurs in towns and cities such as Columbus and Augusta had already erected diversion dams, created small artificial ponds, and laid the foundations for an industrial New South upon the banks of southern rivers during the 1840s. By focusing on the natural history and agricultural dimensions of the southern landscape, Muir obscured the early industrial legacy of the energy-water nexus in the American South.[6]

Throughout the nineteenth century—and in the centuries before—Savannah River valley inhabitants depended on the river to survive. As John Muir traveled leisurely through multiple southern river valleys, he passed through a peopled and working landscape that had been shaped as much by Indian, African, and European hands as it had been shaped by droughts and floods. All of these human and natural influences crafted a Savannah River valley that was an agricultural and industrious place before the American Civil War.

Antebellum Georgians, South Carolinians, and their industrial allies began a process that fundamentally transformed the region's free-flowing rivers into a collection of pools and reservoirs encumbered by dams or channeled in new directions to generate industrial energy and remap social power. The Southeast was rich in organic energy—soil, timber, and wildlife—but lacked abundant and easily transferable mineral fuels—coal and oil—required to generate energy. Participants in America's famed market revolution, however, brought organized capital and mainstream dams south in the 1840s. Entrepreneurs amassed private investors' capital or entered into public-private partnerships to build diversion dams along the region's fall-line urban centers, including Columbia (S.C.) on the Congaree River and Augusta on the Savannah River, to fill canals and supply muscle-powered factory laborers with water and renewable industrial energy.

Water and power have been linked for a long time in the American South.[7] Muir may have observed Augusta's emerging hydraulic waterscape, and had he decided to float the Chattahoochee River from the Georgia mountains to the Gulf of Mexico, he would have discovered similar infrastructure in Columbus. Aside from this speculation, Muir did describe an agricultural landscape, and in so doing, he missed key physical industrial artifacts that were the building blocks of the American South's modern waterscape and political economy. As he descended the Savannah River valley, Muir would eventually encounter the spirit responsible for transforming antebellum waterpower into "New South" hydroelectric power, a process that built a water and power nexus with alacrity.

The Savannah River Basin

The Savannah River watershed encompasses approximately 10,500 square miles in Georgia, South Carolina, and North Carolina. Like a funnel, the watershed consolidates water seeping from underground springs and rain that falls on the ground and drains from northwest to southeast. Water flows quickly to the Atlantic Ocean, since this watershed travels the shortest distance from mountains to sea of any mountain-to-sea river basin in the southeastern United States. Blue Ridge Province streams and creeks descend from Western North Carolina's ancient mountains (5,500 feet above sea level) to the Piedmont Province (elev. 1,000 ft.). Gathering speed, the rugged Southern Appalachian headwater streams give rise to Georgia's Tugaloo River and South Carolina's Seneca River before these two form the 300-mile-long Savannah River. Serving as the dividing line between Georgia and South Carolina, the Savannah River then pushes through the Piedmont and over rocky shoals before cascading over the fall line at Augusta, Georgia (elev. 200 ft.). Below this city, the rocky Blue Ridge and Piedmont clays give way to the Coastal Plain's softer alluvial soils. The gradient change causes the rushing Savannah River to decelerate and slowly twist back upon itself to form serpentine "oxbows" throughout the remainder of the river's journey to Savannah, Georgia (elev. 42 ft.), and the Atlantic Ocean.

Intense geological energy and force created the southern landscape and the Savannah River watershed more than 200 million years ago, when what are now the North American and African continental plates repeatedly collided with each other before separating for the last time. These faulting and thrusting collisions—whereby the plates slid under or over each other—created uplift in the earth's crust and resulted in the formation of the Blue Ridge Mountains, which some geologists think may have been as tall as the Rocky Mountains. Over the following millions of years, erosion—rain, snow, ice, and wind—slowly whittled the Blue Ridge, contributing to creation of valleys that drained through the rolling hills of the southern Piedmont and the more moderate Coastal Plain gradients to the Atlantic Ocean, or drained through the ridge and valley to the Gulf of Mexico.[8] The tectonic forces were important for creating deep valleys and narrow gorges—important landforms that can constrict stream flow—but these actions alone could not form lakes as found elsewhere in North America.

Glacial movement in conjunction with tectonic forces carved the landscapes necessary for natural lakes in other parts of North America, but these combined forces did not sculpt a southern landscape to create natural lakes. During the great Ice Age of the Pleistocene epoch (20,000 to 9,000 years ago), a giant ice sheet stretched from coast to coast but never advanced from the polar north beyond present-day Ohio. Nearly three miles thick, it sliced valleys and pushed soil to build low ridges. As the giant ice sheet began to recede and melt 16,000 years ago, it left behind midwestern and New England waterscapes pocked with natural lakes from Minnesota to Maine and flooded the Mississippi River valley with meltwater. Like tectonic forces, the glacial retreat did not scrape the southern landscape and leave behind a waterscape of natural lakes.[9] Geological and climatic events were not the only conditions that influenced the form and composition of the southern landscape. People also shaped the Savannah River valley for thousands of years before any lakes or artificial reservoirs appeared on the landscape.

William Bartram, the American South's best-known southern naturalist, provided the most complete picture of the Savannah River valley, having traveled from the Atlantic port of Savannah throughout the valley's Piedmont and Blue Ridge headwaters between 1773 and 1775. Endowed with a gifted botanical eye and an artful pen, Bartram observed how planters organized the valley's land, water, and human energy resources.[10] African slavery—initially outlawed in colonial Georgia before legalization in 1751—made it easier for Euro-Americans to capitalize on the valley's natural resources and enabled Georgians to directly compete with South Carolina in production of agricultural and export commodities such as rice.[11]

Bartram called on one diversified South Carolina plantation, located near the present-day town of Bordeaux but now partially under Clarks Hill's reservoir, which was "situated on the top of a very high hill near the banks of the river Savanna." From Frenchman Mons. St. Pierre's house, Bartram looked down and across fields of corn, rice, wheat, oats, indigo, and sweet potatoes on "rich low lands, lying very level betwixt these natural heights and the river." Other reports suggest Bordeaux—located about

3.5 miles from the Savannah River in McCormick County, South Carolina—was primarily inhabited by up to 700 Huguenot transplants who
attempted silk cultivation and wine production. But after the American
Revolution, the region turned to cotton as a staple crop. Bartram provided
no sense of the size of this or other plantations, but these settlements required more than the river valley's soil and free-flowing water to survive.[12]
On another stop, Bartram called on one slave owner downstream from
Augusta who deployed African labor into the "ancient sublime" longleaf
pine and cypress forests. There they cut and prepared timber for export
downriver to Savannah and beyond to the "West-Indian market." Euro-
Americans and African slaves consistently cultivated the valley's rich soil
and water resources for international markets, and those basic resources
became significantly more valuable after the American Revolution.[13]

Once European colonists arrived in the Savannah River valley, developments designed to reap southern rivers' currents began to follow patterns
familiar in other regions, such as New England. In the colonial and early
national periods, private investors improved water resources at specific
sites, constructing single mills or small factories alongside natural waterfalls or shoals. Millwrights undertook similar projects in watersheds
adjacent to the Savannah. Like Native American anglers who congregated
around rocky shoals to capture fish and like farmers who planted the valley's mineral-rich bottoms and floodplains, Euro-American mill builders
utilized specific sites and the river's energy to serve limited geographical
markets.[14]

Well into the antebellum era, private individuals and investors continued to harness the Savannah River's water energy to power gristmills,
lumber mills, and cotton gins. Planters such as James Edward Calhoun,
who owned and operated the Millwood Plantation, erected low dams to
drive mills and machinery. James, the cousin of South Carolina's John C.
Calhoun, who is remembered for steering the nullification and state's
rights crisis of 1833 prior to the American Civil War, owned property that
stretched for seven miles and covered more than 10,000 acres on both
sides of the Savannah River in Abbeville (S.C.) and Elbert (Ga.) Counties. This property included small dams and diversion structures that
channeled water to small mills that sat on riverbanks. Unlike some of the
plantations Bartram visited high on bluffs above the river, Millwood sat in
the Savannah River's floodplain below the mouth of the Rocky River and
about sixty miles upstream from Augusta. Calhoun's many small diversion
dams, which did not run from bank to bank, simply redirected a portion of

Millwood Plantation, n.d. (photographer unknown). In Sharyn Kane and Richard Keeton, *Beneath These Waters: Archeological and Historical Studies of 11,500 Years along the Savannah River* (Savannah, Ga.: U.S. Army Corps of Engineers and the Interagency Archeological Services Division, National Park Service, 1993). Image from Richard B. Russell Study Files, University of Alabama Museum, Moundville.

river to run multiple mills and assorted machinery starting in 1832, and by 1850, mill manager Delancy Chisenhall produced cornmeal, wheat flour, lumber, and leather for Calhoun.[15]

Before the Civil War, Calhoun diversified his crops and succeeded because he ordered the energy of slaves, tenants, and soil to produce the plantation's primary product—cotton—in addition to peas, corn, turnips, and oats. Calhoun's diversification may have been an aberration in comparison with other plantation owners in the region, but his and his neighbors' staple cotton crop anchored central Georgia's and South Carolina's economy. As cotton replaced tobacco, the influence of upriver villages such as Petersburg, Georgia, declined. Throughout the region, planters like Calhoun often erected cotton gins and gristmills and allowed local farmers to use the facilities on a cash or exchange basis.[16] These operations remained local affairs and only began to change as planters cultivated a new variety of cotton, developed new ginning and power sources, and found themselves plugged into the nineteenth century's growing global commodities exchanges.

Textile professionals favored the high-quality, long-staple Sea Island cotton produced on the coast, but farmers and planters in the southern Piedmont could not grow Sea Island cotton. This dynamic soon changed. The convergence of a cotton variety (short-staple), improved ginning technologies, and access to international markets contributed to an explosive moment for antebellum Piedmont cotton production.[17] But the increased output also led to soil depletion, erosion, land consolidation, and outmigration. Farmers—those who owned no or few slaves—who could not keep up with soil improvement or land rotation cycles or purchase new land and slaves moved farther west into Alabama and Mississippi. Between 1810 and 1850, there was a massive white exodus and a corresponding increase in black labor throughout South Carolina's and Georgia's Piedmont. Some of those planters who remained assumed leadership positions in the region, and those who continued to farm in the bottomlands—the agricultural reformers like Calhoun—enjoyed greater returns on their crops because of direct links to markets in Augusta and Savannah.[18]

Calhoun's access to the Savannah River facilitated his grasp of power in the local marketplace, but it also linked him to the region's unpredictable water flows. The summers between 1832 and 1834, according to his journals, were particularly dry. Calhoun's cotton and corn suffered ten weeks without rain from May through August 1832. The Savannah ran "unusually low and for a long time" in the fall of 1833, and Calhoun again was "wanting rain" to sustain his cotton in October 1834.[19] When the Savannah River was flowing, Calhoun's hired white and slave laborers could manufacture material items necessary to keep the whole operation running, but they also constantly reacted to the river's behavior. Flooding—or "freshets"—damaged floodplain fields, and the river rose "as high nearly as in Dec. 1831 which exceeded any Freshet for many years before."[20] Calhoun repeatedly contracted with individuals to reinforce and maintain his dams because he was "uneasy about . . . [their exposure] to the whole force of the River during freshets." Calhoun's personal proto-industrial activities did not necessarily contribute to a southern market revolution on a scale equivalent to what emerged in Massachusetts's Lowell mills. But his experience illustrates the complex quality of his relationship with capital and the Savannah River. The waterway could run dry or flood, and both events threatened to ruin his financial investments. Calhoun—a man rich in real property but perpetually short of cash—apparently dreamed of building a large textile mill on the Millwood site. But he ultimately left that task to downstream investors and "men of capital" with access to deeper pockets.[21]

Lowell of the South

By the nineteenth century, the Savannah River valley looked like other American river valleys with small agricultural and growing industrial communities. The Savannah River had flowed freely until the decades before the American Civil War, and the Augusta Canal diversion dam signaled the beginning of a new relationship between water and power—and a new organic energy regime—in the southern Piedmont.

The city of Augusta, affectionately anointed "the Lowell of the South" by the *Augusta Chronicle*'s editors, successfully redirected the Savannah River's energy-rich current on a much larger scale than Calhoun alone could have ever achieved. Augusta's prominent city boosters secured the local political will, the necessary financial resources, and the appropriate technological advice to begin construction on the Augusta Canal in the 1840s less than 100 miles downriver from Calhoun's Millwood Plantation.[22] Georgia and South Carolina generally lagged behind other states during the canal-building era when compared with New York (Erie Canal, 360 miles long) or Maryland (Chesapeake and Ohio Canal, 185 miles long). Georgians and South Carolinians only constructed a handful of transportation canals: the 22-mile-long Santee and Cooper canal (constructed between 1793 and 1800); the 15-mile coastal Savannah-Ogeechee-Altamaha canal (1825–30); and a 12-mile canal connecting the Altamaha River with the port at Brunswick, Georgia (1834–54). All of these canals suffered for financial reasons and as a result of railroad competition.[23] However, the Lowell of the South was motivated by this canal-building era and the original Lowell's emergence as the epicenter of North American textile manufacturing.

Augustan Henry Harford Cumming merged the political, financial, and technological powers necessary to move the Augusta Canal from an idea in the 1830s to a reality in 1845.[24] More than anything, Cumming wanted to anchor Augusta's mercurial economy and to reverse the city's dependence on northeastern cities and the southern ports of Savannah and Charleston. Cumming sensed that Augusta could compete with Lowell, where investors built twenty-eight water-powered mills and massed 8,000 workers to operate 150,000 spindles and 5,000 looms by 1839.[25] Cumming and other regional entrepreneurs like South Carolinian William Gregg reasoned, Why send raw cotton to New England when it could be processed closer to the fields where it was harvested? Gregg had toured Lowell in 1844 and decided to mimic the system in the Horse Creek valley ten miles east of Augusta on a Savannah River tributary in South Carolina. Operations at the Graniteville Manufacturing Company and mill village where Gregg employed over 300 white workers to operate 9,000 spindles and 300 looms eventually began in 1849.[26] In the years leading up to Gregg's decision to build his first mill, people like Cumming understood that the region's large pool of restless and landless labor—a perceived problem in its own right—could be redirected from farms to the factories fueled by water.

In the wake of the 1830s national financial panic and regional soil erosion, many Georgia and South Carolina farmers began to flee the state for the "black belt" soils of Alabama and points west. This exodus threatened the region's political economy.[27] To stop the hemorrhaging, local leaders advocated for investment in additional projects and a shift to a nationalized and diversified commercial economy. Augusta's Henry H. Cumming advocated on these lines of reasoning and believed new railroads would ultimately favor cities like Augusta. All of these factors—access to raw materials, local labor, and transportation links to international markets—led Cumming, Gregg, and other men of capital to employ the Savannah River valley's water to drive a diversified commercial economy during the nineteenth-century southern market revolution. Antebellum southerners were beginning to balance agriculture with industry—within an organic energy regime—long before Muir passed through the region in 1867.

In Cumming's mind, the Augusta Canal could tame a short section of an unpredictable river and fuel factories while achieving two other connected goals. First, as a transportation conduit, the canal provided a limited bypass through the fall line. The canal was a limited navigational solution because boats could enter the canal upstream of Augusta but could not exit the canal into the Savannah River below Augusta. As a navigational waterway, the canal facilitated movement of agricultural products between Augusta and upstream communities. Once goods arrived in Augusta, they were off-loaded, processed in Augusta, and reloaded onto Savannah-bound riverboats or Charleston-bound railroads. Traveling the upper Savannah River's reaches by boat was daunting; shoals, rocks, and unpredictable water levels made travel hazardous at best. Despite many sources of water such as springs and rainfall, seasonally fluctuating water flows hampered commerce on nearly every river in the American South. Rivers typically ran low in the spring and summer and could rise with autumn tropical storms and winter rains. Not enough rain made navigating the upper Savannah River's shoals difficult with cargo-laden boats, and too much water could turn rivers into torrents.

The Augusta Canal provided seven miles of safe passage through the Savannah River's fall line and around one of the river's longest sets of shoals regardless of water levels. The technology necessary for this endeavor, as for canals in other parts of the American South, came from outside the region. A community of transnational engineers, including Loammi Baldwin Jr., Charles H. Bigelow, James Bechno Francis, and William Phillips, who were associated with designing water infrastructure in Lowell and elsewhere helped build the antebellum South's water schemes to provide water security.[28]

The engineers and individuals like Cumming who contributed to the southeastern hydraulic waterscape also demonstrate what the market revolution and transition to capitalism looked like in one part of the American South. Scholars have typically reduced the market revolution to a conflict either between the interests of coastal merchants and yeoman famers or between cotton planters, poor yeomen, and slaves.[29] The Augusta Canal's example illustrates that middle class, urban professionals—like Cumming and Phillips—do not fit into those categories. According to historians Tom Downey and Bruce Eelman, these individuals were the men of capital who shaped the southern waterscape and the antebellum South's diversified market revolution. "Men of property"—those elite individuals who owned slaves, stands of timber, or small mills throughout the South—represented one layer of southern industrialists who increasingly ceded political power in the late nineteenth century to the new group of capitalists. The men of capital—like Cumming and his South Carolina neighbor William Gregg—symbolized the new southern industrialist mentality that gained significant political clout before the American Civil War. On the war's eve, the valley's political economy had begun to shift from favoring men of property—who were rich in slaves and real estate—to include men of capital who pooled resources and built incorporated institutions like mills and factories.[30]

The Augusta Canal's men of capital also secured their financial resources from various sources to couple water and power. Since no federal or state funds were available for canal construction in Georgia, the newly formed Canal Board of Commissioners turned to Augusta banker William D'Antignac. Through interlocked social and financial relationships, D'Antignac lured additional investors from the Bank of Augusta,

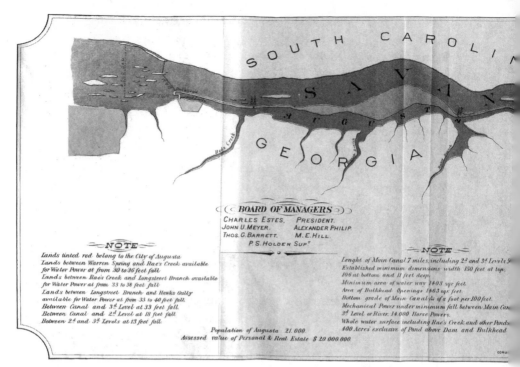

The Augusta Canal, 1875. The diversion dam channeled the Savannah River's water through the canal head gates and the canal's single lock (*upper left corner*) to Augusta. Factories and municipal departments withdrew water from the canal to drive waterwheels and for water supplies, and they deposited the water back into the river. Canal vessels could not access the river from the canal in downtown Augusta. In Byron Holly, *The Enlarged Augusta Canal, Augusta, GA: Its Capacity and Advantages for the Manufacture of Cotton Goods, with Map of Location* (New York: Corlies Macy & Co. Stationers, 1875). Courtesy of Hargrett Rare Book and Manuscript Library, University of Georgia Libraries, Athens.

Georgia Railroad Bank, Augusta Insurance and Banking Company, and Bank of Brunswick. Each of the four entities invested $1,000, and the City Council of Augusta agreed to issue bonds worth $100,000—and raise city taxes to repay those bonds and to finance construction.[31] By April 1845, construction companies had signed contracts and broken ground on a city waterway designed to generate waterpower and regulate navigation. Local individuals, entities connected with the Georgia Railroad, and northeastern stonemasons were contracted to build sections of the canal. Irish laborers, African American slaves, and Georgia citizens performed low-skilled work, and Italians often completed higher-skilled tasks such as masonry work.[32] When the laborers completed the canal in 1847, it

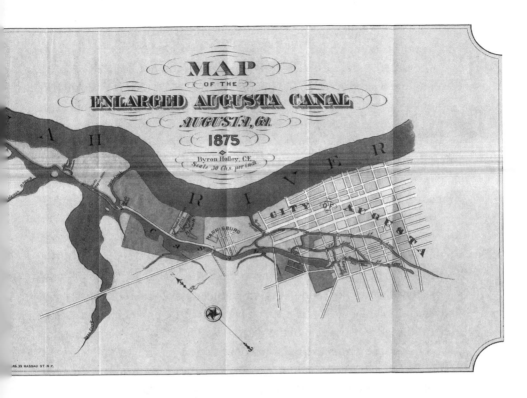

was forty feet wide at the surface, twenty feet wide at the bottom, and five feet deep and ready to move commerce.[33] Cotton may have been king for the financial economy, but this monarchy inflicted serious damage on the political economy and the environment.

While reports from South Carolina's Piedmont and Blue Ridge region have suggested the Keowee River was "the most beautiful river" in South Carolina's upstate with "pure and transparent" waters in 1859, land use and soil management soon complicated river navigation and flows downstream in the Savannah and other rivers.[34] South Carolina and Georgia farmers and planters demanded much from a soil that was not deep enough to continuously perform to human or market expectations. Piedmont tobacco and cotton agriculturalists participated in a cycle of land-clearing and cultivation that resulted in high yields followed by varying degrees of soil erosion and land abandonment; they tapped the soil of its energy. A late-nineteenth-century survey of potential waterpower sites in the United States noted that the rivers in the Santee and Savannah Rivers' headwaters were "in many places rapidly filling up with detritus—sand and mud—which is washed in from the hill-sides, so that many shoals [were] being rapidly obliterated, and at many places, where within the memory of middle-aged men there were shoals with falls of from 5 to 10 feet, at present scarcely any shoals can be noticed." The federal surveyor pointed to deforestation and "a superficial method of cultivation, by which this soil is also rendered less cohesive and more liable to washing."[35] Whether agriculturalists were "soil miners," "land killers," or victims in an "erosional tinderbox," human behavior and labor deployed on land had consequences for the function of all rivers.[36] Erosion and sediments raised river bottoms, contributed to new and ever-shifting sandbars, blanketed old or created new wetlands, buried shoals, and compromised spawning runs for the river's migratory fish such as shad and sturgeon.[37] As farmers, planters, and slaves continually cleared new Piedmont land, they sent more soil into the Savannah River and its tributaries, which only increased sedimentation, further compromised river navigation, and altered the composition of riparian ecology throughout the basin.

Seasonal water flow and sediment-induced navigational hazards were not the only challenges to river transportation in the early nineteenth century. Railroad construction in the 1840s posed formidable competition for riverboat traffic. Extensive railroad construction reconfigured the flow of capital in the Southeast, and a growing network of railroads redirected cotton away from Gulf of Mexico ports to eastern Atlantic ports such as Savannah and Charleston.[38] This situation would seem to have benefited the upper Savannah River basin as cotton and other staple products flowed to the river's metropolitan namesake. However, Savannah River waterborne commerce was limited by the same unpredictable water flows that affected other southern rivers.

From the town of Petersburg, Georgia—located upstream from Augusta at the confluence of the Broad and Savannah Rivers—boats navigated tricky shoals to deliver cotton, corn, grains, and tobacco downriver to the Augusta Canal's entrance. The return trip required three days of upstream poling through those same difficult shoals.[39] River men and boat builders combined forces to create a specialized "Petersburg" boat designed to shoot the river's rapids. The boats were sixty to eighty feet long and seven feet wide with a shallow draft to clear the shallow and rocky river bottom when burdened with up to sixty bales of cotton. The pilot, with an additional crew of six men, drove the boat from the stern with a long trailing oar. The deckhands deployed poles to keep the boat from crashing on the rocks, and their bodies were often left bruised, battered, and exhausted from fighting the river.[40] South Carolina slaves "familiar with all the shoals and other obstructions" on the river piloted some of these boats, often traveling unaccompanied over seventy-five miles between Andersonville (S.C.) and Augusta to deliver cotton.[41] Augusta city records from 1817 also suggest that before the advent of steam power, Augusta's riverborne trade with Savannah was "fueled by the energy" of predominantly free African American river men. Of the 176 free blacks required to register with the city, "boating and carpentry" were the most common occupations among men.[42] These men fought and negotiated the river's currents, and many drowned as a result.[43] Cumming's Augusta Canal provided limited upstream navigational improvements and eliminated some of these dangerous experiences for black and white Petersburg boatmen. The Augusta Canal would certainly help Cumming reach one goal: better transportation options.

A second goal was closely aligned with the Lowell system's ability to turn river water into energy for new industrial applications. Despite boosters' calls for increased industrial diversification before the American Civil War, Augusta remained utterly dependent on agricultural production of tobacco and cotton in the city's hinterland, as illustrated by merchants' $700,000 export of these products to Savannah in 1817. But by 1853, the canal's managers were also selling canal water to five customers: the Augusta Manufacturing Company's two textile mills, the Granite Mill's flour mills and sawmills, the Cunningham Flour Mill, the Augusta Machine Works, and the T. J. Cheely Grain & Cotton Gin.[44] Cumming's canal vision succeeded in bringing industry to Augusta on a scale much smaller than that of the real Lowell in Massachusetts. But like the Merrimack River valley—complete with dozens of dams and power canals, as well as dozens of mills and thousands of operatives—the Savannah River's water became an instrument for industrialists while other river users found themselves at a disadvantage. For example, anglers throughout the basin understood that the Augusta Canal dam contributed to the loss of a once-vibrant shad fishery.[45] Once the water entered the canal, the water belonged to the city of Augusta; the waterpower generated from the canal was "owned entirely by the city" and was "leased to the different mills."[46] These antebellum industrial dreams produced a hydraulic system capable of serving an industrial factory system and war machine.

The survival of the Confederate States of America depended on the Savannah River and the Augusta Canal. Augusta had many desirable natural advantages at the outbreak of American Civil War. The city's environment made Augusta and other southern fall-line cities like Richmond and Columbus critical Civil War towns. The Confederacy tapped Augusta's resources to build a war machine because the city was far from the front lines, was a major stop for east-west railroads, and possessed a canal capable of providing ample renewable waterpower for industrial applications. The Confederacy's Ordnance Bureau built and managed the Confederate Powder Works along the Augusta. Savannah River waterpower helped fabricate and stitch the Confederate Army, supporting the manufacture of pistols, uniforms, locomotives, rolling stock, wheelbarrows, and knapsacks, as well as gunpowder. Men's and women's hands—more than 700 women worked in Augusta's factories during the war—assembled these products with help from the river throughout the war except for one short period. In February 1862, nature temporarily derailed the Confederacy's war industries after heavy rains produced rising waters that breeched the Augusta Canal, thus compromising factory production until workers completed repairs in March.[47]

Augusta was not alone in harnessing the water of southern rivers to drive hydraulic systems and industrial machines before or after the American Civil War. Similar facilities emerged along riverbanks across the southern fall line from Prattville, Alabama, to Richmond, Virginia.[48] These early factories paid white men and women wages and also depended on the hands of black slaves. But these factories likewise relied on a material environment; they could never move far from the flow of southern rivers and their renewable energy source. While these industrial communities and cities suffered decline immediately after the Civil War, they would become examples for a New South built on antebellum visions of diversified agriculture, manufacturing, railroads, and urban growth powered by organic energy sources such as water.

The preceding examples illustrate some of the American South's deep interconnected histories of people, land, water, and power. Water problems—such as drought or flooding—occurred and affected discrete communities. And human activity in the Savannah River basin demonstrated how energy choices resulted in new environmental realities, affected social relationships, and produced a new waterscape. Southern rivers remained predominantly free-flowing rivers with occasional pools formed behind mill dams, but the region lacked the major lakes or reservoirs that mark the twenty-first-century's landscape. Cultural choices and environmental change in the Savannah River basin followed a path generally paralleling that of other American regions such as New England. The southern region remained primarily agricultural with proto-industrial mills along small creeks, but cities and towns across the Southeast increasingly attracted greater concentrations of capital and people in industrial environments fueled by water. By the late nineteenth century, the American South continued a slow process of agricultural and industrial economic diversification. King Cotton still reigned, but cotton factories increasingly processed the fibers regionally and did not export all raw materials to distant mills. Additionally, investors looked into forests for additional products such as timber and pulp that encouraged formation of new industries, technologies, and products like synthetic textiles in the early twentieth century. These new developments all required increased energy supplies and endless capital reserves. In response, southern boosters stumping for the New South continued to turn to the region's rivers for organic energy supplies and social power.

Throughout the discussions over how to build and fund the Augusta Canal, supporters used the canal as an example of how the city could define itself. The canal would enable Augusta to diversify its agricultural and industrial economy and to free itself from dependence on other cities and regions. Augustans shared a sentiment with others that coalesced into a "New South Creed" and mantra in the decades between Reconstruction and the early twentieth century as southerners looked for additional means to build a profitable and productive economy.[49] Soon after the American Civil War, visionaries proposed new ways to power southern society, and we can see this in an unlikely source.

From Waterpower to "E-lec-tricity"

As John Muir traveled the agricultural, industrial, and postbellum South in 1867, he encountered a landscape in transition. Muir had breezed through Augusta, Georgia, on his own march to the sea and perhaps never understood the workings of the Augusta Canal or the existence of the diversion dam and subsequent loss of the shad fishery.[50] If he had, Muir would have immediately recognized that the Savannah River was not like the free-flowing Chattahoochee River on which he sailed and harvested wild grapes for his muscadine wine. While that section of the upper Chattahoochee River was unencumbered and free flowing, the industrial Savannah River was dammed, redirected, and turned into a renewable organic energy machine before the American Civil War. Muir certainly would have encountered mill dams on the middle Chattahoochee River in Columbus, Georgia, had he proceeded to the Gulf of Mexico by boat as he had contemplated. Perhaps Muir was even surprised or uncomfortable with the industrial and technologically modern South he discovered and the people he met.

One of the individuals Muir encountered on his travels between Augusta and Savannah provided a window into the South's future. Muir stopped to sleep or eat with folks who had resources and interest in his cash, and at one of these stops Muir encountered a nascent New South booster named Mr. Cameron. In comparing Muir's interest in botany, Cameron disclosed his own: "My hobby is e-lec-tricity." Cameron—well in advance of the majority of his contemporaries—held a vision for a future South where "that mysterious power or force, used now only for telegraphy, will eventually supply the power for running railroad trains and steamships, for lighting, and, in a word, electricity will do all the work of the world."[51] While Cameron did not explicitly link his electric dreams with the early industrial Savannah River or consider the larger implications of an electrical society for human labor and nature, his unsolicited and prophetic outlook meshed with the industrial advocacy of the antebellum men of capital and emerging New South capitalists hungry for regional independence at the end of the nineteenth century. Neither Muir nor Cameron could foresee what an electrified and modern New South might look like, nor could the two men have conceived of the consequences for southern water and southern power. Those changes in southern history took place under the watch of none other than the New South's preeminent spokesman and journalist-orator.

Henry Woodfin Grady consistently functions as one of the New South's symbolic anchors. Beginning in the 1880s, Grady promoted more than industrial and agricultural diversification, racial compromise, and regional reconciliation. Grady, not unlike his antebellum predecessors or those who followed him, recognized the full array of environmental resources—soils, forests, minerals, and human labor—that stood ready to fuel the New South's economic move out of dependency. Grady also understood in 1881 that the region's abundant "water-powers" were necessary for industrial growth and functioned as reliable instruments, since the Southeast's water "was never locked a day by ice or lowered by drought."[52] Grady's half-truth was based on the assumption that private investors could quickly modernize the New South because ample waterpower would provide cheap energy for new or relocating mills and factories. When Grady looked at the region's waterways, he saw rivers as tools for private investors dedicated to the New South revolution.

To grasp whom Grady was talking to and for what purpose, one must revisit basic industrial geography and energy history. Before 1890, American mills and small factories remained physically connected to the rivers from which they derived energy—or waterpower, in the language of the day. Early-nineteenth-century textile and other manufacturers from Lowell, Massachusetts, to the Lowell of the South had derived waterpower from rivers and canals to drive factory machinery. And in cities where mills, factories, and other commercial enterprises could not access large quantities of water or build on riverbanks, factory managers generated energy, and eventually electricity, on-site in isolated steam plants dependent on imported coal, railroads, and groundwater. Waterwheels and isolated steam plants may have laid the foundations for the New South's initial industrial boom, but they were soon surpassed by growing systems and modern technologies requiring substantial financial backing, multiple generation stations, transmission networks, and larger artificial reservoirs that could conserve extensive reserve supplies of water.[53]

By the late 1880s and 1890s, privately financed energy companies throughout the United States began incorporating water storage and hydroelectric production with long-distance transmission lines to move electricity from rivers to distant mining, agricultural, and urban areas. The nation's first long-distance transmission line (fourteen miles) went into service when the Willamette Falls Electric Company completed its diversion dam and powerhouse in 1889 to power electric lights in Portland, Oregon.[54] Some writers have suggested that southern California led the way in privately financed electricity transmission systems because after 1892 mining facilities and new urban centers incited a "demand for power" for mining equipment, industrial machinery, and electric lights.[55] Others have linked California's agricultural production to private utility companies: Fruit growers needed electricity to pump groundwater to irrigate crops.[56] But streetcar patrons, more than lighting consumers, were the greatest engines of change for urban energy consumption, particularly after Richmond, Virginia, put the first commercially viable electric streetcar line in the United States into service in 1888.[57] Initially, coal-fired steam plants powered these transportation networks, but as these systems expanded in cities such as Atlanta, cheaper water-generated electricity supplemented or replaced coal-generated electricity. And by 1896 the world's most anticipated, politicized, and publicized hydroelectric project—Niagara Falls— began generating and transmitting electricity to Buffalo, New York.[58]

Engineers laboring in the American South joined colleagues working around the country and continued to improve upon existing technological systems that reconfigured the industrial geography of energy production and consumption. On June 22, 1894, the Columbia (S.C.) Cotton Mill's owners could boast of having electrified the first cotton mill in the Southeast. Engineers designed a small hydroelectric station along the Columbia Canal to transmit electricity to a cotton mill only 800 feet from the Broad River's current.[59] New and continually modified technologies, including turbines, generators, transformers, high-tension transmission lines, and electric motors, increasingly enabled factories and mills to slip the restraints of geography and move from riverbanks to towns of all sizes. Despite these improvements, the basic process of making hydroelectricity has not changed. Dams store water before directing it through a penstock—that is, a large pipe—to a turbine. After succumbing to gravity in the penstock, the falling water turns a turbine that is connected to a generator, where spinning magnets produce electricity. Transformers step up the voltage and send the electricity out and across transmission lines to another transformer that decreases the voltage for use in homes, businesses, or factories to drive electric motors in appliances and machinery. Hydroelectric systems in the Southeast, a region with plenty of water, became increasingly organized and capitalized after 1890, with plenty of room for technological innovations at each of these stages. With larger arrangements came highly centralized management, capital, and corporate power.[60] Privately managed water conservation regimes quickly began to rearrange regional industrial geography and energy consumption as well as social and environmental relationships between people and waterways in the New South.

William Church Whitner (1864–1940) was the New South engineer who significantly upscaled the production of hydroelectricity. Unlike earlier waterpower and hydroelectric projects—such as the Columbia, South Carolina, cotton mill—that supplied energy to factories located along rivers, Whitner's Savannah River basin projects injected significant distance between energy production and consumption, and he leaned on transnational technologies and ideas to do so. The Anderson Water, Light & Power Company commissioned Whitner, a civil engineer and graduate of the University of South Carolina, to design and build a coal-fired steam power plant for the municipal waterworks in Anderson, South Carolina. As Whitner completed this project, he considered the late-nineteenth-century debate over the costs and benefits of steam energy versus waterpower. George E. Ladshaw, an unabashed waterpower booster and one of Whitner's contemporaries, encouraged engineers to forgo coal-fired and steam-generated energy altogether in the Carolinas, where Whitner toiled. Ladshaw argued that since southern river systems received greater annual rainfall than northeastern river systems, "southern rivers yield a greater amount of power per square mile." Based on this logic, he assumed individual southeastern mills and factories could always produce their own energy by conserving water behind mill dams, thus freeing independent mill owners from "water power companies" such as Whitner's employer. And with water under sound management, mill mangers could then turn to exploiting what Ladshaw saw as the New South's other well-advertised advantage and energy source: "Labor is cheap, abundant and tractable."[61] Whitner considered Ladshaw's advice to monopolize human and river energy locally via waterpower at single mills, but Whitner ultimately chose a private waterpower company's deep pockets and credit connections over an individual mill's limited scale and scope.

After completing the waterworks project, Whitner determined the Anderson Water, Light & Power Company could eliminate its dependence on imported coal and the mineral fuel's associated railroad freight costs. He convinced his fellow company executives to invest in two pioneering Savannah River valley hydropower and organic fuel projects. Successfully incorporating new generating technology with alternating-current transmission lines, Whitner's High Shoals Hydro Station on the Rocky River (operational, 1895) and the Portman Shoals Hydro Station (1897) on the Seneca River were the first projects in the American South to transmit electricity over long-distance transmission lines.[62] Whitner fitted an old Rocky River gristmill with a turbine, and he designed the new Portman Shoals low dam to generate hydroelectricity that was transmitted over ten miles of lines to Anderson to fuel textile mills, drive municipal water supply pumps, and brighten city lights. At Portman Shoals, which is now buried under Lake Hartwell, Whitner's laborers built a run-of-river dam more than twenty feet tall to create a small reservoir and divert water into turbines to generate electricity; during high-water periods, water also flowed over the rubble-masonry dam's crest and spillway before continuing downstream. Whitner completed the two Anderson hydropower projects, and then he applied his experience across the New South. Traveling throughout Georgia and as far north as Richmond, Virginia, he manipulated waterways, spurred economic growth, and constructed critical infrastructure for an evolving number of powerful southern energy companies after 1900.[63]

At the beginning of the twentieth century, William Church Whitner bridged two communities, one regional and one transnational. Whitner and his contemporaries in the energy industry were powerful New South actors who pushed the region's economic development "beyond planters and industrialists."[64] Whitner was a founding member of the New South's emerging middle class, whom one scholar called "town people." Whitner's hydroelectric projects ultimately contributed to building a "new world" of Piedmont mill towns, and he laid the groundwork for an "embryonic urban civilization" that would support cities like Atlanta and Charlotte. Finally, Whitner helped introduce a new industrial-social order to a region formerly dominated by agricultural production. The core owners and labor pool in South Carolina's industries at the turn of the century were "southern," but an eclectic mix of individuals in the energy industry influenced the future of Piedmont rivers, the New South textile boom, and an electrical utility industry long before the advent of the well-known Tennessee Valley Authority in 1933. Whitner was an influential member of a powerful regional South Carolina community responsible for the new hydroelectric-energy-dependent industrial-social order that emerged in manufacturing towns.[65]

Whitner was a member of a transnational engineering and energy community as much as he was a regional member of the South Carolina town-building community of industrialists. The southern manufacturing industry's financial investment arrived mostly from outside the region, and the energy sector's executives and engineers derived experience and knowledge from all over the globe; the technology that Whitner relied on to build the New South knew no regional boundaries. International engineering trade journals, blossoming in number in the late nineteenth century, demonstrate that projects like Whitner's emerged in other parts of the world.[66] Before building his generation projects in Anderson and elsewhere, Whitner studied these journals and apparently traveled to New York to meet Nikola Tesla, a Croatian immigrant who is credited with devising in 1888 the alternating-current transmission technology that remains an industry standard today.[67] Engineers like Whitner who did not go abroad could travel through the journals and gain indirect exposure to the work of a transnational energy and engineering community.

Many of the men responsible for shaping the American South's energy infrastructure and hydraulic waterscape before 1930 read such journals, and these professionals circulated throughout the United States and overseas to inspect, engineer, and manage energy projects. For example, the Alabama Power Company emerged in 1906, and after 1911 the company looked less like a "southern" and more like an American company influenced by transnational ideas. Canadian-born James Mitchell (1866–1920), one of the company's three core founding executives, got his start in the energy industry with the Massachusetts-based Thomson Houston Company in the railway motor division, traveling around the United States troubleshooting railway motors and new street railway projects.[68] In the early 1890s, Thomson Houston assigned Mitchell to South America to spur sales in street-lighting and power-generating equipment.[69] He worked for the company until 1901 when he assumed the general manager position for the Canadian-owned São Paulo Tramway, Light, and Power Company, where he worked until 1906.[70] After about sixteen years in Brazil, Mitchell moved to London, where he worked with longtime friends and the principals of the Sperling & Company investment house. The firm soon sent Mitchell to Japan, where he spent four months surveying potential dam sites.[71] When he returned to the United States, Mitchell took a southeastern waterpower tour through South Carolina before he encountered former riverboat Captain William Patrick Lay (1853–1940), who had founded the Alabama Power Company in 1906, and Thomas Wesley Martin (1881–1964), a riparian legal expert and, like Lay, a native of Alabama. With Martin's help, Mitchell reorganized Lay's fledging company in 1911 and used his transnational experience and credit connections to turn the financially deprived energy firm into a regional and national force. William Church Whitner, James Mitchell, and others represent a range of transnational experiences that cemented the bond between southeastern rivers and the energy sector.[72] Many of the New South engineers who worked for the region's most successful energy companies during the first half of the twentieth century made the companies distinctive, not necessarily because the companies were southern or for cultural reasons, but because the companies employed individuals informed by global experiences.

William Bartram, John Muir, Henry Grady, and William Church Whitner recognized the value human and water power added to community growth. The Lowell of the South, the New South's men of capital, and transnational engineers learned about the world's diverse organic energy projects and built new North American systems with improved waterwheels and turbines, more efficient generators and motors, taller dams that increased "head" (the height that water falls through a penstock before striking a turbine), longer transmission lines, and an increasingly complex numbers of dams, diversion tunnels, pipeline conduits, and reservoirs necessary to generate and deliver energy to agricultural and industrial consumers. Corporate executives and engineers consciously replaced free-flowing rivers with artificial reservoirs throughout the Southeast. They consolidated economic power in a decidedly unexceptional process and built a modern hydraulic waterscape, as their counterparts did in locales across the globe.[73] The nineteenth-century mill dams and water-powered facilities served as economic and technical foundations for New South boosters whose capital-intensive hydroelectric generation projects grew in scale and scope. The New South's power brokers ultimately combined human and animal muscle power with agricultural production and waterpower to build a versatile organic energy regime. But the utilities' dedication to energy supplies fueled by boundless reserves of "white coal" blinded them to environmental realities. The boosters, executives, and engineers soon learned new lessons about the benefits and risks of an organic energy system that depended on renewable energies and human labor.

CHAPTER 2

Dam Crazy for White Coal
in the New South

In his 1932 book, *Human Geography of the South: A Study in Regional Resources and Human Adequacy*, Rupert Vance declared that "there are two great economic complexes that may be expected to force" states to abandon selfish or provincial attitudes in exchange for regional or national outlooks. Vance's study provided solutions for building a modern region and challenging long-standing assumptions that the South was a colonial outpost bedeviled by race relations and that it could be nothing more than a poor land inhabited by poor people. Born in Arkansas, Vance contributed to the liberal strain of regionalist analysis at the University of North Carolina in the 1930s; he saw a way out of the regional backwardness as the United States entered the global Great Depression. As the first complex, Vance considered continued railroad network development for connecting crops and peripheries to markets and central cores. More recently, scholars have examined the economic, cultural, and environmental consequences of America's railroads and have demonstrated that transportation and technical systems integrated those regions into the national fabric. But Vance's second complex, hydroelectric development in the humid and generally water-blessed Southeast, is still poorly understood as a force of change in the first three decades of the twentieth century. In a region well-endowed with flowing water, Vance argued, rivers were prime renewable energy resources that could be "harnessed" to benefit farmers and factory workers. Vance's travels and collaborative research throughout the Southeast revealed an extensive privately capitalized network of hydroelectric dams, reservoirs, and transmission lines that stretched from North Carolina to Mississippi. Relying on these observations, Vance advocated for a publicly funded and publicly owned regional hydro-complex that mimicked the private energy corporations' modern systems. When Vance looked across the "Piedmont crescent of industry" one year before

President Franklin D. Roosevelt created the Tennessee Valley Authority (TVA) in 1933, water appeared as one of the most underutilized natural resources and as a renewable energy source monopolized by a few private energy companies and industries. Vance saw the fruits and inequity of the New South economy, and he embraced hydroelectric power and cheap organic energy as tools to shape a new future.[1]

White coal, in Vance's estimation, could redefine the New South's relationship with the rest of the nation and improve southerners' daily lives. Reassessing Rupert Vance's ideas provides a new interpretation of southern modernization. First, regionalists such as Vance influenced the shape of the TVA and liberal New Deal river development in the 1930s. Second, the TVA project inspired subsequent federal waterway and energy programs in the Southeast and across the nation after 1945. But more important, Vance opens a window into an early period of regional modernization that has been overshadowed by the TVA's high-modernist experience, by repeated assertions that the South was the nation's top economic problem, and by the federal largesse that built the Sun Belt after 1945.

This chapter examines who hitched the New South to white coal in the Savannah and other river basins during a crucial period in the region's history between 1890 and 1933. We should seek out the origins of Vance's hydroelectric "complex" and "the Piedmont crescent of industry" because waterway manipulation and energy generation were critical components of southern modernization after the American Civil War. For millennia, human beings have produced energy from a variety of sources—primarily by burning biomass (peat moss or trees) and fossil fuels (coal, oil, and natural gas). During the nineteenth-century industrial revolution, people around the world began producing energy by burning fossil fuels with the express intent to transform boiling water into steam for locomotion and generation of electricity. By that time, regardless of the fossil fuel source, water was the critical component for generating energy in steam engine boilers on riverboats, in locomotives, and on factory floors. The Blue Ridge and Piedmont South, however, lacked economical access to coal, oil, and gas reserves necessary to fuel this watery transformation. Between 1890 and 1925, water, not burning fossil fuels, was the most important energy fuel source in the New South. Eager investors and glassy-eyed boosters like Henry Grady had generally assumed the Southeast—a humid place with many rivers—had all the water they could dream of.

Rupert Vance provides a launching point into the New South phase of southern water and power. Vance's second great complex—hydroelectric technology driven by New South capitalists' thirst for a privatized, indigenous, and cheap energy source—made energy corporations and southeastern rivers integral players in the region's history. The New South was hardly exceptional, but the scale and degree by which the energy sector sustained industry with water-generated energy made the region uniquely powerful and vulnerable. James B. Duke, the tobacco king and private university benefactor and Vance's most detailed example, started one of the most prolific energy companies that continues to operate more than 100 years later. Duke Power Company's founding goal in 1904, according to the company's namesake himself, was to harness "white coal" from rivers that previously flowed unused as "waste to the sea."[2] Today, the artifacts of the region's hydraulic waterscape reveal much about the legacy of southern water and southern power in the decades before the advent of the TVA in 1933.

After 1900, New South energy companies invigorated the process of mill and town building that William Church Whitner contributed to in the 1890s in the upper reaches of the Savannah River valley. Numerous companies—including the independent Tennessee River Power, Alabama Power, Georgia Power, Duke Power, and other smaller companies—planned and developed multiple-dam and sometimes multiple-purpose projects across the region to redirect river energy to factory hands and machines. "Water power," Rupert Vance declared in *Human Geography*, was "the one unifying force underlaying industrial development" in the southern Piedmont.[3] Vance observed this development through North Carolina's James B. Duke (1856–1925), and Duke Power Company was among the first and most successful corporate enterprises to couple waterpower and industrial development. Dr. Walker Gill Wylie (1849–1923), a South Carolina native, New York City physician, president of the Catawba Power Company, and Whitner's former business partner, presented the self-made American Tobacco Company king with the idea of developing a series of hydroelectric dams and reservoirs on the Catawba River.[4] Together, Wylie and Duke tapped William States Lee (1872–1934), a Citadel graduate and engineer who had previously worked alongside Whitner at Portman Shoals and who had completed Wylie's Rock Hill (S.C.) Catawba Power Company hydroelectric project in 1904, to provide the technical know-how.[5] Not unlike other company founders who merged technical skill, river knowledge, and financial resources, the Duke trio started building a system in 1905 and within six years had linked four hydroelectric plants (three on the

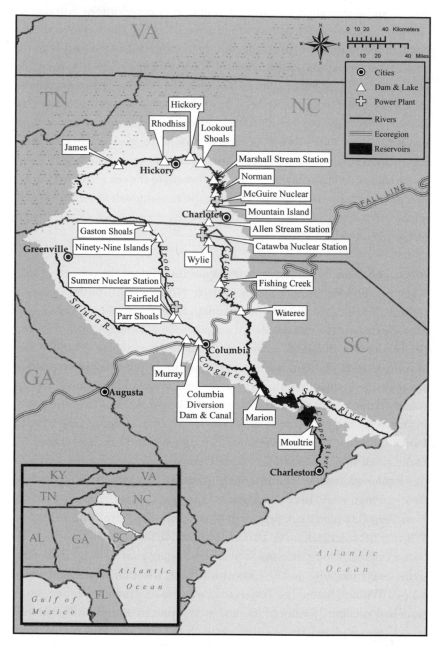

River basins in North and South Carolina, 2013, showing selected sites in the Saluda-Broad, Catawba-Wateree, and Santee-Cooper River basins (map by Amber R. Ignatius)

Catawba River) and two auxiliary coal-fired steam plants in the Carolina's Piedmont.[6] By then, Duke Power Company's Catawba (Lake Wylie) and Great Falls projects stored water behind dams before turning falling river water into energy for distribution over 700 miles of transmission lines to reach more than 100 cotton mills.[7]

James B. Duke did not wait for markets to emerge to justify massive capital investments in hydropower; he cultivated industrial consumers. Duke's company, and other companies that followed, had never envisioned providing service to rural or residential customers. Instead, as Duke historian Robert Durden has demonstrated, Duke invested directly in new textile mills or subsidized the electrical conversion of old mills to use electric equipment to ensure a market for his company's electricity and to attract New England's manufacturers to the Southeast. Industrial sociologist Harriet Herring, one of Vance's Chapel Hill colleagues, concluded that Duke Power "became a veritable Chamber of Commerce in advertising the advantages of the area for manufacturing." Duke Power's influence was "more positive and concrete than any Chamber of Commerce," in Herring's opinion, since the company could "offer attractive inducements to potential customers" in the days before public utility commissions regulated utility rates and service areas. In another example of Duke's influence, one company subsidiary, the Mill Power Supply Company, provided low-interest loans and ample credit to mill owners who abandoned the on-site steam plants they originally used to generate energy and converted to using energy produced and delivered by the Duke network. Duke Power executives were formidable economic players eager to feed the Piedmont's industrial base with energy derived from a changing southern waterscape.[8]

So why did Duke and his contemporaries in the Southeast initially cast their lot with white coal instead of rock coal? The Northeast and Rocky Mountain West had turned to fossil fuels—heavy fuel oil and coal—before and after the American Civil War as canal, railroad, pipeline, and coal mining operations shared corporate ownership and evolved in tandem.[9] Southeastern energy history was equally complicated and for different reasons. Pennsylvania, Alabama, and southwest Virginia miners cut bituminous coal for southern railroads, municipal waterworks, the metallurgical industry, the electric industry, and other heavy manufacturing regions stretching from the Carolinas to Texas that were coal and oil poor before the 1890s. New energy sources soon emerged as the clear winners in the early twentieth century, leading these regions to turn to alternative fossil or organic fuel sources. For example, Los Angeles and Houston declared energy independence from expensive coal imports from Canada, Australia, and Pennsylvania and tied their economic futures to locally available heavy fuel oil or natural gas after 1900.[10]

Southeastern railroads, factories, and homes certainly burned Alabama coal between 1890 and 1925, but coal was not yet king.[11] Alabama was the only major coal-producing state south of Tennessee and Virginia, and in 1900, Alabama produced a mere 8.3 million tons of coal when national production hovered just under 270 million tons. By 1929, Alabama had increased production to 17.7 million tons when national production surpassed 600 million tons.[12] And, Alabama's coalfields primarily supplied the state's Birmingham-centered metallurgical industry. At least one transnational railroad executive considered Alabama coal supplies unreliable and "of uneven quality" as locomotive fuel.[13] Other southern cities, from Atlanta to Charlotte, were hamstrung by coal's freight costs, particularly when post–World War I global demands sent the price of coal sky-high after 1919. Coal costs and fuel efficiency were frequent topics among Georgia railroad managers, whose company publications implored white and black employees to monitor their own coal handling.[14] Furthermore, the late-nineteenth- and early-twentieth-century coal sector was plagued with labor strikes and by poor management. For example, the coalfield wars and United Mine Workers' organized national strikes in Pennsylvania, Colorado, and Alabama between 1890 and 1920 affected coal production, shipments, and markets.[15] In this context, coal supplies, deliveries, and costs were unpredictable when workers went on strike. This volatile muscle-powered and mineral-fueled market helped New South capitalists make a choice and shift from soot-producing coal as a primary energy source to a renewable organic energy environment that eliminated some variables. The new fuel in the Southeast was the old waterpower transformed into slick hydroelectricity generated with white coal.

James B. Duke was just one of many industrial boosters who equated clean hydroelectric production with textiles and light-manufactories in the New South. J. A. Switzer, a professor of hydraulic engineering at the University of Tennessee, believed that luring industry to the New South, including "the industrial expansion already attained," was a result of "the cheapness of water-power already developed." And additional industrial growth—in textiles and other manufactures—would "greatly stimulate the further development of the remaining latent waterpowers" throughout the New South.[16] Thorndike Saville, another engineer and booster, commented in 1924 on corporations' total energy production and consumption in North Carolina, which, since 1912, had rapidly "surpassed its neighboring states." Furthermore, he noted, "this output is a sensitive index of industrial development and reflects the acknowledged superiority of North Carolina in this respect."[17] Cheap organic energy clearly lured textile and other producers to the Southeast. Companies mothballed many cotton mills in New England, and "the Piedmont's share of the total number of textile workers rose from 46 to 68 percent" between 1923 and 1933.[18] The New South's energy supply was renewable and cheap, was more easily manipulated than human labor, and was a major factor in this recentering of the American textile industry before the Great Depression. In other words, cheap renewable energy hastened the initial textile boom, and the continued industrial and energy developments paralleled each other. Maintaining cheap energy rates helped the Southeast remain competitive.

Before engineers and executives could develop all of the potential waterpower sites in the New South, they had to build privately owned and state-based systems. One hydraulic expert and booster noted in 1912 that Duke Power maintained 1,380 miles of transmission lines over a territory that "stretche[d] 200 miles from east to west and 150 miles from north to south" to deliver electricity to 156 cotton mills, homes in forty-five mill towns, municipal street lights, and an interurban railway with about 150 miles of track in North Carolina and South Carolina.[19] And by 1924, 80 percent of Duke's electricity went to textile facilities, while other factory operations (such as tobacco and furniture) consumed 10 percent and municipal systems absorbed the remaining 10 percent.[20] Duke's energy company was initially the most successful at harnessing a single southeastern river with a series of dams and artificial reservoirs placed one after the other in a series, but the institution soon faced stiff competition as other investors also raced to deploy transnational technologies, conserve New South water resources, and consolidate corporate power.

Private companies in Tennessee, Alabama, Georgia, and South Carolina followed Duke in the complex task of environmental manipulation and energy production.[21] Each individual company incorporated old and new ideas to create dam, reservoir, and transmission networks that fit site-specific environments in different watersheds. Every business assumed nature's energy—falling water—would always generate electric power, but they all learned that rivers did not always participate willingly in conservation regimes. When water did not cooperate, corporate bottom lines were threatened, productivity on factory floors faltered, and the fate of public-private development schemes was uncertain. Rupert Vance had informed his regionalist-inspired readers that "while the greatest potential water resources of the area" could "be found in the Tennessee River system, the highest actual development ha[d] been reached on the Catawba River" by Duke's company.[22] But in contrast to the situation in North Carolina, according J. A. Switzer, "there were no hydroelectric plants in operation in the State of Tennessee" in 1905.[23]

In Tennessee, one river project demonstrates the environmental, institutional, and technological difficulties involved in manipulating water and generating energy on a grand scale in the New South. The Hales Bar development underscored the dangers of public-private schemes while accomplishing many engineering firsts by 1914. Hales Bar, built between 1905 and 1913 by the Tennessee River Power Company, was the nation's "first case" where engineers combined hydroelectric generation with navigation, according to one industry periodical.[24] Chattanooga boosters and businessmen had conceived of plans for a dam and navigation lock in the vicinity of their city after observing "the progress of the development of water power in various parts of the country." The boosters then lobbied Congress and received a ninety-nine-year lease from the federal government in 1904 to complete a Tennessee River energy and navigation project that also required inspection and approval by the U.S. Army Corps of Engineers.[25]

The Corps, after all, was initially tasked by Congress with a civil works mission to improve navigation on the nation's waterways. Army engineering units have served the U.S. military since the American Revolution, but it was not until 1802 that Congress formally established the Corps of Engineers. Between 1900 and the 1930s, the Corps' civil works mission expanded to include flood control, but the Corps could participate in flood control projects only if the improvements enhanced navigation and benefited the national economy. Corps engineers were not oblivious to the waterpower and navigational potential of the Tennessee River valley, but the national leadership of the Corps was wary of multiple-purpose projects like Hales Bar and had not yet joined the private sector as dam builders. Until the 1930s, the Corps' primary civil works responsibility was to grease the wheels of commerce by keeping the nation's navigable waterways such as the Tennessee River open for boats and barges.[26]

Despite the Hales Bar project's collaborative and engineering successes, this corporate attempt at a massive dam and reservoir scheme faced many environmental challenges. Industrialists succeeded in completing the multiple-purpose project, but as one Corps of Engineers historian has explained, the dam and powerhouse encountered construction tests that left the Corps responsible for navigational facilities in a structure it considered a potential liability.[27] The region's porous Bangor limestone and sedimentary rock presented engineers and workers with no shortage of problems as they attempted to set the dam's and the powerhouse's foundations. This limestone was apparently "soluble in the river water," according to one technical writer, and "had a geological exploration been made, this condition would" have likely resulted in the project's termination. But the project continued as engineers and laborers drilled hundreds of vertical holes up to fifty feet deep before pumping cement grout under pressure into the holes to fill horizontal and lateral fissures. Workers used more than 200,000 bags of cement to manufacture "solid rock" for the dam's foundation. This solution worked in the short term, but in 1914 four "boils" emerged below the dam, indicating that water continued to enter limestone crevices in the riverbed above the dam, flow through limestone channels under the dam's foundation, and reemerge from the riverbed immediately downstream.[28] Engineers fixed isolated spots, but new boils continued to emerge on the dam's downstream side. Between 1919 and 1921, engineers injected asphalt-grout under the dam's foundation to depths of 130 feet. This method—apparently used elsewhere only once before—stopped the major leakage and reduced the overall number of boils, but it still could not seal all of the leaks. Seepage represented not only lost storage and potential energy. The leaking foundation also signaled that private industry was not entirely capable of financing and engineering multiple-purpose projects of this magnitude.

This limited public-private venture into multiple-purpose planning and water conservation in the Tennessee River valley did not bode well for future collaborations, since the initial projected cost of $3 million mushroomed to an actual cost of $11 million. "At the time of construction, Hales Bar was a great precedent setting project," noted TVA engineers in 1941. Excepting some western dams and the Niagara Falls project, Hales Bar was the "largest single hydroelectric development in the South" when the complex was completed in 1914.[29] But the engineering failures, from site selection to water storage problems, did not inspire future confidence in public-private conservation or power-sharing schemes. Furthermore, private corporations and their investors discovered the range of financial and environmental dangers inherent in building massive dams, navigational locks, powerhouses, and reservoirs. This realization kept some companies on the sidelines and provided ammunition for Progressives who were critical of the private energy sector's monopolistic tendencies.

This was serious business: Tennessee hydraulic engineer J. A. Switzer understood in 1912 that it did "not require the prophetic vision of a dreamer to suppose that the day will come when practically the entire length of such rivers as the Tennessee will be linked to water wheels, and so be forced to contribute their maximum to the country's supply of power." Switzer continued: "Nor is it visionary to say that the next great step will then be the building of enormous reservoirs at the headwaters of the rivers to impound the flood waters now going to waste, and by means of them doubling or trebling the power susceptible to utilization at all such sites as Hale's Bar. Just as certainly as that the Government will complete the Panama Canal will the Government in due time undertake this work."[30] The prescient Switzer envisioned not private enterprises but instead extensive government valley and headwaters projects throughout the nation, starting with the Tennessee Valley.

As the lead federal institution in the Tennessee River valley at the time, the Corps of Engineers approached multiple-purpose dams and projects with trepidation. While the Corps today manages hundreds of multiple-purpose dams and reservoirs, it amassed this responsibility very slowly, beginning in 1918 at a place downstream of Hales Bar called Muscle Shoals, Alabama. Throughout the nineteenth century, individuals and investment groups had presented the federal government with plans to improve navigation and harness Muscle Shoals's immense waterpower potential. Before and after World War I, successive administrations were mired in conflict over how to acquire, develop, manage, and then dispose of federal property at Muscle Shoals. To clear the environmental, financial, and technical hurdles evident at Hales Bar, some Muscle Shoals promoters had suggested public-private partnerships in which the federal government would pay for navigational improvements and a large dam, while energy corporations would finance generation and transmission facilities. Hales Bar's environmental and staggering financial challenges, however, made public-private schemes at Muscle Shoals a tough sell.[31] After the Great War commenced in 1914 and the nation's participation was imminent, Congress eventually acquired two dam sites from the Alabama Power Company and approved construction of two nitrate production facilities at Muscle Shoals and a dam to generate electricity for wartime industry. As construction proceeded, intense national debate ensued over the federal government's entrance into the fertilizer and energy production business, and this well-documented New South battle at Muscle Shoals between big business (namely the Alabama Power Company) and Progressive reformers (led by Nebraska senator George W. Norris) influenced the ultimate shape of the liberal New Dealers' TVA.

The debate over the fate of Muscle Shoals was an important national exercise involving many public and private participants who contributed to the TVA concept, but the creation of the TVA all too often overshadows other aspects of this earlier dispute. Understanding the pre-TVA role of private hydroelectric power illustrates what private energy corporations stood to lose during this famous dispute over Muscle Shoals, as well as why private interests continued to vilify federal hydroelectric energy projects as symbols of New Deal liberalism in the following quarter-century. As Preston J. Hubbard has concluded in his detailed analysis of the debate, Muscle Shoals occupied "an important place" in U.S. history because the conflict was essentially about who should control energy markets and conservation of the nation's natural resources.[32] It is also worth repeating that when the Corps of Engineers built Wilson Dam at Muscle Shoals, the agency was not devoted to multiple-purpose dam building or energy production. According to David P. Billington and Donald C. Jackson, the national leadership of the Corps considered multiple-purpose projects like Muscle Shoals "controversial" well into the 1920s because of a national debate about public versus private energy production and the financial costs. While the Corps' resident Tennessee Valley engineers thought massive dams could serve many beneficial purposes, not until the 1930s did officers in Washington, D.C., recommend that Congress seriously consider federal multiple-purpose projects.[33]

Other Tennessee River valley energy firms and transnational corporations manipulated the state's waterways to generate energy and consolidate economic power in the urban-industrial New South. Private corporations, including the Aluminum Company of America (Alcoa), built at least twenty-one hydroelectric dams on the Tennessee River's tributaries between 1905 and 1928.[34] The Great Depression derailed all companies' plans to fully develop southeastern rivers and disrupted private water storage and management projects throughout the New South. However, Tennessee and other energy companies were not the only organizations to deploy transnational technologies and consolidate corporate power throughout Rupert Vance's "Piedmont crescent of industry" in the 1920s.

One last example illustrates the scope of corporate power and the scale of environmental manipulation in the New South before the genesis of the TVA. The Georgia Power Company's engineers and laborers captured the Savannah River's headwaters and transformed the Tallulah and Tugaloo Rivers into a series of artificial lakes behind multiple dams to generate electricity for transmission to faraway consumers. During the Tallulah-Tugaloo project's formative stage in the early 1900s, one writer noted that the company planned a "vast network of interconnected hydroelectric power systems . . . along lines similar to those of the" Duke Power Company.[35] Georgia Power's ventures on rivers throughout the state were like other companies' projects in Tennessee and throughout the Carolinas: Georgia Power's schemes required external capital and transnational engineering expertise, and the company's choices further solidified the energy-water nexus in the region.

Big dams that diverted water into long pipelines and powerhouses were not exceptional, but the scale of Georgia Power's project was unique for the Southeast.[36] Starting in 1910, Georgia Power completed six dams and filled six reservoirs along the Tallulah and Tugaloo Rivers in the upper Savannah River basin. When the company completed the last dam and reservoir project in 1927, Georgia Power's Tallulah-Tugaloo system constituted "the most completely developed continuous stretch of river in the United States," according to company historian Wade H. Wright.[37] The corporation's artificial reservoirs and hydroelectric plants worked together to produce electricity on demand, as one company executive claimed, for "many thousands" of industrial employees and for more than sixty-five Georgia municipalities.[38] More than 800 miles of transmission lines strung throughout Georgia connected the Tallulah-Tugaloo hydraulic system's falling water to these consumers. To see a map of this hydroelectric machine, or to see it from the air, was to peer into the future of another southeastern river valley just a few miles away on the other side of the Eastern Continental Divide. Georgia Power's system in the Savannah basin—like other New South private utility companies—was a prototype for the New Deal's signature modernizing tool: the TVA.

Preston S. Arkwright Sr. (1871–1946) recognized the power that he wielded as a broker of water and energy. Arkwright estimated that the Tallulah-Tugaloo integrated system directly benefited Atlanta's citizens and the region's textile employers, and he explicitly linked consumers to the northeast Georgia project's water supply and electrical production. Arkwright—born in Savannah, Georgia, and perhaps a distant relative of Richard Arkwright, who invented a water-powered spinning frame

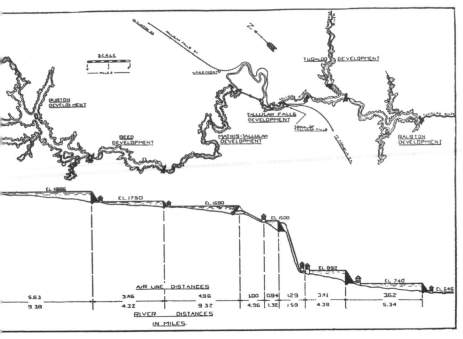

Tallulah and Tugaloo Project, 1921. In Benjamin Mortimer Hall and Max R. Hall, *Third Report on the Water Powers of Georgia*, Geological Survey of Georgia, Bulletin No. 38 (Atlanta: Byrd Printing Company, 1921).

in late-eighteenth-century England—declared that "electricity puts at the finger tips the force of the mountain torrents and . . . energy stored" for centuries.[39] This energy, he continued, was "a silent and unobtrusive servant in the home—always ready, without rest, vacation, sick leave or sleep; eager for its task, tireless, day and night." Arkwright believed hydroelectricity could "banish drudgery and bring convenience and comfort and ease and cheer and joy to human beings." As an instrument for domestic consumers still dependent on human labor, hydroelectric energy was like having servants "on tiptoe" behind a wall waiting to spring "forth at your summons, waiting to do your bidding." Hydroelectricity, in Arkwright's thinking in 1924, might create a domestic and industrial labor utopia free of racial and class conflict. After the brutal 1906 Atlanta race riot left dozens of African Americans dead, and after post–World War I cuts in textile mill production and wages led white mill workers to strike between 1919 and 1920 throughout the Southeast, Arkwright was not the only person to pin the future on white coal. But Arkwright's assumption—and that of his contemporaries in the energy, agricultural, and industrial sectors—that water resources could benefit his company's customers and help solve the New South's manufactured race and labor problems was more dream than reality. Transmission lines ran from dams to urban-industrial areas, skipping an intermediary agriculture zone cultivated by sharecroppers and poor farmers and leaving them without electricity for another decade or more. And textile worker strikes in Elizabethton, Tennessee, and Gastonia and Marion, North Carolina, in 1929 proved that white coal was no panacea for industries that continued to stretch and squeeze energy out of people. In the near future, the company's other urban and industrial customers also learned how a dependence on hydraulic systems like the Tallulah-Tugaloo's waterscape could be dangerous.

When Henry Grady's New South was hitched to white coal, falling water nearly 100 miles from Atlanta benefited urban dwellers and workers increasingly dependent on electricity and the corporate transmission system that delivered that energy. For instance, electric elevators served metropolitan low-rises and "large office buildings" as early as the 1890s, when more than 65,000 people lived in Atlanta.[40] Atlanta's streetcar companies had begun to shift from mule-drawn streetcars to electric streetcars and trolleys after 1890, hastening the development of the Georgia Power Company and new streetcar suburbs like Inman Park.[41] Like most major urban areas in the late nineteenth century, Atlanta also increasingly turned away from gas-powered to electric lighting. By the early 1900s, the generation and transmission of electricity made commercial and residential consumption possible while powering ice-making, electric sewing machines, bakeries, and printing offices.[42] These applications enabled entrepreneurs and boosters to enthusiastically partner electricity and industrialization with a modern New South in the pages of the *Manufacturers' Record, Electrical World,* and *Engineer News Record.* One such cheery writer could boast that Atlanta's approximately 235,000 residents enjoyed the "third lowest average power rate" of any city in the nation in 1924. Furthermore, Georgia Power's interconnection with other regional energy corporations assured the city's "industries against any interruptions in service."[43] Could all this occur in a backward region? To the contrary, Georgia Power's access to a renewable energy source, its engineers' incorporation of transnational technologies, and the company's interconnected hydraulic electrical generation system linked the state's hinterland resources and factories to Atlanta's urban-industrial core. This modern—and inequitable—system also delivered energy to a far larger constellation of New South hinterlands and hives.

Energy companies around the country began experimenting with interconnected production facilities and transmission grids in the early decades of the twentieth century. Powerful southeastern energy corporations, however, put the most complete system into operation. Electrical engineer William S. Murray promoted one such system, called a "superpower zone," to coordinate energy production and distribution throughout the Northeast's metropolitan corridor and across state lines. In a 1921 U.S. Geological Survey report, Murray asserted that a coordinated and privately managed energy grid could facilitate technological standardization and assure reliable service. Northeastern energy executives, however, were reluctant to participate in electrical interconnections in their region.[44] In stark contrast, the major southeastern energy companies—Alabama Power, Georgia Power, Duke Power, and Tennessee Power—did not share this reluctance. In an example of extraordinary business acumen, these independent companies began interconnecting in 1912 and assembled a fully connected Super Power grid by 1921. According to utility trade journal editors and water professionals such as Thorndike Saville, the New South's pre-1930 Super Power system was "unparalleled in the world" and represented "a more complete integration of power-producing and transmission capacity" than any other system on the planet.[45]

Production and distribution interconnections were not uncommon in the United States and Canada, but the southeastern system's scale and scope were remarkable. Private energy executives enlarged, and engineers consciously built Super Power during the roaring 1920s by way of corporate consolidation. In 1924 the Southeastern Power and Light holding company reorganized the Alabama Power Company and other utilities, including two firms that subsequently made up the Georgia Power Company at its founding. Then in 1929, the New-York-City-based Commonwealth and Southern Corporation assumed a 40 percent ownership of the Southeastern Power and Light and all of its subsidiaries, including Alabama Power and Georgia Power.[46] Duke Power Company also consolidated smaller energy utilities in North Carolina and South Carolina but was never financially tied to larger regional or national utility holding companies.[47]

Super Power—or what Vance in 1932 defined as a hydroelectric complex—was a lot like another complex that tied regions together. Super Power proponents, such as Alabama Power Company president Thomas Martin, defended these massive corporate linkages and the electrical production infrastructure by equating Super Power with the railroad systems that moved people "across the continent without change of cars," and he likened individual energy companies to independent railroads that shared standardized railroad tracks and equipment. Each energy company, Martin argued, was "independent, assumes a duty to its own customers, provides its own management, adopts and pursues its own policies, attends to its own financial affairs and is subject to the authority where it operates as to rates and service and security issues. The component companies merely draw from and contribute surplus energy to others which otherwise would go to waste and benefit no one."[48] By 1924, the well-organized southeastern interconnected grid relayed electrical power over 3,000 miles of high-voltage transmission lines and served 6 million people in a 120,000-square-mile region encompassing a half-dozen states.[49]

Critics condemned the early interconnections and the vast Super Power network. These networks, in the words of historian Sarah T. Phillips, consolidated "power—electric power, manufacturing power, economic power" in urban-industrial centers at the expense of rural consumers and citizens.[50] Progressives and liberal reformers shifted their criticism from railroads to electrical utilities, since the new enemy, like the former one, was a natural monopoly. Customers were compelled to purchase services from a single unregulated provider that faced no market competitors. Industrial proponents considered these energy companies and utilities natural monopolies because competitors recognized there was no economic incentive to duplicate service and capital-intensive infrastructure in the same market territories. A congressionally approved 1916 study by the Department of Agriculture, as well as others that followed, confirmed many critics' early claims.[51] Based on a comprehensive study of the nation's public and private electric generation installations and ownership patterns, the report concluded, "There are several lines of evidence which show a continuously increasing tendency toward concentration in the control of the development, distribution, and sale of electric power. Each year shows a greater percentage of electric power being produced by" privately owned entities. The report illustrated that distinct regions were under the control of companies like Duke Power and Carolina Power and Light (the two companies were responsible for generating and distributing 66 percent of all electricity in North Carolina).[52] Progressive and social reformers criticized state agencies and fledgling public utility commissions for allowing corporate consolidation to accelerate in the 1920s. The individual energy companies may have operated independently, as Thomas Martin of Alabama Power claimed, but the interconnected electrical grids looked a lot like Stephen J. Gould's railroad empire and bore a striking resemblance to Udo J. Keppler's Standard Oil octopus. Indeed, in 1913 the editors of the *Southern Farming* periodical superimposed a "Water Power Trust" octopus over a map of the United States and offered a rallying cry: "Do not let the New Octopus Monopolize the inexhaustible supply of white coal in our Southern States."[53] Super Power visionary William S. Murray surely stoked agrarian, populist, and Progressive rage when he observed that "electricity is the True Agent of Power" and "no business ever succeeded without good agents." Southeastern energy companies, however, took this model to heart.[54]

Not to be outdone, Progressive reformers offered an alternative to Super Power as business structures evolved in other American regions. Pennsylvania governor Gifford Pinchot and Morris L. Cooke were among the most visible proponents of so-called Giant Power. This idea emerged in 1924 as a public power program that could check corporate greed and monopolistic utilities, reduce electrical rates, electrify rural areas, and promote conservation of natural and energy resources. The program envisioned publicly owned coal-fired electrical generation plants in coal mining areas and high-tension transmission lines that would link the mouth-of-mine thermoelectric steam plants with rural and urban customers. As originally conceived, Giant Power went down in flames, derided as a communist fantasy.[55] While Giant Power never fully materialized, its liberal backers did eventually influence New Deal initiatives such as the Rural Electrical Administration (REA) and TVA. Until that time in the New South, large energy corporations and natural monopolies used Super Power and its good agents to build a southeastern urban-industrial region.

Alabama and Georgia energy companies exported a high percentage of excess electricity via the New South Super Power system to the Carolinas, where regional textile mill growth and electrification were greatest in the early years of the twentieth century, thanks in part to James B. Duke's industrial subsidies and incentives that cultivated industrial customers. Because of the region's Super Power transmission and distribution geography, Atlanta became "the chief city on this system and a center of utility activity" by 1928, according to hydroelectric booster L. W. W. Morrow.[56] The Georgia Power Company occupied the center of this vast hydraulic system and linked an elaborate hydraulic hinterland that stretched across Mississippi, Alabama, Florida, South Carolina, North Carolina, and Tennessee.[57]

Environmental conditions in Georgia and North Carolina soon tested the system and the individual energy companies. This Super Power grid did more than connect multiple states and a half-dozen different energy companies capable of producing more than 1 million horsepower. These interconnections also provided more than a means to transport surplus electricity: They functioned as lifelines. The interconnected systems quickly justified themselves when region-specific droughts struck the New South and significantly reduced hydroelectric generation between 1921 and 1925.[58] In response to the drought, the water-dependent energy companies used the Super Power grid to manage river flows in "separate and distinct water sheds."[59] Water conserved and run through turbines in one state's watershed produced energy that could be transferred over high-tension transmission lines across another state to facilitate energy delivery to yet a third state hundreds of miles away. This was Super Power in action.

The late summer drought of 1925 led to "one of the greatest power shortages in the history" of the American South, according to the *Atlanta Constitution*.[60] Droughts had previously affected cities and towns like Atlanta and Augusta, where textile mills sitting on riverbanks and dependent upon local river flows frequently ceased production as water levels exceeded or dropped below operable levels.[61] For example, the Savannah River's water flow itself had dropped precariously in 1918 and threatened "a general close down" of industrial and commercial operations in Augusta because the Stevens Creek hydroelectric dam and other small plants along the Augusta Canal could not generate enough energy to keep factories running and workers employed.[62] But the option of shutting down twentieth-century businesses or not providing expectant customers in a major metropolitan area with reliable electrical or streetcar service was unsustainable for corporations with significant capital investments. Geographically isolated nineteenth-century outages only threatened individual urban-industrial nodes, but the droughts and rolling "blackouts" of the 1920s presented a broader problem requiring a shift in corporate strategy.[63]

At the time of the 1925 drought crisis, Georgia Power executives declared that a mere four weeks' supply of water remained in the Tallulah-Tugaloo project's "giant hydro-electric reservoirs" of northeast Georgia. Despite claims from company officials in 1920 that such dams could conserve water supply through "the severest drought," the 1920s circumstances presented the grim reality of an energy-water nexus choke point.[64] While generating every possible kilowatt of energy from the company's

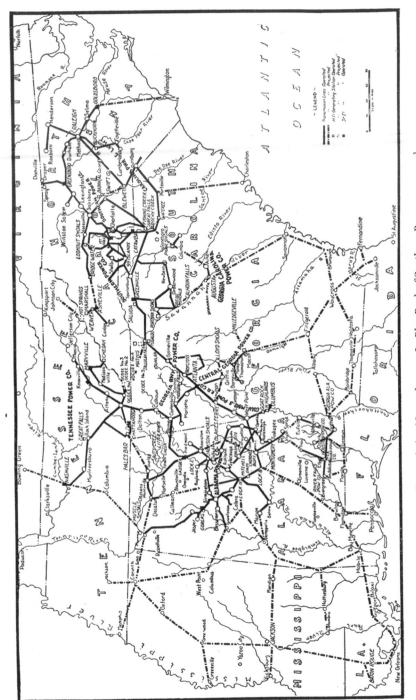

Super Power Transmission Network, 1924. In *Blue Book of Southern Progress*, 1924 ed.
(Baltimore: Manufacturers' Record, 1924). Courtesy of Conway Data, Inc.

operable hydro facilities and auxiliary coal plants, Georgia Power in 1925 imported "hundreds of tons of coal . . . to meet any emergency which might be caused" if operations exhausted the limited remaining supply of renewable energy. Georgia officials also discussed the situation with executives from "textile mills, brick, marble, granite mining and other industries," and the corporate customers agreed to limit their energy use "as much as possible and to operate at nights" for the duration of the drought-induced "crisis."[65] Atlanta's consumers also agreed to follow restrictions in place between August 21 and September 7, and full streetcar service did not resume for another month.[66]

When Atlanta producers and consumers faced this crisis, the interconnected Super Power transmission network ultimately averted more draconian orders. "To the relief of Georgia industries," the state's energy companies imported electricity produced in Alabama and Tennessee in August 1925.[67] The federal government sold energy generated in the Sheffield coal-fired steam plant and from the newly operational Wilson Dam (Muscle Shoals) to the Tennessee Electric and Power Company and the Alabama Power Company, who in turn transferred the energy—some of which could be classified as "coal by wire"—to Georgia and the Carolinas.[68] The droughts of the 1920s threatened New South water conservation and consumption plans, but the Super Power grid enabled electricity to move seamlessly from one state to another. This technological network linked wet hinterlands and cores with drier neighbors and thus allowed energy-dependent consumers to avoid thinking too hard about the energy sources and infrastructure that sustained the modern New South. The Super Power grid integrated the region but had not integrated the region into the nation, as railroads had done elsewhere and as regionalists like Vance had hoped would happen. Instead, the Southeast became a new destination for factories and businesses hungry for cheap natural energy, liberal tax incentives, and tractable human labor. During the 1925 drought, energy companies learned the hard way for the first time that southern rivers, not unlike mill workers, could, in fact, go on strike.

The droughts of the 1920s not only highlighted the utility of interconnected grids; they also revealed a water supply problem, the limits of hydropower, and a technological plateau. James B. Duke and other energy company executives had championed white coal as a solution to southeastern economic development and energy independence, but after the 1925 drought, Duke no longer accepted hydroelectric dams as the energy-generating standard.[69] Both Georgia Power's and Duke Power's hydroelectric expectations and risk management shifted radically in the following years, particularly as black-coal-fueled steam technology became an increasingly efficient and economical method for generating base loads. Despite continued investment in hydroelectric dams to produce peak power when consumer demands exceeded base load supply, the 1925 southeastern drought led the companies on a technological path from a hydro plateau back to coal-fired steam generation plants. The shift away from renewable energy to fossil fuels as the primary energy source might look like an abrupt about-face, but when the companies transitioned back to coal, they never distanced themselves from southeastern rivers or existing artificial reservoirs. Energy producers stopped relying on water falling on turbines to produce energy and turned instead to burning coal and transforming liquid water into pressurized steam to spin turbines. Throughout the remainder of the twentieth century, southeastern energy companies—specifically Duke Power—built coal-fired and nuclear power plants on the shores of the same reservoirs engineers originally built to conserve water for hydroelectric generation, and the companies also built some new reservoirs for new coal-fired plants.[70] Furthermore, after the 1925 drought, Georgia Power's chief executive abandoned plans to build new hydroelectric white coal projects on north Georgia's Chattooga and Coosawattee Rivers and instead invested in black coal plants on the Chattahoochee River upstream of metro Atlanta and on the Ocmulgee River near Macon.[71] White coal was no longer the industry standard, but water supplies remained critical for black coal electrical generation facilities.

The droughts of the 1920s also forced engineers to think differently about water supply. Engineers who maintained the elaborate hydraulic systems increasingly learned how to conserve and utilize water to maximize their companies' profits while also protecting expensive infrastructure. After nearly twenty-five years of managing dams, artificial reservoirs, and auxiliary coal-fired steam plants along the Catawba River, Duke Power employees understood that "the principal problem is to operate" the combination of storage reservoirs and run-of-river hydroelectric "plants in connection with the steam plants so as to secure the maximum kilowatt-hour output from the available river flow." The region's climate and rivers' behavior made it clear that not only was there great "variation in river flow from wet to dry season," but there was "also a considerable variation from year to year," making "it very difficult to map out" energy production schedules and "secure the maximum output from the hydro plants." In other words, weather and consumer behavior were unpredictable. Playing the seasonal calendar, Duke employees typically filled artificial reservoirs during the wet season (January through May), kept them partially filled between May and September because summer or tropical storms could produce flooding during this time of year, and then drew the reservoirs down during the dry months between September and January.[72] On average, the lowest period of rainfall occurred in the late summer and fall, but "even this phase has no regularity," engineers observed. Evidence illustrated that North Carolina's early 1920s droughts were followed by "exceptionally heavy precipitation" and "one of the greatest floods" in the Catawba River's recorded history in the late 1920s.[73] The private power company executives and engineers learned how fickle New South rivers straitjacketed with multiple dams had become by 1930. Water managers had almost fully engineered and controlled the region's rivers and thus white coal and energy production without major disruption. But the companies' success also pointed to a new southern problem and to a pre-TVA New South that was anything but exceptional. The region—a humid place assumed to have plenty of rain—also had a water problem that required water resource management and engineering on a scale once only associated with water-poor regions like the arid American West.[74]

Corporations financed interconnected hydraulic systems stretching from the Carolinas to Florida and across Georgia to Mississippi, and they changed the New South's rivers and economy in the process. The New South's private Super Power energy system and liberal Giant Power alternative also influenced the shape and character of the region's well-documented New Deal water management institution: the TVA. Engineers from the Corps and other federal entities could look across the New South at a vast privately organized and financed electricity generation and distribution system that was more than three decades old when the TVA emerged in 1933 as a high-modernist solution for regional economic, social, and environmental problems.

Once engineers from the TVA and Corps embarked on their own New Deal–style hydroelectric projects in the 1930s, they solicited advice from academic experts, company executives, and professional engineers.[75] Rupert Vance was one of those advisors. On the eve of the TVA's creation, Vance continued to promote hydroelectric possibilities in the region while also acknowledging the inherent dangers of relying on a renewable energy source to sustain urban-industrial development. Vance had identified water as a primary energy source to fuel economic engines, but he was not ready to fully accept the prospect of water scarcity or the "Piedmont crescent of industry's" shift to coal after 1925. In 1935, three years after Vance published *Human Geography*, he collaborated on a study of the Catawba River valley for the TVA. In one of the study's appendices, titled "The Consumption of Coal in Relation to the Development of Hydroelectric Power in the Carolinas," Vance concluded that "the Carolinas had to develop hydro power or nothing" because "cheap power attracts industries." Vance acknowledged that a "tremendous consumption of coal in 1927" reflected Duke Power's response to "a drought which affected" river flows and thus hydroelectric production in what his coauthors called the Catawba River valley's "hydro-industrial empire."[76]

The southeastern physiographic environment—which was fossil-fuel poor but rich in renewable energy like water—had presented Vance's urban-industrial contemporaries with limited tools to make the New South bloom and glow. Vance, however, still believed in hydropower ten years after the Southeast's worst drought underscored regional water insecurity. In *Human Geography*, Vance advised TVA technocrats to build one of the nation's only regional planning experiments, and that they employ large hydroelectric dams as primary energy generators. But at the same time, New South energy companies had turned to black coal to generate the majority of their customers' electricity. TVA directors and progressive engineers, however, had been so clearly influenced by a legacy of New South white coal projects that they initially embarked on a federally subsidized program that was behind a technological curve from the beginning. Private energy companies never abandoned their old hydroelectric facilities or stopped building new ones, but renewable hydro sources increasingly functioned as secondary or peak power sources. Operators could bring hydro facilities online immediately during moments of high energy demand while capital-intensive facilities used coal and other fossil fuels at a steady clip to generate primary, or base, loads. Only after World War II did the TVA once again follow private companies' technological lead and begin building coal and nuclear plants to keep up with the New South's fast-growing industrial, commercial, and residential consumer demands.

William Church Whitner, James B. Duke, and Preston Arkwright each understood that water-generated electricity in the Southeast was, as William S. Murray claimed in 1922, an "Agent of Power."[77] The Super Power grid as developed in the Southeast made this clear. The electrical production and distribution grid supported a regional corporate power structure that was at least as influential as individual states, politicians, planters, and industrialists, and the hydraulic system facilitated the concentration of capital and labor in specific places. The individual energy companies and their transnational employees did not rule an exceptional empire, but they did build a remarkable region defined by radial transmission lines that provided individual companies with a service and product that became indispensable in business operations and daily life. In the process, corporate power and technology wove energy production and water supply into a structure largely invisible to laborers and consumers who lost sight of the energy and water connection after the 1930s.

Unless there was a problem, early-twentieth-century consumers expressed indifference toward questions of where their energy and water came from. And professional, service, and industrial workers took advantage of electric streetcars, elevators in skyscrapers, electric fans, and electrified machinery.[78] The New South's new environmental conditions—artificial reservoirs and urban drought—had reached a point where diminished water supplies threatened daily industrial and commercial functions in metropolitan settings. Urban drought years not unlike 1925 emerged frequently throughout the twentieth century, and they continued to shape private and public energy regimes in the American South well after 1945. Rivers and falling water were significant instruments for New South developers and conservationists who used the hydraulic waterscape to concentrate labor for the benefit of the textile and other industries. These utilitarian boosters and energy sector leaders consistently transformed tumbling waterfalls into waterwheels, rocky shoals where migratory fish spawned into turbines, and free-flowing rivers into "slack-water," artificial reservoirs plied by recreational pleasure craft.[79] Dam-crazy private energy company executives and engineers thought they had tamed southeastern rivers and solved regional water problems while cultivating a new modern urban-industrial landscape linked by Super Power transmission lines. Southern rivers, however, displayed a persistent capacity to function by their own rules, to trump the romantic beauty of waterfalls and the efficiency of corporate turbines with an unwelcome reality of dry riverbeds and raging floods. Southern water and southern power were hardly secure.

CHAPTER 3

New Deal Big Dam Consensus

The Savannah River valley's residents were accustomed to the river running dry or high in the twentieth century. Augusta's factory managers had sent workers home for weeks after shutting down waterpowered operations along the Augusta Canal during previous droughts. And the 1908 flood alone had done enough damage to convince the city government to investigate, finance, and construct an eleven-mile levee to keep the Savannah River's almost annual flood surges out of the city.[1] Given these past weather events, the prolonged, heavy, and cold rains of September 1929 surely looked threatening to residents of Augusta, Georgia, and Hamburg, South Carolina, who had lived through previous bouts of water anxiety and insecurity.

The Savannah River valley's weather swung hard in the direction of rain after the New South's 1925 drought of record. Over the course of thirty-six hours beginning September 26, 1929, nearly nine inches of rain fell across the upper Savannah River valley's landscape. Countless dry gullies, numerous small creeks, and broad rivers swelled beyond capacity and sent a forty-six-foot flood crest down the Savannah River's main channel. The surge breeched the Augusta levee a few miles below the central business district. Water flowed from the river through the levee and into the city and proceeded to back up the city's stormwater drains and flood homes and businesses. The first flood wave passed, and the rain briefly abated. Then, on October 1 and 2, a second storm—this time the tropical remnants of a Category One Gulf of Mexico hurricane—moved across the southeast from Apalachicola Bay in the Florida panhandle to Augusta and dropped another eight inches of rain on an already saturated landscape. Unable to absorb any more water, the land shed the deluge, and the Savannah River rose again to send a second, larger flood crest downstream to the Augusta metro area. The Great Flood of 1929 plowed through the Piedmont, easily surged over the low Stevens Creek and Augusta Canal dams, but broke the Augusta Canal's bank above the city and washed away bridges intentionally loaded down with heavy freight trains. Across the Savannah River from Augusta, William Gregg's antebellum-era Graniteville and other Horse Creek valley mill dams broke loose and washed a handful of South Carolina factory homes from their foundations. Despite fears that the sodden and compromised Augusta Levee might fail catastrophically during the flood, it did not.[2]

The small town of Hamburg, immediately across the Savannah River, was not so lucky. The South Carolina community had attempted to surpass its colonial-era Augusta neighbor in an economic rivalry over which town would serve as the upper valley's commercial and transportation hub before the Civil War. Henry Shultz, a white German immigrant, founded the small town in the 1820s, named it after his German birthplace, and invested significant personal capital to promote its economic development. He secured exclusive rights to operate the Savannah River's only riverboat between his town and Savannah, Georgia, and the town briefly served as the terminus for the Charleston and Hamburg (S.C.) Railroad before an 1834 bridge carried trains directly into Augusta.[3] After the Civil War, Hamburg's demographics shifted, and the town soon lost its economic luster in the shadow of Augusta. Hamburg became known as a center for African American political activity and was the site of a dramatic riot instigated by armed white men who "attacked a legally constituted black militia" on July 4, 1876.[4] This incident made national headlines and signaled the beginning of the end for Reconstruction and how whites would redeem the South from what many called northern aggression; it foreshadowed the violent rise of white supremacy. With no political power, Hamburg remained an unleveed town in the Jim Crow South until 1929.

The Great Flood's second crest, which topped out at nearly forty-five feet, settled any lingering antagonism between the two river communities once and for all and completely swept the unleveed "negro [sic] settlement" away after the residents had already fled. Multiple facilities associated with brick manufacturing, a store, two churches, three filling stations, a railroad yard, and "many of the houses of Hamburg . . . were carried away" or damaged, thereby rendering the "occupants . . . homeless."[5] The Savannah River's historic floods and droughts of the 1920s illustrated dramatic weather, human sacrifice, the inequity of the regional political economy, and water insecurity in one place. The response revealed persistent racial friction as well as new solutions. Hamburg's story also revealed how race, liberal politics, and the hydraulic waterscape were historically bound on the eve of the Great Depression and would remain linked in the Savannah River valley's near future. Hamburg was an example of how white New South citizens, like their national neighbors, had haphazardly managed river systems to meet private needs while serving self-identified public goods.

During the interwar years (1918–41) an alternative emerged. Massive federally backed multiple-purpose dams evolved into the ideal technological tools for organizing river basin resources equitably and managing risk. Above all, these structures delivered to the devoted a trio of benefits—hydroelectric production, flood control, and improved navigation—that New South capitalists had conveyed inefficiently at best. Progressives and New Dealers in Georgia and South Carolina leaned on structural solutions first developed by New South free enterprise to generate energy, but they now coveted designs that managed a variety of needs. From this new policy ecosystem emerged a national New Deal big dam consensus—buttressed by Muscle Shoals (completed in 1924 on the Tennessee River), Hoover Dam (1936, Colorado), and Bonneville Dam (1938, Columbia)—that championed mammoth Corps and Bureau of Reclamation public works projects to tackle interlocking cultural and natural challenges.

In the Southeast, the legacies of New South capitalism shaped New Deal liberalism as Americans redesigned the nation's waterways and energy infrastructure during depression and war. U.S. Army Corp of Engineers staff recommendations contributed to this process but held the agency back from energy, water, and multiple-purpose river dam development in the Savannah River valley. Droughts, floods, and economic crisis were not enough to persuade the Corps to switch from river studies to actual implementation of the studies' recommendations. Only orders from above could, and eventually did, set in motion plans to build upon the New South's piecemeal and fragmented waterscape.

Like many other American institutions old and new, the forces and individuals who advocated for the big dam consensus were reacting to social, economic, and environmental conditions during the Great Depression. New Dealers responded to the free market's failure and ensuing global Great Depression by systematizing the big dam consensus in the Tennessee Valley Authority (TVA). As a grand experiment, one of the TVA's express goals was to limit New South capitalism's monopoly power in the energy sector while simultaneously improving southern social and environmental conditions. Regional planners and southern Democrats enthusiastically embraced big dams as cornerstones for an equitable postdepression economy that would balance production and consumption in urban and rural areas. As the national New Deal big dam consensus lurched forward in the coming years, it would, however, encounter resistance from within the New Deal Democratic coalition and the private sector.

The New Dealers' water and energy agenda began to change form nationally after 1935, and this movement was a reflection of how significant natural resource and energy policy had become to the administrative strategy of President Franklin D. Roosevelt (FDR).[6] Southern Democrats resisted some elements of New Deal liberalism but generally accepted multiple-purpose dams and rural electrification. By the mid-1930s, conservative Democrats were willing to accept limited agricultural relief and improved rural equity for the greater regional benefits that large federal infrastructure projects delivered.[7] The Savannah River valley's residents had clearly experienced natural disasters, but these disasters were only partly natural. Floods, like droughts, revealed "human complicity" in constructing a landscape subject to nature's fury and whim where the human victims were often poor and the beneficiaries were often economically powerful. Augusta's citizens accepted flooding and drought as temporary inconveniences, and they initiated narrowly focused projects like a bigger Augusta Canal that produced more waterpower and a taller Augusta Levee to manage localized flooding. Levees, funded by either community or federal sources, represented one form of technology for risk management and, as environmental historian Ted Steinberg and Hamburg residents might recognize, "risk-production."[8] As the United States entered the Great Depression, a great debate emerged over who was best suited to manage a river valley's water and energy resources and to manage the hydraulic waterscape. Since the region's flooding and drought problems were partially manufactured, the individuals and institutions that shaped the conversation about causes and solutions exerted considerable influence.

Southern Democrats contemplated their water and energy choices and calculated any pushback as their national party struggled to hold together a coalition of black and white workers and farmers. Anxious to block continued liberal attempts to advance civil rights and labor reform, but still hungry for federal investment in infrastructure, southern politicians repackaged the New Deal big dam consensus. They turned over flood, drought, and energy futures of the Savannah, Chattahoochee, and other river valleys to the U.S. Army Corps of Engineers. The Corps, with new power and practical New Deal training, separated the TVA's idealized social planning from the more practical trio of benefits. Corps engineers operating within their old agency emerged as the new arbiters responsible for balancing the legacies of New South laissez-faire and New Deal liberalism to meet the Sun Belt's anticipated energy demands and water needs after 1944. Before the Corps fully launched this new mission, private and public debate over a place called Clarks Hill disrupted the Corps' self-imposed limits and dragged the agency onto center stage at a time when southerners were growing increasingly frustrated with the region's water problems, the old New South corporate models, and the New Deal's faltering liberal solutions. The American South's water and energy future remained central to this debate as New South capitalism and New Deal liberalism squared off.

A long history of floods convinced Augusta residents, congressional representatives, and federal agents to further evaluate local flood control solutions in the late nineteenth century. Augusta, located at the fall line that divides the Piedmont and the upper Coastal Plain, had experienced high water as far back as 1800. Early Corps surveys, including Lieutenant Oberlin Carter's 1890 investigation, studied flood control and water storage options throughout the Savannah River valley in conjunction with the Corps' primary function: navigational improvement and keeping the nation's waterways open for boats and barges by clearing debris, dredging channels, and battling shifting sandbars.[9]

Carter and his assistant, George Brown, hedged when they considered separating human and natural activity while identifying water problems and offering solutions in the Savannah River valley. They reported in 1890 that "it does not lie within the power of man to remove the causes of the destructive floods in the Savannah River valley, although their evil effects" could be "lessened" with improved agricultural and forestry practices in a region still arrested by globalized King Cotton. Their 1890 report noted river bottoms covered in willow, poplar, and sycamore with dense island canebrakes, in addition to the river's obvious shift from clear to muddied water. The "small gullies" that evolved into "deep gorges" produced turbid water and eliminated "many varieties of fish."[10] Beyond recommendations they could never enforce, such as improved land treatment programs to combat erosion upstream of Augusta, the two men recommended structural engineering solutions: deeper river channels below Augusta to move high water more quickly, protective levees around the city, and flood control reservoirs in tributary streams above Augusta if such structures could be economically justified. However, this 1890 federal risk assessment resulted in no action from federal authorities. The Corps' leadership had historically refrained from using levee and multiple-purpose technologies to manage flooding risks if such improvements did not enhance navigation, serve national defense objectives, or meet basic cost-benefit evaluations. Colonel Dan Kingman of the Savannah District engineers' office, like other Corps colleagues, rejected multiple-purpose flood control options in the Savannah River valley because they were "enormously expensive, and their effect uncertain."[11] The 1908 flood did provide Augusta's leadership with enough justification to plan, finance, and complete the city's levee by 1915.[12] This new structural flood control solution protected the city in 1918 from a thirty-five foot flood surge and nearly failed catastrophically during the great flood of 1929. But the city's levee institution successfully managed their only defined risk: The Augusta Levee Commission maintained and reinforced a functional levee with occasional congressional funding distributed through the Corps.[13] As such, Carter, Kingman, and other Corps engineers limited their own agency's activities to flood control and navigation in the Savannah River valley well into the 1930s.

National disasters tend to influence institutional momentum. The Great Mississippi Flood of 1927 helped clear the way for Congress to empower the Corps to move, on a national scale, beyond single-purpose navigational strategies and into the realm of multiple-purpose navigation and flood control work. Under the terms of the Flood Control Act of 1928, Corps engineers assumed increased responsibility for planning, coordinating, constructing, and maintaining the Mississippi and Sacramento valleys' flood control apparatus; they replaced underfunded and poorly coordinated local levee commissions.[14] Colonel Kingman, however, did not move as quickly into flood control in his valley as Corps engineers did in other basins. Since Corps and Augusta operatives continued to focus only on levee engineering along a single, isolated section of the Savannah River, the city's residents and those with no levee protection continued to face threats associated with flooding and drought because the Piedmont and the central Savannah River valley were not important enough to the nation's economy or defense to warrant any federally organized, basinwide improvement.[15] Major flooding in the Mississippi and other river valleys did not inspire action among Corps officials in Georgia and South Carolina.

Corps and private sector engineers thought narrowly about their water projects before 1930. Until then, there were just a few comprehensive or multiple-purpose domestic and international examples to study.[16] One was actually a Corps experiment: the Upper Mississippi River Headwaters navigation project. Congress approved construction of six dams in Minnesota—three in the headwaters and three more on tributaries between 1880 and 1912—that only marginally regulated the river and navigation for St. Paul, 200 miles downstream.[17] Another example of multiple, single-purpose dams was Arthur E. Morgan's flood control project in Ohio. Morgan, who would later become one of the future TVA's founding directors and lead engineer, designed five single-purpose flood control dams and basins in the Miami River valley to protect Dayton and surrounding communities. The Miami Conservancy District program gained national attention when completed in 1918 because the institution was financed without federal funding.[18] Finally, there were multiple-dam developments such as Georgia Power Company's Tallulah-Tugaloo project and Duke Power Company's activity on the Catawba River.[19] As single-purpose hydroelectric dams, these dams did not provide navigational or flood control benefits; in flood conditions, excess water poured over the dams' crests, rolled down spillways, and flowed downstream, the consequences of which could include Augusta's Great Flood in 1929. In this example, Georgia Power's corporate goal—using specific technology to store water and generate electricity in the hinterlands for urban centers like Atlanta—could never provide public services such as flood control or improve navigation in the lower Savannah River valley.

Talented engineers had initiated more serious experiments with the United States' first modern, multiple-purpose dams in Arizona, Georgia, and Tennessee. The Salt River Valley Water Users' Association, in conjunction with the Bureau of Reclamation, completed the Salt River and Roosevelt Dam project between 1909 and 1911, which was the bureau's first multiple-purpose reclamation (irrigation) and power project.[20] By 1914, single projects in the Tennessee (Hales Bar), Savannah (Stevens Creek), and Mississippi (Keokuk) river valleys combined run-of-river dams, hydroelectric generation, and navigation locks.[21]

Early-twentieth-century civil engineers in the public and private sectors clearly understood how to build multiple-dam projects to manage specific risks or generate specific benefits, but they did not necessarily have the capacity to construct multiple dams to serve multiple purposes. The capital required for multiple multipurpose dams was simply beyond the reach of private investors, and the federal government remained noncommittal to public-private power projects due to the construction and environmental challenges encountered at Hales Bar (see Chapter 2). The post–World War I Muscle Shoals political controversy also made the Corps wary of public power projects. And as long as rail transport remained a viable and cost-effective means of moving freight long distances at low cost, waterborne navigation investment could only justify itself in major corridors like the Mississippi River.

Given these national examples and realities, private and public sector engineers had yet to combine multiple dams with multiple purposes anywhere in the United States before 1933. As an institution, the Corps did not want to manage the Savannah River valley on the scale found in Arizona or Tennessee, nor did the Corps leadership desire to radically reshape the valley's energy and water landscape in the 1930s as Georgia Power and Duke Power had elsewhere. Furthermore, managing flood risks remained a peripheral objective Corps engineers met with levees and not with dams. What dramatically changed for the dam-adverse Corps leadership, and why did they embark on a program to build the massive multiple-purpose flood, drought, and energy structures that exist today in the Savannah River valley and throughout the nation? In short, complex environmental and economic disasters accelerated institutional change already under way.

Legislative representatives who believed in the power of the conservation state approved multiple hydrologic, geographic, and forestry investigations that efficiently cataloged the environmental resources of the nation's river valleys, including the Savannah, between 1900 and 1930. Federal and state professionals looked at the landscape with lenses configured to see flood control mechanisms, navigation structures, and electrical generation facilities, among other things. To grasp the range of the basin's environmental resources, congressional committees relied on trained specialists and engineers to catalog the actual and potential assets, as well as the liabilities and risks, of rivers throughout the country.[22]

Corps officers and engineers continued to harbor skepticism of multiple-purpose dams and reservoirs as viable technologies well into the 1930s and only began to think systematically beyond single-purpose water management options when forced by legislators to explore comprehensive river development. Congress also acted in response to mounting evidence generated by Progressives and populists that utility monopolies were growing not just in Georgia, Alabama, South Carolina, and North Carolina, but across the country.[23] Congressional representatives decided to participate in this national water management and conservation boom in 1925 and instructed the Corps to estimate the cost for a national river and hydroelectric power survey. In what was also known as "House Document 308," the Corps recommended that Congress move quickly so federal agencies could get a head start, or perhaps work in conjunction with companies, in order "to secure adequate data to insure that waterway developments by private enterprise would fit into a general plan for the full utilization of the water resources of" any study river. Congress approved funding in 1927, and over the next decade agents of the conservation state efficiently cataloged nearly every river in the country and produced professional reports affectionately called "308 Reports" in reference to the congressional document that initiated the survey process.[24]

The Savannah River's 308 Report study assimilated corporate and public data that ultimately shaped New Dealers' liberal vision for southern rivers. The Savannah District's engineers reached out to corporate executives and engineers to better understand the New South's energy and water infrastructure. Corps engineers incorporated data, plans, strategies, and information accumulated by corporate representatives during the 308 study. For example, William States Lee, Duke Power's chief engineer and one of the leaders since the company's creation in 1904, explained to Major D. L. Weart how the company managed the thirty-five-mile-long Catawba Station "pond" and hydroelectric facility in North Carolina to control downstream flooding.[25] Beyond correspondence over flood control operations of the New South's dams and reservoirs, Corps and private representatives also shared sedimentation information, blueprints, topographic maps, soil-core samples, and stream flow data related to potential Savannah River valley hydroelectric dam sites.[26] By the 1930s, private and public engineers appear to have communicated more frequently as the Corps gathered information for the 308 Report. The correspondence did not stop with technical or hydraulic data.

As the Savannah District engineers prepared their 308 Report, they also asked Georgia Power Company executives to reevaluate their own water and energy plans for the Savannah River. One particular site, known as Clarks Hill and soon to become a major locus of public and private organizational attention, generated real-estate-related correspondence between Major C. Garlington and J. B. Parker of the Commonwealth and Southern Corporation. The Savannah River Electric Company was a subsidiary of Georgia Power Company, which was part of the Commonwealth and Southern Corporation holding company, one of the nation's largest. It was comprised of more than ten utility companies scattered throughout the nation. Since 1926, the Savannah River Electric Company had planned to build a 90-foot-tall and 2,400-foot-long dam about twenty miles upstream from Augusta, possibly with a navigation lock, and a reservoir capable of holding 9 billion cubic feet of water that would inundate 45,000 acres.[27] Major Garlington wanted to know how much land the company had acquired, how much money the company had spent on property acquisition, and if the company had initiated any condemnation proceedings. Finally, did the company know if the Clarks Hill project would "be undertaken when" the market demanded more electricity? Parker, perhaps keen to the implications of his answers, replied that the company had acquired about "two thirds of the necessary" land for the reservoir but claimed it was "impossible for us to supply the" financial information as requested. And given the nation's declining economic status in early 1933, Parker also noted that "a present overcapacity" of available electrical supply made it impossible for the company "to tell when the" Clarks Hill "development will be needed," since it was "entirely dependent on the pickup in business" and demand.[28] The conversations also initiated Corps engineers to some of the practical functions and operations of these corporate-technological systems. At this moment, New South capitalists provided ample information that would ultimately influence the path of the Corps' New-Deal-inspired energy and water projects. One additional and important moment reflected New South capitalism's legacy, the New Deal's liberal trajectory, and the Corps' 308 Report for the Savannah River.

The TVA, authorized by Congress in 1933, enshrined the New Deal big dam consensus in policy. The TVA's initial program demonstrated how several multiple-purpose dams could reshape a river valley's physical, social, and economic environments with large hydroelectric dams that incorporated navigation locks, generated electricity, controlled floods, and regulated river levels to facilitate transportation. Between 1933 and 1945, TVA engineers oversaw construction of one dozen massive dams and reservoirs to deliver the trio of benefits. The TVA's greatest objective was manufacturing cheap electricity: Electrified farms could embark on a new round of mechanization; electrification would make decentralized industrialization possible and thus mitigate urban and labor woes; and electricity would make mass-produced fertilizer affordable for farmers. The regionally focused programs would heal a poor land and rescue poor farmers from their gullied and unproductive lands. The TVA, however, was not just a regional planning or high-modernist success story.[29] As a federal response to the Great Depression, the TVA made waves and motivated other federal agencies to reevaluate their missions and react accordingly. For example, New Dealers from South Carolina eventually secured Public

Works Administration (PWA) and Works Progress Administration (WPA) funding for the Santee-Cooper project in 1935, a public power and flood control scheme that was also supposed to facilitate shipping between the landlocked capital in Columbia and Charleston's harbor.[30] The Corps' 308 Report could have functioned as an important self-promotional piece, given the TVA's and Santee-Cooper's practical examples of the New Deal big dam consensus in action. But it did not.

Congress received Major C. Garlington's official 308 Report, *Report on the Savannah*, in 1935 as the TVA's first four multiple-purpose dam projects moved through planning and construction phases.[31] The Corps' *Report on the Savannah* reached some predictable and striking conclusions as the Great Depression deepened. The report provided an extensive flood history, but there was little discussion about drought history. On flood control, the Corps continued to view the Augusta Levee Commission's locally managed eleven-mile levee as satisfactorily maintained but also in need of improvement.[32] Next, the Corps lumped hydropower and navigation together in the report. The Corps engineers simply recapped what Georgia Power executives had conveyed in March 1933: "Certain power developments may be economically justified when and if a suitable market" emerged, but until then hydroelectric dams did not make economic sense or deserve federal investment. Then the report identified eighteen potential multiple-purpose dam sites throughout the Savannah River basin above Augusta along the Savannah itself and in its tributaries. The Corps also acknowledged that a coordinated "power and navigation" project at Clarks Hill might be organized by an unnamed private power company and the federal government at some point in the future. This suggestion was not radical, and the Alabama Power Company had proposed a similar arrangement during the Great War and the Muscle Shoals controversy. Ultimately, the Corps hoped private interests would develop the Clarks Hill hydroelectric dam and storage reservoir, which would also "provide a minimum continuous regulated flow" to enhance navigation downstream between Augusta and the port of Savannah. But in the end, Major Garlington recommended "that there be no participation by the United States in the problems of irrigation and flood control" on the Savannah River, that any power projects include navigation improvements, and finally, "that no improvement of the Savannah River below Augusta be undertaken at the present time." New South enterprise and local municipalities successfully managed the river's flooding, droughts, and energy needs while serving industrial and residential customers. In conclusion, the Corps' engineers believed federal involvement in the Savannah River basin was "unwarranted" and that the Corps of Engineers' services were unneeded. By this token, the Depression-era Corps limited its own involvement in directly shaping the river basin for the second time since Oberlin Carter's 1890 survey and in the wake of the Great Flood (1929).[33]

The Savannah River valley's power brokers who valued the Clarks Hill concept found the Corps more relevant than the Corps found itself. In August 1935, about seven months after the Corps released the *Report on the Savannah River*, Augusta's chamber of commerce mobilized the city's boosters to woo New Dealers and their federal dollars. Lester S. Moody (1893–1972) had moved from Jacksonville, Florida, to Georgia in 1926, assumed leadership of the Augusta Chamber of Commerce, and henceforth linked the river to Augusta's economic future. He would later be anointed the "Father of Savannah River Development."[34] In 1935, Moody and the Savannah River Improvement Commission formally asked FDR to appoint a PWA commission to reevaluate the 308 Report's findings. Moody's cohort specifically wanted to revisit the Clarks Hill project's ability to deliver multiple benefits such as "flood control, navigation, prevention of soil erosion, and power development."[35] Citing reports from the Federal Power Commission (FPC), Moody and his team refuted assertions made by Corps and Georgia Power Company officials about regional energy needs. The boosters argued that Georgia and South Carolina actually faced a future electrical deficit. Furthermore, Moody explained, the Georgia Power Company was unlikely to complete Clarks Hill. Moody's faith in the Corps and skepticism of Georgia Power were not without justification.

Between the Great Depression and the end of World War II, energy utilities all over the nation faced an uncertain future and shrinking industrial service demand. Many companies put hydroelectric power projects on hold for at least a decade or tabled plans indefinitely.[36] But a shifting economy also contributed to an energy transition and consumer behavior. The Georgia Power Company continued to make use of the region's water after completing the well-publicized Tallulah-Tugaloo River projects in the early 1920s. For example, the company's massive Atkinson fossil fuel plant on the Chattahoochee River seven miles upstream of Atlanta placed the first of four units online in 1930. While the plant burned coal or natural gas to generate electricity, the plant's boilers used 90,000 gallons of water to produce steam. And to cool the plant's condenser, Georgia Power withdrew 5 million gallons of Chattahoochee River water every hour, which was "four times as much water as the entire city of Atlanta" used in a few hours, according to *Snap Shots*, the company's in-house magazine.[37] Fossil fuel plants looked more reliable and efficient than hydroelectric dams after the 1920s droughts, but even shifting to black coal technology was risky and manufactured potential risk, since the region could never escape its dependence on river water to generate electricity for industrial transplants that brought jobs, and for a growing consumer sector.

Everyday urban Georgians—in Augusta, Athens, and Atlanta—initially benefited from an electrified transportation sector. Georgia Power, for example, got its start in the streetcar business. During the Great Depression, as industrial customers reduced production schedules and manufacturing output, utilities like Georgia Power and Duke tapped a new market to generate revenue. Despite the state of the national economy, Georgia Power and Duke Power launched campaigns to increase residential electrical consumption, a sector that had always been considered secondary. Through a variety of merchandising, layaway, and incentive programs, southern utilities convinced women and men to electrify their homes and to invest in electric irons, refrigerators, water heaters, and other home appliances. Residential electric consumption reportedly doubled between 1934 and 1940.[38] Advertising executives helped generate customers, but the revenue only barely helped keep utilities afloat.

While company engineers completed the organic and fossil fuel projects that depended on water to generate electricity, Georgia Power executives simultaneously acquired land for potential dam and reservoir sites along the Chattooga River—a tributary of the Tugaloo River—in 1911.[39] But rather than reproduce the Tallulah and Tugaloo hydroelectric dams and reservoirs along the Chattooga River as the company originally had intended to do, the Georgia Power Company shifted construction to the Piedmont in a decision that proved to be a fortuitous choice for the company and the future Chattooga Wild and Scenic River. The New South company also moved out of the mountains and into the Piedmont to diversify geographically and to diversify the company's collection of generation facilities.

In addition to purchasing Chattooga River valley waterpower sites and completing the Atkinson steam plant, the Georgia Power Company also turned to Furman Shoals and the Oconee River to balance the company's energy mix. In 1929, the company began building this Piedmont and fall-line project—now known as Lake Sinclair and Dam in Georgia's "Lake Country"—about four miles north of the state's old capital of Milledgeville. In September, the company's president announced plans for a 3,000-foot-long and 90-foot-tall dam to create the state's largest artificial reservoir (12,000 acres of surface area) and to house the company's third-largest hydroelectric generation facility.[40] One month later, Black Tuesday wiped out Wall Street in October, and the company newsletter made no mention of the downward economic spiral. Instead, the company pressed on with construction activities at Furman Shoals.[41] Despite the emerging depression, the company announced plans to spend $16 million on new projects in 1930 "to keep constantly in step with the progress of the state," according to *Snap Shots* writers.[42] Almost a full year would pass before the Georgia Power Company abandoned the Furman Shoals project on the Oconee River on November 30, 1930, because the company could no longer ignore the global Great Depression.[43] The economies of the world and the state not only stalled Georgia Power's plans for Furman Shoals but also had repercussions for the company's other projects in the Savannah River valley.

Lester Moody saw an opportunity to balance New South capitalism and New Deal liberalism at Clarks Hill. When Georgia Power executives placed Blue Ridge and Piedmont projects on hold during the Great Depression, the door opened slightly for another party—the U.S. Army Corps of Engineers—to take part in shaping the South's hydraulic waterscape. Furthermore, Georgia Power officers had "surrendered" their Clarks Hill FPC license in 1932 "because of unfavorable economic conditions and consequent lack of demand for power."[44] At this moment of economic insecurity the Great Depression provided a wedge for the Corps to move into the valley, and people like Augusta's chamber of commerce secretary took advantage of FDR's interest in public works projects that could move the nation's economy forward by any means possible. Private utilities worked to block Clarks Hill at the same time that they battled FDR's TVA.

FDR, eager to see New Deal programs benefit southerners, wasted no time reevaluating the Savannah River's 308 Report and Clarks Hill. The president requested that a special Savannah River board reassess Clarks Hill's fate in mid-August 1935. The special board's members offered a number of recommendations to move the project forward, including an option that would benefit FDR and Georgia Power.[45] The former wanted a project that would provide unemployment relief, and the latter still owned thousands of acres of land on the proposed Clarks Hill site.

Georgia Power president Preston Stanley Arkwright Sr. (1871–1946) walked a fine line as a powerful stakeholder who worked at the junction of energy and water in the American South. Arkwright, a long-serving Georgia Power executive (1902–45), did not publicly reject a federally financed Clarks Hill project, and he eventually backpedaled on his company's initial claim that no utility would purchase the federal project's electricity. He asserted that the Georgia Power Company would at least be ready to buy all the electricity, since the company served the vast majority of Georgia's electrified consumers. When the Savannah River Special Board held a 1936 public hearing, Arkwright—perhaps disingenuously—claimed the Georgia Power Company primarily served rural customers: "It is a rural company. It is a rural state. It is substantially a rural supply company."[46] Georgia was predominantly rural, and the company did indeed serve rural customers; but in the 1930s Arkwright's company primarily envisioned Clarks Hill as a means to serve industrial consumers in urban or isolated rural communities. His statement about rural customers was, however, a critical one for southern Democrats.

With a united front, liberal and conservative New Dealers, picking up where Progressive reformers had left off, condemned corporate energy sector monopolies for refusing to serve rural customers. TVA energy projects and the Rural Electrification Administration (1935)—modeled after the 1920s Giant Power concept—subsidized electrical generation, transmission, and distribution service in rural markets where private energy companies had refused to establish service because "the investment required to serve farms with electricity is very great; the revenue small," according to one of Georgia Power's founding executives, Henry M. Atkinson (1862–1939).[47] Preston Arkwright did suggest that if Georgia Power could purchase Clarks Hill energy and use the company's existing distribution lines, then the federal government would not have to invest taxpayer dollars in a duplicate transmission system. Arkwright was simultaneously defending free enterprise while seeking access to federally subsidized infrastructure that could benefit Georgia Power's monopoly in the short term and the long run. Georgia Power executives—and all of the nation's investor-owned utilities—wanted to maintain market share during the Great Depression and defend themselves from New Deal liberalism.

Clearly not content with the direction in which Clarks Hill appeared to be moving, Georgia Power spokesmen launched a new discussion about plans to revive their own Clarks Hill project and reapply for an FPC license. The *Augusta Chronicle* continued to report on—and advocate for—the federal plans to build a high multiple-purpose dam for navigation, flood control, reforestation, recreation, and energy. Augusta boosters who understood the complexities of multiple-purpose planning and engineering were "doubtful" that the Georgia Power Company "could duplicate the vast program planned under the federal project since the latter involved development of the entire Savannah River valley."[48] The company, after all, still owned a half-completed hydroelectric dam at Furman Shoals on the Oconee River in 1939. Moody and others certainly asked, If the company could not complete Furman Shoals, once billed as the third-largest power project in the company's portfolio, how could the Georgia Power Company again propose to start and finish an even larger and more comprehensive Clarks Hill project?[49]

The real conflict between those in favor of a federal power project and those in favor of a private power project was not new and echoed the arguments surrounding the Muscle Shoals controversy. The Savannah River's Clarks Hill project also illustrated the political minefield FDR confronted when his New Deal administration attempted to right the ship of an overturned economy of the 1930s. If there was one New Deal plan that politicians initially accepted, it was the TVA. Many southerners had welcomed the idea to remake the Tennessee River valley into a decentralized industrial heartland, to control the flooding, improve navigation, and to produce fertilizer to reclaim degraded farmland. The TVA initially looked like a set of programs targeting regional poverty and unemployment while also healing a sick land.[50] But New South free enterprise advocates were not interested in more TVAs. After 1935, their opposition had increasingly tarred the organization as socialistic and anticapitalist and as an institution insulated from competition and protected by government subsidies.[51]

As Georgia Power and Corps staff negotiated Clarks Hill's fate, Commonwealth and Southern's president and future U.S. presidential hopeful Wendell Willkie engaged the TVA's directors on multiple fronts to limit the New Deal's liberal regional planning expansion into the territories of Commonwealth and Southern's subsidiaries. Alabama Power—a subsidiary like Georgia Power—had acquired significant land and ideal waterpower sites along the Tennessee River in the Muscle Shoals area before the Great War, begrudgingly donated the Wilson Dam property to the federal government in 1918, and then entered short-term contracts to purchase federally generated hydroelectric power from the site after 1925. Soon after Congress and the president created the TVA in 1933, Willkie negotiated additional short-term contracts and agreed to sell specific utility properties including Alabama Power's Wheeler Dam site to the TVA for $2.9 million. This agreement set off the Alabama Power shareholder-led lawsuit *Ashwander v. Tennessee Valley Authority* in 1936. Given these complicated relationships between private utilities, their shareholders, and emerging public energy utilities like the TVA, Georgia Power and other energy companies, not to mention Corps engineers, across the country watched Willkie and the TVA board of directors engage in a private-power versus public-power battle that had implications for New Deal liberalism, the nation's rivers, and the Savannah River valley's Clarks Hill site.[52] By the mid-1930s, the TVA looked increasingly like a onetime experiment, but the legal route critics pursued in hopes of testing the constitutionality of and dismantling the TVA failed in 1939. And lobbyists on all sides continued to fight over energy and water, over who would protect private needs and public goods, and over how to manage environmental conditions like droughts and flooding. Clarks Hill was bound up in the TVA fight.

Critics within and outside FDR's administration—particularly within the Department of the Interior and the Corps of Engineers—also expressed concern over TVA expansion beyond electric generation and river planning into forestry and soil conservation. As FDR's programs failed to deliver significant relief or threatened local political structures, agricultural and antiliberal critics derailed the New Deal's water program by lobbying Congress to approve the Flood Control Act of 1936.[53] This legislation called into question the viability of future TVAs and regional planning by dividing comprehensive watershed management between the Corps and the U.S. Department of Agriculture. Congress ultimately designed the 1936 act to limit the expansion of additional valley authorities. The act, however, was an example of legislation born out of bureaucratic conflict because it divided flood control within river basins between the Corps and the agriculture department's Soil Conservation Service. The Corps retained flood control responsibilities on navigable waterways, and the conservation service assumed responsibility for the nonnavigable streams and headwaters. Most important, by dividing watershed responsibilities between the Corps and the conservation service within a given watershed, Congress dealt regional and comprehensive planning a mortal blow.[54] This division delineated agency boundaries to eliminate bureaucratic infighting, but it also presented future critics of the Corps with another wedge. The TVA had solved some of the South's water problems but remained a risky model for regional and global modernization.[55]

FDR faced opposition from other quarters as he attempted to hold the New Deal coalition together with the big dam consensus. This was particularly the case in the "Solid South" where the Democratic Party was euphemistically unified. In reality and like many coalitions, the New Deal coalition was tenuous at best. Utility executives—including those from Georgia Power—rejected the New Deal big dam consensus and liberalism because public power projects threatened corporate profits and shareholders' returns. But white southern Democrats with rural ties had little empathy for the utility monopolies that refused to electrify farms; their primary source of antipathy to FDR and the New Deal rested someplace else. Farmers—independent, tenant, and sharecroppers—and low-wage textile mill workers, black and white, formed the base of the Democratic Party. While African Americans—initially devoted members of Abraham Lincoln's Republican Party—found a new home in the Democratic Party during the Great Depression, relations between FDR and conservative white southern Democrats were increasingly strained when New Deal agricultural, labor, and social programs threatened to erase the divisive color line.

FDR commissioned the 1938 *Report on Economic Conditions of the South* because of frustration over southern intransigence toward New Deal programs and because the New Dealers saw no clear indication that the southern economy had improved. The Agricultural Adjustment Act had injected cash into communities and reduced the total acreage in cultivation, but it also adversely affected tenant farmers and sharecroppers, particularly African Americans. If planters and landlords were able to make the Agricultural Adjustment Administration work for them, then southern industrialists found the National Recovery Administration untenable. They disliked the recovery administration because it elevated wages for all laborers—African American and white—and thereby threatened the racial status quo as well as company bottom lines.[56] FDR turned primarily to southern liberals like Howard W. Odum to help write the *Report on Economic Conditions of the South*. The *Report* noted that thirteen southern states—from Texas and Oklahoma to Virginia and Kentucky—produced much of the nation's mineral fuels in 1938: one-fifth of the "soft coal," two-thirds of the natural gas, and two-thirds of the crude oil. Southern energy companies also produced 85 percent of the region's electricity organically via "waterpower"; by comparison, only 37 percent of the total power produced in the United States as a whole came from hydroelectric sources.[57] Despite abundant water resources and a variety of energy regimes, the report characterized the South as a colonial economy and a place of abundant yet mismanaged human and physical resources. As one historian concluded, "Disguised as an objective analysis of the regional economy, the *Report on the Economic Conditions of the South* was a manifesto" to justify New Deal liberalism's intervention in the southern economy.[58]

White southern Democrats likened the report and the New Deal to another Reconstruction imposed on the region. A number of Democrats—including Senators Walter F. George (Ga.) and Ellison "Cotton Ed" Smith (S.C.)—accepted some New Deal programs. For example, long before the creation of the TVA, Smith had advocated for federal involvement in fertilizer manufacture at Muscle Shoals to benefit southern farmers. But when New Deal liberalism threatened to disrupt white supremacy, conservative Democrats turned against FDR. As a result, the president attempted but failed to influence local elections by purging conservative white southern Democrats—including George and Smith—from the party during the 1938 election because of their reluctance to support his full slate of New Deal liberalism.[59] New Deal politics, involving energy, water, and civil rights, revealed a fractured southern wing of the Democratic Party. And where discussion about future TVAs—including a proposed Savannah Valley Authority—failed to generate traction, support for the Corps was more easily secured.[60] Conservatives dismantled regional planning as embodied in the TVA's mission while elevating the Corps' water and energy program. Where the TVA concept talked about community building and equity, the Corps was directed to address only parts of a whole.

Hamburg was one part of the Savannah River valley. The South Carolina community's path after the Great Flood and on the eve of the Great Depression embodied the consequences of New South capitalism and the possibilities of New Deal liberalism. Recommendations reached in the Corps' 308 Report (1935), the Clarks Hill Commission's advocacy for the dam (1936), and the *Report on Southern Conditions* (1938) would have resulted in limited direct improvement for Hamburg's residents. The Great Flood of 1929 did not produce any structural change for Augusta, a response from the Corps, or a New Deal rescue. The Great Flood did result in change for African Americans who had received no direct benefit from levees or hydroelectric dams but were all too familiar with the tenuous relationship between water, power, and risk. Hamburg African Americans "rendered homeless" by the Savannah River's Great Flood and Augusta's levee were also casualties of racial politics; they sacrificed personal property for the public good of Augusta. While they suffered the consequences of living in an inequitable society, some Hamburg residents also benefited from a unique nonstructural flood control solution in 1929. South Carolina citizens who lived across the river from Augusta were relocated, but not by the federal government and not to make way for a massive structural flood control project.

Floods had inundated Hamburg prior to the Great Flood of 1929. The headquarters and local chapters of the American Red Cross had rendered aid on multiple occasions to about eighty African American families. Most of the men worked in brick manufacturing, and many of the women cultivated large gardens and sold produce across the river in Augusta markets. After one spring flood a Red Cross official took the time to explain why African Americans continued to return to the floodplain after floodwaters receded. Residents did not like living in harm's way, but they occupied their homes "practically rent free." Other Red Cross personnel expressed frustration over the residents' perceived "indifference and insistance [*sic*] in residing in this constantly threatened territory." White observers, however, missed African Americans' pragmatic and rational economic decisions; they were "not only out of sympathy with [African Americans] but are really indignant," according to the Red Cross's John T. McMullen.[61] In essence, the first responders blamed the victims without considering the broader racial, economic, and structural factors that influenced African Americans' settlement in a vulnerable place like Hamburg. None of the Red Cross responders identified Augusta's levee as a risk management technology that produced the risk of flooding in Hamburg. And Hamburg's African American residents had limited housing choices and economic reasons not to relocate after previous floods. The consequences of the double storms and Great Flood of 1929, however, were different.

The collective labor of black and white citizens working across the "color line" saved the Georgia levee from total collapse and paved the way for a new Hamburg in South Carolina.[62] When the floodwaters began to recede and the Augusta levee held, the Aiken and Augusta Red Cross chapter members balked at providing aid that would encourage Hamburg residents to reoccupy the floodplain. Less than one month after the Great Flood of 1929, a solution emerged. Charles W. Carr, the official Washington, D.C., Red Cross envoy in Augusta, and white and black businessmen all agreed that relocation was "the only way to solve the problem."[63] He recommended that the Red Cross facilitate relocation of residents from Hamburg to Carpentersville on Shoats Hill, about one mile away and eighty feet above the floodplain on the South Carolina side of the Savannah River. The assumption was that the Red Cross could purchase and subdivide six acres into at least twenty-two individual properties. Given the options, the history of flooding, and the legacy of floodplain occupation, the Red Cross chose a decidedly nontechnological option to remove people from harm's way.[64]

Newspapers soon began to report on a new Hamburg on the plateau above the Savannah River's floodplain after the Red Cross agents negotiated purchase of a few acres that had been subdivided by an unnamed "local real estate man."[65] In paternalistic, patronizing, and misleading language, an Augusta journalist explained that "the land on which these humble negroes [sic] have elected to call new Hamburg was given them through the generosity of the American Red Cross and the white people of Aiken county [S.C.]."[66] In truth, the Hamburg relocation was only possible with help from Augusta's well-established African American business community. Hamburg's eighty-two families had received food assistance from multiple sources over three weeks, including William "Will" Carpenter, a prominent African American with an extensive social and business network. Carpenter was an Augusta grocer, president of the Georgia Mutual Life and Health Insurance Company (founded in 1908), and president of the Penny Savings and Loan Company.[67] Carpenter did more than provide groceries and food for Hamburg residents; he eventually received many of the construction contracts to build new homes with American Red Cross subsidies.[68] Perhaps most important, Carpenter owned the land under the new Hamburg. He served on the board of directors for the Southern Realty Company, a real estate firm that worked for the African American community, and O. M. Blount, the company's president, was the unnamed "local real estate man" who subdivided the new Hamburg property, which was named Carpentersville.[69] The end of Hamburg's story, however, is complicated.

Haphazard management of the Savannah River valley's water, white supremacy, and the Augusta levee's technology contributed to the manufactured risk in Hamburg and the community's ultimate dissolution. The Augusta levee project protected the city's public welfare but not the South Carolina families—the African American market gardeners and brick makers—who contributed to feeding and building Augusta. For Augustans intent on managing the Savannah River for drought and flood, the obvious solution was to move Hamburg, thereby saving lives and money well into the future. At the time, this move was undoubtedly for the public's—and Hamburg's residents'—best interest, or was it? Belching factories and hazardous landfills have historically shadowed poor and minority communities due to a variety of structural and demographic factors, some intentional and others that evolved gradually over time. Many of these spaces had also been marginal environments to begin with, making them less resilient to natural disasters.[70] The Hamburg postflood resolution was significant because the Red Cross managed a community relocation project that moved an African American community out of harm's way. The solution was not to build levees or other expensive and marginally successful flood control structures that many white communities and urban boosters have historically demanded elsewhere (i.e., in the Mississippi Valley and New Orleans). Instead, the Red Cross successfully engineered a nonstructural solution to eliminate future flood disasters within one minority community with material and financial assistance from local white and black businesses.

The dissolution of Hamburg, however, left former residents without easy access to the same fertile floodplain soil, and the brick factories were gone. It is unclear how the new Carpentersville residents made a living after the Great Flood of 1929. But what is clear is that sixty years later the old Hamburg—safe for white resettlement after Clarks Hill's federally subsidized flood control eliminated a perception of risk—was eventually populated with "executive homes" between the riverfront and the River Golf Club in the late 1990s. Carpentersville—isolated on the hill over the river—was eventually surrounded by industrial facilities and deteriorating strip malls. The powerful people who protected Augusta and controlled the valley's water for industrial and commercial economies turned a handsome personal profit at the expense of others who sacrificed property, occupations, and community. Solutions to Augusta's water insecurity benefited those who defined—and created—the problem in the first place.

Interwar environmental and economic conditions challenged the simplistic divisions between the uncoordinated private and public initiatives that managed some risks while producing magnified problems in places like Hamburg. After Savannah River valley residents gripped by the Great Depression reconsidered their drought and flood history, some looked to the federal government for help building water conservation structures that could manage complex rivers, urban-industrial energy demands, and the risks associated with what were clearly recurring and new environmental conditions.

By the time the Great Depression ended with the nation's entrance into World War II in 1941, New Deal liberal water and energy programs bore fruit for the Corps and its critics in important ways. First, the Corps' leadership had been slowly amassing institutional exposure to public works projects during the New Deal. For example, FDR appointed Colonel Francis Harrington to head the WPA in 1938. When former WPA head Harry Hopkins transitioned to secretary of commerce, he observed that Harrington had the political advantage of appearing as an "'apolitical' army engineer." Harrington, as a former Corps officer and Panama Canal chief engineer (1924), also functioned as a foil that protected FDR and the WPA from conservative criticism.[71] There is a second reason why New Deal liberalism was important for the Corps: The 308 Report forced Corps officers to engage with New South executives, and the collaboration resulted in a federal blueprint for the Savannah River's water and energy future. Before and during the New Deal era, Corps staff learned how to organize public works projects and where these projects—including multiple-purpose dams—might rise in the Savannah River valley's headwaters, tributaries, and main stem. Finally, the Corps' work and experience with New Deal–era public works projects had also provided valuable lessons for critics of regional planning, civil rights, and liberalism. As Georgians, South Carolinians, and other Americans envisioned future energy and water solutions, they recognized that artificial reservoirs had the capacity to produce risk in a new social and environmental climate of postwar "rights-based liberalism."

Southern Democrats and boosters capitalized on the Corps' Great Depression knowledge and experience. They repackaged the New Deal big dam consensus's water and energy program and set the stage—beginning at a place called Clarks Hill—for Sun Belt commercialism. Solving the American South's water problems remained a predominantly private enterprise between the New South era and the beginning of the Great Depression. A handful of private companies manipulated southern waters to generate electricity primarily for urban, industrial, and commercial—not rural and agricultural—constituencies from Mississippi to Tennessee and from Georgia to Virginia. The Wall Street crash and Great Flood of 1929 were the major turning points for the Savannah River valley, and the New Deal provided a wedge for federal agencies to participate in sculpting the future of the nation's hydraulic waterscapes. Managing old and new environmental conditions, and energy and water, would never be the same. The TVA presented an alternative program for resource management, but many Americans and Congress rejected the TVA model, leaving other federal agencies like the Corps to negotiate with multiple stakeholders over the fate of southern rivers. This experience presented all Sun Belt parties—public and private, large and small—interested in southern waterscapes with very different circumstances and new options.

CHAPTER 4

A Keystone Dam and Georgia's New Ocean

Dry months and a lack of water left Georgians with a serious problem and grim choices in 1941. Geographic pockets in the American South had rotated from one alleged natural disaster to another like a broken record since the 1920s. And as with previous multiple-year droughts, observers in the 1940s could no longer pass this one off as a drought that only affected farmers. By the spring of 1941, another *urban drought* threatened water and electrical consumption in homes, businesses, and factories at the very moment that the nation's industrial machine mobilized to provide its European Allies with additional war material. Conditions were so bad that the Georgia Power Company began rationing electrical service to customers via controlled blackouts in Atlanta and Augusta.[1] A rainfall "deficiency" threatened the Blue Ridge's and Piedmont South's rivers. But more important, the drought jeopardized the corporate energy-water nexus by withholding the water supplies necessary for electrical production.[2]

To save the interconnected production and consumption network, Georgia Power Company spokespeople announced a "SAVE ENERGY Plan" and continued to run nearly full-page announcements in the *Atlanta Constitution* and other state newspapers. The Georgia Power Company, a powerful New South energy institution in operation since the first decade of the twentieth century, communicated a serious message to urban residents: "This is not a 'scare.'"[3] The *Augusta Chronicle* editors picked up the company's energy conservation message and implored city officials, business leaders, and the general public to make "sacrifices" for national defense production, since the "water in Lake Burton"—the largest of the Tallulah-Tugaloo River storage reservoirs in the Savannah River basin "where the Georgia Power Company derives most of its hydro-electric power"—was reduced by 40 percent. The company and the editors clearly linked water conservation and energy production with electrical demand

and consumption in urban areas. For example, the company requested that business owners "raise the temperature to 83 degrees" in their air-conditioned shops as a part "of the patriotic power thrift campaign." One Georgia Power spokesperson explained that citywide controlled blackouts—which required shopkeepers to turn off display window lights, reduced streetlight coverage, and cut elevator usage—were necessary to get through "the present serious situation," which had slowly "been approaching a crisis for two years."[4] As the editors noted, "The electric power situation became critical not only because of the abnormal electric power requirements of defense plants" scattered across the southeast and connected by long-distance electrical transmission lines, "but also because of one of the most prolonged and excessive droughts this section has experienced in many years."[5]

The "crisis" intensified before it abated. The Georgia Power Company's executives prepared customers for a draconian plan because conservation had "to work at once," since water levels in the company's Tallulah-Tugaloo project's six artificial reservoirs continued to drop. In Lake Burton alone, the water level had plummeted more than sixty feet below the normal summer level. "Only heavy, widespread, protracted rains" could "correct this condition," since the periodic "afternoon's thundershowers won't raise the level of the great storage lake appreciably."[6] The Chattahoochee River's flows were so diminished that Atlanta's municipal water managers had to channel the diminished flow directly to the intakes. And Georgia Power Company technicians reduced operations at the coal-fired Plant Atkinson.[7] Environmental conditions and an urban drought once again compromised the quality of life for Atlanta's residents (population 302,288).[8]

Eventually, the region pulled out of the crisis for two reasons. First, the Southeast's and the nation's interconnected electrical transmission grid pooled power "from all directions" to save southern electric customers—much as it had in 1925. Second, what amounted to a multiyear drought in north Georgia ended in the spring of 1942 when the rain began to fall across the Blue Ridge Mountains. The parched Peach State received an average of 43.10 inches of precipitation in 1941, while 1942 recorded an average total of 52.34 inches. The sought-after rain replenished the dry Chattahoochee and Savannah River watersheds and busted the drought of 1941.[9]

After a half-century of New South boosters' rhetoric that sold the region to industrial developers predicated on an abundance of water and cheap energy, how could the region still lack adequate water supplies?

And given that recent history, how would post–World War II planners approach water management and energy production differently to avoid future resource rationing? The post-1945 hydraulic waterscapes needed retooling to survive the cyclical and dramatic drought and flood events. For New South capitalists, the answer—massive artificial reservoirs— became the Sun Belt's preferred method of taking federal dollars while maintaining acceptable environmental and social conditions. Southern water problems, both cultural and natural, continued to function as barriers to growth and as pathways to power.

The New Deal big dam consensus resurfaced after 1945. Proponents— namely, prominent southern Democrats—lobbied for multiple-purpose dams and an enhanced hydraulic system. But the rules of the game had changed. The Tennessee Valley Authority (TVA) experiment had run its course and would never be repeated again. As the United States and its Allies anticipated victory over fascism in Europe, Congress replaced New Deal liberalism—and the social and employment programs that defined it—with a more conservative and commercial model of economic development to sustain postwar industry and promote leisure. Something else changed: The New South capitalists and the New Deal regional planners were no longer the primary dam builders. The U.S. Army Corps of Engineers' participation in transforming the Cotton Belt into the Sun Belt after 1945 should not be underestimated. The Corps had experience with wartime military-industrial development and altering river valleys at the behest of local navigational or flood control lobbies. But the Corps was not necessarily prepared to build hydraulic waterscapes that specifically benefited cities, industries, and leisure-seekers at the expense of old agricultural landscapes.[10] The milewide Clarks Hill dam and massive lake on the Savannah River about twenty miles upstream from Augusta was among the Corps' first attempts to remake the New Deal big dam consensus and deliver economic building blocks to the Sun Belt's boosters without disrupting social relations.[11]

Southern Democrats in Congress, state capitols, and chambers of commerce enthralled by the New Deal big dam consensus continued to solicit and plow federal dollars into big-ticket Corps water and energy developments to bust droughts, tame flooding, and boost Sun Belt commercialism. From the beginning, the Clarks Hill scheme appeared to have wide support, but it was a project that took many people into uncharted territory. The Corps was challenged to manage seemingly tangential new objectives and the social engineering required for something like Clarks

Hill on the eve of the modern civil rights movement. This new nature—artificial lakes with attendant recreational possibilities and public health responsibilities—needled the fracture lines within a political party that was less and less solid.[12] Crafting blue lakes from a land of red clay to avoid future droughts and floods in mild Sun Belt climes proved more difficult than anyone anticipated.

Droughts, perceived as natural disasters, like flooding, provided an impetus for southern river valley residents to support dam and reservoir construction across the region after 1945. Drought in 1941 had again demonstrated that environmental conditions, like the oft-cited and manufactured labor and race problems, were among the most important barriers to regional economic growth. The White House, Congress, and the Corps responded by reengaging a modified New Deal land, soil, and water conservation program. Since the 1930s, engineers planned for Clarks Hill to provide electricity, flood control, navigation, and "other beneficial effects," including the opportunity to "eliminate entirely" power "outages" along the Augusta Canal "due to low water."[13] While the Corps may have downplayed its own 308 Report in 1935 (the New Deal–era survey that identified eighteen potential multiple-purpose dams and reservoirs in the Savannah River valley), local boosters won support at various levels of the federal government to achieve real commitments.[14] The Corps completed another round of surveys throughout the valley in the early 1940s and published the results in June 1944 while Allied forces prepared for the massive D-Day landing in Europe.[15] By the end of the year, Congress agreed to fund construction for the Savannah River valley's largest water and energy scheme.

The Clarks Hill site itself was, from an engineering perspective, not challenging. Situated in the Piedmont's rolling hill country, the dam's proposed location was about twenty miles upstream from central Augusta. Clarks Hill was named for John Mulford Clark, who was born in 1813 in the mid-Atlantic and moved to Milledgeville, Georgia, in 1835. A few years later, Clark moved to Augusta and then again in 1841 to Edgefield County (S.C.), where he farmed and opened a general store in a community that eventually bore his name. Clarks Hill, South Carolina was a short distance from the future waterpower site that would also carry his name.[16] There the valley funneled water collected from a 6,144-square-mile watershed above the site, and the river bore down some 225 feet below the adjacent uplands (elev. 400 ft.). Multiple proposed dam sites existed in the vicinity of Clarks Hill; the Georgia Power Company owned a dam site about a half-mile downriver from where the Corps planned a 200-foot-tall and mile-wide dam. The Corps' geologists had already identified the presence of sound granite, gneiss, and quartz for the concrete gravity dam's foundation and good soil for the rolled-earth embankments that would flank the concrete structure on the South Carolina side of the river. The massive reservoir was to inundate fifty-two square miles of the valley (78,000 acres) and stretch nearly forty miles upriver to Trotters Shoals; it would be the largest south of Tennessee and east of the Mississippi River.[17] The Corps was cut out for technical engineering at a well-suited site, but Clarks Hill was more than a technological Sun Belt project.

Southern Democrats and Corps engineers provided many reasons to rally behind and to justify federal financing for the massive Clarks Hill project. Before a congressional hearing in 1943, Corps engineer Colonel P. A. Feringa explained that "without Clarks Hill Dam we will never have year-round navigation in the Savannah River." While defending the dam, Feringa sounded as if he was defending a valley authority whereby the Clarks Hill dam would "fit into any integrated scheme for the full development of the Savannah River." And with a touch of misrepresentation or at least naiveté, the colonel noted, "It is a remarkable dam and reservoir project in that everyone is for it. The reservoir area is composed largely of marginal lands. There is very little real value attached to the lands and a minimum amount of relocation will be necessary. . . . There is no competition with private interests." Georgia Power Company executives, who had challenged federal overtures to build at Clarks Hill in 1936, supported the project in 1943 and continued to claim they were ready to take delivery on the excess power generated by the dam. The Georgia and South Carolina congressional delegations supported the Clarks Hill project.[18]

So, too, did South Carolina's Democratic governor. James Strom Thurmond (1902–2003) was born in Edgefield, South Carolina, which was less than thirty miles from the Clarks Hill dam site. He began his political career as the Edgefield County superintendent of education before serving as the county's attorney and entering the South Carolina legislature in 1933 for five years. Thurmond rounded out his state service as governor between 1947 and 1951 and then moved on to the U.S. Senate, where he remained for more than fifty years (eighteen as a Democrat and thirty-nine as a Republican). As governor, Thurmond advocated for the New Deal until liberalism challenged white supremacy and President Franklin D. Roosevelt attempted to purge southern senators during the 1938 campaign. Thereafter, according to historian Kari Frederickson, Thurmond and many of his contemporaries were "moderately liberal" Democrats who promoted "bureaucratic efficiency and industrial development" because economic development was perceived as the key to the future.[19] Agricultural and industrial promoters in the South and across the nation beat a path to new federal dams and artificial reservoirs throughout an era of depression, unemployment, and war. As the powerful Democratic boosters closed ranks, they nurtured an emerging Sun Belt economy as equally dependent on water and energy as it was on federal engineers and a healthy infusion of federal dollars.

Georgia senator Walter F. George articulated his interest in the Clarks Hill project in slightly different terms. He was fishing on the Flint River when he learned that the senator he would replace, the famous populist Tom Watson, had died.[20] Walter George (1878–1957) was a lifelong Democratic senator (1922–57) and friend of the New Deal big dam consensus, though his bona fides were allegedly influenced by Georgia Power Company campaign contributions.[21] In the long term he believed big dams would provide electricity for dairy farmers and decentralized industrial development. But in the short term, Senator George, like many other Americans, also worried that the end of World War II might bring about a labor shortage and an economic slowdown, so he "advocated taking all precaution through providing employment, by developing industry, and making use of the high resources of the country" to avoid another economic depression.[22] By the end of 1944, a majority-Democratic Congress expressed concerns over how the war might wind down, how to convert war production to meet domestic needs, and how to employ millions of demobilized veterans. In this context, Congress approved of the Flood Control Act of 1944 in December (and had previously approved in June what became known as the G.I. Bill). This mammoth public works legislation presented a master plan for nationwide postwar employment, regional development, and a new round of economic stimulus to avoid a return to Great Depression economics. It was logical legislation that Senator George, who later had a large artificial reservoir on the Chattahoochee River named in his honor, and other Americans could accept.

The Flood Control Act (1944) became a legitimate extension of late New Deal liberalism and the big dam consensus. Americans feared a postwar unemployment spike and anticipated that the government would intervene in the economy and prime the pump, but they favored a curtailed New Deal–like response. Rather than revive "social" Keynesian projects or create new agencies to manage unemployment and economic decline, the postwar local leadership partnered with the federal government to pump up regional economies through "commercial" Keynesian projects, according to one historian. These short-term public works projects subsidized private contractors, created employment primarily for white men, and built a foundational infrastructure for Sun Belt commercialism.[23] Liberal operatives had designed large-scale New Deal public works projects like the TVA to create jobs and inject money into all levels of the economy. Once completed, TVA's dams did generate energy for factories and contributed to production of fertilizer for farmers. In sum, regional planners had hoped that the TVA would create a modern industrial society that complimented a revitalized agricultural sector. Post-1944 multiple-purpose projects, however, would be different.

Congress, via the Flood Control Act (1944), stripped the regional planning model down to a techno-selective river planning model. The Corps' leadership also embraced a limited understanding of comprehensive development and how multiple dams in a single valley could compliment one another. Most important, the Corps' Sun Belt projects did not serve industrial and agricultural production equally, included no soil or forestry programs, and only halfheartedly supported navigation. By and large, boosters and the Corps could promote and tailor individual postwar hydroelectric and flood control projects to meet locally specific needs in ways the TVA never did. As such, the postwar multiple-purpose river projects like Clarks Hill resembled vehicles for pork barrel politics and constituent service. By the end of the war, Congress positioned the Corps to serve as the main agent responsible for placing dams and artificial reservoirs in the nation's watersheds, and the Corps began its post-1945 mission in the Savannah River valley with the Clarks Hill dam and lake.

In the Savannah River valley alone, the Corps bundled together ideas cribbed from the 308 Report (1935) and a June 1944 study before including a recommendation for eleven dams and artificial reservoirs throughout the Savannah River basin in the 1944 Flood Control Act.[24] Starting with the Clarks Hill project and a $35.3 million congressional appropriation, the Corps set a course to reshape the valley.[25] Benefits of this project specifically included the ever-desirable year-round navigation below Augusta, flood protection for that same city, and cheap electricity for Augusta and the lower Savannah River region. Boosters hoped that the dam, like those in the Tennessee Valley and in North Carolina (Yadkin River) erected by private institutions before 1933 and public agencies afterward, might also attract the chemical or aluminum industry, which required access to raw water supplies and low-cost electricity.[26] As a pork barrel project, Clarks Hill combined flood control, hydroelectric power production, and navigational improvements, thus making the public works project an easy sell to various constituencies throughout the valley. Not only would the Clarks Hill dam eliminate the long history of destructive seasonal floods in the Augusta region, according to Corps engineers, but the dam would also stabilize "low-water flows for navigation below Augusta" as well as "produce hydroelectric power for industrial purposes and rural electrification."[27] The dam might also conserve enough water to save the region from future electrical shortages such as those caused in part by the severe 1925 and 1941 droughts. Finally, the Corps and its congressional enablers considered the dam "the keystone"—the first of nearly a dozen dams in a coordinated project that might reorganize the valley's water, people, and economy.[28]

There was clearly support for the federally financed Clarks Hill multiple-purpose project, but a vocal minority of industrial and corporate interest groups initially maintained an aggressive oppositional stance. Georgia Power Company executives—and others from their Savannah River Electric Company subsidiary—soon changed their tune and opposed the federal project by 1944. Furthermore, company spokesmen ignited a firestorm after launching a campaign promoting private enterprise in an effort to sink the public energy, navigation, and flood control project. The energy company had held its first license to build at Clarks Hill between 1926 and 1932, but in a rare and unprecedented move it surrendered the license during the Great Depression when it could no longer afford to move the project forward and the Corps presented a viable plan to do so.[29] The Georgia Power Company publicly floated the idea of reapplying for a second Federal Power Commission license in 1939 but found little support among Augusta's leaders and dropped the idea.[30] But in 1946, the Georgia Power Company again announced plans to reapply for a second license. With depression and wartime sacrifice nearly behind the nation, the Georgia Power Company wanted to revive its version of capitalism—or, as critics would claim, a natural monopoly—through a private Clarks Hill project. After more than a decade's worth of battles with the TVA, companies like Georgia Power took the emerging postwar period as a moment to reassert their definition of free-market fundamentals as private power companies did elsewhere.[31] The Georgia Power Company—the most successful New South water and energy project builder in the Savannah River basin—received ample assistance in its quest to reclaim the Sun Belt's water, energy, consumers, and commercial future.

To fight these battles and push back against the Democratic Party's leadership, the company enlisted supporters around the state to rally for a return to the early twentieth century's private energy and water model. Georgia newspaper editors channeled Georgia Power's message in a coordinated campaign opposing federal projects like Clarks Hill. House editorial boards harped on the same themes of private enterprise and favored taxpaying development over tax-spending and tax-exempt public projects.[32] Many opponents to the Corps' plan argued that if private industry wanted to spend the money, the state should enable it to do so and then collect taxes. "We," the *Milledgeville Union-Recorder*'s editorial board stated, "very definitely believe private capital should have its right to exercise free enterprise, the same kind of pioneering spirit that built this country into the greatest nation the world has ever known." Milledgeville was the Piedmont town near the Georgia Power Company's recently restarted Furman Shoals project on the Oconee River. The company initiated construction at Furman Shoals (now known as Lake Sinclair and Dam) in 1929, stopped in 1930 during the Great Depression, and restarted construction in 1949. And when Georgia Power began operating Sinclair Dam in 1954, Milledgeville benefited from local tax payments. This was enough to justify the editor's opinion that the company was in a better financial "position to develop" Clarks Hill.[33] Despite the crippling 1941 drought conditions, the conversation on Georgia Power's side generally stuck to economic motivations and did not dare suggest that protecting water supply and water quantity was necessary for future economic development.

The Georgia Power Company's move to relicense Clarks Hill took some boosters by surprise and frustrated others. Lester Moody, the secretary of the Augusta chamber of commerce, rejected Georgia Power's proposal in 1946 and championed the federal project thereafter.[34] The Augusta business community and others also rebuffed their adversaries' attempts to link a public energy program with socialism. After the Georgia Power Company called the federal project socialistic, Moody replied: "If working to improve the conditions of the people living in the Savannah River Basin area is socialistic, then I am a socialist." The socialist label, he continued, "was just another version of the old story that is always used when one attempts to do something to improve living conditions for a people."[35] One of Moody's cohorts, *Augusta Herald* publisher William S. Morris Jr., the father of the Morris media empire's current CEO William "Billy" Morris III, endorsed the federal project over the private project. Like Moody, Morris likewise contested Georgia Power's assertion that the federal project was akin to socialism: "We cannot support the power company's argument that the development of the Savannah River constitutes Socialism, because the rivers and streams and all other natural resources belong to the people, and should be developed in a manner which would be most beneficial to all the people."[36] Lifelong southern supporters of private enterprise, Moody, Morris, and others found fellow southern boosters' and journalists' "socialism" and "socialistic" criticisms unfounded, and they recognized the language as a rhetorical leftover from the fight against fascism in Europe and from fears of Soviet expansion, and as a product of dropping temperatures at the onset of the Cold War. Distrustful after years of private energy company monopoly, valley residents rejected the legacy of private hydroelectric dams that had generated power that was, as Governor Strom Thurmond's hometown newspaper declared, "transmitted away" from the hinterlands "for the emolument of people elsewhere" in water- and energy-poor cores.[37] Taxes, free enterprise, and electricity, however, were not the only conversation topics.

Clarks Hill not only moved forward as a project to minimize flood- and drought-induced damages or as an energy and navigation scheme, but it also became a major tool for reshaping the Savannah River valley's recreation future. Recreation became an official part of the traditional multiple-purpose project planning by way of the Flood Control Act of 1944. If the desired troika of benefits insulated humans from seemingly uncontrollable environmental conditions and raging rivers, then recreation—as a means to reconnect people with predictable environmental circumstances and benign lakes—also emerged on an alternate level. The Corps and other agencies discovered that providing recreational opportunities at artificial reservoirs for local, regional, and the highly coveted out-of-state visitors at Clarks Hill was a top priority. They also learned that new working reservoirs and hydraulic waterscapes linked energy, water supplies, recreation, and race.

Public access to outdoor recreation emerged as an important national topic during the interwar period. After World War I, Americans turned to the open road to explore the great outdoors in personal automobiles. State governments built roads and parks, and businesses emerged to cater to and provide roadside services for tourists. Recreation planners generally agreed that leisure opportunities should provide democratic access and physical stimulation. Democratic access—or outdoor recreation for middle-class and working Americans—became a key flash point in these discussions that also focused on creating national outdoor recreation policies for public lands in the American West. This, by default, left local and state outdoor recreation advocates in urban areas—or in corners, including the American South, that lacked such lands—to shape their own recreational plans. However, New Deal programming provided southerners with tools—dollars and labor—to create some enclaves of public land. The Great Depression and New Deal response enabled President Franklin D. Roosevelt to funnel federal dollars and conservation work programs into a vast, national outdoor recreation network on state and federal lands. Local political and economic organizations (such as chambers of commerce) tapped New Deal dollars to fashion interwar outdoor recreation facilities and stimulated local economies while serving visitors of varying means from different geographical regions and with diverse needs.[38]

Following this basic national trajectory, Georgia's state and federal natural resource agencies worked together to acquire, improve, and plan for outdoor recreation areas and unique sites throughout the state. Between 1931 and 1937, the Department of Forestry and Geology acquired and managed approximately nine state properties, including one of Georgia's first state parks, a 1926 240-acre gift from Fred and August Vogel of the Pfister Vogel Leather Company. Between 1937 and 1941, Georgia's state park acreage tripled from less than 5,000 to more than 17,000 acres through donations and estates that sold or donated land to the state.[39] Throughout the period, Georgia's state park facilities and communities benefited from continued Civilian Conservation Corps (CCC) labor in ongoing coordination with the National Park Service (NPS) and the state's Works Progress Administration office. By the end of 1941, Georgia's Department of Natural Resources claimed that "the Federal government had spent through the National Park Service and the Civilian Conservation Corps, $6,300,000 on CCC camps working on State Park areas in Georgia."[40]

Amidst all of this physical activity and parkscaping, Georgia's newly organized Department of Natural Resources and other state and federal agencies assembled a recreation survey in 1939. The *Report on Outdoor Recreation in Georgia* ultimately highlighted the necessity of preservation and a state park system. Acquiring or setting land aside earlier rather than later would ultimately save "large sums of money" needed to research, relocate, and establish state parks, monuments, and historical sites. The authors wanted to learn from other states' experiences, "where rapid development and growth of population, business and industry" had "outstripped the love for recreation." The study's authors concluded, "It appears entirely logical and feasible to anticipate future trends, and look ahead, by at least acquiring, preserving and partially developing areas, which future generations will need for recreation, and probably will appreciate even more than today's generation." Recreation, apparently, was "alive in the hearts of Georgians."[41]

When the authors of Georgia's state park report recognized that recreation was alive in citizens' hearts, they also acknowledged that those hearts were in black and white bodies. Recreation conversations among leisure-seekers, state planners, elected officials, and federal bureaucrats always included discussions about race, class, and gender. Numerous writers have argued that private recreational opportunities were central to the formation of African American identity and community throughout the Jim Crow era. Another has revealed that even the NPS system planned in the 1930s to racially segregate users when they began building southern national parks—including the Great Smoky Mountains and Shenandoah—only to reverse course in 1942 after African Americans lobbied the NPS.[42] State parks—areas not considered by these studies—also became contested ground for outdoor recreation at southern water and energy projects in the Jim Crow era. State park systems throughout the South chose different paths to exclude or include African Americans. And plans for segregated state parks in Georgia and South Carolina—and eventually the Savannah River valley at Clarks Hill—were not without precedent.

North Carolinians may have operated the first state park in the American South—Jones Lake—for African Americans to leisurely interact with the environment in a Jim Crow setting in 1939.[43] While African Americans built and operated numerous private coastal recreational areas and communities, no other southern state legislatures or park systems appear to have created segregated parks for African Americans before 1940.[44] Georgia planners thought a lot like the federal and state officials in North Carolina. Throughout the State Planning Board's *Report on Outdoor Recreation in Georgia* (1939), the writers advocated for segregated recreational facilities based on racial and socioeconomic categories. Due to Georgia's demographics and assumed Jim Crow–segregated future, the authors declared that "separate areas and facilities for education, welfare, recreation, and other activities were required for" white and black residents.

Georgia officials expressed the belief that "every citizen should be provided for." For white "land owners," prime destinations apparently included coastal and mountain destinations "during the warm summer months" and "especially when crop prospects" were favorable. But for "the white tenant class of the farming population," the report observed, "recreation among the men and boys" consisted primarily "of hunting and fishing" and sports. Additionally, these white tenant families—perhaps white wives and girls more specifically—enjoyed "old fashioned church sociables [sic] . . . and special events" such as barbecues. Finally, the authors assessed African Americans, who were not subcategorized as property owners or tenants or by their sex. The authors' racial stereotypes assumed that African Americans' recreation was "peculiar to their racial characteristics" and only "centered around churches." As such, African American recreation facilities only needed to include "simple local developments, such as playfields with barbecue grounds and swimming pools." African Americans, so the thinking went, would not like the beach or mountains, and these prescriptions ultimately limited African American exposure to particular types of outdoor recreation and environments. Based on these combined demographic and assumed social characteristics, Georgia not only needed "two area systems, one for white people" and one for African Americans, but institutionalized facilities for "low income groups" and men who did not have the money, time, or transportation means to travel "very far in search of recreation."[45] According to the *Report*, Georgia had little public land like the American West and needed a recreational plan that played to the region's racial, socioeconomic, and rural realities.

Sun Belt boosters and politicians stumping for the Corps' Clarks Hill project took this recreation advice seriously. They disseminated information about plans for segregated recreation at the Savannah River valley's multiple-purpose dams in anticipation of a postwar leisure boom. By the late 1940s, Augusta's chamber of commerce secretary Lester S. Moody and South Carolina's governor J. Strom Thurmond consistently campaigned for Clarks Hill as a public source of industrial energy and flood control. Both also openly supported the Corps' recreational plans. Moody, in particular, did not underestimate recreation as an economic engine for his region and looked at Clarks Hill as a destination for all overworked and "half sick" Americans seeking a sublime nature. Singling out Clarks Hill, Moody envisioned the artificial reservoir as a "mecca" [sic] for "thousands of visitors" who had the financial means to travel great distances, rent boats, sleep in lakeside cottages, and pump thousands of recreation-related dollars into the Savannah River valley's emerging Sun Belt service economy.[46]

South Carolina's then-Democratic governor J. Strom Thurmond worked the other side of the river and did not limit Clarks Hill recreation and nature appreciation to nonlocal visitors with potentially deep pockets. Thurmond, of course, recognized first and foremost that Clarks Hill would benefit one particular class: industrialists. Clarks Hill would lure industry south, according to Thurmond, because of cheap energy and the region's "freedom from [labor] strikes." But Thurmond also supported the Clarks Hill project because it would provide public recreation space for "the working people, the farmers, textile workers, barbers, [and] mechanics," the very "people on the street who" did not have the money to join golf or hunt clubs or buy "fine horses." Speaking before an Augusta audience familiar with South Carolina's horse country in Aiken County, Thurmond explained that Clarks Hill would include a "16,000 acre park . . . for the recreation and enjoyment of the working man." At Clarks Hill, Thurmond's archetypal "common man" could enjoy free access to public space to "hunt and fish" and thus presumably avoid a legacy of conflict over trespassing on private land.[47] Moody, Thurmond, and others recognized class divisions among recreation enthusiasts and leisure-seekers. But class alone was not the only topic in the discussions about recreational facilities in the Savannah River valley.

Though Moody and Thurmond tipped their hats to the newly proposed waterscape's local and nonlocal users, they did not limit recreational benefits to white nature seekers and water lovers. While campaigning for governor in October 1946 and defending the Clarks Hill project, Thurmond declared the water and energy scheme's recreational aspects as "one of the most important benefits of the project." He added, "If the Federal Government develops the project," as opposed to the Georgia Power Company, the NPS recommended "beautiful parks, for whites and blacks, separate parks."[48] Thurmond should not be identified as a defender of democratic outdoor recreation. In wooing his white constituents, what he ultimately promised to white leisure-seekers was that they would never have to share recreation space with African Americans.[49] Two years later, Corps planners followed the NPS report's advice and announced plans for at least two separate swimming, picnicking, and camping facilities on Clarks Hill's shoreline. In Georgia, the Corps recommended the "Keg Creek Negro [sic] Area," located about thirty miles north of Augusta and about two miles east of Leah, Georgia (now a day-use area). And in South Carolina, the Corps recommended the "Hickory Knob Negro [sic] Area," located about two miles south of Bordeaux, South Carolina, and currently the site of the state's most popular state park, Hickory Knob.[50]

Race, not unlike class, continued to enter recreational planning conversations in conjunction with Sun Belt water and energy developments. Georgia's state park system was a relative latecomer to democratic recreation and operating state parks for African Americans. The state opened its first African American park, George Washington Carver State Park, in 1950 on land leased from the Corps after operations commenced at the multiple-purpose Lake Allatoona project. Georgia also maintained at least three other parks for African Americans by 1955.[51] South Carolina's system, on the other hand, followed closely behind North Carolina's and excluded African American visitors between 1934 and 1938.[52] Thereafter, some parks had "Negro [sic] Areas," such as Lake Greenwood State Park, a reservoir for hydroelectric operations built with New Deal Rural Electrical Administration funds.[53] While these parks provided separate facilities, they were hardly equal. Greenwood's 12,000-acre artificial lake, for example, was for white visitors only. These segregated state parks and swimming areas became flashpoints for civil rights protesters beginning in the late 1940s.[54]

Legal cases emerged in Maryland and Virginia to challenge segregated access to or exclusion from municipal and state park facilities before and after the U.S. Supreme Court's landmark *Brown v. Board of Education* decision declared segregated (so-called separate but equal) education unconstitutional in 1954.[55] A Maryland legal case combined three suits involving exclusion from public pools, bathing areas, and a public beach. Upon hearing the Maryland case after the *Brown* decision, the U.S. Fourth Circuit Court of Appeals (Richmond, Va.) ruled state park segregation unconstitutional on March 14, 1955.[56] The court soon ruled on subsequent Virginia cases and ordered the state's park system desegregated. But rather than consider an integrated arrangement, Virginia leaders elected to follow the path of "massive resistance" and white supremacy. They closed all parks in response to the *Brown* case, and they considered leasing or selling parts of the system.[57] Together, the recreation-inspired legal challenges to segregation demonstrated how state parks and access to water-based recreation served as loci for civil rights activists and massive resistance. African Americans challenged segregation in schools and on buses as well as at state park gates and on shorelines in the 1950s and 1960s.

In the years leading up to the *Brown v. Board of Education* decision, the Corps had planned to segregate black and white nature seekers at Clarks Hill in the Savannah River valley.[58] Two events blocked those plans. First, one South Carolina state park official claimed that "the establishment and development of the two state parks proposed on Clark [*sic*] Hill" would burden the existing system of twenty-one parks that served 3 million visitors and already could not balance maintenance with new construction.[59] The second, primary reason for the cooled discussion about segregated parks emerged when lower courts applied legal precedents and the *Brown v. Board of Education* decision to public recreation facilities. When Virginia officials closed state parks in 1956 to avoid court-ordered desegregation, South Carolina state park administrator C. West Jacocks defended his state's segregated system as it also faced a challenge from the National Association for the Advancement of Colored People's Charleston chapter over access to Edisto Beach State Park. Jacocks justified his operations because he thought the park system provided an equitable geographic distribution of parks and facilities for white and African American visitors. Clearly not interested in park integration, Jacocks threatened, "Should any 'power' eventually bring into being the enforced non-segregated use of the state parks, there is every indication that there will be *no* use." In that event, he intoned, "the parks will be closed."[60] Despite his best face, Jacocks knew that his facilities could never be truly separate and equal.[61] Separate and equal recreation facilities—as recommended for Clarks Hill's Hickory Knob (S.C.) and Keg Creek (Ga.) sites—could never have been possible, given the project's federal authority. Furthermore, any such arrangement would have only delayed an inevitable confrontation over racial inequality evident in other arenas—swimming pools, schools, and public transportation—throughout the United States. Such events forced the hands of administrators like Jacocks, who eventually followed through on threats. South Carolina attempted to close selected parks in 1956 to avoid desegregating the entire system but eventually closed all parks in response to a 1963 U.S. District Court desegregation order.[62] Clarks Hill planning proceeded, but when segregation as a legal instrument died, plans for segregated parks along the lakeshore died as well.

Planning for the recreational future of the Clarks Hill project required significant socioeconomic considerations, corrective action, and time. The Corps and other agency staff all came to realize that creating an artificial lake to generate electricity for industry and provide leisure space in a peopled and agricultural environment was not easy. Implementation of the

Clarks Hill water and energy project clearly roiled environmental questions as much as it confronted social and economic inequalities in Georgia and South Carolina. Plus, the Georgia Power Company executives were not the only voices to protest federal plans for Clarks Hill. Everyone was actually not "for it," and even those who did support the federal Clarks Hill project were not always happy with the Sun Belt environments they got.

The real estate planning and land acquisition process produced conflict when the Corps physically removed people from the Clarks Hill dam and reservoir project area. As Andrew Sparks reported for the *Atlanta Journal Magazine* in 1947, "Although some farm land will be inundated, there are remarkably few home sites in the vast area," since most valley residents "built on high ground" above the valley floor.[63] Corps real estate reports identified more than 500 property owners in the project area: "It is estimated that approximately 45 percent of the reservoir area is owned by individuals, 45 percent by the Savannah River Electric Company, 4 percent by the Twin City River Company, 3 percent by the United States (National Forest) with the remainder in the stream beds." A total of 450 individuals—white and African American—comprised the approximately 128 resident and tenant families requiring physical relocation from a project area that grew to encompass more than 150,000 acres.[64] Based on the initial purchases of 96,000 acres, there was an approximate average of one person for every 213 acres in the Clarks Hill project area. As a point of reference, beginning in the mid-1930s, President Roosevelt's administration began acquiring more than 200,000 acres of abandoned and severely eroded upland in South Carolina to assemble the Long Cane District of Sumter National Forest, which now abuts the Clarks Hill reservoir. That area was not as sparsely populated: According to one source, there were 3,300 families in the area. However, only 25 percent of families owned the land they farmed; 74 percent were renters, tenants, or sharecroppers; and squatters constituted 1 percent.[65] If the same multiplier is applied to the Clarks Hill project, the potential total number of affected individuals rises from 450 to 1,800. This suggests the Corps underreported the number of people affected by its project. Or maybe not.

Other, non-Corps-generated surveys and documents confirm that the Savannah River valley was a sparsely populated but working landscape. In the mid-1940s, the Smithsonian Institution's Bureau of Ethnology initiated a national archeological salvage project known as the River Basin Surveys. The basin survey program evolved from TVA-sponsored archeological activity at New Deal dam and reservoir sites before becoming a formal program applied nationwide to dam and reservoir sites after World War II.[66] In 1947, the River Basin Survey sent two archeologists, Carl F. Miller and University of Georgia professor Joseph Caldwell, into the Savannah River valley to investigate the Clarks Hill dam and reservoir area as one of the Southeast's first major interagency archeological salvage projects. The two men traversed a generally unpeopled landscape in transition, and their narrative descriptions and photographs clearly indicated the used, abused, and abandoned states of the Savannah River valley's landscape.

The area's old domesticated fields and orchards had transformed into a feral landscape. The land was not wilderness; but it was not entirely domesticated, and the territory obscured past uses as much as the land was obviously scarred by some of those uses. As Miller walked across private property and drove state highways in Georgia and South Carolina, he looked for Indian mounds and potential settlement sites on knolls, in fields, and at the junction of watercourses on sandbars, in bottomlands, or adjacent to shoals. He then read back through layers of modern landscapes to find pot shards, human remains, bone tools, and Indian mounds in wooded areas, orchards, cotton fields, and pastures. Miller's notes included brief narrative descriptions of sites, indicated the existence of inconsistent landownership records or occupation status, and noted previous land uses and current property conditions. At the time of Miller's surveys, dated January through April 1949, the survey sites were typically located in cleared and fallow fields. But landowners and tenants or renters clearly continued to use many fields—for cotton, orchards, and cattle—set to be covered by the water stored behind Clarks Hill dam to control downstream flooding, produce energy for distant urban and industrial consumers, and improve navigation in the lower valley.[67]

Miller and his archeological contemporaries also noted land in various stages of use and ecological evolution a few years before University of Georgia biologist Eugene P. Odum—often cited as the "father of modern ecology"—began evaluating old field succession downriver at the Barnwell (S.C.) Savannah River site nuclear bomb factory in 1951.[68] Miller categorized erosion generally and specifically in the Clarks Hill reservoir area. One "badly eroded knoll . . . was covered with broom straw and small pines."[69] Another knoll, near South Carolina bottomland on the Little River, was "marked by sheet erosion" and ubiquitous loblolly and slash pine trees.[70] Some of the "old plowed" fields "had been allowed to grow to pine and shrub" in McCormick County, South Carolina. Other fields identifiably "old" and "terraced" were "partly overgrown in pines and broom straw."[71] Very often Miller found evidence of Indian habitation in plowed fields, pastures, and canebrakes, and at other times he did not.[72] Despite occasionally striking out, Miller consistently observed an agricultural landscape that—in the absence of constant human labor and domestication—had been "allowed to go back to nature."[73]

About the same time that Miller and Caldwell conducted their Clarks Hill investigations, an NPS historian investigated potential historic sites during March and April 1949. Operating independently of the River Basin Survey and the interagency archeological salvage project, Edward Riley investigated and reported on nearly twenty locations in the proposed Clarks Hill reservoir area, including an eighteenth-century military fort, "dead towns," ferry crossings, and cemeteries. Riley's recommendations to the NPS varied from doing nothing with some areas to improving road access for others. For most spots, Riley was a harsh historian: "Archeological investigation of the sites is not feasible. It would probably contribute little to the known history of the towns." To be fair, Riley evaluated these areas for their national significance and not just their local interest, and as such he believed that "none of the sites to be covered by the reservoir has sufficient significance to require preservation." But at a basic level, NPS historian Riley diverged from River Basin Survey archeologists Miller and Caldwell. Riley only recommended "erection of historical narrative markers at the various" historic sites not older than the eighteenth century, since little could "be done to interpret the history of the reservoir area." In contrast, archeologists Miller and Caldwell identified hundreds of pre-eighteenth-century locations illustrating the complex and long environmental history of an area shaped by shifting natural and cultural conditions as well as energy regimes.[74]

Journalist Andrew Sparks later reported from one of the sites Riley considered insignificant and highlighted valley residents' ambivalence about selling their property and relocating. According to Riley, "The only town which will disappear under the dammed-up water" behind Clarks Hill was Lisbon, Georgia, an "out-of-the-way, one-store hamlet" sixty-five miles upriver from Augusta as described by Sparks.[75] Located at the junction of the Broad and Savannah Rivers, Lisbon had been an important tobacco and cotton trading center in the late 1800s but declined as railroads stifled river transportation. In the 1940s, Lisbon still included a working river ferry, a post office, and a handful of other buildings.[76] As Irene

DuBose, a resident from the small town explained to Sparks, "They'll have a hard time pushing us out but I reckon I'll go." Another resident, Lisbon ferryman Jim Evans, commented, "I ain't going to wait for them to start" building the dam or flooding the reservoir; "I'll take my five children and get out. I'll farm somewhere I reckon."

Like DuBose and Evans, individuals and family estate agents, plus other Clarks Hill corporate landowners, including electrical utilities (the Savannah River Electric Company, a Georgia Power Company subsidiary, held title to nearly 40,000 acres) and local banks, eventually sold their property to the federal government. Many individual and corporate sellers willingly worked with the Corps, eagerly sold eroded farms battered about for decades in a volatile agricultural economy, and moved out of the valley. In a procedure familiar in the past and encountered in the future, not all transactions were so smooth. Some individual and corporate landowners reluctantly sold property only under condemnation proceedings or vacated property only as the reservoir's rising waters began to cover their property; they protested the right of the federal government to condemn land as well as the land's assessed economic value, which often did not account for the property's historic or emotional value.[77]

So was everyone "for it"? In 1943, when Colonel P. A. Feringa made this remark about the federally financed Clarks Hill project, he was technically more correct than wrong. Flooding that nearly caused a catastrophic levee failure in Augusta in 1929 and a 1941 urban drought that resulted in a major energy crisis made the multiple-purpose navigation, flood control, and hydroelectric dam development at Clarks Hill more appealing to the Savannah River valley's residents in 1945 than the Georgia Power Company's water and energy scheme. Within a few years, this assumption was briefly challenged, but the Corps' project moved forward and workers poured the first batches of concrete for Clarks Hill dam in 1948. The topography of the Savannah River valley did not call for a tall western dam best exemplified by the iconic Hoover Dam (1936). That Colorado River dam, which stood taller than 500 feet and measured just over 1,000 feet in width, was far different from the Clarks Hill dam. After increasing from an estimated 1944 cost of $35.3 million to a 1954 cost of $78.5 million, the concrete dam and earthen embankment stood just shy of 200 feet tall and nearly one mile (5,280 feet) wide across the Savannah River when completed.[78]

When Clarks Hill dam's floodgates closed and the reservoir began to fill in 1951, the project remained incomplete. In late 1952, an Atlanta journalist declared that the Savannah River was "imprisoned" behind the dam and had turned into "Georgia's new ocean" covering 71,000 acres with more than 1,200 miles of shoreline. At the time, Clarks Hill Lake was the "biggest man-made lake southeast of TVA." Many held out hope that the dam would "tame the river in floodtime, preventing more than a million dollar's worth of damage every decade" and store water for "periods of drought" last experienced in 1941. Others hoped that Clarks Hill would become the Sun Belt's "biggest vacationland between the Blue Ridge mountains and the sea."[79] Supporters, critics, and observers assumed Clarks Hill would serve many interests well into the future, thought this was not readily apparent to everyone.

Clarks Hill began producing energy in 1953, and all dam watchers waited to see what the dam could do. But the project—including park planning, concession contracts, real estate claims and leases, and domestic water supply allocation—was unfinished and contested well into the 1960s. While the Corps eventually acquired all the land titles it needed, there were numerous situations where individual and community support for a federally financed Clarks Hill traveled a difficult path. From road and bridge relocations to public health and malaria control to shoreline aesthetics and timber clearing, there was no shortage of grassroots resistance to the Corps.[80] Citizens successfully won concessions from the Corps to alter road relocations that positively benefited communities affected by the new reservoir, and they also influenced the Corps' timber operations to protect public health. These citizens, not unlike their elected representatives, learned that while they were all "for it" during the conceptual and planning stages, the Corps' execution of Clarks Hill was not simple, clearly explained, or so easily acceptable.

Many of these issues were new and unanticipated by those who conceived of and who supported the Clarks Hill development, and they illustrated the continuing and unintended management issues the Corps, elected officials, engineers, and residents had to confront in their new hydraulic waterscape. And even before Clarks Hill went online, the Corps' next massive artificial Savannah River valley project moved from idea to reality. The Hartwell dam and lake scheme, as recommended in the 1944 Flood Control Act, would also face many of the same endorsements, trials, and rejections the Corps experienced with the Clarks Hill project.

Just as there was no real politically Solid South, Sun Belt boosters found themselves equally divided over the region's water and energy future. The

Georgia Power Company waged an unsuccessful political battle to win approval for a privately financed Clarks Hill water and energy project and to avoid what their surrogates interpreted as the road to socialism. The energy companies and their supporters consistently trumpeted the importance of private enterprise and raised the specter of socialism, though this message was often interpreted as flagrant hyperbole. For example, the *Atlanta Journal* editors surmised in 1947 that the Georgia Power Company was "not only fighting for something" it wanted but was primarily "spearheading a campaign in behalf of the National Association of Electric Companies" lobby and "to stop further development by government of the nation's river systems on the pattern of the Tennessee Valley Authority." In the editors' opinion, the battle over Clarks Hill was just one front on a nearly thirty-year-old war: "Shall there be any further governmental developments like TVA, or shall TVA remain a sort of yardstick or object lesson, and our river systems be developed for power production by private initiative in the manner it deems best for production of profits?"[81] In the matter of Clarks Hill, many supporters clearly sided with public power and rejected private power.

In perhaps the most forceful and clear language, Governor J. Strom Thurmond declared in 1947, "We know the government always completes its projects." In directly calling out Georgia Power Company executives who were then restarting the almost twenty-year-old Furman Shoals (Lake Sinclair) project on the Oconee River, Thurmond reminded South Carolina citizens that they could not always be sure about a private energy company's interest in finishing projects.[82] Thurmond also noted that "opposition to the nation's water development system stemmed from 'bulwarks of wealth and private interest,'" not from those who purportedly held public and community values.[83] Furthermore, the private energy company was apparently selective in calling federal projects socialistic. Thurmond claimed that Georgia Power had not branded the Corps' Allatoona dam in northwest Georgia as "Socialistic."[84] The company may have behaved this way because it was planning new coal-fired plants downstream of Allatoona on the Etowah River, such as Plant Hammond (operational in 1954), and it was keen to have a federal dam regulate the river's flow. Thurmond—more well known for his future leadership in the Dixiecrat revolt, his racial politics, and his eventual jump to the Republican Party in 1964—was a complex character who contributed to the breaking apart of the Democratic Party over the issue of civil rights. This advocacy for Clarks Hill undoubtedly played into Congress's decision to change the name of Clarks Hill Dam and Lake to the J. Strom Thurmond Dam and Lake at Clarks Hill in 1988.

To say that dry and high river years, drought and flood legacies in the Savannah River valley, did not equally shape the Savannah River valley's history as did politics or labor history would be an understatement. Water and its shifting behavior contributed to the reasons why people chose to move into and throughout the valley for centuries. New South boosters had consistently trumpeted the region's stock in plentiful, high-quality water as a reason to call the American South home from the 1890s to the 1950s. As such, devastating flooding in river communities and droughts that compromised electrical production and industrial development did not always strike innocent Georgians and South Carolinians. Water was a top-tier factor in the region's economic growth, and water in the wrong quantities at the wrong times also compromised that growth. Natural disasters—the droughts and the floods in the Savannah River valley—were thus nature's and people's making. Many other manufactured problems—racial inequality, eroded land, the need for bridge relocations, and public health problems—also influenced conversations about the valley's shape, where people lived, and the ability for communities to thrive along the riverbanks and reservoir shorelines.

After completing the Clarks Hill dam and reservoir project, Corps and federal engineers continued to build hundreds of large and small reservoirs throughout the American South for a variety of purposes in places southerners had lived in, farmed, hunted, and appreciated for centuries. In the post-1945 period, the Corps' work in southern valleys tied the region's water and energy future to questions about democratic recreational access. Outdoor recreation discussions also forced some southerners to negotiate the color line and confront socioeconomic realities. If Sun Belt boosters celebrated their ability to segregate public recreation space, then they also defined where and what kind of recreation activities would be available for white and black men and women, rich and poor, during their free time. Unfortunately, this process also determined and limited how Americans engaged with and learned about nature. In a Sun Belt comprised of used, abused, and abandoned landscapes, the Corps and other institutions faced major challenges in creating democratic and accessible leisure landscapes while also building hydraulic waterscapes.

In the last half-century, longtime valley residents, including those forced to move and make way for the Clarks Hill reservoir, had to share a transformed landscape perhaps best described by William Faulkner in his collection of short stories *Big Woods*. In Faulkner's Mississippi, an old hunter could lament that the new fishermen in powerboats had no memory of the old forests and fields below the surface of a "government-built" reservoir. Furthermore, the unappreciative sport fishermen lacked an ethic and simply left sunken bass plugs and beer bottles on the "Big Bottom" itself where the hunter had once tracked deer and bear on foot.[85] The old agricultural economy and landscape had been consumed by human fears of future floods and droughts; it was consumed by corporate dreams of energy independence; it was consumed by insatiable boosters and clever congressional leaders who repackaged the New Deal big dam consensus as a solution to southern water problems.

Flush with public funds and hungry for institutional validation after World War II, the Sun Belt Corps' river planning program manufactured new environmental and social conditions in the Savannah River valley and beyond. However, before the Clarks Hill reservoir had even completely filled up, drought once again struck the American South in the 1950s and cast doubt on the role new reservoirs could play in maintaining adequate water and energy supplies for a region that suddenly did not have enough water again.

CHAPTER 5

Big Dam Backlash Rising
in the Sun Belt

When Governor Sonny Perdue (b. 1946) prayed for rain on the state capitol's steps during Georgia's deepening drought on November 13, 2007, it was not the first time politics, religion, and water scarcity merged in the Peach State. In the 1950s, drought gripped Georgia for a third time in less than thirty years, and Georgians decided to "Pray for Rain" during the driest year in Georgia history since 1925.[1] In a display of sympathy and well-choreographed publicity, Governor Herman Talmadge (1913–2002) personally led a Sunday service designated as a "day of prayer for rain," according to one newspaper. As the multiyear national drought climaxed in October 1954, the drought hit Georgia's farmers and small communities hardest. Atlanta officials restricted city departments' water use, and they developed a plan for rationing municipal water supplies that did not have to be implemented.[2] Fayetteville, a small town about twenty-five miles south of downtown Atlanta in the upper Flint River basin, was not so lucky. The Fayette County seat of 1,200 had to cancel school for the county's 700 students because the town had no water; it was one of at least seven Georgia communities whose municipal water supplies had vanished.[3] Urban municipal water customers were not the only individuals to feel the effects of drought. The state's increasingly diversified truck farmers—including those in the Augusta and Savannah River region—also suffered as their fruit and vegetable crops withered on the vine. Richmond County dairy, cattle, and poultry farmers in the "death throes" became eligible for federal financial assistance.[4] Overall, the state's agricultural economy took a $100 million hit from a so-called natural disaster that *Atlanta Journal* editors characterized as not making "as much noise as fires and floods" or moving "as fast." But the drought's consequences were, in their opinion, "just as deadly."[5]

Georgians—and other southeastern residents—once again encountered a serious water supply crisis, signaling that water insecurity continued to challenge the American South's potential. The 1954 drought, not unlike droughts in 1925 and 1941, compromised urban water supplies and industrial operations, as well as agricultural livelihoods. But the 1954 event was different: It sparked "widespread interest . . . to find not just a temporary or expedient" solution, according to one observer. Many people, including those who served on the hastily formed Georgia Water Use and Conservation Committee, agreed on the need to "develop a long time policy that will be flexible in character and that will deal equitably and effectively" with all water consumers. The often forgotten 1950s Georgia drought occurred at a critical juncture during the so-called Cotton Belt's transformation into the Sun Belt and was partly the result of "slow, but steady, social and economic changes."[6] These changes amplified long-standing environmental realities in a region defined by water and power. The 1950s southern drought and response ignited an intense backlash over how best to balance water and energy supplies as the New Deal big dam and liberal consensus began to unravel. The rising Sun Belt rediscovered an old vulnerability in a period of increasing change: Sustainable growth required a sustainable water supply.

Opposition to the New Deal big dam consensus coalesced nationwide as the U.S. Army Corps of Engineers' plan for the Hartwell Dam energy and water project surfaced in the Savannah River valley. Controversies over dams in the American West sparked resistance across the country. For example, the postwar public-private power debate over the Hells Canyon High Dam served as a critical tipping point for New Deal liberalism and post-1945 conservatism and environmentalism. The Idaho Power Company's legal team successfully mounted a decade-long campaign to win control of the Snake River valley, "unplugging the New Deal" in the process, according to one scholar. The utility lobby trumpeted the economic value of free enterprise, won Republican president Dwight Eisenhower's political support, and secured federal approval for three small corporate hydroelectric dams in 1957. These victories eliminated the Corps' and the Bureau of Reclamation's Hells Canyon High Dam project while simultaneously beating back plans set forth by New Deal–era agencies such as the Bonneville Power Administration. Interest group opposition at Hells Canyon—beginning in 1945 and initially led by an energy corporation—opened the door for other opponents, such as conservationists and ecologists who spoke for salmon and wild rivers. Unplugging the New Deal's multiple-purpose dam program in the Snake River valley empowered old and new stakeholders across the country.[7]

A second western battle further cracked the New Deal's big dam consensus. Successful opposition to one of the Bureau of Reclamation's Colorado River Storage Project dams in Echo Park (Colo.) also convinced an emerging postwar community of environmental stakeholders that federal dam building could be stopped. Activists defended Dinosaur National Monument and the National Park Service's mission from a big dam on the Green River. By 1956, park and river advocates argued in favor of wilderness and questioned the bureau's benefit-cost analysis and technological claims. They defeated the Echo Park dam and launched a national environmental movement led by personalities such as David Brower who championed wilderness and wild rivers for the next two decades. After Hells Canyon and Echo Park, few western dams moved forward without dedicated, professional, and nationalized opposition.[8]

In the Southeast, leaders in the rising Sun Belt doubled down. The New Deal big dam consensus changed tact but plowed forward at full speed to resolve the region's persistent water and energy challenges. An interlocking group of stakeholders—local boosters, energy executives, members of Congress, and Corps engineers—drove the process from multiple angles. First, fast-talking local chamber of commerce agents adept at "selling the South" and long-serving Democratic Party operatives perfected a process initiated during the New Deal that captured federal dollars to finance the region's military bases, airports, factories, and highways.[9] Less-well-known Sun Belt boosters also continuously used water and energy projects to secure federal dollars and sell the region's known commodity: low-cost, nonunionized labor. Second, energy corporations and their allies did not, however, completely unplug the New Deal in the American South during the same time period as they did in the Snake and Green River valleys. Corps and elected officials defended—and corporate executives criticized—publicly funded water and energy programs in the South. At the same time, private sector energy companies contributed to the region's hydraulic waterscape by building their own hydroelectric dams or coal plants downstream from federal dams that regulated unpredictable river flows. The private sector's opposition picked up at Hartwell, but it could not defeat the Corps' two remaining Savannah River valley projects. Southern Democrats had reloaded the New Deal and successfully turned the valley's environmental manipulation over to the Corps. Energy executives, citizens, and other federal agencies challenged the Corps throughout this process, but it would take these collective forces nearly two decades to build a serious big dam backlash to federal energy and water operations. In the 1950s and 1960s, the Corps' victories in the Savannah River valley's public-private power debate were very different from the celebrated outcomes that stopped big government dams in the American West's Hells Canyon and Echo Park. But the free enterprise, fiscal restraint, and environmental rhetoric resonated in the American South.

The backlash and resistance to federal water projects in the Savannah River valley in the 1950s manifested in a complex moment of volatile global, social, and environmental conditions. Southerners articulated water problems—floods, droughts, and soil erosion—in newspapers, correspondence, and public meetings and throughout the levels of state and federal bureaucracies. As New Deal economic liberalism came to an end, according to historian Alan Brinkley, postwar "rights based liberalism" produced a limited regulatory environment while also responding to the civil rights and states' rights movements.[10] Agricultural, industrial, and municipal constituencies affected by water problems expressed a wide range of solutions to protect property rights, the local tax base, private enterprise, and the environment. Individuals and interest groups also wanted to reevaluate water rights in an era in which property rights and states' rights converged with civil rights to redraw political loyalties after the Supreme Court's landmark *Brown v. Board of Education* desegregation case (1954). All of these issues touched as local boosters leaned on politicians to make sure full funding was extended for new Corps projects such as Clarks Hill, Hartwell, and nearly two dozen other major dam, reservoir, and waterway projects across the Sun Belt.[11] The Clarks Hill project—completed between 1946 and 1952 because, reportedly, "everyone was for it"—barely held together the region's long-reigning but clearly fractured New Deal Democratic Party. The Hartwell project's postwar debates over public energy, fiscal responsibility, and rights all contributed to dividing political parties and the states of Georgia and South Carolina. Opinions about the Southeast's hydraulic waterscape could be found in the heart of these debates and continued to shape liberal and conservative discourse in the coming decades. Conservative rights-based ideas—like those espoused in other regions over busing, taxes, and entitlements—also influenced the Sun Belt's energy and water choices while recasting future political affinities after the 1950s drought.[12]

U.S. Army Corps of Engineers technocrats had previously evaluated the Hartwell dam and reservoir site in multiple studies—including the 308 Study (1935) and as one of eleven projects approved in concept by Congress in the Flood Control Act (1944)—before completing the project in the early 1960s.[13] The Hartwell Dam, a 200-foot-tall and 2-mile-long (11,000-foot) structure, is about ninety miles upstream and northwest of Augusta. Congress approved and engineers designed Hartwell to provide the primary trio of benefits like Clarks Hill and other multiple-purpose Corps projects as explicitly approved by the Flood Control Act of 1950 for flood control, navigation improvement, and energy production. They also envisioned a new hydroelectric dam that would impound a 56,000-acre reservoir (2 million acre-feet) to provide nearly endless opportunities for recreation on land and water.[14] In the 1940s, elected officials remained generally mum about Hartwell and other possible federal dams in the river valley during Clarks Hill's planning and construction period. Colonel Paschal N. Strong, on the other hand, did not remain so tight-lipped. Strong believed the Savannah River valley was "a gold mine for electric power." And in 1949, while discussing Clarks Hill, the self-confident Strong declared, "You may be sure that the Savannah River will be developed and the Hartwell dam will be built."[15] Strong was not wrong, and Hartwell got a congressional green light and first appropriation one year later.[16] With money in the pipeline to improve the Sun Belt's water and energy conditions in the Savannah River valley, Corps engineers promptly began finalizing land surveys and construction designs for the valley's second major postwar public works project.

Support for the new Hartwell scheme emerged from predictable directions. First, civic bodies mobilized to promote the project. Georgians and South Carolinians called Hartwell a self-liquidating "cash-register" dam that would pay for itself through electrical sales revenue to rural electric and municipal cooperatives established during the New Deal.[17] The Hartwell Steering Committee—comprised of prominent Savannah River valley movers and shakers—believed the public infrastructure project would jump-start Sun Belt commercial development. Lester Moody, Augusta's tireless chamber of commerce leader, was a primary spokesman, and he peddled promotional materials. For example, *The Hartwell Project . . . Now: Presented to the Congress of the United States by the People of South Carolina and Georgia* defined the social merits and economic benefits of the proposed dam for members of Congress while also adding some others, including soil conservation and recreation. National defense, however, quickly rose to the top as a new vehicle for Hartwell.

National defense likely represented a sincere attempt to secure federal dollars, given the nation's emerging Cold War relations with the Soviet Union. *The Hartwell Project . . . Now* pamphleteers linked the new Communist threat with old fears expressed by their New South predecessors: Georgia and South Carolina lacked coal and petroleum reserves. Thus, the Sun Belt could not support itself during a national war emergency, and industrial operations could "be paralyzed" by striking miners or rail workers.[18] The committee's argument that hydroelectric facilities were good for national defense because river water was always available ignored the fact that rivers could, in fact, shrink considerably as they did in the past. Regardless of history, boosters interpreted Hartwell as a critical tool for national defense and energy security. When the promoters released *The Hartwell Project . . . Now* in 1949, they may not have known that the Atomic Energy Commission (AEC) planned to locate a nuclear weapons material manufacturing plant on the Savannah River downstream from Augusta. However, the Hartwell cheerleaders surely recalled that Congress was quick to approve New Deal and World War II public works projects when such projects supported national defense objectives.[19] And if they did not remember, Georgia senator Richard B. Russell would have certainly provided the institutional memory.

Born in Winder, Georgia, Richard B. Russell Jr. (1897–1971) was elected to the state legislature in 1920, governor in 1930, and U.S. senator in 1932. He served in the Senate for nearly forty years until his death. As a New Deal Democrat, Russell supported agricultural programs and the Rural Electrification Administration's enabling legislation. But by 1938, he was casting a critical eye on the New Deal after President Franklin D. Roosevelt attempted to purge Georgia's other senator and southern Democrats who valued white supremacy over liberalism and civil rights.[20] After World War II, Russell came into his own, and he mastered the Senate's rule-making and legislative process as a member of two powerful committees—appropriations and armed services—where he served for decades and at times as chairman. Russell excelled in his ability to win allies; he lobbied for their projects and expected their debts to help pave the way for his own interests. For example, Russell helped Oklahoma's Robert Kerr, an equally savvy and powerful senator, win federal dollars in the 1950s for water projects. Half-jokingly Russell noted, "If any is left over after you . . .

get through with the Treasury, I hope to get a few dollars for Georgia." Dam and water schemes were an instrumental part of this horse-trading process that Russell tapped to build out Georgia's hydraulic waterscape.[21] Russell and the Savannah River's boosters worked hand in hand to build an industrial and commercial sector in the valley and to meet their collective vision for a commercial Sun Belt.

To the boosters' advantage, the Savannah River valley did accrue strategic capital when it became a part of America's modified Cold War "garrison state."[22] After the Soviet Union tested its first fission atomic weapon in 1949, National Security Council Resolution 68 outlined the U.S. military response and included a call for a new generation of nuclear weapons: hydrogen bombs. By the end of 1950, the federal government had selected a site twenty miles east of Augusta in Aiken and Barnwell Counties (S.C.) and contracted Delaware-based E. I. Du Pont De Nemours & Company to operate a new nuclear facility—the Savannah River Site (SRS)—to produce tritium for the next wave of nuclear weapons.[23]

The Hartwell boosters and the Corps grafted the SRS project into their promotional materials to fortify their cause in the halls of Congress while inadvertently sowing confusion.[24] South Carolina's and Georgia's Democratic leadership initially connected Hartwell and the SRS defense facility in the early 1950s based on projected regional electrical needs.[25] The real connection between the two facilities, they soon learned from the AEC, was not electrical supply but Hartwell's ability to help regulate the Savannah River's flow of water into—and ultimately out of—Clarks Hill's reservoir. As one AEC spokesperson explained to South Carolina senator J. Strom Thurmond (D), Corps engineers' combined operations at Hartwell and Clarks Hill would ensure water releases at a minimum flow of 5,300 cubic feet per second. These regular releases of cold water were necessary for the SRS's water withdrawals and critical nuclear reactor operations.[26] These details mattered, but Sun Belt boosters and politicians ultimately branded Hartwell as a national defense project that also promised commercial development throughout the central Savannah River valley's much larger hydraulic waterscape.

Another group of Sun Belt movers and shakers lined up in support of Hartwell's recreational promise. This new crew was not interested in the traditional trio of benefits or national defense; they wanted to invest in property adjacent to the Sun Belt's newest working reservoir. As Corps real estate agents began acquiring and condemning land from hundreds of property owners already living within the Hartwell dam and reservoir area in 1958, a small band of professionals and contractors eager to carve a new lakeside community from old farmland began corresponding with South Carolina's Senator Thurmond. This new pro-dam crowd inquired about specific shoreline land management policies, such as property owners' rights to access the public reservoir from private land.[27]

It is important to point out at this juncture that the Corps incorporated a buffer or collar of land between the reservoir's high-water line and adjacent private property lines for nearly every project all over the country. Working reservoirs—public and private—maintain these buffers primarily to protect water quality and to keep dirt from running off, accumulating in the reservoir, and compromising water storage capacity.[28] The distance between these lines or the amount of land contained within the buffer and collar could be a few hundred feet or more, depending on topography, a surveyor's skill, and the final agreement between sellers and Corps real estate agents. Finally, and most important to understand, the Corps' collar lands were (and are) public land and therefore open to general access. This final point made the real estate investors and property owners apprehensive about purchasing land abutting the collar or relinquishing ownership and riparian rights to land corralled within the buffer. Most property owners and investors ultimately wanted to build docks and boathouses, clear vegetation in the collar to improve the view, and enhance property values set to be further inflated due to proximity to a massive taxpayer-funded artificial amenity lake. Could property owners purchase or use the federal property in the buffer area between the water line and a private property line to build a dock? Senator Thurmond's constituents inquired.[29] According to one Corps officer, private property owners adjacent "to the project boundary" had "the same rights as the general public in using the Government lands and access to the water." The general public, in turn, could also access the collar from the lake itself. Corps officers also explained to Senator Thurmond that property owners could build floating docks, walkways, access roads, and other structures in the buffer areas on a permit application basis and as long as the improvements did not imply "exclusive use" or prevent public use of the reservoir or adjacent public lands.[30] As such, some property owners and real estate investors were positioned to gain significant financial benefit from the reservoir, and they supported the New Deal–inspired public works project because of the anticipated private rewards that came with Sun Belt leisure activities in a postindustrial waterscape.

Promises to serve national defense, dreams for personal playgrounds, and the reported trio of traditional benefits propelled Hartwell forward after 1950. These advocates—from chamber of commerce secretaries and media personalities to lawyers and general contractors who often landed lucrative federal construction contracts—functioned as cheerleaders for Hartwell dam for different reasons in the postwar period.[31] Boosters, elected officials, and Corps engineers believed that Hartwell was one of the federal government's most important Savannah River valley endeavors. Many people also understood that Hartwell was a relic of the New Deal big dam consensus, and a crop of critics emerged to oppose the venture after Hartwell received its first dedicated appropriation. As with opposition to Clarks Hill, a vocal group of conservative challengers opposed Hartwell when the project's costs exploded and the Corps' plans threatened property and water rights.

The backlash mobilized along multiple fault lines. In 1951, the Clemson College (currently known as Clemson University) board of trustees was anxious to learn how the Corps' proposed Hartwell project might affect the school. Clemson commissioned alumni Cecil L. Reid, A. G. Stanford, and Ed D. Sloan, and their internal report determined that the Hartwell project threatened the college's future. Reid and Stanford were both engineers; the latter worked for the Atlanta-based Robert and Company, an engineering outfit with direct ties to World War II defense factory contracts (e.g., the Marietta, Georgia, Bell B29 Bomber factory) and postwar civil infrastructure contracts (Atlanta Hartsfield International Airport).[32] In their report, the alumni argued that the Hartwell dam's regularly scheduled water releases for electrical generation would surround Clemson College with unsightly and insect-prone mudflats. Second, as water rose behind the Hartwell dam, the new high-water level would render the college's raw drinking-water intake and sewage treatment facilities inoperable. Finally, and an issue that soon threatened to halt the project forever, the authors determined that the new reservoir's water would inundate thousands of acres of college property. In their final assessment for the Clemson board of trustees, the three men believed a dike or levee— built and maintained by the Corps—was the best solution to keep the rising waters off campus property and out of the Tigers' football stadium.[33]

Reid, Stanford, and Sloan then used information from the private Clemson College report to publish their own publicity piece. The tone of the two documents could not have been more different, and *The Truth about "Hartwell"* reads like a red-smearing vituperative rant. The 1952 cover page alone made the mission clear: "SAVE CLEMSON from being surrounded by a sea of mud; SAVE SOUTH CAROLINA from Federal Control, from so-called Civil Rights, from Socialism and Communism; SAVE STATES RIGHTS." Buried in the rhetoric were nuggets of truth. The three authors correctly identified a well-founded criticism of multiple-purpose dams: "A full reservoir cannot regulate floods and an empty reservoir cannot generate power."[34] Managing a reservoir to collect flood-waters might mean keeping the reservoir low or nearly empty, but in order to produce electricity on a regular schedule, reservoirs need to be full. Since Hartwell was initially considered a flood control structure with additional benefits for power production and navigational improvements, the concern was legitimate. What, the authors asked, would the reservoir's fluctuating level mean for Clemson—the mudflats, the mosquitoes, the sewage and water lines, and the relocation of buildings and roads? When Reid and his coauthors specifically targeted the Corps' projected water levels, they landed clear opinions on the federal government's encroachment on race relations, property rights, and the free enterprise system. Concerns about a new working reservoir served as key elements of the Sun Belt backlash against liberalism that critics concentrated on the crumbling New Deal big dam consensus.

Hartwell opponents used the Tennessee Valley Authority (TVA) much as those who opposed public water and energy projects like Clarks Hill had a decade earlier. *The Truth about "Hartwell"* explained that the TVA did not pay taxes, was a federally subsidized electrical company, and threatened the competitive marketplace. The TVA, Clarks Hill, and now Hartwell represented the slippery slope: "If the government can go into the power business and charge itself no interest and practically no taxes it should pay, why cannot it also go into the Oil, Bread, Shoe, Transportation or Insurance business. When it does this, is that not state socialism?" The conservative authors recommended that the Corps abandon its project or, at a minimum, reduce the height of the dam to keep the Clemson campus high and dry.[35] After school officials and alumni waged a nearly five-year, well-choreographed, and at times misleading public battle portraying Clemson College as a victim, the Corps eventually built the levee initially recommended by Reid et al. to keep Hartwell Lake's rising waters from flooding portions of campus.[36] Regardless of the actual physical outcomes, *The Truth about "Hartwell"* ultimately preached one conservative conclusion: New Deal–inspired public energy and water projects threatened individual rights and compromised the free market.

South Carolina representative William Jennings Bryan Dorn (1916–2005) did not directly respond to *The Truth about "Hartwell,"* but he did put his own spin on the socialist and conservative rhetoric. Dorn, a New Deal Democrat who served thirteen congressional terms between 1948 and 1974, explained to one constituent that his visits to the TVA's and the Columbia River's multiple-purpose water and energy projects had hardened his resolve to see the Hartwell development through to completion. He believed Hartwell would deliver prosperity to "the desperately poor people of the Savannah Valley. . . . It will help small industries and in aiding small industries and the rural people, it most certainly helps those people to be independent and will help them to resist Socialism and Communism." For Dorn the emphasis behind public projects and postwar liberalism's goal was to put individuals back on their feet, promote local industry, and thus provide jobs for able-bodied white Americans who could then ascend to middle-class status. This was the Sun Belt's operative goal for many southern Democrats.[37]

Executives with the Charlotte-based Duke Power Company did weigh in on the Hartwell situation, but not because they were directly threatened at the moment. Duke Power, not unlike Georgia Power after 1945, wanted to revive its version of capitalism and eliminate competing energy proposals in the Savannah River valley associated with the lingering New Deal big dam consensus. Duke, of course, cut its corporate teeth in the New South era and turned the Catawba River valley into a vast "hydro-industrial empire," according to one observer.[38] The company also provided hydro- and coal-generated electrical power to the majority of upstate South Carolina. Given this experience, Duke's executives offered technical analysis to South Carolina's politicians regarding Hartwell's hydroelectric value in comparison with the company's proven steam technologies. According to one Duke executive, the company had shifted to coal and steam generation after 1940 and had additional plants in the pipeline. Based on a long operations history, company employees understood the complexities of planning new facilities, managing generation, and attracting future customers. David Nabow recognized "that the large increases in the demands for electric power in the Company's service area [had] outgrown the limited hydro-electric potentialities in this area." As such, "the primary dependence must therefore continue to be placed on large and efficient steam-electric generating plants" and "economical hydro-electric sites" if necessary. In short, steam technology was more cost-effective and efficient than hydroelectric systems.[39] These market and environmental conditions led Duke executives and Hartwell opponents alike to begin merging their concerns and to ask big questions: If private enterprise and technology outperformed public hydropower projects, then why did the federal government continue to promote energy-inefficient big dam projects that symbolized a colossal waste of taxpayer money and an affront to water and property rights? A backlash that began with Clemson's fear of mudflats, Reid's states' rights argument, and now Duke's cost-benefit analysis began to coalesce.

The Truth about "Hartwell" and other individual voices represented a new conservative vanguard that articulated opposition to the Hartwell development, the lingering New Deal big dam consensus, and postwar liberalism. Even when Georgia and South Carolina delegates championed federal water projects as solutions for water problems, citizen support for public energy developments did not come very easily. Not all boosters shared the same vision of shaping the region's economic future through water and energy endeavors like Hartwell. Civic bodies such as the Hartwell Steering Committee had enjoyed cross-border alliances in the past. However, and over the course of the next thirty years, South Carolinians increasingly became spoilers, and they defended private enterprise while rejecting Georgians' vision of public energy and federal public works projects in the Savannah River basin. Property rights, water rights, and fiscal issues continued to dog Corps and elected officials. But did other solutions exist to resolve the Southeast's water insecurity?

Hartwell critics latched onto flood control and water supply solutions in a competing federal agency's neopopulist programs that embraced low-tech options. Taxpayers, such as S. Maner Martin, feared government expansion and bristled at spending public funds on a massive "fish pond" like Hartwell to solve the Sun Belt's water problems.[40] Lucile Buriss Watson, who considered herself among the "reputable engineers" and "thinking voters," opposed Hartwell because it represented "a major step toward Socialism and an extravagant waste of the taxpayers' money." Watson admitted her opposition to the project was grounded in self-interest because she did not want "the beauty and peace of our landscape spoiled by mosquitoes, mudbanks, motor boats, and hoards of fishermen!"[41] Calling the proposed Hartwell reservoir a "fish pond" sounds like a misrepresentation of a body of water that would eventually inundate more than 50,000 acres and produce more than fish. But Martin's and Watson's choice of words about the massive Sun Belt working reservoir tapped into a larger discussion about the federal government's role in resolving national water problems and what water storage and irrigation tools to use.

The 1950s drought was a turning point in the American South. As the lack of rain and competing demands exacerbated water scarcity in Georgia, some farmers turned to farm ponds to survive the water crunch in 1954. As journalist Bill Allen said in 1953, if midwestern states could claim the title of the "Land o' Lakes" then Georgia was the "Paradise o' Ponds." By one account, Georgia could claim 12,000 farm and fish ponds that inundated 40,000 acres. Not only did the ponds produce nearly 450 pounds of fish per acre for anglers; farmers also used the ponds to water livestock, combat erosion, and control floodwaters. But these water supply tools should not be confused with the Savannah River valley's enormous Hartwell or Clarks Hill reservoirs.[42] These smaller impoundments and structures also revealed a growing competition for water among a variety of agricultural, industrial, and municipal water consumers vying for a common public resource. Farmers, factory managers, and city water managers clashed throughout the state as water supplies evaporated or dwindled. When farmers built ponds to water livestock upstream of factories, the reduced downstream flow compromised factory operations. In one county, an upstream farm pond so reduced downstream flows that five commercial enterprises were without water for nearly five months. In Newton County (Ga.), one upstream farm and irrigation pond consumed so much water that a downstream factory had to shut down because it could not produce enough energy in an onsite steam plant. And finally, some fish pond owners complained about the lack of dilution for pollution that washed downstream—from military installations, factories, homes, and other farms—into their ponds and killed fish or threatened livestock health.[43] Water problems in Georgia's ponds in the 1950s were not limited to quantity; quality was an emerging and real concern.

The drought also affected urban and agricultural communities in the Savannah River valley and around Georgia. Newspapers published a grim report of urban drought in the summer and fall of 1954 before Governor Herman Talmadge's prayer service in Macon. For example, the city of Washington's water supply was so depleted that the city council considered "a complete shutdown of water service during certain hours of the day as a necessary conservation measure." City ordinances also banned "unnecessary" water use activities such as car washing and lawn and garden watering and threatened $100 fines.[44] By the fall, the metro Atlanta community of East Point purchased and transferred 85 million gallons of water from Douglas County.[45]

The drought was caused not only by a lack of rainfall but also by the region's historical shift from the so-called Cotton Belt to a diversified Sun Belt. Southern farmers, of course, had always produced crops other than cotton, such as tobacco, vegetables, and fruit orchards. And boosters had been attempting to balance industry with agriculture since the nineteenth century. But Sun Belt economic choices accelerated and exacerbated a shift away from old monocultures such as cotton and the textile industry.

Livestock was one example of new growth in the post-1945 agricultural sector. In 1954, South Carolina agricultural officials thought the state's 437,000 head of cattle consumed 8.5 million gallons of water per day, and this figure did not include other animals such as hogs and poultry. Water, as journalist W. D. Workman declared, was an irreplaceable "commodity" necessary for industrial, agricultural, and municipal development. But, water's "vital importance" had been neglected by "layman and law-maker alike." In South Carolina, like Georgia, the water problem was "not so much one of supply as of distribution and regulation." In a refrain often repeated at the time and again in the future, Workman claimed that "the quantity of water which falls annually as rain" was enough to supply South Carolina's "industrial, agricultural, commercial and residential potential." However, increased demands for irrigation, energy production, and manufacturing; from dish- and clothes-washing machines; and for "modern plumbing facilities" all boosted water and energy consumption "terrifically."[46] The Sun Belt South's water problems had clearly reached a tipping point in the 1950s, but there was disagreement over the solutions and the utility of major reservoirs and small farm ponds.

Georgians directly confronted their water insecurity in the midst of the 1950s drought when the annual rainfall was twenty inches less than average. In late 1953, attendees of Georgia's Association of Soil Conservation District Supervisors meeting discussed the state's "water problems" and water law. Participants hatched an idea, and within months they assembled the Georgia Water Use and Conservation Committee to promote water "conservation" and "wise use" to protect the state's future water supply. For clarification purposes, "conservation" in the 1950s equated with increased storage capacity, not necessarily a reduction in consumption. But the committee was honest about the water problem: Members did not blame the drought on "nature" and instead acknowledged the region's historically "erratic" water supply and conflicting water usage as the cause.[47]

In other words, the drought was the result of colliding environmental and cultural factors: a lack of rain and high demands on a limited supply.

To solve the state's water woes, Water Use and Conservation Committee members recommended additional storage capacity, improved wastewater treatment, and possible changes to the state's riparian water law. The committee—comprised of professors, lawyers, judges, business owners, extension agents, and federal employees—also suggested that the governor or the legislature create a water administration office that could conduct a statewide study to ascertain how much water the state had, withdrew from the ground, and consumed in different sectors. The committee was cognizant of the state's diverse geography and that no single plan could solve all of the state's water issues. They all agreed a plan was necessary for future economic growth and that the General Assembly needed to resolve the state's water problems as soon as possible.[48]

While the Georgia Water Use and Conservation Committee advocated for state action to protect Georgia's future water supply, some members recommended and accepted any and all federal assistance. Columbus-based Jim Woodruff Sr. (1879–1963) was a radio station owner and chairman of the Georgia Waterways Commission. Woodruff, who has also been referred to as "the Father of the Chattahoochee," wanted the state to "build multi-purpose dams on tributaries" of the major rivers where the Corps was already building large dams and reservoirs, including the Allatoona, Clarks Hill, Lanier, Seminole (Congress officially named the reservoir's dam in Woodruff's honor in 1957), and other projects throughout the Sun Belt.[49] Other participants were not as sanguine about additional massive dams and reservoirs as solutions to drought-proof the South.

Two alternatives to massive dams and reservoirs emerged with the backlash and represented methods to solve the Sun Belt's water problem: irrigation and small watershed projects. First, Dr. George King, a University of Georgia irrigation engineer, corrected a misinformed historical comparison about the Southeast and the American West. "Until recently," he explained to a Rome (Ga.) reporter in 1954, Georgians thought "irrigation was . . . something pertaining to the arid western states." But after Georgia moved through "three drought years in succession" with a final year "of extreme severity," state agriculturalists reconsidered the value of irrigation in the humid American South. King was really only rediscovering a problem already identified by a much older colleague. Georgia hydrologist Benjamin M. Hall noted in 1908, "In Georgia and other Southern and Eastern States the rainfall is much greater and more evenly distributed through the year, but, nevertheless, the lack of rain at the proper time often cuts a crop to one-half or one-third what it would have been." Hall explained how "a small amount of water in storage and ready for use" would be beneficial for southern farmers but would also require a substantial investment that might not be as easily justified as irrigation was in the arid American West.[50] In the 1950s, King and others believed that Georgia's water supply was "reasonably fair to copiously ample" south of a line drawn from the fall-line cities of Columbus through Macon to Augusta, and in parts of the Georgia mountains. The Piedmont area between the Coastal Plain and the Blue Ridge, however, faced serious challenges "obtaining enough water for general irrigation." The state generally had plenty of water, but the water was not always in the right place at the right time.[51] And King, like his predecessor Hall, understood the financial barriers to irrigation. So where would the new water supply infrastructure, water, and financing come from?

U.S. Geological Survey technician M. T. Thomson had an answer: Georgia's Citizens and Southern bank began "financing irrigation installations" and urged "farmers to avail themselves" of the new revenue source and technological solution "where conditions justify."[52] Georgia's farmers received loans from local banks for equipment, but federal tax dollars funneled through the Soil Conservation Service (SCS) of the U.S. Department of Agriculture (USDA) bankrolled the state's farm and fish ponds that filled irrigation lines. SCS engineers, who had been providing technical consultation for nearly two decades, helped build 1,289 Georgia farm ponds in 1953. To build a pond, farmers contacted the SCS for advice and, for a few hundred dollars, paid for an earth-moving equipment operator, the pipe, and the necessary material to build a small embankment dam. If the farmer declared the pond was intended to support livestock or to irrigate fields, the USDA's Production Marketing Administration paid up to $300 (or about $2,500 in 2012 dollars) of the pond's construction cost.[53] Additionally, farmers had access to free fish, including bass and sunfish, from the U.S. Fish and Wildlife Service and the Georgia State Game and Fish Commission to stock the ponds. Farmers could also obtain loans—facilitated through the USDA's Farmers Home Administration—for diesel pumps, aboveground sectional irrigation piping, and wheeled pump-gun sprinklers to irrigate fields or more easily move water to farm animals. Farmers who utilized these federal tools irrigated between 15,000 and 25,000 acres of Georgia cropland by the mid-1950s.[54] Farm ponds, however, were pawns in a much larger game.

Letters from opponents to the Corps' Hartwell dam and reservoir increasingly included the second alternative to solving the Sun Belt's water problem highlighted by the 1950s drought. Some critics wondered why Congress continued to support the Corps' colossal flood control plans over an emerging alternative.[55] Southerners had learned about the USDA's emerging Small Watershed Program as the 1950s drought shifted from the middle of the country to the entire nation. In response to deteriorating national drought conditions, President Dwight Eisenhower approved expansion of multiple USDA financial farm assistance programs. The first initially provided drought relief in seventeen specific western states, and another made loans available to communities across the country.[56] Of greater significance to South Carolinians who were critical of Corps projects such as Hartwell, Eisenhower made permanent a USDA program that provided technical and financial assistance to local watershed groups who took "responsibility for initiating, carrying out, and sharing the costs of upstream watershed conservation and flood control."[57] Known alternately as "The Small Watershed Program" or PL-566, its benefits included technical and financial support for flood control and soil conservation for agricultural projects. The USDA technically administered this federal "assistance" program, but local committees and districts were initially responsible for sharing some costs and managing the projects. Unlike the Corps' reservoir schemes that required top-down acquisition of private land, which did involve unwilling sellers and condemnation proceedings, the USDA's bottom-up farm pond incentives and Small Watershed Program catered to willing landowners and local community organizations interested in local control. The small watershed program was also cheaper and more democratic on paper, and this neopopulist and agrarian solution did offer flood control within specific watersheds.

The regional debate over who would build small or large dams was hardly confined to Sun Belt farmers during the Cold War. Luna Leopold and Thomas Maddock Jr. plunged into the national discussion in the early 1950s. Leopold, the son of conservationist and wildlife biologist Aldo Leopold, was a well-known geologist and engineer. He and Maddock (also an engineer) coauthored a book, *The Flood Control Controversy* (1954), to clarify what caused floods and how to best manage them. The two authors suggested that small watershed projects and land treatment methods (terracing, kudzu planting, etc.) would indeed manage flooding and soil in the headwaters, but these measures would do little to prevent flooding downstream, where large dams best alleviated flooding. Regardless of the technology, flood control did "not mean the elimination of floods," in their professional opinion.[58] Big dam critics compared small watershed impoundments with the Corps' big dams as though they were the same fruit, but Leopold and Maddox thought the options were more like apples and oranges. The Corps' main-stem multiple-purpose reservoirs and the SCS's small watershed projects were ultimately compatible, but they were not interchangeable. Despite this objective assessment, not all southerners were convinced, and many believed small watershed plans were economically and politically more valuable than multiple-purpose Corps dams. South Carolinians labeled the Corps' projects as nothing but "big dam foolishness," a characterization they picked up from a midwestern journalist who popularized opposition to the Corps' general program of water management. Elmer Peterson published his book, *Big Dam Foolishness*, in the same year Leopold and Maddock published theirs. One particular USDA small watershed project in the Savannah River valley illustrates how the process worked and was infused with Peterson's rhetoric.[59]

The Twelve Mile Creek watershed project in Pickens County, South Carolina, located high up in the Savannah River's watershed, contained 790 farms spread over 67,000 acres. According to one cheery Greenville newspaper writer, farmers and soil conservationists worked "to see how efficient a job man can do with Nature's help in storing as much water as possible in the land where it falls and thereby reducing the flood flow with accompanying damage to land." Journalist David Tillinghast toured the watershed, and he bristled at the cost of the Corps' Hartwell dam and reservoir while enthusiastically trumpeting the benefits of the small watershed program. The Twelve Mile Creek project, which included small dams on headwater farms and land treatments in erosion-prone areas, was technically a much cheaper flood control option when compared with Hartwell.[60] Other editors followed Tillinghast's lead in a statewide campaign. The *Charleston News and Courier* editor was more inclined to see federal money spent on multiple smaller watershed projects throughout the state. Smaller farm ponds in particular would provide a better "method of conserving water, and controlling floods at the source." This type of watershed planning "could be adapted to the entire state with excellent results at half the cost of Hartwell Dam," because the USDA's small watershed project costs were "shared by local and federal sources."[61] Another columnist concluded that the cost-sharing alone made the small watershed program more democratic because farmers and conservation district members worked with federal engineers to complete projects and manage local water supplies.[62] Local control—or a hyperfocused states' rights attitude—soon infused the debate of water and power in the Savannah River valley.

Georgia's and South Carolina's 1950s drought not only highlighted competition among water users and potential alternatives to massive reservoirs; the drought also uncovered anxiety about water rights at a moment when states' rights and civil rights agendas converged. One constituent explained to Senator Olin Johnston that the acquisition and management of the collar and buffer lands that surrounded Corps reservoirs represented a fundamental seizure of property: The "transfer of local ownership to centralized governmental ownership was Socialism to say the least." Furthermore, "big Federal Dams take from the local people ownership and access to lakes or streams except as regulated by Washington."[63] Washington bureaucrats, however, were not the only people responsible for determining water rights.

The Georgia Water Use and Conservation Committee recommended that the state legislature consider amending Georgia's riparian legal tradition, a legal construction that entitles a property owner along a watercourse to use or control access to water so long as they do not diminish the overall flow or significantly impair downstream property owners' access to water supplies. This tradition is more common in the eastern United States as compared with the western water allocation process of prior appropriation, whereby an individual holds access rights to water and can move large quantities over great distances.[64] The Georgia Water Use and Conservation Committee ultimately recommended that laws not be changed until the committee uncovered specific problems. However, the committee did argue that Georgia's industrial development was handicapped by the "uncertainty as to the rights and duties of the users of Georgia's water resources." As such, "this uncertainty discourages investment in beneficial water use, and constitutes perhaps the greatest weakness in our law as it exists."[65] The Georgia Water Use and Conservation Committee was not alone in articulating this aspect of the water problem. Whereas the USDA-funded farm ponds and small watershed projects vested water supply management responsibilities in adjacent landowners and local soil conservation district operatives, the Corps' projects redrew property lines and thus transferred water supply management responsibilities to the federal government on behalf of the nation's citizens.

As Corps and South Carolina officials debated the future of farm ponds, small watershed projects, and Hartwell's reservoir in the midst of drought and power struggles, the Clarks Hill project moved into the operational phase. A serious topic emerged immediately that would affect all federal reservoirs: How would communities or industries access the physical water in the reservoir managed by the Corps? McCormick, South Carolina, was the first Savannah River valley community to broach the question. The Clarks Hill dam and reservoir was not originally authorized to provide a municipal water supply for any specific community in South Carolina or Georgia. McCormick officials convened a meeting in 1955 with Corps engineers to discuss the city's proposal "to acquire water" from Clarks Hill after the reservoir was completed and operating, and because of a recent local water supply crisis. Corps staffers plus Senators Strom Thurmond and Olin Johnson ultimately helped McCormick leaders obtain specific legislation from Congress authorizing the Corps to divert 600 acre-feet (196 million gallons) per year from the reservoir to McCormick customers for an annual sum of $500.[66] City and local leaders appreciated the access to the reservoir but soon soured when they attempted to increase their water withdrawals and acquire surplus reservoir lands because the county wanted to woo industrial prospects; they entered a bureaucratic maze.

By the late 1950s, the Corps' process for evaluating water supply requests had evolved according to the terms of the newly established Water Supply Act (1958). McCormick County executives and lawyers were irritated when they had to ask for permission a second time.[67] To be fair, McCormick County had sacrificed more than a fifth of the county's taxable land for the Clarks Hill project, and many residents in the region were increasingly frustrated with the Corps' management style.[68] Nonetheless, the Water Supply Act enabled the Corps to reallocate storage in federal reservoirs—like Clarks Hill—for uses that were not specifically included in a project's authorization, such as domestic and industrial water supply. As Brigadier General William F. Cassidy explained to Senator Thurmond, after receipt of an application, Corps engineers would determine if water allocation would "'seriously' affect the purposes for which the project was authorized or would involve major structural or operational changes." If a proposed request would ultimately alter operations at Clarks Hill, congressional approval was "required before a water supply agreement could be finalized." And the final decision would hinge on the quantity of water removed and the quality of the water returned, as well as if the water would be returned to a different watershed.[69] In the opinion of the McCormick chamber of commerce, the federal government had to resolve what the chamber considered a federal reservoir water supply and water rights problem because county officials and boosters needed to convey to industrial reps searching for new sites that water was available from Clarks Hill and how much that water would cost.[70]

As the Hartwell dam and reservoir project moved through the planning phases upstream on the Savannah River, South Carolina congressman William Jennings Bryan Dorn communicated with the Corps about the new reservoir's water allocation process in light of the Clarks Hill and McCormick situation. Since Congress did not initially authorize Hartwell to provide a municipal water supply for any community in South Carolina or Georgia, Corps officers explained how the water allocation process worked, much as engineers had explained it to Senator Thurmond months earlier.[71]

In light of these water allocation negotiations and drought conditions, some South Carolinians reduced the issue to a question of states' rights. One informed the McCormick chamber of commerce that federal control of water supply in federal reservoirs was symptomatic of "the gradual attrition of the individual states' historical rights to control water resources."[72] Frank E. Harrison, McCormick County's attorney, offered the same opinion in no uncertain terms to a group of Corps engineers. Harrison was particularly interested in the legal instrument that fundamentally altered water management and legal access to water in Clarks Hill, the planned Hartwell, and any future federal reservoir. Harrison wanted water management turned over to a "local water authority so that the common law rights as to water use can be restored to the people." Harrison articulated how federal reservoirs, ringed by the buffer or collar of public land, fundamentally changed Sun Belt riparian rights. Communities and property owners lost access rights to water contained within federal reservoirs when the Corps acquired the shoreline. As such, Harrison and others respectfully argued that federal management of Clarks Hill's water supply discouraged industry from locating in McCormick County because industry would have no direct access to the water supply without congressional approval. Harrison labeled the Corps "a military branch" that threatened to inflict "great damage to our country" by assuming "political power and economic control over large areas of our economy."[73] To many southern Democrats frustrated by the New Deal's disruption of race relations and labor norms but interested in water and energy projects, the Corps initially represented a better alternative to the TVA. By the late 1950s, however, even the Corps' reputation was slipping, and the engineers appeared as intractable diplomats of federal domination.

Damage, of course, is relative. McCormick got the water it wanted from Clarks Hill, and as of 2013 two dozen other communities, utilities, industries, and golf courses also eventually obtained water from the Corps' three major Savannah River valley reservoirs.[74] To some people, the Corps dominated the valley when it built the Hartwell dam, a 2,451-foot-long concrete and 10,000-foot-long earthen embankment structure. Behind the dam, a reservoir covered 56,000 acres. Clemson College, once concerned about the prospect of losing portions of the campus and stadium to rising reservoir waters, was protected behind a series of earthen levees built by the Corps. Furthermore, the Corps compensated Clemson College $2.2 million for nearly 8,000 acres of land and structures buried by Hartwell's water, which represented a sliver of the more than 27,000 acres the USDA had deeded to Clemson for $1.00 in 1954 to help the school meet its land-grant mission.[75] But most property owners did not get the same treatment. The land required for the reservoir area necessitated the removal of 560 urban and rural families, "or a total population of 2,800" in a project area with a population of seventeen people per square mile. Not all landowners were excited to make way for the dam and reservoir project that required them to sell their property.[76] For example, one landowner was frustrated that he could not recoup the market value for the property he needed to sell. He pleaded with Senator Thurmond, "I am told the dam is to benefit this area, but why should I be pushed out of my home without being given full value, or enough to replace my home in the same general locality?" Harold Timms clearly understood the real estate dynamics at work, or at a minimum how they worked against him. Surrounding property values were destined to increase as more folks like him competed for remaining property or "due to higher value placed on resort type property." Thurmond worked his magic by contacting the Corps' real estate managers in an effort to ameliorate his constituents. Eventually, the Corps offered to acquire Timms's property earlier so he might better plan his relocation while also allowing him to remain on the property during the project's construction phase.[77] Not all situations had such happy endings.

Land condemnation cases blossomed during the Hartwell land acquisition process as other landowners fought to establish fair prices for their land. According to U.S. District Court case file transcripts, many property owners primarily struggled to establish fair per-acre values for land through condemnation proceedings, not unlike those who challenged federal real estate agents at Clarks Hill and other reservoir locations.[78] Based on selected transcripts, some of these farms were profitable for pulpwood, cattle, corn, and hay, and these property owners wanted to make sure they got fair value for what they considered good river bottomland. Condemnation proceedings favored white landowners who had the resources to fight in court, and people with good land had little incentive to sell. But property owners with poor land, or minority landowners with no resources to fight, took the money when offered.[79] Others held out until the bitter end, including seventy-eight-year-old Eliza Brock and her daughter, who leveled a shotgun at the workers who arrived to clear her land. Brock eventually settled out of court and accepted the Corps' original offer for her property before moving.[80] As Clarks Hill and Hartwell land condemnation issues worked their way to resolution, constituent uproar did encourage Senators Olin Johnston and Strom Thurmond to repeatedly attempt to introduce legislation to reconvey to former owners the surplus lands the Corps no longer needed for project operations.[81]

But real estate issues alone would not hold up the dam's construction, which the Corps had begun in 1955 and completed by 1962, when the reservoir filled and power generation commenced. The initial estimated cost of $68.4 million (in 1948 dollars, or more than $653 million in 2012 when adjusted for inflation) jumped to a final $89,240,000.[82] But the Corps claimed in 1989 a return of more than $118.4 million from power sales to electrical cooperatives and other customers. While the development incited a conservative backlash and was not popular with all area residents, the Corps reported that nearly 750,000 people visited Hartwell in 1962. And in 2005, Hartwell Lake was among the top five most popular Corps projects in the nation, drawing in more than 10 million visitors. The boosters' dream to build a recreational and leisure paradise while solving the Sun Belt's water insecurity in the Savannah River valley appeared to have come true. The recent 2006–9 and 2011–12 droughts, however, combined with the Great Recession and volatile fuel prices, reduced the lake's volume and communities' ability to recover once-humming recreational, real estate, and associated roaring service economies of the past.[83] The valley's hydraulic waterscape was clearly expansive, functional, and successful by some metrics.

The 1950s southern drought, not unlike the 2007 drought and Georgia governor Perdue's prayer service, replayed the region's old water and power challenges. For decades, southern boosters sold the New South and Sun Belt by offering up cheap and tractable labor, downplaying white supremacy, and showcasing bottomless stores of natural resources like water. Despite their best face, the boosters and politicians discovered that the region's water problem—like the race and labor conflicts—persisted and was manufactured. After 1945, New Deal–inspired solutions for public water management encountered stiff resistance from Sun Belt conservatives and champions of private enterprise. As civil rights and states' rights politics merged, conservative rights-based ideas influenced conversations about solutions for the Sun Belt's water challenges in Georgia and South Carolina. The water rights issue was a real and legitimate concern for rural communities looking to compete in the growing commercial Sun Belt. Local leaders believed they were entitled to the Savannah River's water that had always flowed past their communities long before the Corps—a representative of an unwanted expanding federal power in the 1950s—arrived on the scene. And neopopulist farmers who opted for farm ponds or to participate in small watershed projects contributed to limited water supply improvements on their own terms without ceding physical property to the federal government. In the end, no amount of political backlash or commercial success could ensure the region's water supplies because social and economic decisions were not the only factors at play.

Droughts, not unlike floods, influenced the region's economic development and the waterway's environmental future. Massive Corps reservoirs, large utility reservoirs like Georgia Power's, medium-sized SCS watershed projects, and thousands of small farm ponds served municipal, industrial, and agricultural constituents. The schemes produced electricity, delivered water to industry, reduced flooding down the valley, irrigated fields, became recreation destinations, and supported domestic animals, fish, and wildlife. Today, Georgia ranks fifth nationally—behind Texas, Kansas, Missouri, and Oklahoma—for the total number of inventoried dams, with more than 4,600 structures. Collectively, all of these economic developments also fundamentally altered the region's hydrologic cycle. Certainly the Savannah River's watershed was never pristine or unaltered by those who depended on the basin for survival. However, the scale to which Georgia's watersheds were altered after 1945, and particularly after the 1950s drought, had been unmatched. As one state employee concluded, "The measurements of low flows made during the drought of 1954 are important because on many small streams they are probably the only such measurements that will ever be made under predominantly natural flow conditions during an extreme drought. Since 1954, the flows of streams in

Georgia have become more and more affected by manmade [*sic*] regulation from innumerable small ponds and by diversions for water supplies and irrigation."[84]

The Sun Belt's elaborate hydraulic system of ponds, reservoirs, dams, canals, locks, levees, and channelized streams supported the region's wide-ranging demographic and economic constituencies. But without any comprehensive management vision, this system would always be beholden to dramatic climatic, hydrologic, and political cycles. Environmental conditions—too much or not enough rain—had clearly visited the ever-growing region before and during Georgia governor Herman Talmadge's time much as they would in the future during and after Governor Sonny Perdue's.

As the Clarks Hill and Hartwell multiple-purpose projects demonstrated, not everyone supported these large water supply and infrastructure schemes. By the time the Corps and advocates for the valley's next and final project moved forward, the social, political, and environmental landscape had shifted dramatically. The benefits, needs, and assumptions regarding what Sun Belt dams and reservoirs could deliver and for whom changed. The New Deal big dam consensus was crumbling, and vestiges of New South capitalism persisted. Innovative solutions for Sun Belt water problems emerged as the region's energy and water plans encountered a new level of backlash.

CHAPTER 6

Countryside Conservatism and Conservation

"Darkness pressed against the car windows, deep and silent, and I couldn't help but think I was seeing into the future when much of this land would be buried deep underwater," Sheriff Will Alexander contemplated while responding to a Jocassee Valley bar brawl in the opening pages of Ron Rash's novel *One Foot in Eden*. At the end of the story, Alexander's bitter deputy drives out of the same valley "for the last time if I had any say in the matter. I wouldn't be coming back here to fish or water ski or swim or anything like that. This wasn't no place for people who had a home. This was a place for the lost."[1] Rash's mountain drama was set in the South Carolina upstate after the Korean War, and the narrative stretches into the late 1960s, when "Carolina Power" finished acquiring mountain property, sawed timber from steep coves, and flooded the previously populated Jocassee Valley to complete a massive hydroelectric project. The narrative ranges immediately from emotional floods of posttraumatic stress and death to moments of lust and recovery. There was physical flooding too: autumn rain and a muddy creek surging into a Blue Ridge Mountain cabbage patch as a new artificial lake filled. These floods left trails of debris and spurred new discoveries as well as signaling the arrival of new social and environmental relationships in the Sun Belt's hydraulic waterscape.

Like all excellent fiction, Rush's novel relies on threads of fact. North Carolina–based Duke Power Company began acquiring property in the Savannah River valley's mountainous and peopled headwaters in 1916. But it would be a long time before the trees and people were cleared from company land to make way for reservoirs in the South Carolina upstate. Between 1970 and 1990, Duke built three hydroelectric dams—and three nuclear reactors—including the Lake Jocassee project. Not unlike Georgia Power's New South endeavor in the Tallulah and Tugaloo Valleys a few miles to the west, Duke's Sun Belt schemes unfolded during a private phase of southern waterway development. Duke was not the only institution to bury parts of the Savannah River's watershed deep under water.

As the North Carolina company initiated its own capital-intensive master plan, the U.S. Army Corps of Engineers embarked on its third and final energy and water project down-valley at a place called Trotters Shoals between Hartwell (completed 1963) and Clarks Hill (1952). While independent and beholden to different constituencies, Duke and the Corps were also tied together; they both designed technological systems that complimented the existing energy and leisure waterscape in the same valley. And after 1960, both organizations reached the end of an era. When the Corps completed the Trotters Shoals dam (now known as Richard B. Russell dam) in 1983 and Duke finished the Bad Creek Reservoir (1991), there were no more worthy sites to build massive hydroelectric dams in the Savannah River valley, the American South, or the United States.[2] The big dam era was over, and countryside conservationists and environmentalists could claim victories during a transition in energy regimes.

If the New South capitalists and liberal New Dealers generated energy, managed water quantity, and alleviated some valley residents' fears about uncontrolled flooding or slow-moving drought, then both parties also invited a big dam backlash and encountered a new water problem in the Sun Belt's waterways: poor water quality. When the Corps moved forward on the Trotters Shoals multiple-purpose dam and reservoir, it was compelled to address a new factor as the political landscape shifted under its boots and bulldozers. Before 1945, private and public engineers primarily approached water quantity as an environmental challenge when designing energy and water projects: How much water could operators store to generate electricity, facilitate navigation, or mitigate flooding? In other words, the traditional trio of benefits—hydroelectric generation, navigation, and flood control—promoted efficient water conservation and storage with only secondary concern for water quality. Corps engineers had previously worked with state and federal agencies in the Savannah River valley to manage fisheries and control malarial conditions at reservoir sites, but promoting recreation and public health was not the same as protecting clean water.[3]

The story of Trotters Shoals was different from that of Clarks Hill and Hartwell in two important ways. First, Congress dismantled the New Deal big dam consensus's traditional trio of benefits. It officially authorized the Sun Belt scheme for power production and recreation and only incidentally for flood control or navigation. Second, the project was situated in the middle of the Savannah River valley's Piedmont Province, and the shoals were among the last undammed twenty-eight miles of the Savannah River between the upper reaches of the Clarks Hill reservoir and the base of the Hartwell dam. Industrialists, conservationists, and environmentalists all weighed in on the function, benefits, and value of free-flowing water; they influenced the technocrats' final execution of the Trotters Shoals dam along this unique stretch of river. Deliberation over the upper section of the Savannah River's fate began as early as 1959, persisted until authorization in 1966, continued before construction began in 1974, and was far from finished when the dam began generating electricity in 1985. This lengthy twenty-five-year political drama involved powerful old and new actors who used equally archaic and novel arguments to lay claims on the Savannah River's water and energy resources.

Environmental historians have long considered the post-1945 period as a turning point, whereby technical conservationists who promoted wise use of natural resources gave way to professional environmentalists who promoted beauty, health, and permanence. Domestic and urban expatriates who lived part time in the post-1945 countryside have been singled out as important contributors to the nascent environmental movement. Following this path of urban-to-rural migration, middle-class suburban homeowners have also been considered as the progenitors of modern environmentalism. In both interpretations, new arrivals in the countryside were motivated to protect their bucolic rural or new suburban landscapes from reckless and environmentally damaging development. As these part-time and suburban pioneers watched the destruction outside their plate-glass windows, they turned to local, state, and federal authorities to help alleviate the destructive cycles for which they were partly responsible. Most of these narratives involved liberal, white citizen activists in the mid-Atlantic and Northeast who leaned on scientific and political networks to resolve environmental problems, and these localized interest groups generated national environmental sensibilities and action. What about in the Southeast?

One limited regional comparison suggested that a general "weakness in environmental interest" existed in the Southeast. Samuel Hays attributed this sentiment "to the region's agricultural roots, the persistence of rural attitudes and institutions, and the slower growth of urban populations with newer interests and values." Only by the 1980s did the citizen engagement in environmental issues look like the engagement found in New England, the mid-Atlantic, and the Pacific Coast, but then only in the urban South.[4] The events and actors involved in the Trotters Shoals and subsequent water and energy episodes demonstrate why conservationists and environmentalists in the Savannah River valley Sun Belt countryside did not wait until the 1970s or 1980s to begin balancing appropriate economic development, water quality, and environmental protection.

The New South and Sun Belt eras have a rich conservation and environmental political history. For example, Georgians led grassroots opposition to Georgia Power's Tallulah Falls hydroelectric dam (1911).[5] The interwar period was particularly fertile: Georgia volunteers organized one of dozens of Appalachian Trail clubs (1930) to complete the national trail, and the idea for the Wilderness Society was hatched outside Knoxville, Tennessee (1934).[6] Marjory Stoneman Douglas, Herbert Stoddard, Archie Carr, and Marjorie Carr campaigned for, respectively, restoration of the Everglades, sustainable longleaf pine ecosystems, the conservation biology field, and the defeat of the Cross Florida Barge Canal.[7] Also active during the interwar era, regionalists Rupert Vance, Howard W. Odum, and others repeatedly linked human behavior with environmental problems and solutions. Following in their father's footsteps, ecologists Eugene P. and Howard T. Odum studied old agricultural fields and freshwater springs in the 1950s before helping translate ecosystem principals into a more easily consumed and international vernacular after 1970.[8] These examples illustrate how countryside conservationists, outing clubs, academics, and scientists contributed to an environmental culture and legacy reaching back to the New South. An engaged Sun Belt citizenry continued this long legacy of environmental awareness and actively negotiated post-1945 commercial development and water problems in the shadows of dams inspired by New South capitalism and New Deal liberalism.

Sun Belt countryside conservation and environmentalism involved a wide range of participants concerned about the Savannah River valley's beauty, communities, and commercial future. The people who participated in the Trotters Shoals battles between 1960 and 1970 lived in small towns, growing suburbs, and emerging urban centers, and they linked together the Sun Belt's energy regimes, economic development, and environmental conditions. "Unlikely environmentalists" in Congress crafted federal water pollution control legislation in the 1950s while laying the foundation for the landmark Clean Water Act (1972). And sportsmen and recreationalists certainly leaned on Sun Belt state agencies to fight pollution in the 1940s and 1950s.[9] However, the less-well-known participants—county lawyers, corporate executives, university employees, and journalists in the Savannah River valley—also weighed in on the value of dams, water pollution, and the Sun Belt's future while congressional committees and staff built their own cases. The countryside conservationists and environmentalists repeatedly used water quality to justify a range of positions. They had an appetite for economic development, but not at the expense of southern waterways and certainly not at the expense of water quality in the massive federal reservoirs that were supposed to drive the Sun Belt's growing recreational and service-based economy.

The Sun Belt's environmental movement was diverse and was not solely focused on how best to manage the Savannah River valley's water resources or how to protect wilderness. As historian Samuel Hays observed, "Internal Democratic party variations were especially noteworthy in the South, where rapid social change was creating new urban views within a more traditional rural climate."[10] While he placed this friction in the 1970s and afterward, the long sweep of Trotters Shoals's history illustrates how the region's conservationists, liberal environmentalists, and their conservative critics reflected internal debates within the Democratic Party over issues such as what constituted appropriate federal spending, the public good, and adequate regulation of private enterprise. Boosters, elected state and national representatives, agency bureaucrats, corporate executives, and citizens all spoke for the river because the water continued to represent potential energy for industrial production and offered new leisure environments. The Corps' Clarks Hill reservoir and Hartwell dam also created a new river environment in between at Trotters Shoals. At this geographic location, along this last undammed stretch of the Savannah River's Piedmont section, countryside conservationists and environmentalists challenged the Sun Belt economic juggernaut and powerful interests born of the New South and New Deal eras. The regional fight had implications for the rest of the country, the Democratic Party, and southern rivers.

As a New South institution, Duke Power Company maintained a vested interest in the Savannah River valley's watershed and market territory. Based in Charlotte, North Carolina, the company had been responsible for coordinating the Catawba River valley's water and energy since 1904 and also owned thousands of acres and a handful of waterpower sites in the Savannah River basin. Between the 1920s and 1960s, company real estate agents had amassed more than 100,000 acres along the Keowee River in South Carolina and thousands of acres downstream along the Savannah.[11]

The utility had been providing the South Carolina upstate with electricity since the early 1900s, linking Greenville's and Spartanburg's economies with Charlotte's. Duke's Sun Belt industrial and residential customer base continued to grow in South Carolina, but the company had no major electrical generation facilities in the valley or this portion of the company's service area now known for its BMW, Michelin, and other transnational corporate citizens.[12] Not unlike Georgia Power Company executives who challenged public power at Clarks Hill immediately after World War II (and lost), Duke Power executives had Sun Belt plans for their property and challenged public power directly at Trotters Shoals after 1960. Duke Power Company ultimately succeeded in capitalizing on its Keowee and Savannah River properties but not without a fight and compromise.

Duke Power Company, like other private utilities, considered the public power models exemplified by the Tennessee Valley Authority (TVA) and the Corps' two new Savannah River valley projects as competitive threats to corporate monopoly. Since 1904, Duke's executives had successfully engineered the Catawba River's multiple dams to generate electricity, provide limited flood control relief, and supply water to municipalities and industries for free. Engineers also operated company reservoirs to eliminate malarial conditions, a forestry division managed more than 200,000 acres of working forest, and the public had access to ten company lakes by 1960.[13] As Duke's public relations executives liked to boast, the company built this elaborate hydraulic waterscape "without government subsidy," and the public enjoyed many of its benefits "free of charge."[14] Today, Duke maintains eleven major dams and reservoirs along the 200-mile Catawba River (a major tributary in the Santee River basin). No federal agency maintains any facility on this river.[15] Duke Power Company was compelled, however, in the 1960s to compromise with Congress and the Corps at a place called Middleton Shoals, a long series of shallow rocks below the Hartwell dam, to get what it wanted upstream of Hartwell in the Keowee and Jocassee River valleys.

Middleton Shoals became a flash point between private and public power advocates in the 1960s. Duke Power Company owned thousands of acres at Middleton Shoals, located eight miles downstream from the Hartwell dam and twenty miles upstream from Trotters Shoals in Anderson County (S.C.) and Elbert County (Ga.). As construction continued at the Hartwell dam, rumors of additional Savannah River valley dams generated both support and opposition to projects in the vicinity of Middleton and Trotters Shoals.[16] Given their successful monopoly track record in the

Catawba valley, Duke executives continued to publicly oppose any federal project that impinged upon private manipulation of the water and energy resources of the upper Savannah and Keowee Rivers. Numerous pro-Hartwell supporters believed utility executives and their surrogates were among the "many people using the Clemson issue" to stop the Hartwell dam project in the 1950s and 1960s.[17]

Duke executives had discussed building a coal-fired steam plant to generate electricity on the South Carolina side of the Savannah River for many years, and Middleton Shoals was the most promising site. Duke's plans included a $289 million Appalachian-coal-fired thermoelectric steam plant capable of generating 700,000 kilowatts by 1965, with plans to expand to 2 million kilowatts.[18] However, the energy company did not have the power to develop the river on its own. Because Middleton Shoals required a diversion dam that would stretch partway across the navigable Savannah River and redirect river water into the steam plant's boilers and once-through cooling system, Duke Power needed congressional approval to proceed. The company had failed, despite support from South Carolina's delegation, to obtain this right in 1962 because Georgia's senator Richard B. Russell Jr. (D) blocked authorization in the Senate. Russell argued that Duke's Middleton Shoals project conflicted with multiple theoretical federal dam and reservoir projects the Corps had recommended for that stretch of the Savannah River in the 1944 Flood Control Act. Given this resistance, Duke lobbied hard to win the favor of South Carolina's congressman William Jennings Bryan Dorn (D) and Senators J. Strom Thurmond (D) and Olin D. Johnston (D).

Many South Carolinians generally favored the Duke facility at Middleton Shoals and were opposed to new federal water and energy schemes. River basin residents rightfully asked, Why build another dam and reservoir with the Corps' preexisting Clarks Hill and Hartwell facilities already in place? The often-repeated reasons to support a private project included increased tax revenue, in this case $2 million per annum for Anderson County, South Carolina.[19] The company also claimed the fully completed coal plant would generate more than $15 million annually in local, state, and federal taxes. But what no elected official wanted to admit, and what Duke president William B. McGuire (1910–2012; Duke employee 1933–71) divulged in a private meeting, was that Middleton Shoals would operate "tax free for the first three years." Furthermore, McGuire acknowledged that "it would be a long time before they would actually put the ultimate capacity of this plant into operation," and thus tax payments would remain low until Duke operated the plant at full capacity.[20] Most South Carolinians—influenced by the media campaigns of Duke Power and other industrial advocates—supported private industry's agenda. Some Georgians, along with their cross-river neighbors, also supported Duke's Middleton Shoals project because they assumed that free-market principles and free enterprise would enlarge the local tax rolls and spur job creation on both sides of the Savannah. Many of these same people were probably not aware that their states were subsidizing industrial development by offering liberal tax incentives to create a friendly business environment for companies like Duke Power that were always quick to champion the invisible hand.

Duke enjoyed great support throughout South Carolina and in Georgia. According to opponents of federal development on the Savannah River, additional publicly financed dams and reservoirs wasted taxpayer dollars, eliminated potential industrial sites, and introduced unequal competition in the energy sector. Governor Ernest F. Hollings was one of successive South Carolina governors who opposed additional federal projects, and his "strenuous opposition" in 1960 led the Corps to scrap their initial plans to build two dams on this stretch of the Savannah River.[21] The editors of the *Augusta (Ga.) Chronicle*, an institution that had enthusiastically supported the older Clarks Hill and Hartwell programs in the 1940s and 1950s, quickly switched sides and favored Duke's private investment goals.[22] Given these cheerleaders and formal positions, Duke's Middleton Shoals project appeared well supported and pragmatic. However, the Corps' dam projects were not dead yet.

Not to be outdone by the South Carolina political establishment or Duke Power Company, Augusta's chamber of commerce executive Lester Moody and former Georgia state senator Peyton Hawes capitalized on Senator Richard B. Russell's leadership to obtain a restudy of the Savannah River between the Clarks Hill and Hartwell dams. Hawes (1903–90) was a longtime political operative from Elbert County who served on the state supreme court and, in the 1950s, as chair of the Georgia chamber of commerce. After the prompt restudy, Corps investigators recommended "that the United States construct the Trotters Shoals Dam and Reservoir with a hydroelectric power installation."[23] But there was a catch: The height of the Trotters Shoals dam threatened to flood part of Duke Power Company's Middleton Shoals steam plant site as well as other proposed industrial sites on the Savannah's remaining undammed twenty-mile stretch of Piedmont river. The Corps' restudy sparked an outcry from South Carolinians.

The Corps' Trotters Shoals and Duke's Middleton Shoals, however, were not exclusive projects, according to many professionals. This fact made Duke's drive to terminate Trotters Shoals all the more difficult. For the next three years, Duke Power Company and other stakeholders in South Carolina and Georgia debated the merits and benefits of public energy at Trotters Shoals and corporate energy at Middleton Shoals. When Corps engineers ultimately released their plans for Trotters Shoals in 1962, engineers dismantled the old New Deal big dam consensus's trio of benefits connected to every preceding multiple-purpose scheme.[24] The Corps did not recommend Trotters Shoals as a flood control or navigation structure; Hartwell upstream and Clarks Hill downstream provided those benefits. Instead, Corps technocrats sold Trotters Shoals's public energy and recreation benefits. As such, Trotters Shoals remained a water-quantity project that would soon become entangled with notoriously dirty pulp and paper mills.

In the late 1950s, South Carolina congressman William J. B. Dorn (D) launched an economic development mission to sell the Savannah River valley to the pulp and paper industry. Dorn never tired in his quest to bring jobs to his upstate South Carolina district and to increase tax revenues to benefit community businesses, schools, and roads. And he never stopped reminding people that the pulp and paper industry had a future in the region because cotton farmers had "gone to pine trees and cattle."[25] As early as 1956, Dorn arranged a tour for executives from the Mead Corporation, based in Dayton, Ohio; Duke Power; and South Carolina's economic development team, all in an attempt to hook Mead and land a new industrial plant.[26] Mead had already purchased property in the valley, and after the Dorn tour in 1956, the company announced plans to build a pulp and paper mill in South Carolina at the confluence of the Rocky River and the Savannah River between the Hartwell dam and the upper reaches of Clarks Hill reservoir.[27] Dorn was pleased with the results of his industrial tour.

The Mead Corporation's plans to harvest valley timber and manufacture paper products along the Savannah River also complimented Duke Power's plans for a steam plant at nearby Middleton Shoals. Mead had purchased Savannah River valley property and timber from Duke and was positioned to purchase Duke's electricity to energize the new mill. But

Mead executives also felt threatened like Duke, since the Corps' Trotters Shoals reservoir was set to flood some company assets, including one of Mead's proposed mill sites. Duke's and Mead's objective—to develop a coal plant and a mill along the last undammed section of the Savannah River in the Piedmont—initially made Dorn's and other boosters' opposition to the Corps' Trotters Shoals water and energy scheme easier. However, this effort to bring industry to this stretch of the Savannah River sparked more backlash.

Georgia politicians and boosters were dubious of Duke's and Mead's intentions. Georgia Democrats were also incredibly successful and almost unmatched in landing federal dams. Between 1950 and 1963, the Corps completed seven hydroelectric, flood, and navigation projects along Georgia waterways.[28] This put the South Carolinians at a disadvantage, but Dorn, a reluctant public power supporter, eventually brokered a compromise with Georgia's Senator Russell and Congressman Phil Landrum (D). For Georgians, giving up on the Corps' Trotters Shoals and supporting Duke's Middleton Shoals was a losing proposition, since the latter project would really benefit only South Carolinians. As one astute South Carolina attorney observed, "A large number of people have asked me why the people of Georgia are so whole heartedly" in support of Trotters Shoals and opposed to Duke's Middleton Shoals project. "The obvious answer is that Duke Power Company has no influence in the State of Georgia."[29] Furthermore, Georgia Power Company and Georgia's pulp and paper industry may have weighed in on this issue only in private, since the companies had little incentive to publicly support competitors in adjacent market territories. But it should also be clear that many Georgians supported Trotters Shoals on one condition. Newspaper editors, business interests, and Georgia governor Carl Saunders explained that they would prefer private development and industry in the Savannah River valley. But if companies like Mead could not make firm commitments, Georgians vowed to endorse Trotters Shoals.[30] Mead's and Duke's wavering in the Savannah River valley eventually tipped the scales in favor of Trotters Shoals, Georgia, and the Corps.

Breaking the impasse over the Middleton Shoals coal burner and Trotters Shoals hydroelectric dam ultimately involved another water and energy site Duke coveted in the upper Savannah River valley, on the Keowee River. In 1965, Duke Power Company president William B. McGuire announced plans to build a $700 million Keowee-Toxaway hydroelectric and thermoelectric steam plant complex. Congressman Dorn enthusiastically pronounced the Oconee and Pickens County project "fantastic and almost incomprehensible."[31] As reported in local papers, the company claimed the Middleton Shoals coal plant was still on the table while also promising to build two new hydroelectric dams to create Lakes Jocassee and Keowee in addition to three steam plants on Lake Keowee's new shoreline. This was a strange twist for Duke executives to discuss new hydroelectric dams after spending five years criticizing the Corps' Hartwell and Trotters Shoals hydroelectric facilities on economic grounds or because hydro facilities were inefficient compared with steam facilities. (See Chapter 5.) But according to news reports, "The Duke president said his company needed hydro plants for use in peak hours and could use steam plants" throughout the rest of the day to maintain base loads (i.e., "peak hours" would include morning/evening or the hottest/coldest part of the day, when consumer demand can spike above the "base load").[32] When the company formally submitted an application to the Federal Power Commission (FPC) for a license to build the energy complex, Duke alluded to the possibility that future steam generation might be produced by nuclear fission reactions instead of pulverized black coal.[33] Sure enough, one year later, Duke submitted a formal application to the Atomic Energy Commission (AEC) to build three nuclear reactors, which now comprise the Oconee Nuclear Station. As the company began to move the Keowee-Toxaway hydronuclear energy complex project through the FPC and AEC licensing processes, electrical cooperatives established during the New Deal objected to further privatization of the Savannah River valley's energy and water.

Congressman Dorn broke the impasse. Under his stewardship, the electrical co-ops relented because Duke Power Company agreed not to oppose the Corps' Trotters Shoals dam. When Dorn announced the "Trotters Shoals, Middleton Shoals, and Keowee-Toxaway" compromise terms in July 1966, he pledged to support authorization for Duke's Middleton Shoals diversion dam, Duke's Keowee-Toxaway project in Oconee and Pickens County (S.C.), and the Corps' Trotters Shoals development. When Dorn was done, after fighting for nearly a decade, he could claim, "This entire development, both Federal and private, will be second to none in the world."[34] On one level the compromise was novel and created a climate for public and private power to co-develop the Savannah River's hydraulic waterscape. Congress soon authorized $84.9 million for Trotters Shoals in the Rivers and Harbors Act of 1966 and approved Duke's Middleton Shoals diversion dam. Then the FPC approved Duke's Keowee-Toxaway application.[35] After 1966, the Savannah River valley's comprehensive development plan of mixed corporate and federal institutions looked complete, and the Sun Belt's commercial future looked bright.

The compromise, however, did not address a nagging water problem that had emerged in the years leading up to the 1966 agreement: water quality. As with previous federal water and energy projects in the Savannah River valley, boosters formed a committee—the Trotters Shoals Steering Committee—to promote the dam and lake. Georgia's Peyton Hawes, picking up where Augusta's Lester Moody left off, chaired the new committee and tackled water pollution head-on. He explained that Trotters Shoals, like the other two Savannah River dams, was designed to provide cost-effective peak electricity, water for municipal and industrial use, recreational opportunities, and a stimulus for economic development. Another anticipated benefit included projected increases in land values and the use of lakefront property for recreation and vacation homes. Hawes also proclaimed that the industrial sites along the free-flowing Savannah River between Clarks Hill reservoir and Hartwell dam were inappropriate for most industrial companies such as Mead.

Peyton Hawes explained in 1963 that chemical and pulp paper mills required clean water for production and fast-moving water for disposal and assimilation. As such, "Industries needing free flowing water" were often "polluting industries." This kind of industrial development, Hawes argued, would turn the slow-flowing Savannah River below the Hartwell dam and the Clarks Hill reservoir into cesspools. And because Hawes and his allies believed the region was "one of the few areas in the nation where clean, fresh water is still available in substantial supply," they wanted to "develop and conserve these great resources expeditiously and judiciously."[36] In their opinion, the solution to avoiding pollution and to saving this section of the Savannah from industrial effluent was not to harden effluent regulations or the enforcement apparatus. Instead, Hawes wanted to eliminate industrial sites by transforming the river into a clean water pool between two existing reservoirs.

Water pollution in the Savannah River valley was not necessarily a new problem. Water quality had long been on the minds of Savannah River valley residents. Since the nineteenth century, fishermen had lamented a decline in migratory fish, and Corps engineers observed sediment deposits throughout the upper and middle sections of the river. Lower Savannah River valley residents had also connected water pollution from Savannah, Georgia, with the pulp and paper industry in the 1930s.[37] In the 1940s, U.S. Fish and Wildlife biologists again linked soil-filled rivers with lackluster Savannah River fisheries, and the Public Health Service provided the Corps with malarial control suggestions for the Clarks Hill project.[38] Municipal and industrial pollution was not yet a serious concern in the upper Savannah River valley for these engineers, biologists, and public health officials. Water quality, as fishermen and professionals illustrated at the time, had more to do with sediment and muddy waters than with untreated municipal and industrial wastes. Put another way, water pollution initially resulted from a long legacy of soil management choices made by Savannah River valley farmers or forestry managers.

By the 1940s, serious water pollution began migrating upstream in southern watersheds like the Savannah and Tennessee systems and was no longer simply a land management problem.[39] Beginning in the late 1930s, TVA technicians discovered that the majority of the upper Tennessee River valley's water pollution originated from textile, cellulose, and paper manufacturing operations located upstream of Knoxville in the Holston, French Broad, and Pigeon Rivers that stretched into southwestern Virginia and western North Carolina. Some of these river stretches were, according to Daniel Schaffer, "so polluted that they were unsuitable for industries requiring clean water, could not be used for swimming," and had reduced former trout streams to carp waters. By 1945, untreated industrial and municipal waste flowed downstream, entered TVA reservoirs, and compelled officials to act. However, the TVA's board of directors was hamstrung by a hostile anti-TVA and conservative political climate that scrutinized any attempts to enlarge the institution's 1933 legislative mandate. The New Deal institution was powerless to combat Sun Belt pollution, since TVA regulations could not supersede state water quality regulations. Agency engineers and consultants did provide data and technical details to state authorities, and they left enforcement to state agents with authority to negotiate with municipal and industrial polluters.[40] The Savannah River was an interstate river like the Tennessee, but valley residents did not have a TVA-like actor that could work with Georgia and South Carolina to assess and manage water pollution. The Corps was an unlikely enforcer.

Corps engineers were aware in the 1950s that communities and industries in the Trotters Shoals reservoir area dumped untreated and partially treated waste into the Savannah River. As an institution, the Corps was not responsible for enforcing the Federal Pollution Control Act (1956), but Corps engineers were not oblivious to water pollution. In the Corps' *Savannah River, Georgia Review Report*, staff noted that while the dumping of wastes was "currently permitted or tolerated" in the proposed reservoir's footprint, discharges in reservoirs elsewhere in the county resulted in public outcry, requests for federal assistance to build treatment plants, and other "corrective measures" that might bring too much attention to industrial operations.[41] To avoid this, the Corps recommended that state and local agencies take the lead responsibility on water cleanup or face federal enforcement action. Under the terms of the Federal Water Pollution Control Act, the first step in enforcement involved a "conference phase" where state and local authorities attempted to resolve water pollution problems. If state and local authorities could not resolve the problem, the U.S. surgeon general (Public Health Service) could take the alleged polluter to court. This happened only once before 1966.[42]

The pollution issue helped build support for Trotters Shoals. South Carolina countryside conservationists rallied behind Trotters Shoals, and they cited the potential for industrial pollution as the single most important reason to support the federal dam and reservoir project. As early as 1962, one group of South Carolina citizens rejected Mead's plans for a pulp and paper mill on the Savannah River. Attorney James Nickles wrote to Georgia's Senator Russell and stated, "The people of Abbeville County are not the least interested in" Mead's mill because the company planned to "pour their poison chemicals" and industrial wastes directly into the Savannah River.[43] The Corps regulated the Savannah River's flow between the Hartwell dam and Clarks Hill reservoir, and Nickles's allies argued that Mead's proposed location was unacceptable "because there is no CONTINUOUS flow of water in the Savannah" due to the Hartwell dam's regulation of the river.[44] Like Georgia's Peyton Hawes, these South Carolina countryside conservationists cited the potential for water pollution as a justification to dam the Savannah River and build a new reservoir that could fill with high-quality clean water. The Corps' Trotters Shoals project, however, was still not a guaranteed project after Congress approved the Rivers and Harbors Act of 1966 and authorized the $84.9 million Trotters Shoals project. In the legislative and budgetary process, authorization to proceed is never the same as appropriation of the required monies; funding would come in fits and starts until the project was operational in the 1980s. The boosters, politicians, and citizens who defended Trotters Shoals and rejected polluting industries for twenty years faced a new issue after the private-versus-public-energy, jobs-and-free enterprise, and pollution challenges.

Sun Belt environmentalists rallied in the 1970s. The individuals who opposed Trotters Shoals on new environmental grounds differed slightly from the countryside conservationists. Local citizens plus university professors, state agency employees, and representatives from national conservation and environmental organizations raised a new tool in the name of Sun Belt environmental health and challenged previously powerful actors.[45]

A new piece of federal legislation invited public participation in massive federal public works projects. Congress—with a Democratic majority in the House and Senate—passed, and President Richard Nixon (R) signed into law, the National Environmental Policy Act (1969) three years after Congress authorized Trotters Shoals. NEPA, as the act was known, created the Council on Environmental Quality to set the nation's environmental policy shortly before Nixon crafted additional legislation to form the Environmental Protection Agency in late 1970 to manage both the Council on Environmental Quality's and NEPA's mandates. NEPA, according to supporters and critics, threw a wrench into the gears of major federal public works projects across the country because the new policy required a pre-construction environmental assessment or environmental impact statement (EIS) that evaluated potential environmental effects and considered the advantages of alternatives, including the benefits of abandoning the given project. The assessment process also opened a federal agency's entire construction process to two rounds of review. The first round was an internal review to resolve interagency quarrels. For example, federal agencies such as the Fish and Wildlife Service could weigh in on how a Corps project might impact the agency's mandate to protect fish and wildlife. The second round was an external evaluation that provided citizens with access to the same information used by agencies to complete a project's initial assessment. The public could also submit formal responses that had to be included in the public record, and if any aspect of an assessment was incomplete, they could sue the agency.[46] NEPA established a project review process that forced the Corps to consider the environmental effects of their projects "in unprecedented detail." Environmental historian Jeffrey Stine's observation comes in the context of the Tennessee-Tombigbee Waterway, a massive navigation project that linked the Gulf of Mexico with the Tennessee River via Alabama and eastern Mississippi. The Tenn-Tom was one of the Corps' first major water projects "built entirely under the auspices of NEPA."[47] Trotters Shoals dam and reservoir was also subject to the EIS process not only once but multiple times.

Corps engineers began building Trotters Shoals after 1970, so Trotters was the Corps' first Savannah River valley project subject to compliance with NEPA. Trotters's first EIS laid bare the Sun Belt's water-quality challenges. Corps engineers defended the massive Trotters Shoals dam and reservoir project in the *Draft Environmental Impact Statement* while simultaneously arguing that the project would produce complicated new environmental conditions. Artificial reservoirs are, after all, convoluted environments. These working reservoirs do indeed create good fishery habitat and a new environment for anglers, pleasure boaters, campers, swimmers, and second-home owners to appreciate. But juggling the services—hydroelectric generation, flood control, and recreation—of the dams and lakes also hindered the reservoirs' ecological functions. The new reservoir environment of the artificial lakes required technological solutions beyond hatchery science to maintain new sport fisheries, and one of the most significant problems was insufficient oxygen for aquatic organisms. Large artificial southeastern reservoirs behave differently from natural lakes in colder regions. Whereas some lakes and reservoirs experience a circulating inversion of hot and cold water twice a year (particularly lakes that have freeze-thaw cycles), southeastern reservoirs typically experience a single seasonal inversion. This single inversion, when combined with manipulated water levels and intensive solar heat gain, leave southern reservoirs oxygen-poor. For example, the Savannah River's reservoirs "stratify" during the summer and fall, and cold water sinks to the bottom and warm water rises. By late fall and early winter, an inversion takes place that helps mix the water more completely. But before this mixing, water discharged from the dams—typically from the deepest portion of a reservoir near the dam—in the summer season has very little dissolved oxygen. The EIS authors expressed concern that low dissolved oxygen levels and cold water released from Trotters Shoals directly into Clarks Hill would further reduce dissolved oxygen, water temperatures, and water quality in the latter reservoir.[48]

Fishery health and oxygen levels were also related to the Sun Belt's commercial explosion. The Trotters Shoals *Draft Environmental Impact Statement* observed that the region's primary industrial sector—the textile industry—utilized significant "quantities of water for manufacturing and processing." The Corps identified eleven textile mills in Georgia and nine in South Carolina that discharged industrial wastes into water bodies that would ultimately affect Trotters Shoals's reservoir water quality. Industry was not the only pollution culprit: Seven municipalities also discharged municipal wastes into tributaries that would feed Trotters Shoals's reservoir. The Trotters Shoals dam and reservoir moved ahead, but water quality, pumped storage, dredging, and earthquake engineering issues generated subsequent EIS reviews.[49]

Boosters tried to fight back after facing the new environmentalists and multiple EIS reviews that threatened to bring the Trotters Shoals dam and reservoir project to a halt. The first booster to do so was James R. Young. When the dam was threatened by another EIS review related to a proposed Savannah National Recreation Area in 1971, Young, an associate editor of the *Elberton (Ga.) Star*, communicated with an ally about an upcoming public meeting. Young did not "want the ecology opposition to arrive with any scheme to make an adverse issue of Trotters Shoals." If other topics arose, such as pollution, commentators would be told to hold those subjects for a "subsequent hearing."[50] Young was not the only Savannah River valley resident who was put off by the new Trotters Shoals opposition community. Even old hands like Congressman William J. B. Dorn (D) were unsure of Trotters Shoals's future, and he encouraged his allies to "keep fighting or this 'far left' crowd will kill everything."[51] Finally, Robert L. Williford, like the other old-school Trotters Shoals supporters, was equally concerned about the emerging and powerful environmentalists' voices that threatened his water and energy project as well as local authority. In late 1971, the *Elberton Star* editor expressed frustration over the Georgia Press Institute convention's organizational decision to allot two hours to environmental issues as requested by the Georgia Conservancy, an Atlanta-based nonprofit founded in 1967 (see Chapter 7). Williford branded the Georgia Conservancy "a highly controversial group of environmentalists who are fighting the activities of the US Corps of Engineers, the Soil Conservation Service and other agencies engaged in such projects as stream improvement, flood control, harbor improvement, snagging operations, watershed conservation and mosquito control." As a newspaper man and Trotters Shoals supporter to the core, Williford "strongly" opposed the conservation agenda item, and he requested that the time slot be reassigned to "something of more value and interest to newspaper publishers." Clearly frustrated, Williford called the Georgia Conservancy "a special interest group which came requesting time to promote their beliefs and programs." In exaggeration mode, he did not think "we should provide a forum for such groups, and certainly not in response to their request," because if the Georgia Conservancy got airtime, "Why not the Black Panthers, religious groups, or one of the thousands of others who have some 'special kick' going?" Williford was not the first person to associate the Sun Belt's environmental concerns with civil rights problems.

Countryside conservationists and environmentalists who rallied around water quality were only the latest manifestation of opposition to Corps water and energy projects.[52]

Frank Harrison was among a small group of regular writers to South Carolina's congressional delegation who linked the Savannah River's water and energy history to the nation's civil rights conflict and postwar rights-based liberalism beginning in the 1950s. As a concerned constituent, Harrison was not alone in his critique of the Corps' Hartwell and Trotters Shoals projects. Unlike some of his fellow writers who were prone to hyperbole, Harrison pointed logically to a new conflation of "rights" that eventually converged more concretely downstream at Trotters Shoals. First and foremost, Harrison opposed the Hartwell project because the economics did not make sense. The Corps wanted to build a taxpayer-funded and tax-exempt dam that produced electricity less efficiently than thermoelectric coal-fired steam plants as advertised by Duke Power Company. His protest bubbled from a collection of circumstances including his observation of the Corps' Clarks Hill project land condemnation and purchase process as well as the Corps' acquisition of water rights. Harrison had been personally involved in McCormick County's (S.C.) fight for congressional authorization to legally draw water from Clarks Hill, and while ultimately successful, this experience only added to his sense that the federal government was usurping states' and local municipalities' water rights.[53]

As Harrison succinctly summed up his concerns, "The taking of huge areas of private property by the Federal Government is becoming increasingly dangerous especially in view of the recent Supreme Court decision and other actions of the administration in attempting to continue the centralizing of power in the Federal Government." Harrison was referring to nothing other than the Supreme Court's May 17, 1954, *Brown v. Board of Education* ruling that declared "separate but equal" facilities unconstitutional. Harrison thought he saw the writing on the wall and connected states' rights, water rights, and civil rights: "The widespread increase of federal public use and recreation areas may result in serious political repercussions in this state and other states because these areas may become areas which cannot be used to any extent by members of the white race."[54] Harrison was not alone. For example, when the Georgia Farm Bureau assembled to set the 1955 state farm lobby's agenda, they "expected to make a stand on four major issues—water resources, segregation, rural electric and telephone appropriations, and price supports on basic commodities," according to one journalist. Farmers who had suffered through the 1954 drought were interested in "legislation for establishment of water rights" because existing law was unclear, out of date, and often pitted municipal, industrial, and agricultural users against one another.[55] By the late 1950s, Georgians and South Carolinians saw states', civil, and water "rights" converging across the Sun Belt's hydraulic waterscape.

Water projects are an unlikely place to look for this conflation of rights and were far removed from the suburbs of Charlotte (N.C.), Atlanta (Ga.), and Orange County (Calif.), where others have found the roots of the New Right and modern conservatism.[56] In the southern countryside, communities considered access to the Savannah River's water as a critical component to their continually diversifying and growing commercial Sun Belt economy. Water politics was another site to locate social power, and the Savannah River valley's water remained highly contested by those who supported federal energy projects and those who advocated for corporations. According to critics, the Corps' public water and energy schemes made water access more difficult and directly challenged states' rights and strangled local economic development. The *Brown* decision only exacerbated the southern water and power dynamic.

By the 1960s, southerners' frustration with federal water politics threatened an already fragile Democratic Party. Constituent disappointment with Clarks Hill and reluctance with Hartwell morphed into a full-bore big dam backlash against the Trotters Shoals water and energy program. When the John F. Kennedy and Lyndon B. Johnson administrations began to address civil rights between 1960 and 1965, some southern Democrats became confused about the party's direction. As one letter to Senator Olin Johnston asked, "How can you kick Kennedys [*sic*] civil rights Bill and at the same time condone this power take over by the federal government" at Trotters Shoals? Another asked him to "oppose the so-called 'public-accommodations' legislation proposed by the Kennedy family," while also asking him to reconsider his support for Trotters Shoals.[57] While Johnston supported Trotters Shoals, his partner in the Senate, Strom Thurmond, did not. Trotters Shoals was the first of the Corps' three Savannah River valley dams that Thurmond did not back, and he bolted the Democratic Party in favor of a Republican affiliation in 1964 because of the Democrats' direction over civil rights.

Trotters Shoals's opponents connected civil rights with Sun Belt water and energy projects. One letter commended Senator Olin D. Johnston on his decision not "to support the President on the Civil Rights package legislation demanded of Congress." In the author's opinion, the senator's action proved "to me that you are not willing to submit to the influence of the mob, and of the Kennedy Dynasty. You, as a representative of the South and of the state of South Carolina, must help curb the growing power of the 'liberals' and help restore the system of governmental checks and balances." South Carolinians, like Frank Harrison from years earlier, understood that if federal water and energy projects included recreation areas, then carefree recreation for whites would be impossible. Any public recreation areas at Trotters Shoals built with public funds or "any thing that has Federal money in it will have to be open to all races."[58]

The public debate over Trotters Shoals incorporated New Right rhetoric and antiliberal arguments found in other parts of the United States in the 1960s. Clarks Hill, Hartwell, and Trotters Shoals opponents grafted water projects into a discourse of states', civil, and water rights in the post-1945 period. Conservative constituents from small towns and rural counties used language that included throwbacks to the past while wrestling with the Sun Belt's long-chronicled race and water conflicts. These responses from the urban and rural Southeast trumpeted the merits of privatization and free enterprise while criticizing public energy projects and federal intrusion into the nation's economy; they also conveniently ignored the local incentives used to lure industry to the region. Finally, the conservatism stirred by water and energy projects in the Savannah River valley paralleled the thoughts and activities of grassroots activists sitting at kitchen tables who organized around taxes, zoning, and busing in the other parts of the country. The conservative letter writers who shared their ideas about Trotters Shoals and environmental politics identified entitlements—to local self-determination, to peaceful segregated recreation, or access to the water supply—as fundamental rights.

Trotters Shoals spanned a critical era in American environmental and Sun Belt history. Countryside conservationists and environmentalists faced formidable challenges in the post-1945 period. They were not alone. New South capitalists and liberal New Dealers had promoted dams as solutions for the region's water, energy, and economic problems; they repeatedly met opposition. Whereas countryside conservationists concerned about water supply and quality helped put Trotters Shoals on the map, post-1970s environmentalists threatened to erase it to save an undammed stretch of river in favor of a National Recreation Area. When Trotters Shoals's proponents packaged the project in the 1960s, they never could have imagined that a local, Savannah River project would become a national symbol.

Eventually, Corps engineers transformed the Savannah River's Piedmont between the Hartwell dam and Clarks Hill reservoir. Corps project managers let the first construction contract in 1974 as they continued to purchase land for the project area from at least sixty families and property holders, including twenty-five farms.[59] Trotters Shoals dam was renamed the Richard B. Russell Jr. Dam shortly after Russell died in 1971 to commemorate the senator and to make it very difficult for the congressional Public Works Committee to turn down future appropriations for a project named for one of the Senate's most senior members.[60] The Corps constructed a series of earthen and concrete dams stretching 6,000 feet across the Savannah River, and when water from the 26,000-acre reservoir first flowed through the dam's four generators in January 1985, a nearly 100-year quest to maximize public benefits of the Savannah River basin neared completion.[61] Today the Corps operates this hydroelectric dam—one of the largest east of the Mississippi River—only as a peak-power producer (with pump storage capability) during periods of high demand and does not operate it continuously.[62]

The Savannah National Recreation Area that would have preserved a section of free-flowing river in the Piedmont never materialized. When the Corps completed Trotters Shoals dam, it buried one of the last stretches of Savannah River shoals. In the 1960s and 1970s, however, Georgia countryside conservationists and environmentalists did win concessions for free-flowing rivers. Advocates fought for the Georgia Scenic Rivers Act of 1969 that named four rivers to a state scenic river system and recommended further study of others, and the legislation was modeled after the National Wild and Scenic Rivers Act (1968).[63] The Georgia act prohibited dams, reservoirs, diversions, and other structural changes on the Jacks, Conasauga, Chattooga, and Ebenezer Rivers and was designed to help expedite rivers named at the state level more quickly through the national wild and scenic designation process. Another important Georgia river was missing from this list. The Flint River shared similarities with the Savannah River, namely, the Corps had plans to build more multiple-purpose dams, including one at Sprewell Bluff in the Piedmont. But the Sprewell Bluff and other dams never grew from the Flint River's Pine Mountain bedrock. One Georgia governor's big dam backlash helped make that history.

As Georgia's governor from 1971 to 1975, James Earle Carter took on the Sun Belt's water problems. As a candidate for governor, Jimmy

Carter stood barefoot and ankle-deep in South River raw sewage to draw attention to one of metro Atlanta's polluted rivers, identifying problems he would fix as governor, and to woo environmentally conscious voters.[64] While campaigning, he was also convinced to paddle the state's rivers. Based on his personal experiences paddling the Chattahoochee, Flint, and other Georgia rivers, Carter "immediately fell in love" with the state's waters, according to one writer.[65] Within years and in what was a seminal environmental activist moment in Georgia history, Governor Carter stopped the Corps on the Flint. He primarily cited an economic—fiscally conservative—argument to protect the Flint River from the Corps' decades-old plan to build a multiple-purpose dam at Sprewell Bluff. Carter received thousands of letters and telephone calls from like-minded Georgians, as well as those who were concerned about the project's potential to cause "environmental damages." The decision was not easy for Carter. He had previously served as the chairman of the Middle Flint River Planning and Development Council that, in his words, "was instrumental in securing passage of" congressional legislation authorizing the Flint River dams in the first place.[66] Carter stopped the Corps' Sprewell Bluff dam project on the Flint River because "the construction of unwarranted dams and other projects at public expense should be prevented."[67] On the other side of the state, however, the Trotters Shoals water and energy project got a green light from Governor Jimmy Carter's office up until his last day.

U.S. President Jimmy Carter (1977–81) thought differently and executed his own version of a big dam backlash. He announced his famous "hit list" in 1977 after less than six months in office and threatened to eliminate any water project in the country that was fiscally irresponsible, based on faulty cost-benefit accounting, an engineering folly, or detrimental to the environment. Among the more than thirty nationally targeted pork barrel projects—previously promoted by chambers of commerce, local steering committees, the Corps, the Bureau of Reclamation, and legions of elected Republicans and Democrats—was the Trotters Shoals development the former peanut farmer had supported as Georgia's governor.[68] As the nation's chief executive, Carter placed the Trotters Shoals dam and reservoir project—already scrutinized by liberal and conservative critics for more than twenty years—under the microscope again. Previous opponents had tried to eliminate the Corps' last major Savannah River valley project by championing free enterprise, defending potential industrial sites and new jobs, and raising the EIS shield. As such, President Carter's newfound opposition to the Savannah River valley project represented only the latest attempt to kill Trotters Shoals. His hit list, however, soon crumpled under the weight of a congressional backlash by members of his own party and Republicans who hailed mostly from the American West. Before the end of 1977, Carter compromised with the Senate, and nearly all of the water projects—including Trotters Shoals—were fully funded.

Journalists, former aides, and scholars have repeatedly asserted that Governor Carter's decision to reject the Corps' Flint River project in Georgia informed his decision to critically examine the economic feasibility and environmental consequences of the nation's water projects in 1977.[69] But President Carter was unable to apply those same lessons and convince Congress to rein in spending even as the national deficit grew. As Guy Martin, the former assistant interior secretary during the Carter administration intimated, Carter failed because he pushed environmental issues more than economic issues. According to Martin, "Most Congressmen" did not "really care about wild rivers," and "the New Deal mentality [was] entrenched up there—even the right-wingers" treated dam and reservoir projects as entitlements. Governor Carter's rejection of a single water and energy project on the Flint River was bold and formative, but President Carter could not easily apply the same logic on the national stage when pork was on local tables.[70] As an outsider—part countryside conservationist and part environmentalist—Jimmy Carter could not overcome Capitol Hill's political and institutional momentum or implement revolutionary ways to think about water and energy.

Savannah River valley residents had organized for centuries to criticize and oppose elements of Georgia's and South Carolina's hydraulic waterscape. Aside from the Flint River case, southerners had a poor success rate when it came to beating dam proposals. Early-nineteenth-century fishermen protested antebellum dams in the 1850s, and anglers attempted to save migratory fish runs in the 1880s at the Augusta Canal diversion dam. Progressive preservationists unsuccessfully fought the Atlanta-based Georgia Power Company's New South–era Tallulah Falls project in northeast Georgia in the 1910s. These events mirrored grassroots preservation and federal conservation moments observed in other parts of the nation. President Jimmy Carter's attempt to apply a Georgia solution to the nation's water problems likewise failed. But in the Sun Belt period, states' rights, antipollution, conservation, and environmental activists became unaffiliated countryside associates dedicated to shaping the Savannah River valley's Piedmont. Southeastern water problems had evolved beyond conserving water for energy production, channeling water for navigation, controlling floodwaters, and storing water to bust droughts. Sun Belt countryside conservationists, environmentalists, and conservative critics represented streams of a big dam backlash that recast the contours of national water and power politics. That was no small feat. By 1970, the nation's water problem encompassed the old problem of water quantity, a lingering water quality problem, and a new demand. At that moment, Sun Belt commercial boosters—influenced by New South capitalists and New Deal liberals—were torn as some valleys were flooded to build lakes for water-ski boats and others were saved to balance working reservoirs with recreational, scenic, and wild rivers.

CHAPTER 7

Taken and Delivered
The Chattooga River

Water is a prime factor in most outdoor recreation
activities. . . . Recreation on the water is increasing.
—*Outdoor Recreation for America* (1962)

After nearly fifty fires burned across northeast Georgia's mountains on a single weekend in 1976, National Forest Service supervisor Patrick Thomas tried to make sense of the 800 smoldering acres of Rabun County's public land. With more forest burned in the first two months of 1976 than in the previous two years combined, Thomas linked the recent "fire style protest" to the 1974 creation of the Chattooga Wild and Scenic River. Thomas also empathized with the group of local mountain residents allegedly responsible for the fires, noting, "I would think it was a hardship, someone taking away access to a place I'd always been able to take pleasure in." Thomas did not explicitly identify the "someone" who benefited from the Chattooga River's new identity, but his comment communicated that the process was not entirely equitable or welcomed by those living in the Savannah River valley's extreme upper reaches.[1] The fires did make clear how federal implementation of the Wild and Scenic Rivers Act of 1968—a new watershed management strategy—stirred community protest and class conflict in the southern Appalachian mountains. This episode illustrates how one solution for the Sun Belt's evolving water problems signaled a change for old corporate and federal powers, empowered new grassroots environmental organizations, and invited "Retro Frontiersmen" to spark fire on the land in response.

The Chattooga River—James Dickey's famous *Deliverance* river—brings the Southeast's nearly century-long water and energy history full-circle. The Chattooga is unlike virtually all other southern Appalachian rivers within a fifty-mile radius: It escaped the lumber cribs, concrete, spillways, turbines, generators, transmission lines, and reservoirs' drowning waters found in nearby watersheds such as the Tallulah-Tugaloo. New South executives and New Deal regional planners had also identified the river as a waterpower and hydroelectric energy source for decades. Anglers, day-trippers, and canoeists had regarded the Chattooga River as a unique and endangered river for decades, complete with swimming holes, breathtaking scenery, superior trout fishing, and white-knuckle rapids. This history was immediately relevant after Congress enacted the National Wild and Scenic Rivers Act (1968) and directed the U.S. Forest Service to evaluate rivers worthy of protection across the country—including the Chattooga as one of the American South's only representatives—for inclusion in this new federal land protection category.[2] Forest Service staff discovered tremendous support for a protected Appalachian river among local county governments, state agencies, and a segment of the Georgia and South Carolina public. Furthermore, environmentalists who participated in the Chattooga National Wild and Scenic River campaign joined a national movement dedicated to solving water problems in the 1960s. Given this wide spectrum of enthusiasm, the Chattooga easily moved from a study river in 1968 to an official wild and scenic river in six quick years. The undammed river represented a scarce commodity for these interest groups, and thus they considered the Chattooga an extremely valuable chunk of southern wilderness worthy of federal protection.

This victory was surprising. The Chattooga River was not saved exclusively by crusading preservationists or wilderness advocates, such as those who successfully fought the Bureau of Reclamation's Echo Park dam project (Green River, Colo.) in the 1950s.[3] Instead, nearly every party involved in the Chattooga's case—multiple federal and state agencies, new environmental groups, and many county residents—agreed that Congress should confer wild and scenic river status on the river. The process was made much easier when the traditional enemies—private utilities and federal agencies intent on building hydroelectric dams—intentionally avoided a fight during a national energy transition. A victory for one set of players rang hollow for others, as demonstrated by the burning forest. Everyone may have agreed the Chattooga River was a scarce and valuable resource, but not everyone agreed with how the Chattooga Wild and Scenic River should be used. And most people acknowledged that the valley, after centuries of land use and habitation, was no wilderness. Based on arson events and Patrick Thomas's observations, one might assume that top-down conservation rangers remapped the Chattooga River's watershed and resources without local input or consent.

Resistance—including clandestine acts of arson and vandalism or formal community and labor organization—has been linked to transitions in land and resource use, ownership, and management throughout the United States.[4] Thus, in the Chattooga's case, arson might look like a local anti-statist protest in response to the taking of private land or the disruption of local subsistence economies. However, the story behind the northeast Georgia fires was much more complicated than a monolithic-state power narrative. The fires set within and around this southern Appalachian river's narrow corridor were the consequence of turning a site of local leisure along the Chattooga River into a national destination popularized by the 1972 screen adaptation of James Dickey's novel *Deliverance* and protected by the Wild and Scenic Rivers Act in 1974. The fires, like historic acts of resistance, did not occur during the negotiation and designation process to preserve a special environment, nor were they the result of declarations of eminent domain. While the Chattooga had always represented a leisure commons for many people, the reluctance of old river users to adhere to new federal management policies—plus the crush of Sun Belt visitors stimulated by Hollywood's visual representation of the Chattooga's wild landscape and rapids in *Deliverance*—sparked a violent response during a management stage that was not nearly as smooth as the designation phase.

The Chattooga River's story illustrates how landscape transformations, social relations, and energy choices were bound together with the Southeast's hydraulic waterscape. First, national citizen action and engagement in water politics had ramifications for how people thought about and interacted with wild rivers like the Chattooga. For example, river advocates argued that free-flowing rivers had ecological and economic values that benefited local environments and service economies. Second, the nation's electrical utilities continued to shift away from hydroelectricity to coal while also experimenting with emerging civilian nuclear technologies. The new fossil fuel and mineral energy sources still depended on water, but not always directly on dams, to generate base loads. Whereas the Georgia Power Company had built a hydraulic system that expropriated energy from the adjacent Tallulah and Tugaloo Rivers in the 1920s, the company delivered the Chattooga River to the environmental and paddling community for safekeeping in the 1960s. Not all of the Sun Belt's water problems

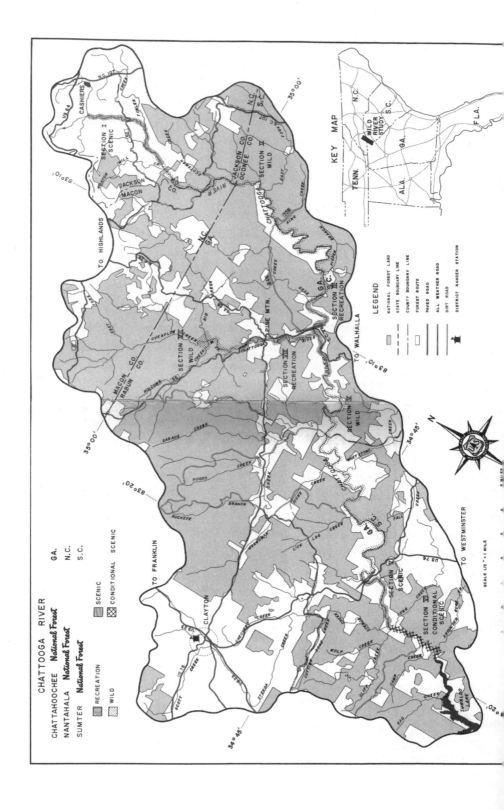

could be solved so easily, but the Chattooga River's history illustrates how water and power continued to cycle in the Southeast with important consequences for Sun Belt rivers and communities.

Private energy corporations and federal agencies built large dam projects in every cardinal direction and every southern Appalachian watershed neighboring the Chattooga's before 1970. The Chattooga River tumbles from the Eastern Continental Divide and the base of Whitesides Mountain's 700-foot granite rock face near Cashiers, North Carolina. The river's tributaries drain an 180,000-acre watershed ringed by mountains that reach nearly 5,000 feet above sea level and can receive over eighty inches of annual precipitation. (The Pacific Northwest is the only other area in the lower forty-eight states that receives this much precipitation.) The majority of the river forms about forty miles of the South Carolina and Georgia border. The Chattooga flows between the two national forests, crashing over boulders and ledges before the current slacks and fills the Georgia Power Company's Lake Tugaloo—an uninspiring, flatwater reservoir behind a hydroelectric dam that fills the former Tugaloo river valley—one of many short stops on a 300-plus-mile journey to the Atlantic Ocean via the Savannah River.

A bird's-eye view of the southern Appalachian headwaters clearly illustrates how the Chattooga River differs from other Blue Ridge watersheds. To the south and west, the Georgia Power Company effectively transformed the Tallulah and Tugaloo Rivers into one large water-storage pond between 1913 and 1927 to supply Atlanta with electricity to power a New South. On the west and north, the headwaters of the Tennessee River feed the Gulf of Mexico on the other side of the Eastern Continental Divide. There, Alcoa, the Tennessee Electric Power Company, and other New South energy corporations dammed the Tennessee River system's southern Appalachian tributaries—the Tuckasegee, Nantahala, Little Tennessee, and Hiwassee Rivers—extensively before 1930. The more well-known Tennessee Valley Authority assumed control of that river and tributaries after 1933 and initiated a comprehensive plan to build more

(opposite) Chattooga River (Study River Proposal), 1970, including designated wild, scenic, and recreational sections. The Chattooga River's headwaters can be located in the upper right corner of the map (below Cashiers, N.C.), and the river flows to the map's lower left corner (Tugaloo Lake) along the Georgia and South Carolina border. In Forest Service, United States Department of Agriculture, *A Proposal: The Chattooga, "A Wild and Scenic River"* (March 3, 1970). Courtesy of Hargrett Rare Book and Manuscript Library, University of Georgia Libraries, Athens.

than twenty multiple-purpose dams to provide agricultural, navigational, flood control, and hydroelectric benefits for purportedly democratic and decentralized economic development in one area of a larger region labeled the "nation's no. 1 economic problem" by New Dealers.[5]

Turning east from the bird's-eye vantage point back to the Savannah River's headwaters, Duke Power Company began building Sun Belt hydroelectric dams in Appalachian valleys to create Lakes Jocassee and Keowee by drowning South Carolina's Whitewater, Toxaway, and Keowee Rivers in the late 1960s. To the south, and farther down the Savannah River valley itself, the Corps' three massive hydroelectric installations appear. Engineers built these Sun Belt projects above the river's fall line between 1945 and 1985. In contrast to these adjacent watersheds, the fifty-mile Chattooga River flowed wild and free as an anomaly, undeveloped by corporate or federal energy institutions. The Chattooga remained a river surrounded by a sea of reservoirs.

The Chattooga may have been alone in the Southeast, but wild rivers across the country were equally threatened by agricultural and energy interests. Environmental historians have long considered the battles over Hells Canyon and Echo Park as critical national battlegrounds. At both locations—in Idaho and in Colorado (see Chapter 5)—the Army Corps of Engineers and the Bureau of Reclamation planned large multiple-purpose dams for the Snake River and the Green River in the 1950s. Organized protest that defeated both projects contributed to the rise of postwar environmentalism, and the skills opponents marshaled "carried over into subsequent wilderness and water controversies," according to Mark Harvey.[6]

The wild and scenic river system was one such example. In the late 1950s, brothers John C. and Frank E. Craighead Jr. formalized a river classification system that directly influenced the National Wild and Scenic Rivers Act (1968). They were avid outdoorsmen, naturalists, and wildlife biologists best known for their lengthy grizzly bear study in Yellowstone National Park in the 1960s. But their personal experiences also connected these two scientists with rivers. They spent much of their childhood playing and fishing in the eastern Potomac River and their adult lives in Wyoming's Snake River valley. The brothers also developed an intimate knowledge of the American West's waterways, and the Craigheads acted as they watched the nation's rivers deteriorate after 1945.[7]

At the same moment that the Craigheads spoke for wild rivers, members of Congress linked water quality and scarcity with national economic development in the 1950s. John Craighead spoke before the traveling Senate Select Committee on National Water Resources that toured twenty-four American cities and towns to hear about water pollution in 1959. John leaned heavily on evolving ecological systems theory when he characterized watersheds as "both ecological and economic entities" where the whole was "equal to more than the sum of its parts."[8] John believed that those best equipped to identify rivers in need of protection were people like himself and others at "the grass roots."[9] In individual statements before the Senate Select Committee, in *National Geographic* publications, and in academic articles, the Craighead brothers made the case that free-flowing rivers had to be protected for educational and recreational purposes and to maintain a clean and healthy water supply.[10] Combined, these conditions would stimulate an outdoor recreation economy that could tap the 44 percent of Americans who preferred "water-based recreation activities over any others."[11] In short, congressionally designated wild and scenic rivers like the Chattooga could help solve the nation's wide-ranging water problems.

Beginning in the late 1950s the Craigheads helped develop and write an equivalent to the Wilderness Act (1964) for the nation's undeveloped rivers, since the legislation had intentionally excluded rivers. John stated in an interview with river historian Tim Palmer that he "had worked on the wilderness legislation with Olaus Murie, Howard Zahniser, Stewart Brandborg, and others . . . but they were not interested in rivers" and were more focused on wilderness areas that lacked "rivers because the lands were at high altitudes." The more he became involved, John continued, "the clearer it became that we needed a national river preservation system based on the wilderness system but separate from it." So the Craigheads joined forces with Sigurd Olson (Wilderness Society), Joe Penfold (Izaak Walton League), Bud Jordahl (a close colleague of the late senator Gaylord Nelson), and Leonard Hall (Missouri journalist), and together they bent the bureaucratic ears of Ted Swem (National Park Service) and Ted Schad (staff director, Senate Select Committee on National Water Resources).[12] Collectively, these river enthusiasts, recreation professionals, and water experts drafted the first wild and scenic rivers act, which was a component of President Lyndon Baines Johnson's *Special Message to the Congress on Conservation and Restoration of Natural Beauty*. In retrospect, the president's February 1965 message was a quaint start for a Congress that would address water pollution, watch riots engulf cities, expand civil rights via the Voting Rights Act, and face public opposition to an escalating conflict in Vietnam.[13] Nonetheless, by 1968, congressional members approved legislation and created the National Wild and Scenic River System. The act immediately protected eight rivers (and four tributaries); slated twenty-seven as "study rivers," including the Chattooga; and requested reports describing the characteristics that made study rivers worthy of designation.[14] The Craigheads had successfully shepherded a new land management designation through Congress to benefit the nation's rivers and those intent on solving water problems.

While wild and scenic river proponents like the Craigheads worked with Senate colleagues in the early 1960s to produce the Wild and Scenic Rivers Act, the U.S. Department of the Interior announced a national "Wild River Study" of twelve rivers. In 1964, Interior staff tasked the Department of Agriculture's Forest Service with executing an investigation that included the Savannah River's Georgia and South Carolina tributaries.[15] Secretary of the Interior Stewart Udall was well aware of the Corps' plans for hydroelectric dams in Sun Belt river valleys, and of Duke Power's specific proposal to build Lakes Jocassee and Toxaway plus the adjacent Oconee nuclear power station.[16] Udall "strongly" believed "that at least one major tributary of the Savannah River—the Chattooga—should be preserved in its free-flowing condition for the benefit of future generations and for the purpose of giving needed balance to the comprehensive development of this river."[17] At this juncture in 1965, the Department of the Interior went on record and recommended that any corporate or federal agency seeking approval to build any dam in the Chattooga River valley be denied a Federal Power Commission license. But Udall and the Department of the Interior were not the only ones interested in protecting the Chattooga in the 1960s.

Georgians and South Carolinians joined the initiative as Udall promoted a national wild rivers study group. Jack Brown, the Mountain Rest (S.C.) postmaster, wrote Congressmen W. J. Bryan Dorn (D) claiming that he was "born and raised here near the Chattooga River" and that he thought a fully designated wild and scenic river would be good for the region. Brown expressed a keen interest in how "tourist potential" might be developed. But he supported Forest Service acquisition of additional land only if such land was necessary for "something like the National Wild River System which I understand will preserve and develope [sic]" the property for recreation. Brown's correspondence exposed his opinion that the National Forest Service's general land management process could limit timber cutting, and thus forestry-related jobs, but the wild and scenic river idea seemed to balance recreational jobs and preservation.[18]

Other conservationists such as Ramone Eaton also acted on behalf of the Chattooga's watershed. Eaton—a pioneer in southeastern boating culture, a former Atlanta educator, and then an American Red Cross executive in Washington, D.C.—reminded Greenville, S.C., attorney C. Thomas Wyche in 1967, "You may remember that the Toxaway Gorge area was lost to the Duke Power [Company's dams and reservoirs] because of the complete indifference of the South Carolina citizenry."[19] Wyche also encouraged Congressman Dorn and counterpart Senator Ernest F. Hollings (D) to support inclusion of the Chattooga in the 1968 Wild and Scenic Rivers Act because, he feared, "too often South Carolina does not have a voice in matters of this sort simply because there is no organized group in this area that has any interest in such things and we let matters of this sort go by default."[20] Brown, Eaton, and Wyche recognized that the Chattooga, unlike the downstream Savannah River, where two hydroelectric dams had come online between 1954 and 1962, could remain wild and dam-free. The unimproved Chattooga's scenic attributes, exemplary whitewater, and lack of development perfectly fit the specifications of the national wild, scenic, and recreational rivers policy promoted by the Craighead brothers in the 1950s.

The Chattooga River's 1968 designation as a study river fits well within the larger national process that produced the Wild and Scenic Rivers Act. River advocate Tim Palmer has written extensively about the U.S. river and conservation movement and how national dam planning and construction initiated in the 1920s slowed during the Great Depression only to resume with intensity in the 1950s. These public water development programs typically placed secondary emphasis on recreation, water quality, and the free-flowing rivers Eaton and Wyche valued. The existing wild and scenic river narrative also follows wilderness crusaders who were against dams and "for a river," as the famous environmentalist and former Sierra Club executive David Brower once said.[21] In this contest, the Chattooga's story closely paralleled the nation's other wild and scenic river stories. Many Sun Belt countryside conservationists and environmentalists organized and challenged river development at places like Trotters Shoals on the Savannah, in North Carolina's upper French Broad River valley, and along the New River in southwestern Virginia. They all spoke on behalf of "their" river or rallied to protect unique landscapes. Sun Belt Georgians and South Carolinians who spoke for the Chattooga River in the 1960s and 1970s had much in common with other countryside conservationists and environmentalists in their own regions and around the country.

In Georgia, two institutions established in the 1960s reveal how Sun Belt residents cultivated cooperative relationships with corporate and federal agents to reshape the balance of water and power. These countryside conservationists utilized state agencies, grassroots initiatives, and scientific expertise to speak for a wild and scenic Chattooga River. The Georgia General Assembly established the first institution—the Georgia Natural Areas Council—in 1966 to survey the state's rare and valuable plant and animal species, "or any other natural features of outstanding scenic or geological value."[22] Georgia State University ecologist and trout fisherman Dr. Charles Wharton drafted the council's founding legislation, which freshman state senator and future governor Zell Miller introduced.[23] The council, composed of eight members selected from four state agencies and four Georgia institutions of higher learning, possessed no explicit regulatory or direct management authority over natural resources and served primarily in an advisory capacity to the state. Robert Hanie, the council's first executive director and a recipient of multiple Emory University degrees, collaborated with state resource managers and university scientists like Wharton and Eugene P. Odum to make recommendations on what "natural areas" the state should consider protecting. Hanie maintained a skeleton staff of volunteers and academic scientists who also developed policy and legislative tools such as the Georgia Scenic Rivers Act (1969).[24]

If the Georgia Natural Areas Council championed the Chattooga River as a prime example of a *state* natural area worthy of protection, a second institution, the Georgia Conservancy, molded opinion on behalf of the river as an irreplaceable *national* resource. The Georgia Conservancy played an important role as a mechanism for change during the Chattooga's wild and scenic river study phase and campaign. James A. Mackay—a former City of Decatur legislator and member of Congress—served as the founding president for the Atlanta-based nonprofit Georgia Conservancy in 1967, an organization modeled after the Western Pennsylvania Conservancy (established in 1932) and the nationally oriented Nature Conservancy (1951).[25] The Georgia Conservancy was primarily an advocacy and educational organization, and though the organization did purchase land—the first such deal involved Panola Mountain, which is now a Georgia state park—land acquisition was not a primary objective. Members considered the conservancy a "purposeful organization" dedicated to active participation in the democratic process, but a cadre of former members established a splinter group in favor of aggressive lobbying tactics, shedding corporate influence,

and improving organizational strategy.[26] The Conservancy's members—
most of whom were white, affluent, and well-educated "businessmen,
housewives, scientists, teachers, artists, naturalists, sportsmen, botanists,
students, and young people"—gathered every fourth Saturday to explore
their state's wild, scenic, and recreational areas.[27] The conservancy promised to provide "members a living awareness" of given ecological problems
"by conducting field trips to natural areas," including a well-attended mid-
1967 outing to the Chattooga River. In the Chattooga's case, the conservancy teamed up with the Georgia Canoe Association (established in 1966)
on more than one occasion to sponsor canoe and hiking trips for members
and the general public, as well as state and federal officials. The Georgia
Conservancy's and the Georgia Natural Areas Council's members provided
advice, expertise, and resources to keep the Chattooga free of hydroelectric
dams and commercial development and, more importantly, running wild
for all to enjoy.[28]

The Georgia Conservancy and Georgia Natural Areas Council shared
members, executive officers, and scientific experts who likewise influenced
the way people understood regional environments. These organizations
also influenced the relationship between southern water and southern
power in a democratic society managed by narrowly focused special interests. For example, Robert Hanie organized a "Chattooga River Seminar"
at the Dillard House in Dillard, Georgia, in November 1968, two months
after the National Wild and Scenic Rivers Act declared the Chattooga an
official study river. He pulled together bureaucrats and special interest
groups, including forty representatives from the Forest Service, the Bureau of Outdoor Recreation, and state development organizations, and
resource managers from three states to discuss how they might collectively
shift the Chattooga from study river to wild and scenic river. Lynn Hill,
the Georgia Conservancy's director, and William Dunlap, assistant to
the president of the Georgia Power Company, also attended the meeting.
Dunlap, a longtime executive with the company, frequently paddled the
Chattooga's whitewater, and his respect for the conservation community
and his relationship with the company made him a valuable member of
the river lobby in the late 1960s.[29] This November meeting initiated a collaborative and cooperative coalition between federal and state bureaucrats
and public and private interest groups who would continue to speak for
Georgia's environment well into the future.[30]

The Georgia Power Company was one of those interests. Long a player
in state water and energy issues, Georgia Power was a major and unique

actor in the Chattooga River's story. Beginning in the 1920s, the company had acquired approximately 37 percent of the property (5,690 acres) necessary for the Chattooga's fifty-mile-long and approximately three-mile-wide protective wild and scenic river corridor; the National Forest Service owned the majority of the remaining property.[31] The New South company intended to build a series of hydroelectric dams and replicate the Tallulah-Tugaloo project. But a chronology of factors—including the public-private power debates over Muscle Shoals during and after World War I, the 1925 regional drought and subsequent shift to coal-fired generation, a lack of capital during the Great Depression, and the post-1945 development of civilian atomic energy technology—led Sun Belt Georgia Power executives to forgo developing five potential hydropower sites along the Chattooga.[32] By the late 1960s, the fast-growing company became embroiled in a racial discrimination suit and feared competition as other energy companies such as Duke Power also invested in nuclear energy. To further muddy the company's public face, Georgia Power encountered customer resistance to a proposed rate increase to finance future power projects—including Plant Hatch's twin nuclear reactors on the Altamaha River (construction began in 1968) and Plant Bowen's four coal-burning units on the Etowah River (1971)—while simultaneously reporting high revenues and profits.[33] In light of these challenges, and after over half a century of landownership in the Chattooga watershed, the Georgia Power Company looked for a way out in 1968. Anticipating the Wild and Scenic Rivers Act's passage, a Georgia Power Company spokesman announced that the company would "be most willing in the matter of land ownership to cooperate with groups interested in the Chattooga River," and that the company did not intend to develop the river's hydropower potential because such projects were "marginal from the economic view point."[34] With this decision, a wild river's greatest enemy in the 1960s—the dam builders—backed away from the Chattooga during a national energy regime transition.

The wild and scenic river process presented Georgia Power with an extraordinary opportunity to extract itself from the Chattooga watershed. The situation provided the company with a chance to swap its Chattooga land with Forest Service property adjacent to the company's Tugaloo Lake and the inundated Tugaloo River. This combined land purchase and exchange signified that the Chattooga land held little value for the company; indeed, it may have actually represented a liability from the perspective of management and state tax payments.[35] The Tugaloo land, on the other hand, increased and consolidated the company's land holdings in a recreational and leisure waterscape owned primarily by Georgia Power. The cooperative relationship between Georgia Power and the Forest Service served very narrow recreational ends, on one hand. The swap also protected a unique river and provided additional ecological and community benefits as envisioned by the Craighead brothers.

However, this network of private businesses, public officials, and environmental stakeholders included few full-time Rabun County (Ga.) and Oconee County (S.C.) residents. Both counties were in the midst of striking economic shifts, and these Sun Belt transformations only intensified after 1970. Rabun County experienced a nominal population increase of just over 900 people between 1960 and 1970, when it had a total population of about 8,300 people. The 370-square-mile county's shift from agricultural and forestry employment was more significant; the county lost more than 175 positions and witnessed a corresponding increase of nearly 500 manufacturing positions, primarily in the "textiles and fabricated textiles" sectors.[36] On the South Carolina side of the Chattooga River, the nearly five times more populous Oconee County (over 40,000 residents) grew much more slowly. But Oconee (650 square miles) gained more than 2,000 manufacturing positions while losing over 1,000 agriculture-related jobs. In these Sun Belt demographic shifts, the Chattooga River was an excellent retreat for a large body of nonagricultural employees in two states who lived within sixty miles of the river and may have already enjoyed this recreation destination. Rabun and Oconee County residents found themselves increasingly tied to time clocks that not only kept track of hours worked but also limited their recreational time in easily accessible southern Appalachian recreation commons like the lightly managed Chattooga River corridor.

Rabun and Oconee residents participated in discussions pertaining to the Chattooga's federal designation to varying degrees. The "locals" who had long visited the river to fish or socialize or for other community uses had been described by wild and scenic river advocates as nonparticipants in the many private or public discussions about the river's future. One nonparticipant, John Ridley, grew up on the Chattooga's South Carolina bank, just upriver from the Highway 28 bridge; he attended Clemson University in 1961, where he received a horticulture degree. According to him, South Carolina and Georgia locals who had lived near the river did not participate in the process for two reasons.[37] First, there was limited communication between folks who lived along the river and those who lived in Walhalla, Oconee's county seat. As an illustration of this disconnect, his family never had a phone and did not receive electricity until 1952, despite the Southeast's extensive electrical generation and transmission system. Their neighbors—the Russells—obtained the first community phone connection in 1968 before selling their property to the Forest Service in 1970.[38] Second, Ridley interpreted the Chattooga's transformation in a larger historical context of southern Appalachian community reaction to Forest Service policy. The Forest Service's history of land condemnations in Georgia and South Carolina dating back to 1915 had left an impression with local residents that when the Forest Service threatened to condemn property, little could be done to stop the process. This early fear likely dated back to the Forest Service's condemnation of thousands of acres of private property when it began to acquire land under the auspices of watershed protection and the Weeks Act (1911).[39] It is worth noting that the Wild and Scenic Rivers Act (1968) made land condemnation for river corridors very difficult, but land adjacent to and outside the future corridor—including in-holdings—was indeed condemned.[40] Given this context, local people "did not think they could do anything or did not know about the process," in Ridley's opinion. Furthermore, farming families like his, who lived along the river before moving out in 1970, "lost interest after losing their land." These families may have chosen not to participate, but that did not mean they did not care about the river. Ridley believed the "locals knew they took better care of the river" and that the "general public doesn't take care of the property." He also claimed that today's visitors from outside the region—mostly raft, kayak, and canoe recreationists—leave their trash along a river that once provided his family with trout.[41]

Ridley was not alone in the opinion that local residents who cared about the Chattooga did not vocalize significant opposition to the river's designation. Newspaper editors and their coverage on both sides of the river portrayed the initial wild and scenic river designation process as a love fest, with one paper noting "almost no opposition" at advertised public "listening sessions" as the study process kicked off in 1968.[42]

But beginning in 1969, conservation-minded critics—particularly from South Carolina—warned the Forest Service officials facilitating study sessions and public hearings that designating the Chattooga a wild and scenic river would require users, including local residents and outside visitors, to adjust their behavior within the protected river corridor.[43] Attention to planned road and trail closures on the South Carolina side of the river, as well as potential restrictions on hunting and fishing access, occupied more than passing conversation at a Clemson meeting and foreshadowed future points of contention.[44] Tension flared at yet another Chattooga-related public meeting when a lawyer from Greenville—a South Carolina city located about sixty-five miles east of the river—attacked the Forest Service's clear-cutting policy, only to be rebuffed by resident loggers in the audience who responded that clear-cutting operations improved the forest's health and provided jobs for South Carolinians. These South Carolina meeting participants—countryside conservationists to varying degrees—clearly identified the river as a local leisure and labor landscape and worried that the river's official designation might result in reduced recreational access or a loss of forestry-related jobs in the face of increasingly centralized federal authority.[45]

River enthusiasts from Atlanta to Greenville, however, envisioned the river primarily as a leisure waterscape for nearby Sun Belt residents. Members of the Georgia Conservancy, paddlers from the Georgia Canoe Association, Georgia Power employees, and the Sierra Club's Joseph LeConte Chapter formed a coalition. Private interests that cast themselves as publicly minded—such as the Georgia Conservancy—spoke for more privileged local and nonlocal folks.[46] For example, conservancy member Fritz Orr Jr. lived part-time in Atlanta, and North Carolinian Frank Bell spoke before Congress in support of the river.[47] Orr and Bell, both pathbreaking southern paddlers, also owned and operated summer camps that utilized the Chattooga's headwaters. The network was indeed deep: One of Orr's Atlanta neighbors was Georgia Power executive Harlee Branch Jr.[48] These nonlocal advocates were not the only river enthusiasts. Greenville attorney Ted Snyder, who grew up in Walhalla, twenty miles east of the Chattooga, had spent time on the river as a young adult and understood that the Chattooga represented the last of its kind in the mountain South. He spoke for the river on behalf of the local Sierra Club chapter and before congressional committees in Washington, D.C., as a Walhalla transplant living in Greenville.[49]

The Chattooga also had attentive friends in Washington who learned about the river's value and popularity. In mid-1973, Congressmen Roy A. Taylor (D-N.C.), William Jennings Bryan Dorn (D-S.C.), James R. Mann (D-S.C.), and Phil Landrum (D-Ga.) cosponsored a bill to add the Chattooga River to the official list of wild and scenic rivers.[50] This was in response to the favorable Forest Service staff report titled *A Proposal: The Chattooga, "A Wild and Scenic River"* (1970).[51] This legislation sparked a congressional hearing process, and Dr. Claude Terry—an Emory University microbiologist, avid whitewater boater, and Georgia Conservancy spokesman—testified before a subcommittee charged with hearing public input on the Chattooga's wild and scenic status in late 1973. Terry followed standard discourse on the need for balanced water management and declared, "Using a river for power production, building industries or homes along its bank or in its flood plains . . . are all consumptive uses which damage or destroy the stream itself."[52] The Georgia Canoe Association's Cleve Tedford echoed concerns over development on southern rivers while shifting his focus during the hearing: "If the watershed of the Chattooga is not protected, then many of the values for which the wild and scenic river is cherished will vanish even though the stream bed and banks are preserved." He expanded the discussion of river protection in language not unlike John and Frank Craighead's back in the 1950s, and Tedford distinguished between river protection and watershed protection in an effort to push his congressional audience in the direction of the latter.[53] He tapped into a growing ecological systems theory expressed by scientists like Terry but more clearly articulated by University of Georgia ecologist Eugene Odum, who viewed whole watersheds and activity on the land above the riverbank as more valuable and influential than protection of individual streams or rivers. Terry and Tedford presented persuasive arguments to shift the Chattooga from a study river to a wild and scenic river. They also got some help from Georgia governor Jimmy Carter, who had paddled the Chattooga not just once but multiple times. And Carter, an evolving countryside conservationist who would put a stop to Flint River dams, proved to be instrumental in lobbying congressional committees on the Georgia Conservancy's behalf.[54]

South Carolina's and Georgia's congressional delegations also spoke for their constituencies in less scientific terms to support free-flowing rivers. James R. Mann (1920–2010), a five-term (1968–78) congressman from Greenville most well known for his drafting of President Richard Nixon's articles of impeachment, recalled recreating on the riverbanks "since [his] earliest years as a school boy." Senator Herman E. Talmadge (1913–2002) described the Chattooga as a "primitive, free flowing river" that offered excellent recreational values. Talmadge's junior counterpart, first-term senator Sam Nunn (D-Ga.), painted a slightly different picture and worried that visiting crowds threatened the Chattooga's recreational integrity. In Nunn's opinion such overuse and impact justified federal management and "development of the proper facilities."[55] Each of these spokesmen communicated important reasons for maintaining a Wild and Scenic Chattooga River as one solution for the Sun Belt's water challenges. Their interests in balancing the old policy of constructing dams, preserving wild watersheds, and maintaining watershed integrity joined two other major foundational aspects of the Wild and Scenic Rivers Act—recreation and ecological restoration—as intended by the act's authors, the Craighead brothers. The act did not specifically use ecological terminology but stated that "each component of the national wild and scenic rivers system shall be administered in such manner as to protect and *enhance*" the characteristics that contributed to a river's inclusion in the national system.[56] To enhance implies some degree of improvement or a landscape in need of hands-on management after centuries of human activity. The Chattooga indeed had been worked over by the lumber industry at the beginning of the twentieth century and was not the primitive wilderness many supporters claimed. But in the case of the Chattooga River, Senator Nunn and natural resource agency staffers were less interested in watershed protection and more interested in hands-on management to deal with the hordes of inexperienced paddlers who soon descended upon the river. Recreation—at the expense of ecological restoration—became a central part of the Chattooga's story, but not necessarily in the "educational and spiritual" sense expressed by the Wild and Scenic River Act's authors.[57] The river's popularity was a problem in and of itself.

The book and film versions of James Dickey's *Deliverance* help explain the role recreation played in pushing the Chattooga from study river to wild and scenic river in 1974 and why the forest burned in 1976. Dickey's novel (1970) and his subsequent screen adaptation (1972) introduced the country to the stunning and adrenaline-pumping Chattooga River. The basic story followed the epic trials of four suburban Atlanta professionals who floated the fictional Cahulawasee River before a hydroelectric dam and reservoir drowned the wild river forever. The film opened with construction images of Duke Power Company's Jocassee dam (one component of the Keowee-Toxaway hydronuclear project) as a stand-in for the fictional Cahulawasee's dam. Lewis, played by Burt Reynolds, intoned in an opening voice-over that the Cahulawasee was "just about the last wild, untamed, unpolluted, unfucked-up river in the South."[58] Dickey effectively communicated his opinion about special rivers like the Chattooga, and his narrative revealed the risky transformative powers that a wild South could bestow on people disconnected from nature. As the soft, inexperienced, and domesticated Sun Belt suburbanites descended an increasingly chaotic river, one member of the party was raped by a woodsman, two others committed murder, and a third drowned after the party "voted" to bury the first casualty without notifying the authorities. In the process of commenting on modernization's dulling effect on individual freedom and the perilous consequences of wilderness exposure, Dickey's screenplay also reinforced negative Appalachian stereotypes about a land of dueling banjos and backward mountain people.[59] But despite the dark tale of male rape and murder on the Cahulawasee that leaves today's campers apprehensive about spending a night in the watershed, the wild and raging riverscape on the big screen attracted thousands to the real Chattooga River.

In 1971, the year before the *Deliverance* film was released, the Forest Service estimated that 800 people visited the river annually. During the wild and scenic river study process, one Georgia State Game and Fish staffer commented on visitor projections, and he worried that a "loss of space and tranquility due to use by excessive numbers of people" was among the "greatest" dangers "on this river." Furthermore, Claude Hastings believed that improved access to the river would actually invite recreational conflict between experienced and inexperienced river users.[60] Time would prove Hastings right. Many of these early visitors undoubtedly learned about the unmanaged river from local and regional newspapers such as the *Atlanta Journal Constitution*. Others discovered the river via a network of paddlers and national boating journals like *American Whitewater*, which published two Chattooga boating guides prior to the river's wild and scenic designation.[61] The first generation of southern paddlers—including Fritz Orr Sr., Ramone Eaton, Randy Carter, Hugh Caldwell, and Frank Bell—had also introduced new boaters to the river as early as the 1950s. Many of these men either owned or worked for summer camps, such as Merrie-Wood and Camp Mondamin, in the southern Appalachians. This older generation initiated succeeding generations of paddlers—including Payson Kennedy, Fritz Orr Jr., Claude Terry, and Doug Woodward—to southern rivers, and they in turn established the most prolific guiding businesses of the 1970s that still operate today: the Nantahala Outdoor Center (Kennedy) and Southeastern Expeditions (Terry and Woodward).[62] The film, however, introduced the river to a much larger and more inexperienced throng of leisure and thrill seekers. After *Deliverance* popularized the Chattooga's wild rapids—with Terry, Woodward, and Kennedy hired as body-paddler-doubles for Jon Voight and Ned Beatty—river visitation jumped to an estimated 21,000 visitors in 1973.[63] The movie infected would-be paddlers with a "Deliverance Syndrome" that led many to their deaths, according to Terry.[64]

Recreation, risk, and tragedy nudged the Chattooga closer to formal wild and scenic river designation. According to a *Georgia Outdoors* writer, the movie spawned traffic jams "and all but choked every access point; the river filled with jaunty adventurers in varied vessels—in kayaks and canoes, in rafts and rickety inflatable contraptions—each seeking in one way or another to prove himself (or herself)" equal to star Jon Voight or the other lead superstar. On screen, Burt Reynolds was the movie's wet-suit-clad, cigar-smoking, bow-hunting-survivalist, and whitewater-paddling embodiment of 1970s masculinity. The Chattooga's popularity, however, led to an increased number of recreation-related fatalities on the river. The banks "echoed the calls of search parties seeking the remains of those whose carelessness or naiveté proved terribly expensive," according to T. Craig Martin.[65] Some whitewater guide companies, including Claude Terry's newly established Southeastern Expeditions, and other paddling clubs had formed explicitly to provide visitors with a safe introduction to the river. But not all river-runners sought guides or advice, and the mounting recreational dangers and a proliferation of guide services ultimately contributed to the river's use, abuse, and upgrade from study river to full wild and scenic river. In response to the hordes and persistent lobbying by advocates and agency staff, in May 1974 the Chattooga Wild and Scenic River became an official component to the national system of protected rivers. And with congressional authorization, the Forest Service deployed river ranger staff and instituted a permit system to better manage guide companies and individual river-runners.[66]

Saving the Chattooga in the 1970s—made possible by the combined efforts of the Forest Service, the Georgia Power Company, and new environmental institutions—was clearly not entirely about saving wilderness. When the river was officially folded into the National Wild and Scenic River system in May 1974, the end of the designation chapter signaled a general agreement over the river's unique qualities. But the management chapter chronicled the deteriorating relationship between the river corridor's users and managers. The public and private network that shifted the Chattooga from a study river to a wild and scenic river did so in a self-contained manner that increasingly alienated a body of local river enthusiasts. According to Max Gates, the first official Chattooga Wild and Scenic River ranger, "mostly outsiders" supported the river's designation. The former Sumter National Forest (S.C.) land manager explained that the Forest Service sponsored multiple, well-advertised public meetings in three counties in the three states adjacent to the Chattooga River before 1970, as well as additional meetings after 1974.[67] But apparently only a "few locals" from North Carolina, South Carolina, or Georgia attended. Furthermore, the Forest Service had solicited comments from the newspaper-reading public before 1971 and received more than 1,000 responses supporting the designation, with only three outright dissents.[68] While Gates may have exaggerated the lack of local participation, he adequately described the conflict that emerged after designation as a result of a "clash of classes," or a clash between the local folks who preferred the ease of recreating on the banks and the growing number of visitors intent on traveling the whole corridor's length on the river's back.[69]

As Georgians and South Carolinians moved through the Chattooga Wild and Scenic River designation process in 1974, they took part in a much larger regional discussion about public land management. For example, at the time the Forest Service was revising national policy in the late 1960s and early 1970s. That topic is beyond this book's scope, but it is sufficient to say that the Forest Service was in the midst of reshaping national forest management policy in an effort to balance even-aged timber management—also referred to as clear-cutting—with recreation, wildlife, and biological diversity.[70] Nobody liked clear-cutting, according to Max Gates, and some local forest users chastised Forest Service officials for cutting hardwood trees that produced nuts. Game hunters and anglers in particular thought clear-cutting was bad for squirrel populations and fish. Indeed, Forest Service public relations specialists published regular columns in local newspapers in an attempt to convince Rabun County residents that forest management and clear-cutting improved conditions for wildlife. The Forest Service also provided locals with access to free firewood for personal consumption.[71] But in the end, and in Gates's opinion, local people resisted anything that disrupted the "way of life" in what they considered their forest community, despite the fact that many of the river's recreational spots had historically rested on Georgia Power's private property or public land.[72] Or more plausibly, as historian Kathryn Newfont has observed in other southern Appalachian communities, rural and mountain residents understood the forests and rivers as places "to live rather than to visit." For people who lived close to the Chattooga River, the valley was a space for baptisms, picnics, and relaxation; it was undoubtedly "a part of the fabric of everyday life rather than a retreat from the ordinary."[73]

In the larger federal policy context, the southern Appalachians also became a battleground in the 1960s and 1970s as repeated intrusion by external interests threatened the composition of mountain communities. Not only did outsiders move in, buy second homes, and erect "No Trespassing" signs, but federal policy also imposed restrictions on public and private land use. New policies included declarations of eminent domain to acquire Appalachian Trail lands (National Trails System Act [1968]); the creation of eastern wilderness areas (Roadless Area Review and Evaluation I [1972] and the Eastern Wilderness Act [1975]); and a proposed extension of the Blue Ridge Parkway along Georgia's ridgelines.[74] Furthermore, at the time of the Chattooga's full wild and scenic river designation in 1974, parcels of South Carolina's public land near the river—such as Ellicott's Rock and more than 37,000 acres in the Chauga watershed— were under consideration for wilderness and roadless designations. In both cases these federal designations would have eliminated logging and forestry jobs in those specific areas, a point articulated by local wilderness opponents as early as 1971.[75] Against this backdrop, Rabun County (Ga.) and Oconee County (S.C.) communities thought they were besieged by the federal government's reach into the mountain landscape. In response to these encroachments, residents on both sides of the Chattooga River began to vent their frustrations over increasingly restrictive land management policy that dated back to the Weeks Act (1911), when the Forest Service began acquiring property in the southern Appalachians, but that now centered on the Chattooga's 1974 designation as a wild and scenic river.

No other issue sparked greater confrontation in the Chattooga region than the Forest Service's October 1974 decision to close roads that crossed Forest Service land and entered the Chattooga's new wild and scenic river corridor.[76] Under the terms of the Wild and Scenic River Act (1968), river sections designated as "wild" were supposed to be "generally *inaccessible except by trail.*" Scenic and recreational sections could be "*accessible in places by roads.*"[77] The Chattooga's wild and scenic corridor—or the distance between the riverbank and the corridor boundary—was rarely more than one-quarter mile wide, and the corridor itself was generally surrounded by thousands of acres of Forest Service land. Chattooga River study personnel intent on meeting the designation standards first introduced the idea to close corridor roads and selected foot trails in 1969 and immediately encountered resistance from state fish and game managers who were concerned about how they would reach the river to restock fish or check hunting licenses. And in 1971 the Forest Service proposed closing up to thirty miles of roads.[78] Despite the expressed concerns, Oconee County (S.C.) commissioners eventually transferred all the required road rights-of-way to the Forest Service prior to 1974, but their Rabun County (Ga.) counterparts did not. As early as 1972 the Rabun County commissioners had begun to hear arguments from both the Forest Service's Max Gates and county residents on the issue of future road closures.[79] By October 1974, Chattahoochee National Forest (Ga.) supervisor William Patrick Thomas facilitated a localized and back-channel road-closure agreement between Rabun County commissioners and Chattooga's wild and scenic river managers. Georgia senator Herman Talmadge, chairman of the Senate Committee on Agriculture and Forestry who was embarking on his fourth and last term (1956–80), helped Thomas and Rabun County commissioners broker a deal that closed some state and country roads while keeping others open in spite of the Wild and Scenic Rivers Act's requirements.[80] Plus, the Forest Service maintained three bridge crossings—including one U.S. highway, one state road, and one Forest Service road—within the protected river corridor for management and logistical reasons. Many longtime forest users, however, did not understand the uneven road closure policy.

After 1974, Forest Service managers continually used a public safety argument to justify the selective road closures in Georgia and South Carolina. In light of the high fatality rates and drowning incidents that resulted from the popularity of *Deliverance*, Forest Service personnel wanted to limit easy access to the river's dangerous sections where visiting hikers and swimmers might (and did) get swept over rapids or pinned by the river's current. Most of the local users did not float the river, but they had used the old roads to access favorite campsites, swimming spots, and picnic areas. Or as former Forest Service recreation planner Charlie Huppuch recalled, people would drive vehicles into the Chattooga River and wash them.[81] When the Forest Service finally gated roads after 1974, most trout fishermen faced less than a one-mile walk "to their favorite holes."[82] These restrictions and user policies did coincide with the river's evolution from a site of local leisure to a regional and national destination for select visitors or well-equipped river-runners. Despite the Forest Service's and local newspapers' attempts to explain the road closures before and after the fact, local residents who may not have chosen to participate in the designation process responded to what they interpreted as a continued loss of local control and traditional access rights to the river.

"Retro Frontiersmen," as defined by the late Jack Temple Kirby, who had watched individuals, corporations, and federal agencies close the "open range" and enclose resources once considered freely accessible for generations, turned to an old tool and instrument of protest. The forest fires that raged between 1974 and 1978, according to one local historian, were arsonists' responses to the Chattooga's final designation as a wild and scenic river.[83] Arson as a form of protest was certainly not new to the Chattooga River's valley. In early 1972, two men and one woman were caught "setting woods fires" in the Warwoman Dell Wildlife Management Area.[84] Wet conditions, however, thwarted attempted arson in the spring and fall of 1975, but drier conditions in February 1976 contributed to more than fifty fires that burned 800 acres on a single weekend in Georgia's Rabun County. Chattahoochee Forest Service supervisor Thomas attributed the arson to a "fire-style protest of state and federal restrictions" by a minority of "angry mountaineers" deprived of access and "exiled" from the Chattooga River corridor. But he also linked the fire-style protest to the past, dating to 1911, "when the Forest Service began regulating timber cutting, closing access to protect rivers and blocking off old logging roads." In the course of two short months during 1976, Georgia's Chattahoochee National Forest lost 3,800 acres to fire in three counties—approximately as much forest burned in sixty days as had been burned in the previous two years—all in part of the larger local reaction to forest policy and federal intrusion throughout the mountain region in the 1970s.[85] According to another source, between 1969 and 1973, South Carolina's Andrew Pickens Ranger District—which the Chattooga River borders—incurred a yearly average of five fires with 18 acres burned. But in the five-year period between 1974 and 1979, twenty-three fires burned an average of 687 acres in the same district.[86] After 1974, South Carolina and Georgia residents—initially respectful of the local recreational commons—assumed similar tactics to protest forest policy in Sumter and Chattahoochee National Forests, with residents displaying signs proclaiming: "You put it in wilderness and we'll put it in ASHES."[87]

Arson in the Chattooga River's corridor represented latent protest against turning a local recreational commons into a federal recreational commons. It is important to remember that in the Chattooga's case, the Forest Service did not "take" private land from unwilling sellers by declaring eminent domain; the Wild and Scenic Rivers Act made this tactic extremely difficult to implement but never impossible to threaten. Prior to the road closures, Georgia Power and the Forest Service already held title to 84 percent of the proposed wild and scenic river corridor, including some roads, and theoretically controlled access to existing informal campsites, swimming spots, and fishing holes.[88] But after 1974, the conflict between insiders and outsiders, and between privileged locals and nonlocals, materialized over the issue of what constituted appropriate recreation in Georgia's and South Carolina's expanding and popular national forests.

The Wild and Scenic Rivers Act (1968) was a useful instrument for Sun Belt citizens who pushed back and against a half-century of the modern hydraulic waterscape's assembly. The network of public and private ambassadors from the Georgia Power Company, the Georgia Natural Areas Council, the Georgia Conservancy, and the Forest Service participated in local and national hearings, communicated with elected officials, and mobilized a grassroots constituency to achieve a specific end. These parties—the "someone" Patrick Thomas identified as responsible for "taking away access" to the Chattooga—justified the river's federal protection on post-*Deliverance* safety concerns, but more importantly because the Chattooga was, in fact, the last major undammed river surrounded by a sea of reservoirs in the mountain Sun Belt.[89]

The process also did not accommodate all local recreational realities and elicited a response that left the woods burning when the river corridor became a linear recreation space that catered to national and nonlocal consumers. Initially a fragmented local landscape composed of fishing holes and camping spots, the Chattooga became a unified wild and scenic river with clear start and end points for paddlers and boaters that visually muted the older intermediate recreation spaces. The Forest Service closed roads to secret spots and campsites and transformed fishing trails along the river's edge into hiking trails on parallel ridgelines. This imperfect process maintained a wild and free-flowing river, but some local users lost a perceived freedom to access the river. While the Chattooga River's story highlights how a private and public coalition transformed a local commons into a federal commons, the story also illustrates that the conflict did not revolve around *whether* the river should have been conserved but over *how* this federally managed and unique river would be used and by whom.

New South, New Deal, and Sun Belt economic interests had attempted to resolve the region's water and energy challenges with canals, dams, reservoirs, levees, and deeper channels. Private and public engineers changed rivers' shapes, forms, and functions to cope with problematic flooding and drought. Another coalition of postwar southerners reevaluated those old supply solutions to the region's water problems and moved in a completely different direction. Like allies around the nation, the Sun Belt's countryside conservationists and environmentalists thought dams and river structures *were the problems* and not the solutions. For these engaged activists, the Wild and Scenic Chattooga River solved a new problem: In a region that lacked significant free-flowing rivers, the Chattooga's new designation broke with the past and illustrated a new relationship between southern water and southern power.

Author John Lane has described his personal Chattooga experiences to illustrate why the river attracts people and what the river delivers to those who know and use it today. As a nature writer, Lane tapped into what people have taken from and what expectations people have of the river shed, including water quality concerns of longtime headwaters residents; observations of the riverscape by literary and academic visitors; backcountry experiences sought by backpackers; and the ambivalence of the residents of Clayton, Georgia, over the impact of *Deliverance* on their community. Ultimately, he interprets the southern landscape as sublime on its own terms, in terms that Rabun and Oconee County residents from yesterday and today would agree with, including those residents who continue to believe the river was taken from them.[90] Bearing Lane's context in mind, we should remember that in the end, through a series of choices in a century of energy regime transformation, the spectacular Chattooga River, the star of *Deliverance*, was consciously left wild, or at least undammed by the Georgia Power Company and the U.S. Army Corps of Engineers, and was delivered to the national whitewater boating and environmental community for safekeeping.

Water and Power

As 2012 came to a close after two dry years, many Georgia water watchers thought the region was poised to return to the dry years of 2007 and 2008. Reservoir levels dropped, and farmers worried once again about the next growing season. According to the U.S. Drought Monitor, 65 percent of Georgia was somewhere between "severe" and "exceptional" drought in January 2013. Then the rains came much as they had in 2009 after three years of drought. By late April 2013, the drought was officially over—and yet the rains kept coming. In the first six months of 2013, more rain had fallen in many Georgia communities, including the metro Atlanta region, than had dropped from the clouds in all of 2012.

There were consequences of extreme "weather whiplash"—a term coined by climate science writer Andrew Freedman—from drought to flood. A number of earthen dams, some dating back to the 1930s, failed along the Ogeechee River and upstream of Lake Lanier in the Chattahoochee River basin. No lives were lost, but sediment flushed downstream and washed out roads. In the Savannah River basin, the Corps' three major lakes refilled and began releasing water from flood storage. Neighborhood creeks, community parks and boat ramps, and homes in the Augusta area flooded before and during the subsequent dam releases. And the rain kept falling throughout the summer, leaving many farmers with flooded fields and an expectation for lower yields come harvesttime. Dams, reservoirs, levees, and ponds built long ago worked double-time throughout the drought-flood whiplash period—storing water for consumption, managing floodwaters, and generating electricity—much as they have during past whiplash events.[1]

Nearly all of the dams and reservoirs conceived by municipal leaders behind the Augusta Canal and levees, Georgia Power executives at Tallulah Falls, Duke Power's draftsmen in the Carolina upstate, Corps officers in the upper Savannah River valley, U.S. Department of Agriculture

(USDA) Small Watershed Program leaders, and other engineers across the Southeast between the mid-nineteenth and late twentieth centuries continue to operate and function today. The region relies on a vast hydraulic waterscape of artificial lakes, agricultural ponds, working reservoirs, and levees. While this manipulation has replumbed southern waterways to match energy choices and solve water problems, it has also clearly created new problems.

Water and power, topics common in histories of the American West, have been equally intertwined throughout the American South's long environmental history. In the antebellum Old South, energy production and consumption in organic regimes took place where fires burned or at riverside mills and gins. In the middle of the nineteenth century, in parts of the nation described by Henry David Thoreau and John Muir, fishermen with an agrarian past clashed with dam operators, who represented a new economic force. Dreamers also identified electricity as a key to the New South's post–Civil War economic reconstruction and resurrection.

During the late nineteenth and early twentieth centuries, New South energy companies separated energy production and consumption. New transmission and electrical generation technologies—not to mention concentrations of capital—made it possible for factories to slip the restraints of geography. As the organic energy regime evolved, electricity became an invisible power for residential, commercial, and industrial consumers across the nation. This separation—made possible due to transmission lines—increasingly masked white coal's role in Henry Grady's and William Church Whitner's New South economic juggernaut. During the critical New South period, textile mill owners and energy company executives laid claim to the area's rivers and put families to work in factory towns scattered across a Piedmont region cultivated by tenants and sharecroppers.

Divergent visions of the New South's future hardened between the wars. Thomas Martin and William S. Murray considered the privatized Super Power electrical transmission system as a symbol of modernization. They clashed with Rupert Vance and Howard W. Odum, who countered the old water and power dynamic with their own modern liberal economic planning models. The regional planners and New Dealers looked at the monopolistic Super Power system and responded with a big dam consensus, the Tennessee Valley Authority (TVA) experiment, the Rural Electrification Administration, and similar programs designed to use and distribute resources equitably while balancing industry with agriculture. Only after the dramatic droughts of the 1920s did energy generators begin a shift from organic energy sources back to fossil fuels. In the process, the New South abandoned the long quest for an energy regime fueled by renewable and indigenous sources. The New South capitalists initially embraced a diversified energy mix but eventually turned to a system dominated by black coal.

The end of World War II empowered the old independent utility operators. Private energy companies fired back and successfully lobbied against the TVA, but their success emboldened a sleeping giant as water and power continued to drive the Sun Belt's economic and environmental future. After 1945, the U.S. Army Corps of Engineers embarked on a program to build multiple-purpose dams and reservoirs born out of New Deal regional planning but transformed into pork barrel projects. Some of those projects had higher value, while others—such as the Mississippi flood control reservoir William Faulkner lamented—had narrow missions. In this context, the energy corporations found a new enemy in the Corps' public energy mission. The Corps and investor-owned utilities soon squared off in the Savannah River valley. They clashed over who would control water supplies, the necessary ingredient for the organic energy systems the Corps set out to complete and for Duke Power's planned Middleton Shoals (coal) and Keowee-Toxaway (nuclear) generation facilities. Who would get to manage and dictate solutions for Sun Belt water problems—and thus influence commercial development—got increasingly complicated after another major drought in the 1950s.

The private utilities discovered unlikely allies in the postwar environmental and conservative "rights" movements. Some Sun Belt conservatives defended free enterprise and championed freedom from federal intervention in economic matters. Others, who called the Corps' energy and water projects "big dam foolishness," turned to the USDA. The USDA's Small Watershed Program, in some critics' opinions, represented a better and more democratic plan to control water where it fell on the land. Luna Leopold watched the national flood control debate unfold and believed the two federal water control programs worked together in harmony better than one in the absence of the other. Other critics also emerged. Sun Belt countryside conservationists and environmentalists challenged the old corporate and the new federal dam builders. They defended free-flowing watercourses in the Savannah River watershed from pollution and energy development. They organized their local communities, not around the old issues of water quantity and conservation but around water quality. They recognized that free-flowing water and lots of clean water were critical components for emerging Sun Belt commercial and leisure economies. "Locals," particularly those with no political power, no interest in water-skiing, or no desire for whitewater rafting, did not see value in levees, reservoirs, or protected rivers that eliminated existing communities or limited individual behavior. Within this conservative and environmental discourse, the Sun Belt's few wild rivers—such as the Chattooga National Wild and Scenic River, best described by James Dickey's fiction and John Lane's nonfiction—revealed a power to engage communities and empower individuals, for better and worse.

These loosely constructed time periods produced particular projects to meet particular needs or to solve a particular problem—southern, water, or other. As has been clear throughout this book, the hydraulic water-scape tells us three things about southern environmental history. First, water supply solutions have almost always been linked to energy choices. Second, drought history tells us water supply had never been secure, and increasing supplies or controlling floods only represented short-term solutions. Southern droughts have a history, too, and the recent droughts were not one-offs but part of a longer pattern of cycles and weather whiplash. Finally, water will continue to drive the regional political economy as population and an increasing array of economic sectors demand additional water resources. Conflict over water—for energy, economic development, and recreation—is not new.

Given this history, the future of regional water quantity and quality will continue to demand the public's attention and engagement across the modern U.S. South. Today's citizens increasingly ask the region's private and public water and energy managers to operate projects and provide benefits for which they were never designed. The legal tussle over Lake Lanier's official designation as a municipal water supply source during the mid-2000s drought and metro Atlanta's subsequent flooding in 2009, in addition to the Carolinas' settlement in a brief bi-state water war, poignantly demonstrate the persistent nature of the Southeast's water problems and political landscape.[2] Georgians, South Carolinians, and their neighbors have toiled for more than a century to use and control water resources to manage flooding and drought risks. But for all the corporate, state, and citizen investment, the flooding and droughts continue to compromise ever-growing communities, cut into corporate bottom lines, and mold river valleys. Flooding and drought, the so-called natural disasters, have shaped the Southeast's political economy for more than a century and a half. As time has demonstrated, droughts and flooding will return, and these anticipated environmental conditions make our future energy, agricultural, and municipal energy and water choices matter.

Southern energy companies and the Corps continue to define and obscure the relationship between water and power. Energy utilities' authority and vulnerability surfaced dramatically in 2007, just as they had in the 1920s and 1940s. As a stinging drought dried out the region's rivers, including two major river basins embroiled in protracted water wars, representatives from the Southern Company, Duke Energy, Progress Energy, South Carolina Electric and Gas, Santee Cooper, Dominion (Virginia Power), East Kentucky Power Cooperative, PowerSouth Energy Cooperative (Alabama Electric Cooperative), the TVA, the Southeastern Power Administration, the Federal Energy Regulatory Commission, the U.S. Army Corps of Engineers, and the Environmental Protection Agency convened at Atlanta's Hartsfield-Jackson International Airport to discuss "drought in the Southeast and the potential electricity sector impacts." When asked by federal representatives about the drought's anticipated influence on energy generation and utility operations, delegates from the Southern Company responded, "The issue is how much water are we gonna get" from the Corps' five facilities that worked in sequence with the company's fifteen hydroelectric, coal, natural gas, and nuclear generation facilities spread throughout the Apalachicola-Chattahoochee-Flint (ACF) river basin. In other words, the investor-owned company's organic, fossil, and mineral energy regimes wholly depend on the federal government's publicly financed water storage operations at Buford Dam (Lake Lanier) and other Corps hydroelectric, flood control, and navigation projects. Beyond the ACF's example, the major goal for the meeting's private and public representatives remained figuring out how energy utilities—from Alabama to Virginia and from the Carolinas to Kentucky—would continue generating electricity for millions of Americans in the face of diminishing water supplies in all of the region's major river basins. The attendees also controlled what the public would learn; they did not want "any P.R." regarding the meeting.[3]

Messaging is important for any institution. The nation's two largest utility holding companies have a far-flung family of current and former employees who remain close to the region's political structure. Duke Energy (the nation's largest utility) and the Southern Company (and its Alabama Power, Georgia Power, Gulf Power, and Mississippi Power subsidiaries) do more than generate energy for residential, commercial, and industrial consumers. They lobby state capitols and the Capitol in Washington on a variety of issues—environmental legislation, climate change science, federal subsidies for clean energy—by spending millions of dollars every year to enlist super-lobbyists such as Haley Barbour (who was a Southern Company lobbyist before he became Mississippi's governor from 2004 to 2012) to bend the ears of elected representatives and regulators from Mississippi, Alabama, Georgia, and the Carolinas. Southern Company reportedly spent $13 million in 2013 lobbying federal and elected officials.[4] Without cheap and reliable energy sources and unfettered access to water with minimal regulations, the utilities are apt to argue, their home states cannot lure industry and stimulate economic development.

This closeness among the regulators and the regulated community at the energy-water nexus carries significant risk for energy companies and communities. In early 2014, North Carolina governor Pat McCrory—a former Duke Energy executive of almost thirty years who also accepted more than $1.1 million in campaign contributions from the company—was implicated in the state's failure to regulate Duke's thirty coal ash storage ponds after the one pond at a retired steam station failed and sent almost 40,000 tons of ash into the Dan River. Coal ash is generated when coal is burned to boil water and generate steam for electrical production. Coal ash is highly toxic and contains heavy metals. Subsequent coal ash pond investigations at other Duke facilities in North Carolina revealed violations to the federal Clean Water Act as well as state regulations. Furthermore, a federal grand jury has since opened a criminal investigation and subpoenaed Duke's executives and McCrory's agency staff. As one editorialist noted, Duke has not faced this much public or regulatory attention since the 1930s when populists and New Dealers targeted utility monopolies nationwide for their resistance to rural electrification. A full analysis of the coal ash situation in North Carolina is a long way off. What is evident now is how coal ash storage along major southern waterways illustrates the intertwined legacy of water and energy choices and the long-term economic and environmental consequences of those choices for communities tied to southern rivers. Furthermore, the relationship between the regulators and regulated communities needs additional scrutiny and oversight.[5]

In Georgia, water and energy relationships among decision makers are not secret. Two years after the Atlanta airport water and energy meeting in 2007, Governor Sonny Perdue appointed Georgia Power's former CEO Michael Garrett to manage the state's response to Judge Paul Magnuson's decision in 2009 that Lake Lanier was not congressionally authorized as a water supply project (Perdue's chief of staff at the time was also a former

Georgia Power lobbyist).[6] Southern and other investor-owned utilities clearly influence the flow, quality, and availability of water supplies. In Georgia, Southern Company's water footprint includes fifteen fossil fuel and nuclear facilities plus nineteen hydro stations that withdraw water from eight major rivers. One estimate puts Georgia's electrical plant water withdrawals at 3.3 billion gallons per day (Duke's companywide withdrawals may reach 3.9 trillion gallons a year). Thermoelectric (coal and nuclear steam) power plants are the largest water users nationally and withdrew 200 billion gallons of water per day in 2005.[7] While the bulk of the utilities' water "withdrawals" are returned to waterways via once-through (open-loop) cooling systems, millions of gallons are also "consumed" and lost through the evaporative cooling processes (primarily in closed-loop systems). Given the energy sector's water withdrawal and consumption rates, companies like Georgia Power and Duke Energy are in a position to help consumers and policy makers see the critical connection between water security and energy security.

To the company's credit, Georgia Power has begun—after more than a century in the generation business—to systematically analyze water usage. In 2011, the company opened the Water Research Center at its thirty-plus-year-old Plant Bowen on the banks of the Etowah River. What the center will produce for public consumption is unknown at this juncture. Bowen is considered the second-largest generation facility in North America, is one of the top producers of carbon dioxide, and is home to the largest smokestack scrubbers in the world (Bowen was also the site of a coal ash spill in 2002). Now, Bowen engineers and technicians will conduct water withdrawal, consumption, and return rate experiments—and hopefully begin producing full water budgets for all of the company's generation facilities. According to plant manager Tim Banks, "Water is vital for the prosperity of Georgia, and our company wants to continue to contribute to that effort."[8]

Energy companies and major industries across the U.S. South have influenced regional rivers for far longer than any federal or state agency. Georgia Power and its larger corporate utility family depend on fifteen rivers, including the Coosa, Tallapoosa, Chattahoochee, Flint, Apalachicola, Altamaha, and Savannah. The company's vision to stand as "A Citizen Wherever We Serve"—an old motto since 1927—and deliver useful, relevant, and timely research findings pertaining to water usage and quality could help improve public awareness and better inform future energy choices.[9] These private interests continue to play a critical role in shaping the region's water and energy policy, and they will also influence how people interact with and think about southern rivers, electricity, and community health. Energy companies keep the lights on and smartphones powered up so consumers can go about their lives. However, if energy utilities cannot lead the way into a new energy regime that includes less-water-intensive solar and wind sources that can arrest our changing climate, utilities stand to lose more ground before public utility commissions and environmental, conservative, and consumer advocate coalitions.[10]

But who else uses southern water and energy? Following national trends, energy utilities and the agricultural sector share the top two slots as the largest water users. Nationally, all types of agricultural irrigation-water withdrawals amounted to 128 billion gallons per day in 2005, second only to the energy sector.[11] In the Southeast and after the 1950s drought, many people in the agricultural community assumed that enhanced water supply technologies, such as massive Corps reservoirs or USDA-funded farm ponds, would save them in the future. Some farmers adopted irrigation technology in Georgia and Florida after the 1950s drought, but many continued to think irrigated farming was not an economically viable prospect. For example, one agricultural researcher concluded that Florida citrus irrigation was not profitable for growers unless they used irrigation technology systematically and followed proscribed watering schedules. Additionally, portable pipes, pump guns, and groundwater pumps were expensive and labor-intensive to operate and refuel. But by the mid-1960s, irrigation had changed. Florida growers experimented with systematic irrigation systems and were rewarded with improved yields that justified the expense. Furthermore, Florida growers adapted efficiency-minded microsprinkler irrigation systems pioneered in South Africa in the 1970s. Microsprinkler irrigation spread quickly in Florida when growers learned that the systems served dual purposes: Scheduled watering improved yields and provided fruit with frost protection. With these revelations, well-capitalized growers and farmers tapped surface and groundwater supplies to expand irrigated farming throughout the Southeast.[12]

In Georgia, farmers primarily irrigated tobacco and peanuts in the 1950s before increasingly watering cotton, peanuts, and corn. Over time, the geography of irrigation farming spread from southwestern Georgia eastward across the Coastal Plain. By the early 1960s, more than 6,400 Georgia farmers irrigated 110,000 acres of tobacco, corn and other vegetables, orchards, hay, and pastures. This was a significant, fivefold increase; farmers had irrigated approximately 20,000 acres only a decade earlier. To water these expanded crops, landowners relied on streams and groundwater wells, but 66 percent of irrigation water came from farm ponds.[13] As for the technology, in the 1960s, tobacco farmers who irrigated used labor-intensive portable pipe sections and petroleum-fueled pump systems. Soon thereafter in 1967, at least one well-capitalized farmer installed the state's first center-pivot system, a technology imported from the arid Great Plains. Farmers deployed more cable-tow and center-pivot systems, though center-pivot systems carried a hefty price tag of $78,000 to $80,000. Regardless of the system, the number of farmers using irrigation technologies increased by 12 percent after 1970.

Farmers irrigated approximately 975,000 acres of cotton, peanuts, soybeans, pecans, peaches, and sod farms in 1980. To power these systems, most farmers initially relied on diesel- and gasoline-powered pumps before turning to electric systems. According to agricultural research professionals, Georgia had "the fastest rate" of growth in irrigation in the Southeast in the 1980s. Many factors contributed to farmers' shift to irrigation, including increased corn prices, fertilizers, herbicides, pesticides, and center-pivot irrigation technology. Drought in the 1980s, however, was once again paramount among the factors that induced growers to invest in irrigation technology.[14] According to a 2008 survey, growers irrigated about 1.5 million acres in Georgia. Eighty-one percent of that acreage was watered by more than 16,000 center pivots, and corn, cotton, and peanuts constituted 67 percent of all irrigated crops.[15] Energy generation and agriculture production require a tremendous amount of water, but they are not alone.

Nationally, municipal drinking water systems demanded 44 billion gallons of daily water withdrawals in 2005.[16] The Southeast faces a series of energy, agricultural, and population challenges, and the region's water future is tied to Georgia. Atlanta, the South Carolina upstate, Charlotte, and Houston—the Sun Belt's economic powerhouses—have been locked in a regional economic civil war for some time over aquariums, halls of fame, major athletic events, auto plants, national political conventions, and corporate headquarters. When the Great Recession hit, a number observers suggested that Atlanta's competitors had seized the upper hand.[17] The Great Recession did indeed hit metro Atlanta particularly hard in one of the state's foremost commercial sectors: real estate. This major economic blow—and a lack of new utility ratepayers—has in turn rippled into turbulent energy markets shaken by the plummeting cost of natural gas, by conservative activist support for solar generation, and by the flagging nuclear renaissance.[18] But the fate of these two industries ultimately remains linked to another historically contentious issue: water.

If Georgia's political and economic leadership cannot resolve or head off three simmering cross-border conflicts, then the state's water-rich regions and immediate neighbors will feel the repercussions. In the first conflict and at the time of this analysis, Georgia's leadership sees no advantage to a tristate resolution with Alabama and Florida over allocation of the ACF river basin. In late summer 2013, Florida filed suit in the U.S. Supreme Court against Georgia seeking equitable allocation of water in the ACF. In late 2014 the Court accepted the case. Florida's governor claimed he wanted more water for the panhandle to support future growth and to protect the state's declining commercial oyster industry.[19] Long-term water supply planning everywhere remains a guess at best without an ACF water-sharing compact or a similar agreement for the Alabama-Coosa-Tallapoosa basin, where a second conflict with Alabama may lie in wait. In a third possible conflict, groundwater withdrawals from the Floridan Aquifer underlying the Southeastern Coastal Plain have compromised one of the Atlantic coast's primary shared drinking-water sources. Savannah, Ga., and South Carolina communities tap the Floridan, but the region's collective municipal and industrial groundwater pumping has allowed salt water to contaminate and compromise many municipal wells in Hilton Head, S.C. While the two states have been studying the movement of salt water for decades, in the spring of 2013, the director of South Carolina's state environmental agency threatened to sue Georgia unless the states can reach an agreement to protect and share groundwater more equitably.[20]

Politicians, agency staff, private sector consultants, and water professionals have proposed a number of solutions to resolve these conflicts. Many of the solutions, however, may only produce more problems. For example, any proposed interbasin transfer will continue to threaten interstate and intrastate regional relations. One of the most talked-about interbasin transfers involves moving Tennessee River water to serve metro Atlanta customers. Aside from the costs associated with construction (estimated in 2009 at more than $2 billion) and operations including the energy to move millions of gallons of water ($98 million annual operating costs), this proposal is complicated by a nineteenth-century surveyor's mismarking of the Tennessee-Georgia border that may only be resolved by the U.S. Supreme Court.[21] Another option, a 2012 state agency initiative to operate a complex aquifer storage and recovery project in the Flint River basin's agricultural region, exacerbated intrastate urban-rural relations.

The agency initiative proposed a water exchange as a long-term benefit for metro Atlanta 200 miles away. This was followed in 2013 by a legislative sidecar that initially threatened property rights with a proposal that would have altered the state's centuries-old riparian water rights tradition.[22] Transferring water from the Savannah, Tennessee, or Coosa River basins into the Chattahoochee to serve metro Atlanta and privatizing surface water in south Georgia may solve some of the state's short-term difficulties and benefit a few landowners and corporate interests. But taken together, these choices will manufacture more fundamental problems inside and outside the state.

In 2011 the chairman of the Metro Atlanta Chamber of Commerce stated that Georgia "grew along ridgelines and railways, not riverbasins."[23] If you look closely at a relief map of Georgia—one that depicts elevation via contour lines—you can read the state's historic development in the landscape. Many roads, railways, and towns in the Coastal Plain and Piedmont are indeed perched on a high point, bluff, or ridgeline above broad yet shallow valleys. Among the many reasons for this human geography: Freshwater springs can gush from high points; ridges do not flood; ridges lifted Georgians above miasmatic or malarial wetlands; and based on personal experience, ridge walking conserves energy otherwise lost traversing valleys. Georgia's ridgeline civilization, however, could never have existed without river basins, and Georgians should not forget the fall-line and downstream urban areas that preceded ridgeline cities like Atlanta.

Southern Water, Southern Power illustrates why human manipulation and use of river basins was critical for the region's modernization between the New South and Sun Belt eras. Fertile river basins pleased corn, tobacco, and cotton farmers, or their grazing livestock, as well as fishermen. People also dredged, diked, and blasted rivers to control flooding, improve navigation, and facilitate the transport of timber from inland sources to coastal markets. Urban boosters, corporations, politicians, and fall-line citizens in Augusta, Milledgeville, Macon, Albany, Columbus, and Rome all depended on the Savannah, Oconee, Ocmulgee, Flint, Chattahoochee, and Coosa Rivers to grow and prosper. Life changed during the famous New South period (1890–1930). Georgians depended increasingly on railroads, but the ridgeline occupants never hid their affection for river basins. For example, recall a Georgia Power Company predecessor that built six hydroelectric dams in the upper reaches of the Savannah River basin. From these northeast Georgia facilities—built between 1910 and 1927 and still operating today—the company channeled electricity ninety miles south over high-tension transmission lines to Atlanta. Georgia Power also built new coal plants, including Plant Atkinson (1930), on the Chattahoochee to power Atlanta by an organic and mineral energy mix. All of these energy-generation facilities—the renewable and the fossil fuel systems—depended on water, and all were interconnected via transmission lines. These "networks of power," to borrow historian of technology Thomas Hughes's phrase, furnished Atlanta's busy bees with electricity and what were considered modern conveniences in the 1920s: Street lights and electric fans gained popularity, but electric streetcars and factories captured the lion's share from this versatile hydraulic waterscape.[24]

The Southeast's hydraulic waterscape and environmental history provide a perspective for future decisions. Nearly all of the region's cities, regardless of their geography or size, have depended on river basins and shared water supplies for a long time. Federal agencies may control the Chattahoochee River's floodgates at Buford Dam and other facilities, but ridgeline corporations—including those that participated in the 2009 Georgia Water Contingency Task Force—all have a vested interest in making sure there is enough clean water in the ACF river basin, the Savannah River, and other valleys across the Southeast. If history is a guide, these corporations are not mere players on the ridgelines; they transformed the energy of many rivers in many states into a variety of agricultural products, industrial hard goods, and services in the past, and they are as focused today on securing clean water for tomorrow. Finally, Alabama, Georgia, and Florida have been mired in tristate water skirmishes for more than two decades. If Georgia's leadership continues to avoid a resolution with Alabama and Florida, other regions might begin to look more appealing for investors.

By running away from a tristate compact for decades, Georgia's leadership has pulled the state and region into a trap. There is an old western adage that water flows uphill to money, that is, from the Colorado River to California's irrigated fields and municipal water pipes. Georgians and their neighbors learned their own version of this maxim when they figured out how to turn water into electricity at hydroelectric dams and coal-fired power plants and then transmit energy to an urban-industrial Piedmont built atop a withering cotton South. In recent years, all Georgians and their regional neighbors have been learning how water itself might flow from distant river basins to money via interbasin transfers, an interconnected neo–Super Power network of water distribution lines, or other water exchanges. Solutions to the regional water puzzle lie in Georgia and involve a complex combination of policy, infrastructure, and individual behavioral modifications that will also be required of everyone everywhere to meet U.S. water demands in the twenty-first century.[25]

Georgia policy makers, for example, have built an impressive framework over the last decade to improve water supply management now and into the future. The state could serve as an example if other regions could find value in Georgia's policy instruments such as statewide water planning and water conservation through legislation. However, observers must recognize that with limited enforcement and anemic funding mechanisms in place, Georgia is a poor example and is not preparing its citizens or regional water planning councils to follow through and implement lasting solutions. Among federal water quality tools at their disposal, natural resource agencies must enforce Clean Water Act permit requirements and fine offenders. Strong clean water policies protect and improve water quality, and strict enforcement will ultimately result in less costly treatment—and lower drinking-water utility bills for consumers—while benefiting communities' long-term economic and environmental health. Federal engagement in water supply management is also critical. Times have changed at federal sites such as Georgia's Lake Lanier and Buford Dam, and federal water managers must clearly redefine authorized uses for these water projects. And since there is no such thing as a free lunch, federal reallocation for municipal water supply must require existing and future permitted users to alter behavior. For example, communities that derive water from federal water projects must demonstrate an aggressive reduction in consumption and water loss as a condition for access. Finally, water is a numbers game: State and federal regulators calibrate water withdrawal and pollutant discharge permits to river flows. But a critical sticking point has existed for a half-century. In the United States, the nation's groundwater and surface water supplies and use have never been fully and systematically quantified because reporting is spotty, states do not have adequate in-stream flow standards, and communities and commercial entities do not always know how much water they actually consume. Honest and transparent water budgeting across all economic sectors—municipal and private water and energy utilities and agricultural and industrial interests—is incredibly difficult but is imperative for future policy decisions.

Nationwide our transportation and water infrastructure—our roads, bridges, dams, and pipes—is crumbling. New technologies, such as new reservoirs or extensive pipeline networks to move water, can provide short-term solutions for the region's water supply deficiencies. Flood control solutions such as floodplain zoning, improved municipal sewage and stormwater management, and "green infrastructure" that better manages water where it initially falls will also help. These adaptations will manage risks but could also manufacture future risks and create new environments that will require additional hands-on attention. Building new working reservoirs to increase water supplies or piping water to consumers far from original sources can also create a false sense of security and assumptions about future availability. Like levees and flood control measures, water supply technologies can benefit specific constituencies and shift risk without eliminating hazards or fully identifying root problems.

Communities everywhere would be best off maintaining and repairing existing infrastructure to maximize existing supply and delivery systems. Repairs should supersede new construction where practical. But why the rush to create new supplies? A public water utility manager has a tough job: delivering inexpensive cheap water to customers' homes and businesses today while preparing for tomorrow. Clean water is expensive to make and deliver, but managers are expected to keep water bills low. However, developing a new water supply, such as a reservoir, is not as easy as it sounds. As a colleague once said, "Building a new reservoir is like opening a new bank account. Without an influx of rain or cash, the reservoir and account will be empty." So what can communities in drought-prone regions do before investing in a reservoir? In terms of municipal water supply, there is a "hidden reservoir" filling underground because of broken water mains, leaky pipes, and faulty water meters.[26] If communities can identify and fix those problems first, then they might be able to avoid costly alternatives that may not have been justified in the first place or could become prohibitively expensive for local tax- and ratepayers in the long run. There are also many reuse options—so-called gray and purple water systems—that utilize treated water for specific applications such as irrigation and energy generation, thus freeing up costly treated water for human use. Water suppliers utilizing these first-level and low-hanging-fruit options have grown supply in tandem with population growth.

Last but not least, individual behavior matters. Just as individuals make history, they also make critical decisions about energy and water on a daily basis. Water problems and solutions are local, but that does not mean that nonlocal ideas and proposals will not work. At a minimum, all decisions must be informed decisions: Citizens must have a basic understanding of where their drinking water comes from and where it goes for treatment, the energy costs of delivery and treatment, and why what happens on the land or what is discharged into streams affects water quality, the cost of water treatment, and economic health. Furthermore, since climate change will present another suite of challenges, our energy and water behaviors matter. According to the National Climate Assessment, southeastern communities face the threat of sea level rise, excessive heat events, and continued water stress. Choosing less-water-intensive energy systems, such as solar or wind generation, can reduce water stress and help arrest climate change.[27] With this knowledge, there is a good chance individuals will adopt smart energy and water behaviors.

If these policy, infrastructure, and individual steps were implemented to their full potential in Georgia, then some might foresee a symbolic end of Georgia's reign as Empire State of the South. However, given the boosters' historical record of selling the South, modern Sun Belt cooperation on energy and water issues throughout the ACF, Savannah, and other multistate river basins will be just as good for business as competition. Southern water has been harnessed to generate energy and spectacular growth for a long time. Sun Belt citizens benefited from the steep curve and are increasingly aware that conflict over water and unilateral attempts to control water and energy are not good for their communities, state, or region. Informed Sun Belt citizens are engaged with these issues and eager to cooperate if the goal is equitable water and energy policy for all.

When it comes to conflict over water, the American South is not exceptional. Historic water problems, such as flooding and droughts, are the products of material environmental conditions. Low-pressure tropical storms and heavy rain at any time can produce record rainfalls and flooding, and high-pressure systems can generate record heat waves and droughts. As environmental factors, these climatic events became problems for people after rivers flooded built and domesticated environments, when urban and industrial centers faced electrical shortages, and more recently, when municipal or poorly designed stormwater systems failed or water supplies nearly ran dry. Energy and water choices played a major part in the American South's history, and if that is a guide, water and energy choices will continue to affect one another well into the future. When considered this way, the humid Southeast, the arid West, and the other parts of the country wrestling with their own water problems and weather whiplash do not look so different. In this context, the American South has much to share with and learn from other regions grappling with what are clearly national problems.

Notes

CFM   Carl F. Miller Files, River Basin Survey Collection, National Anthropological Archives, Smithsonian Institution, Suitland, Md.

GAA   Georgia Archives, Morrow

GNAC   Georgia Natural Areas Council Records

JEC   John Ewing Colhoun Papers, Southern Historical Collection, Manuscripts Department, University of North Carolina, Chapel Hill

JMP   James A. Mackay Papers, Special Collections Department, Robert W. Woodruff Library, Emory University, Atlanta, Ga.

LMC   Lester S. Moody Collection, Augusta Museum of History, Augusta, Ga.

NAS   National Archives Records Administration, Southeast Region, Morrow, Ga.

NAII   National Archives Records Administration II, College Park, Md.

NMAH   National Museum of American History, Smithsonian Institution, Washington, D.C.

OJP   Olin DeWitt Talmadge Johnston Papers, South Carolina Political Collections, The University of South Carolina, Columbia

RG   Record Group (National Archives)

RRC   Richard B. Russell Jr. Collection, Richard B. Russell Library for Political Research and Studies, University of Georgia, Athens

RWC   Robert L. Williford Richard B. Russell Dam and Lake Project Files, Richard B. Russell Library for Political Research and Studies, University of Georgia, Athens

STP   Strom Thurmond Collection, Strom Thurmond Institute, Clemson University, Clemson, S.C.

WDP   William Jennings Bryan Dorn Papers, South Carolina Political Collections, University of South Carolina, Columbia

1. "Georgia's Water Crisis: The Power of Water," *Atlanta Journal-Constitution*, November 18, 2007, A1. E-mail announcement, attendee list, and agenda minutes for the "Southeastern Drought and Reliability Meeting" (November 16, 2007) provided to the author by Southeastern Power Administration, Freedom of Information Act Request #2011-0032.

2. "Drought Stricken Georgia Says It Will Sue over Water," CNN.com, December 2, 2012, http://edition.cnn.com/2007/US/10/18/pip.atlantadrought/index.html (July 14, 2013); "Water Worries: Ban on Use Tighten," *Athens Banner Herald*, September 15, 2007, http://onlineathens.com/stories/091507/news_20070915060.shtml (July 14, 2013); "Drought-Stricken South Facing Tough Choices," *New York Times*, October 16, 2007, http://www.nytimes.com/2007/10/16/us/16drought.html (July 14, 2013); "Drought Anxiety Rises as Water Levels Fall," *USA Today*, November 4, 2007, http://www.usatoday.com/weather/news/2007-11-01-drought-anxiety_N.htm (July 14, 2013).

3. "Metro Atlanta's Need for Water: Three Months from a Mud Hole," *Atlanta Journal-Constitution*, October 11, 2007, A1; "Coke, Pepsi: Big Cuts in Water Use Unlikely," *Atlanta Journal-Constitution*, October 23, 2007, 1D; Dale E. Dodson, map, "Heavy Demands on Our Water," *Atlanta Journal-Constitution* (October 26, 2007), http://www.ajc.com//metro/content/metro/stories/2007/10/26/watermap.html (April 10, 2012).

4. "Watering Ban Now the Widest: 'Unprecedented' Situation," *Athens Banner Herald*, September 29, 2007, http://onlineathens.com/stories/092907/news_20070929061.shtml (July 14, 2013).

5. "Rain Stops, but 8 Are Dead in Southeast Floods," *New York Times*, September 22, 2009, http://www.nytimes.com/2009/09/23/us/23rain.html (July 14, 2013); "Atlanta Flood: After Drought, Residents Caught by Surprise," *Christian Science Monitor*, September 24, 2009, http://www.csmonitor.com/USA/2009/0924/p02s02-usgn.html (July 14, 2013); "Flood Death Toll at 9," *Atlanta Journal-Constitution*, September 26, 2009, http://www.ajc.com/news/flood-death-toll-at-142739.html (July 14, 2013); "Federal Officials: September's Flood 'Off the Charts,'" *Atlanta Journal-Constitution*, November 4, 2009, http://www.ajc.com/news/news/local/federal-officials-septembers-flood-off-the-charts/nQYyH/ (July 14, 2013); "Failure to Control Storm Water Makes Floods More Likely," *Atlanta Journal-Constitution*, February 21, 2010, http://www.ajc.com/news/failure-to-control-storm-318983.html (July 14, 2013).

6. U.S. District Court, Middle District of Florida, *Memorandum and Order, Re: Tri-State Water Rights Litigation*, Case No. 3:07-md-01 (PAM/JRK), Document 264, July 17, 2009, 11 (Hartsfield quote), http://www.atlantaregional.com/File%20Library/Environment/ep_tri-state-water-litigation-order-090717-mdfla-07md1-doc-264.pdf (December 2, 2012). Georgia parties successfully appealed this order (Re: MDL-1824 Tri-State Water Rights Litigation, U.S. Court of Appeals for the Eleventh Circuit, No. 09–14657, D.C. Docket No. 07–00001 MD-J-PAM-JRK, June 28, 2011, http://www.ca11.uscourts.gov/opinions/ops/200914657.pdf). Alabama and Florida parties asked the U.S. Supreme Court to review the appeal, but the court declined to hear the case; see "High Court Grants Georgia Water-Wars Victory," *Atlanta Journal-Constitution*, June 25, 2012, http://www.ajc.com/news/news/local/high-court-grants-georgia-water-wars-victory/nQWmm/ (July 14, 2013).

7. "Perdue Forms Team to Fight Water Ruling," *Atlanta Journal-Constitution*, July 23, 2009, http://www.ajc.com/news/news/local-govt-politics/perdue-forms-team-to-fight-water-ruling/nQJFH/ (July 14, 2013). Garrett retired from Georgia Power, and his corporate bio is no longer available: http://www.georgiapower.com/about/ceo.asp (March 9, 2010).

8. "Judge: States' Water Talks Can Be Secret," *Atlanta Journal-Constitution*, January 8, 2010, http://www.ajc.com/news/judge-states-water-talks-270323.html (July 14, 2013).

9. The Atlanta Regional Commission covers a 10-county area with 4 million residents; see http://www.atlantaregional.com/. The Metropolitan North Georgia Water Planning District covers a slightly larger area, including 15 counties; see http://www.northgeorgia water.com/. The Metro Atlanta Chamber of Commerce shepherds 28 counties and 5.3 million people; see www.metroatlantachamber.com/.

10. Governor Sonny Perdue, *Water Contingency Task Force: Final Report*, December 21, 2009, 9–12, and Appendix 3, *Findings and Recommendations*, 123–41, http://sonny perdue.georgia.gov/00/channel_modifieddate/0,2096,78006749_154453222,00.html (July 14, 2013).

11. "Watch Out for Our Water," *Augusta Chronicle*, December 6, 2009, http://chronicle .augusta.com/stories/2009/12/06/edi_558272.shtml (July 14, 2013); Senator Jim Butterworth, "Hey Atlanta, Hands Off Our Water," *Atlanta Journal-Constitution*, December 12, 2009, http://www.ajc.com/opinion/hey-atlanta-hands-off-237175.html (July 14, 2013); Representative Alan Powell, "Hands Off the Savannah River," *Savannah Morning News*, December 12, 2009, http://savannahnow.com/column/2009-12-12/powell-hands-savannah-river (July 14, 2013).

12. The General Assembly considered SB462 and HB1301. An interbasin transfer (IBT) moves water from one river basin into another. For example, some of the IBTs discussed here would have moved raw water from the Savannah River basin, which drains into the Atlantic Ocean, into the Chattahoochee River basin, which drains into the Gulf of Mexico. For reference, data from the Georgia Environmental Protection Division shows that in 2008, one dozen IBTs transferred more than 1 million gallons per day from one basin to another. See Georgia Water Coalition, "Interbasin Transfers: Briefing Document," November 2010, http://www.garivers.org/gawater/pdf%20files/GWC%20Interbasin%20Transfers%20Briefing%20Document.pdf (July 13, 2013); "Water Transfers Need Supervision," *Atlanta Journal-Constitution*, March 3, 2010, http://www.ajc.com/news/news/opinion/water-transfers-need-supervision/nQdc8/ (July 13, 2013).

13. "Rural Legislators Push Interbasin Transfer Rules," *Atlanta Business Chronicle*, April 22, 2010, http://www.bizjournals.com/atlanta/stories/2010/04/26/story4.html?b= 1272254400^3235961&s=industry&i=energy (July 13, 2013).

14. The American South has also been a vessel for race, labor, and economic "problems"; see James C. Giesen, *Boll Weevil Blues: Cotton, Myth, and Power in the American South* (Chicago: University of Chicago Press, 2011), and Natalie J. Ring, *The Problem South: Region, Empire, and the New Liberal State, 1880–1930* (Athens: University of Georgia Press, 2012).

15. Thomas P. Hughes, *Networks of Power: Electrification in Western Society, 1880–1930* (Baltimore: Johns Hopkins University Press, 1983).

16. David E. Nye, *Consuming Power: A Social History of American Energies* (Cam-

bridge: MIT Press, 1998); Alfred W. Crosby, *Children of the Sun: A History of Humanity's Unappeasable Appetite for Energy* (New York: Norton, 2006); Daniel Yergin, *The Prize: The Epic Quest for Oil, Money, and Power* (New York: Simon and Schuster, 1991); Thomas G. Andrews, *Killing for Coal: America's Deadliest Labor War* (Cambridge: Harvard University Press, 2008); Christopher F. Jones, "A Landscape of Energy Abundance: Anthracite Coal Canals and the Roots of American Fossil Fuel Dependence, 1820–1860," *Environmental History* 15, no. 3 (July 2010): 449–84; Daniel Yergin, *The Quest: Energy, Security, and the Remaking of the Modern World* (New York: Penguin, 2011); "Oil in American History," a special issue of the *Journal of American History* (June 2012).

17. See the Sandia National Laboratories website: http://www.sandia.gov/energy-water/.

18. "Tallulah the Terrible," *Madisonian*, July 12, 1912, 4. See also Andrew Beecher McCallister, "'A Source of Pleasure, Profit, and Pride': Tourism, Industrialization, and Conservation at Tallulah Falls, Georgia, 1820–1915" (M.A. thesis, University of Georgia, 2002).

19. Disaster histories include the following: a history of a private dam's failure, David G. McCullough, *The Johnstown Flood* (New York: Simon and Schuster, 1968); a history of an agricultural drought, Donald Worster, *Dust Bowl: The Southern Plains in the 1930s* (New York: Oxford University Press, 1979); and a history of flooding exacerbated by failed levee technology, Pete Daniel, *Deep'n as It Come: The 1927 Mississippi River Flood* (New York: Oxford University Press, 1977), and John M. Barry, *Rising Tide: The Great Mississippi Flood of 1927 and How It Changed America* (New York: Simon and Schuster, 1997). I am only aware of two historical accounts of drought in the American South: One addresses Arkansas, Kentucky, Louisiana, Mississippi, Tennessee, and West Virginia; see Nan Elizabeth Woodruff, *As Rare as Rain: Federal Relief in the Great Southern Drought of 1930–31* (Urbana: University of Illinois Press, 1985). A second addresses irrigation history in Mississippi and Alabama; see Valerie Grim, "The High Cost of Water: African American Farmers and the Politics of Irrigation in the Rural South, 1980–2000," *Agricultural History* 76, no. 2 (Spring 2002): 338–53.

20. Ted Steinberg, *Acts of God: The Unnatural History of Natural Disaster in America* (New York: Oxford University Press, 2006), xvi, xxii; National Weather Service, "What Is Drought?" Public Fact Sheet (May 2008), http://www.nws.noaa.gov/om/brochures/climate/DroughtPublic2.pdf.

21. Few topics have been as central to the growth of environmental history as the relationship of water to power in the American West, and the central debate in western water history largely emerged from Donald Worster's *Rivers of Empire* and its critics. In Worster's interpretation, irrigation in the arid West reorganized communities in ways that were detrimental to both people and nature. The "free" West, a region defined by aridity and settled with an individual pioneer spirit, evolved into a monolithic and oppressive "hydraulic society" where a water elite co-opted federal authority (from the Bureau of Reclamation) and expertise to use water as an instrument of control in a highly capitalized agricultural economy. This interpretation has been challenged as colleagues found Worster's West too specific to California and that he ignored complex cultural and environmental realities that produced diverse water management institutions based on specific local conditions. One critic argued that Worster overstated the presence of omnipotent agriculture-water elites, and another that his depiction of nature dominated by

modern waterworks missed the extent to which environmental conditions reshaped and compromised the very systems designed to control nature. As Worster's critics revealed, river societies in the urban and agricultural American West were never as coercive as the empires he described, nor was nature steamrolled by culturally inspired choices. For example, Richard White has provided the most useful example of a "hybrid" environment where nature and culture left a collective imprint on power relations in the Pacific Northwest. The Columbia River, as an "organic machine," was a dynamic place where different cultures learned about the river's nature through their labor. See Donald Worster, *Rivers of Empire: Water, Aridity, and the Growth of the American West* (New York: Pantheon, 1985); Donald Worster, "Hydraulic Society in California," in Worster, *Under Western Skies: Nature and History in the American West* (New York: Oxford University Press, 1992), 53–63; Norris Hundley Jr., *The Great Thirst: Californians and Water: A History* (1992; rev. ed., Berkeley: University of California Press, 2001); Donald J. Pisani, *To Reclaim a Divided West: Water, Law, and Public Policy, 1848–1902* (Albuquerque: University of New Mexico Press, 1992); Richard White, *The Organic Machine: The Remaking of the Columbia River* (New York: Hill and Wang, 1995); Donald J. Pisani, *Water, Land, and Law in the West: The Limits of Public Policy, 1850–1920* (Lawrence: University Press of Kansas, 1996); Mark Fiege, *Irrigated Eden: The Making of an Agricultural Landscape in the American West* (Seattle: University of Washington Press, 1999).

22. Marc Reisner, *Cadillac Desert: The American West and Its Disappearing Water* (New York: Penguin, 1986; rev. and updated ed., 1993), chap. 9, quote on 307.

23. Thomas Lunsford Stokes and Lamar Dodd, *The Savannah* (New York: Rinehart, 1951); Henry Savage Jr., *River of the Carolinas: The Santee* (Chapel Hill: University of North Carolina Press, 1968); E. Merton Coulter, *Georgia Waters: Tallulah Falls, Madison Springs, Scull Shoals, and the Okefenokee Swamp* (Athens: Georgia Historical Quarterly, 1965); Harvey H. Jackson III, *Rivers of History: Life on the Coosa, Tallapoosa, Cahaba, and Alabama* (Tuscaloosa: University of Alabama Press, 1995); Lynn Willoughby, *Flowing through Time: A History of the Lower Chattahoochee River* (Tuscaloosa: University of Alabama Press, 1999); Edward J. Cashin, *The Brightest Arm of the Savannah: The Augusta Canal, 1845–2000* (Augusta, Ga.: Augusta Canal Authority, 2002); John Lane, *Chattooga: Descending into the Myth of Deliverance River* (Athens: University of Georgia Press, 2004); Doug Woodward, *Wherever Waters Flow: A Lifelong Love Affair with Wild Rivers* (Franklin, N.C.: Headwaters Publishing, 2006); Janisse Ray, *Drifting into Darien: A Personal and Natural History of the Altamaha River* (Athens: University of Georgia Press, 2011). For corporate histories, see Wade H. Wright, *History of the Georgia Power Company, 1855–1956* (Atlanta: Georgia Power Company, 1957); Jack Riley, *Carolina Power and Light Company, 1908–1958: A Corporate Biography, Tracing the Origin and Development of Electric Service in Much of the Carolinas* (Raleigh, N.C.: Edwards and Broughton, 1958); Robert F. Durden, *Electrifying the Piedmont Carolinas: The Duke Power Company, 1904–1997* (Durham, N.C.: Carolina Academic Press, 2001); Martha Elrod and Julie Groce, *Energizing Georgia: The History of Georgia Power, 1883–2004* (Macon, Ga.: Indigo Custom Publishing, 2004); Leah Rawls Atkins, *"Developed for the Service of Alabama": The Centennial History of the Alabama Power Company, 1906–2006* (Birmingham: Alabama Power Co., 2006); and Dub Taft and Sam Heys, *Big Bets: Decisions and Leaders That Shaped Southern Company* (Atlanta: Southern Company, 2011).

24. Broadus Mitchell, *The Rise of the Cotton Mills in the South* (Baltimore, 1921), 263; J. Wayne Flynt, "The New Deal and Southern Labor," in *The New Deal and the South*, ed. James C. Cobb and Michael V. Namorato (Jackson: University Press of Mississippi, 1984); Gavin Wright, *Old South, New South: Revolutions in the Southern Economy since the Civil War* (New York: Basic Books, 1986); C. Vann Woodward, *Origins of the New South, 1877–1913* (Baton Rouge: Louisiana State University Press, 1951); George Brown Tindall, *The Emergence of the New South, 1913–1945* (Baton Rouge: Louisiana State University Press, 1967).

25. David L. Carlton, *Mill and Town in South Carolina, 1880–1920* (Baton Rouge: Louisiana State University Press, 1982); Jacquelyn Dowd Hall, James Leloudis, Robert Korstad, Mary Murphy, Lu Ann Jones, and Christopher B. Daly, *Like a Family: The Making of a Southern Cotton Mill World* (Chapel Hill: University of North Carolina Press, 1987); Allen Tullos, *Habits of Industry: White Culture and the Transformation of the Carolina Piedmont* (Chapel Hill: University of North Carolina Press, 1989); Bryant Simon, *A Fabric of Defeat: The Politics of South Carolina Millhands, 1910–1948* (Chapel Hill: University of North Carolina Press, 1998).

26. James C. Cobb, *The Selling of the South: The Southern Crusade for Industrial Development, 1936–1990* (Urbana: University of Illinois Press, 1993); Bruce J. Schulman, *From Cotton Belt to Sunbelt: Federal Policy, Economic Development, and the Transformation of the South, 1938–1980* (Durham, N.C.: Duke University Press, 1994); Numan V. Bartley, *The New South, 1945–1980* (Baton Rouge: Louisiana State University Press, 1995); Stephen Wallace Taylor, *The New South's New Frontier: A Social History of Economic Development in Southwestern North Carolina* (Gainesville: University Press of Florida, 2001); Sarah T. Phillips, *This Land, This Nation: Conservation, Rural America, and the New Deal* (New York: Cambridge University Press, 2007).

27. Preston J. Hubbard, *Origins of the TVA: The Muscle Shoals Controversy, 1920–1932* (Nashville: Vanderbilt University Press, 1961); Thomas K. McCraw, *TVA and the Power Fight, 1933–1939* (Philadelphia: Lippincott, 1971); Arthur Ernest Morgan, *The Making of the TVA* (Buffalo, N.Y.: Prometheus, 1974); North Callahan, *TVA: Bridge over Troubled Waters* (South Brunswick, N.J.: A. S. Barnes, 1980); Philip Selznick, *TVA and the Grass Roots: A Study of Politics and Organization* (New York: Harper and Row, 1980); Michael J. McDonald and John Muldowny, *TVA and the Dispossessed: The Resettlement of Population in the Norris Dam Area* (Knoxville: University of Tennessee Press, 1982); Erwin C. Hargrove and Paul K. Conkin, eds., *TVA: Fifty Years of Grass-Roots Bureaucracy* (Urbana: University of Illinois Press, 1983); Karen M. O'Neill, "Why the TVA Remains Unique: Interest Groups and the Defeat of New Deal River Planning," *Rural Sociology* 67, no. 2 (June 2002): 163–82. For Corps history, see Jeffrey K. Stine, "United States Army Corps of Engineers," in *Government Agencies*, ed. Donald R. Whitnah, Greenwood Encyclopedia of American Institutions (Westport, Conn.: Greenwood Press, 1983), 513–16, and Martin Melosi, *Precious Commodity: Providing Water for America's Cities* (Pittsburgh: University of Pittsburgh Press, 2011), 12–20.

28. Mart Stewart, *"What Nature Suffers to Groe": Life, Labor, and Landscape on the Georgia Coast, 1680–1920* (Athens: University of Georgia Press, 1996; reprint, 2002); Judith Ann Carney, *Black Rice: The African Origins of Rice Cultivation in the Americas* (Cambridge: Harvard University Press, 2001).

29. See, for example, Daniel, *Deep'n as It Come*; Jeffrey K. Stine, *Mixing the Waters: Environment, Politics, and the Building of the Tennessee-Tombigbee Waterway* (Akron: University of Akron Press, 1993); Barry, *Rising Tide*; Ari Kelman, *A River and Its City: The Nature of Landscape in New Orleans* (Berkeley: University of California Press, 2003); Mikko Saikku, *This Delta, This Land: An Environmental History of the Yazoo-Mississippi Floodplain* (Athens: University of Georgia Press, 2005); Craig E. Colten, *An Unnatural Metropolis: Wresting New Orleans from Nature* (Baton Rouge: Louisiana State University Press, 2005); Karen M. O'Neill, *Rivers by Design: State Power and the Origins of U.S. Flood Control* (Durham, N.C.: Duke University Press, 2006); and Christopher Morris, *The Big Muddy: An Environmental History of the Mississippi and Its Peoples, from Hernando de Soto to Hurricane Katrina* (New York: Oxford University Press, 2012).

30. Donald Worster's well-known book *Dust Bowl* examines the consequences of drought in Kansas and Oklahoma in the 1930s for agroecological systems. I am aware of only two historical accounts of drought in the American South. The first addresses Arkansas, Kentucky, Louisiana, Mississippi, Tennessee, and West Virginia in the 1930s; see Woodruff, *As Rare as Rain*. The second addresses drought and irrigation history in Mississippi and Alabama after 1970; see Grim, "High Cost of Water."

31. David Emory Stooksbury, "Historical Droughts in Georgia and Drought Assessment and Management," proceedings of the 2003 Georgia Water Resources Conference, April 23–24, 2003, at the University of Georgia, Athens.

32. Amber Ignatius, a University of Georgia doctoral candidate in geography, has presented on multiple occasions a spectacular compilation of geospatial data sets that illustrate the historic distribution and purpose of ponds, impoundments, and reservoirs throughout the Chattahoochee River basin in Georgia. Ignatius is currently assessing the cumulative hydrologic impacts of impoundments in the upper Chattahoochee River. For more information, see http://geography.uga.edu/article/big-water-little-water/.

33. "The Great Lakes of Georgia" site is no longer functional (http://www.greatlakes ofgeorgia.com); see also Georgia Public Broadcasting, http://www.gpb.org/georgia-outdoors-classic/georgias-great-lakes (September 3, 2013). For "Georgia's Lake Country," visit http://www.oconee.org/index.php (July 14, 2013).

34. Thomas L. Crisman, "Natural Lakes of the Southeastern United States: Origin, Structure, and Function," in *Biodiversity of the Southeastern United States: Aquatic Communities*, ed. Courtney Thomas Hackney, S. Marshall Adams, and William Haywood Martin (New York: Wiley, 1992), 475–538, esp. 478.

35. Blue Ridge and Coastal Plain environmental histories are more common than Piedmont stories: Jack Temple Kirby, *Poquosin: A Study of Rural Landscape and Society* (Chapel Hill: University of North Carolina Press, 1995); Stewart, *"What Nature Suffers to Groe"*; Donald Edward Davis, *Where There Are Mountains: An Environmental History of the Southern Appalachians* (Athens: University of Georgia Press, 2000); Daniel S. Pierce, *The Great Smokies: From Natural Habitat to National Park* (Knoxville: University of Tennessee Press, 2000); Margaret Lynn Brown, *The Wild East: A Biography of the Great Smoky Mountains* (Gainesville: University Press of Florida, 2000); Carney, *Black Rice*; Timothy Silver, *Mount Mitchell and the Black Mountains: An Environmental History of the Highest Peaks in Eastern America* (Chapel Hill: University of North Carolina Press, 2003); Albert G. Way, *Conserving Longleaf: Herbert Stoddard and the Rise of Ecological*

Land Management (Athens: University of Georgia Press, 2011); and Kathryn Newfont, *Blue Ridge Commons: Environmental Activism and Forest History in Western North Carolina* (Athens: University of Georgia Press, 2012).

36. Matthew D. Lassiter and Joseph Crespino, eds., *The Myth of Southern Exceptionalism* (New York: Oxford University Press, 2010); Cynthia Barnett, *Mirage: Florida and the Vanishing Water of the Eastern U.S.* (Ann Arbor: University of Michigan Press, 2007); Robert Glennon, *Unquenchable: America's Water Crisis and What to Do about It* (Washington, D.C.: Island Press, 2009).

CHAPTER 1

1. John Muir, "Through the River Country of Georgia," in Muir, *A Thousand-Mile Walk to the Gulf* (Boston: Houghton Mifflin, 1916), 48–63.

2. Donald Worster, *A Passion for Nature: The Life of John Muir* (New York: Oxford University Press, 2008), 122.

3. Mart A. Stewart, "If John Muir Had Been an Agrarian: American Environmental History West and South," *Environment and History* 11, no. 2 (May 2005): 139–62.

4. Muir, *Thousand-Mile Walk*. For delineations between organic (animal, wood, water, and wind) and mineral (coal, natural gas, petroleum, and uranium) economies as well as the limits of and transitions between these energy regimes, see E. A. Wrigley, *Continuity, Chance, and Change: The Character of the Industrial Revolution in England* (New York: Cambridge University Press, 1988); David E. Nye, *Consuming Power: A Social History of American Energies* (Cambridge: MIT Press, 1998; 3rd ed., 2001); E. A. Wrigley, *Poverty, Progress, and Population* (New York: Cambridge University Press, 2004); and Alfred W. Crosby, *Children of the Sun: A History of Humanity's Unappeasable Appetite for Energy* (New York: Norton, 2006).

5. Nye argues, "The South chose a less energy-intensive form of industrial development, based on muscle power and local mills," and simplifies that notion by stating that "part of the explanation is geographical [since] the North was better situated to exploit water power" (*Consuming Power*, 49). For alternative interpretations of nineteenth-century mill development, see Bess Beatty, "Lowells of the South: Northern Influences on the Nineteenth-Century North Carolina Textile Industry," *Journal of Southern History* 53, no. 1 (February 1987): 37–62, and Tom Downey, "Riparian Rights and Manufacturing in Antebellum South Carolina: William Gregg and the Origins of the 'Industrial Mind,'" *Journal of Southern History* 65, no. 1 (February 1999): 77–108. For an exemplary interpretation of New England's early industrial and environmental history, see Theodore Steinberg, *Nature Incorporated: Industrialization and the Waters of New England* (New York: Cambridge University Press, 1991).

6. Muir, *Thousand-Mile Walk*.

7. Mart Stewart, *"What Nature Suffers to Groe": Life, Labor, and Landscape on the Georgia Coast, 1680–1920* (Athens: University of Georgia Press, 1996); Judith Ann Carney, *Black Rice: The African Origins of Rice Cultivation in the Americas* (Cambridge: Harvard University Press, 2001).

8. L. L. Gaddy, *A Naturalist's Guide to the Southern Blue Ridge Front: Linville Gorge, North Carolina, to Tallulah Gorge, Georgia* (Columbia: University of South Carolina Press,

2000), 4–6; Leonard M. Adkins, *Walking the Blue Ridge: A Guide to the Trails of the Blue Ridge Parkway*, 3rd ed. (Chapel Hill: University of North Carolina Press, 2003), 3–4.

9. Sharyn Kane and Richard Keeton, *Beneath These Waters: Archeological and Historical Studies of 11,500 Years along the Savannah River* (Savannah, Ga.: U.S. Army Corps of Engineers and the Interagency Archeological Services Division, National Park Service, 1993), 9; Donald E. Davis, Craig E. Colten, Megan Kate Nelson, Barbara L. Allen, and Mikko Saikku, *Southern United States: An Environmental History*, Nature and Human Societies Series (Santa Barbara, Calif.: ABC-CLIO, 2006), 1, 7–8.

10. William Bartram, *The Travels of William Bartram*, naturalist's edition, edited by Francis Harper (Athens: University of Georgia Press, 1998).

11. Betty Wood, *Slavery in Colonial Georgia, 1730–1775* (Athens: University of Georgia Press, 1984).

12. Bartram, *Travels*, 237; Edward M. Riley, "The Survey of the Historic Sites of the Clark Hill Reservoir Area, South Carolina and Georgia" (Richmond, Va.: National Park Service, June 1949), 10–11; Edward J. Cashin, *The Story of Augusta* (Augusta, Ga.: Richmond County Board of Education, 1980), 11.

13. Bartram, *Travels*, 196–98; Timothy Silver, *A New Face on the Countryside: Indians, Colonists, and Slaves in South Atlantic Forests, 1500–1800* (New York: Cambridge University Press, 1990).

14. Henry Savage Jr., *River of the Carolinas: The Santee* (Chapel Hill: University of North Carolina Press, 1968), 331; E. Merton Coulter, *Georgia Waters: Tallulah Falls, Madison Springs, Scull Shoals, and the Okefenokee Swamp* (Athens: Georgia Historical Quarterly, 1965), 84–111; Cashin, *Story of Augusta*, 59; Michael C. White, *Waterways and Water Mills* (Warrenton, Ga.: C.S.R.A. Press, 1995), 202–10; Stewart, *"What Nature Suffers to Groe,"* 71. On shoals and fishing, see Kenneth E. Sassaman, *People of the Shoals: Stallings Culture of the Savannah River Valley* (Gainesville: University Press of Florida, 2006), 114–32; Kane and Keeton, *Beneath These Waters*, 44–49; and George Frederick Frick and Raymond Phineas Stearns, *Mark Catesby, the Colonial Audubon* (Urbana: University of Illinois Press, 1961), 26.

15. Kane and Keeton, *Beneath These Waters*, chap. 3. See also The History Group, Inc., *Historical Investigations of the Richard B. Russell Multiple Resource Area* (Atlanta: History Group, 1981), prepared for the Archeological Services Division, National Park Service, and funded by the Savannah District, U.S. Army Corps of Engineers, 177–89, and Charles E. Orser Jr., Annette M. Nekola, and James L. Roark, *Exploring the Rustic life: Multidisciplinary Research at Millwood Plantation, a Large Piedmont Plantation in Abbeville County, South Carolina, and Elbert County, Georgia*, Russell Papers, 3 vols. (Atlanta: Archeological Services, National Park Service, 1987).

16. Kane and Keeton, *Beneath These Waters*, 174.

17. Angela Lakwete, *Inventing the Cotton Gin: Machine and Myth in Antebellum America* (Baltimore: Johns Hopkins University Press, 2003).

18. Kane and Keeton, *Beneath These Waters*, 176; Steven Stoll, *Larding the Lean Earth: Soil and Society in Nineteenth-Century America* (New York: Hill and Wang, 2002).

19. James Edward Calhoun, Plantation Journal, 1930–1834, Financial and Legal Papers, ser. 2, folder 11, JEC. The 1833–34 summer droughts may have been the initial years of an "extended dry" period that lasted from 1834 to 1861, and the initial years of the

midwestern "Civil War" drought; see Richard Seager, Alexandria Tzanova, and Jennifer Nakamura, "Drought in the Southeastern United States: Causes, Variability over the Last Millennium, and the Potential for Future Hydroclimate Change," *Journal of Climate* 22 (October 1, 2009): 5021–45; Celine Herwiger, Richard Seager, and Edward Cook, "North American Droughts of the Mid to Late Nineteenth Century: A History, Simulation, and Implication for Mediaeval Drought," *The Holocene* 16, no. 2 (2006): 159–71; and N. Pederson et al., "A Long-Term Perspective on a Modern Drought in the American Southeast," *Environmental Research Letters* 7 (2012): 1–9.

20. James Edward Calhoun, Plantation Journal, 1930–1834, Financial and Legal Papers, ser. 2, folder 11, JEC.

21. For Calhoun quote, see History Group, *Historical Investigations of the Richard B. Russell Multiple Resource Area*, 185. For the distinction of "men of property" and "men of capital," see Downey, "Riparian Rights and Manufacturing."

22. "Lowell of the South," *Augusta Chronicle and Sentinel*, January 2, 1845.

23. Savage, *River of the Carolinas*, 241–47; Ronald E. Shaw, *Canals for a Nation: The Canal Era in the United States, 1790–1860* (Lexington: University Press of Kentucky, 1993), 15–18, 123–24; Robert J. Kapsch, *Historic Canals and Waterways of South Carolina* (Columbia: University of South Carolina Press, 2010), 21–53.

24. For the best history of the Augusta Canal, see Edward J. Cashin, *The Brightest Arm of the Savannah: The Augusta Canal, 1845–2000* (Augusta, Ga.: Augusta Canal Authority, 2002).

25. Steinberg, *Nature Incorporated*, 3.

26. Downey, "Riparian Rights and Manufacturing," 93–95.

27. Stoll, *Larding the Lean Earth*.

28. Baldwin and Bigelow, both fixtures in New England's institutional waterpower management, served as investors and consultants in southern canal projects, including the Augusta Canal. Phillips, one of the Augusta Canal survey team members, was a Pennsylvania native whose father had supervised the Delaware and Chesapeake Canal's construction. Francis, the famous Lowell waterpower and canal engineer, also participated in the Augusta Canal's design and consultation process in the 1840s. See Steinberg, *Nature Incorporated*, 88–95; Cashin, *Brightest Arm*, 54; Shaw, *Canals for a Nation*, 124; and Robert L. Spude, *Augusta Canal, Historic American Engineering Record (HAER)*, GA-5 (Washington, D.C.: Department of the Interior, 1977), 7.

29. Charles Grier Sellers, *The Market Revolution: Jacksonian America, 1815–1846* (New York: Oxford University Press, 1991); Harry L. Watson, "Slavery and Development in a Dual Economy: The South and the Market Revolution," in *The Market Revolution in America: Social, Political, and Religious Expressions, 1800–1880*, ed. Melvyn Stokes and Stephen Conway (Charlottesville: University Press of Virginia, 1996), 43–73; Joseph P. Reidy, *From Slavery to Agrarian Capitalism in the Cotton Plantation South: Central Georgia, 1800–1880* (Chapel Hill: University of North Carolina Press, 1992). Harry L. Watson discussed the market revolution's advance in the American South and the consequences for upcountry farmers and fish from the perspective of mill dams; see "'The Common Rights of Mankind': Subsistence, Shad, and Commerce in the Early Republican South," *Journal of American History* 83, no. 1 (June 1996): 13–43

30. Downey, "Riparian Rights and Manufacturing"; Bruce Eelman, *Entrepreneurs in*

the Southern Upcountry: Commercial Culture in Spartanburg, South Carolina, 1845–1880 (Athens: University of Georgia Press, 2008).

31. Cashin, Brightest Arm, 66–68.

32. Shaw, Canals for a Nation, 123–24; Spude, Augusta Canal, 5, 7, n. 25, n. 38.

33. U.S. Department of the Interior, Census Office, Statistics of Power and Machinery Employed in Manufactures: Reports of the Water-Power of the United States, pt. 1 (Washington, D.C.: Government Printing Office, 1885), 127–28.

34. John H. Logan quoted in Stanley Wayne Trimble, Man-Induced Soil Erosion on the Southern Piedmont, 1700–1970 (Ankeny, Iowa: Soil Conservation Society of America, 1974), 57.

35. U.S. Department of the Interior, Statistics of Power, 108.

36. Carville Earle, "The Myth of the Southern Soil Miner: Macrohistory, Agricultural Innovation, and Environmental Change," in The Ends of the Earth: Perspectives on Modern Environmental History, ed. Donald Worster (New York: Cambridge University Press, 1988), 175–210; "land killers" from Edmund Ruffin, quoted in Stanley Trimble, "Perspectives on the History of Soil Erosion Control in the Eastern United States," Agricultural History 59, no. 2 (April 1985): 175; "erosional tinderbox," Stanley Trimble quoted in Kane and Keeton, Beneath These Waters, 172. See also Paul S. Sutter, "What Gullies Mean: Georgia's 'Little Grand Canyon' and Southern Environmental History," Journal of Southern History 76, no. 3 (August 2010): 579–616.

37. Douglas E. Facey and M. J. Van Den Avyle, Species Profiles: Life Histories and Environmental Requirements of Coastal Fishes and Invertebrates (South Atlantic): American Shad (U.S. Fish and Wildlife Service and U.S. Army Corps of Engineers, 1986); John McPhee, The Founding Fish (New York: Farrar, Straus and Giroux, 2002).

38. Lynn Willoughby, Flowing through Time: A History of the Lower Chattahoochee River (Tuscaloosa: University of Alabama Press, 1999), 78. William Cronon charts the flow of commodities and "The Geography of Capital" in his classic Nature's Metropolis: Chicago and the Great West (New York: Norton, 1991).

39. Cashin, Brightest Arm, chap. 4.

40. Ibid., 47, 54.

41. "The Upper River," Augusta Chronicle, February 18, 1888, 8.

42. Cashin, Story of Augusta, 65.

43. "Drowned—Inquest," Augusta Chronicle and Sentinel, April 5, 1859.

44. Spude, Augusta Canal, n. 30.

45. For example, see John H. Logan, A History of the Upper Country of South Carolina from the Earliest Periods to the Close of the War of Independence (Columbia, S.C.: P. B. Glass, and Charleston, S.C.: S. G. Courtenay & Co., 1859), 1:75, and Christopher J. Manganiello, "Fish Tales and the Conservation State," Southern Cultures 20, no. 3 (Fall 2014): 43–62.

46. U.S. Department of the Interior, Statistics of Power, 128.

47. Cashin, Brightest Arm, chap. 7; Charles B. Dew, Ironmaker to the Confederacy: Joseph R. Anderson and the Tredegar Iron Works (New Haven: Yale University Press, 1966). Civil War, environmental, and energy history have converged; see Jack T. Kirby, "The American Civil War: An Environmental View," on the National Humanities Center website, Nature Transformed: The Environment in American History, http://nationalhumanities

center.org/tserve/nattrans/ntuseland/essays/amcwar.htm (February 15, 2013), and Mark Fiege, "Gettysburg and the Organic Nature of the American Civil War," in *Natural Enemy, Natural Ally: Toward an Environmental History of Warfare*, ed. Richard P. Tucker and Edmund Russell (Corvallis: Oregon State University Press, 2004), 93–109.

48. Willoughby, *Flowing through Time*, 88–89; Harvey H. Jackson III, *Rivers of History: Life on the Coosa, Tallapoosa, Cahaba, and Alabama* (Tuscaloosa: University of Alabama Press, 1995), 104, 113–15.

49. Paul M. Gaston, *The New South Creed: A Study in Southern Mythmaking* (New York: Knopf, 1970), 64–70.

50. James W. Milner, Appendix 19, "Report on the Propagation of the Shad (*Alosa Sapidissima*) and Its Introduction into New Waters by the U. S. Fish Commissioner in 1873," in U.S. Commission of Fish and Fisheries, *Report of the Commissioner for 1872 and 1873* (Washington, D.C.: Government Printing Office, 1874), http://penbay.org/cof/cof_1872–1873_xix.pdf (February 15, 2013); "Around Georgia," *Augusta Chronicle*, August 25, 1889, 2; Charles Minor Blackford, "The Shad—A National Problem," *Transactions of the American Fisheries Society* 46, no. 1 (December 1, 1916): 5–14.

51. Muir, *Thousand-Mile Walk*, 60–63.

52. "Greeting Grady," *Atlanta Constitution*, December 25, 1886, 1; Henry W. Grady, "Cotton and Its Kingdom" (1881), in *Life of Henry W. Grady Including His Writings and Speeches*, ed. Joel Chandler Harris (New York: Cassell Publishing Company, 1890), 262–307, esp. 273. See also Grady, "Before the Bay State Club" (1889), in Harris, *Life of Henry W. Grady*, 199–207.

53. Thomas P. Hughes, *Networks of Power: Electrification in Western Society, 1880–1930* (Baltimore: Johns Hopkins University Press, 1983), 2–15.

54. James C. Williams, *Energy and the Making of Modern California* (Akron: University of Akron Press, 1997), 174.

55. F. C. Finkle, "Electrical Development of Hydraulic Power," *Engineering Magazine* 14, no. 6 (March 1898): 1011–26, esp. 1012. See also Williams, *Energy and the Making of Modern California*, 168–70.

56. Robert McF. Doble, "Hydro-Electric Power Development and Transmission in California," *Journal of the Association of Engineering Societies* 34, no. 3 (March 1905): 75–98, esp. 82.

57. "Electric Railroad Development," *Engineering Record, Building Record, and Sanitary Engineer* 23 (May 9, 1891): 383. See also Institute for Electrical and Electronics Engineers (IEEE) Global History Network, "Milestones: Richmond Union Passenger Railway, 1888," http://www.ieeeghn.org/wiki/index.php/Milestones:Richmond_Union_Passenger_Railway,_1888 (April 14, 2012), and David E. Nye, *Electrifying America: Social Meanings of a New Technology, 1880–1940* (Cambridge: MIT Press, 1990), chap. 3.

58. Ginger Gail Strand, *Inventing Niagara: Beauty, Power, and Lies* (New York: Simon and Schuster, 2008), 148–53.

59. George Fillmore Swain, J. A. Holmes, and E. W. Myers, *Papers on the Waterpower in North Carolina: A Preliminary Report*, North Carolina Geological Survey, Bulletin No. 8 (Raleigh: Guy V. Barnes, 1899), 341; Augustus Kohn, *The Water Powers of South Carolina* (Charleston, S.C.: Walker, Evans, and Cogswell, 1911), 37; David L. Carlton, *Mill and Town*

in South Carolina, 1880–1920 (Baton Rouge: Louisiana State University Press, 1982), 46 n. 11.

60. Hughes, *Networks of Power*, 14–17.

61. George E. Ladshaw, *The Economics of the Flow of Rivers and the Development of Hydraulic Power: Water Power vs. Steam Power* (Spartanburg, S.C.: Jones and Company, 1889), 3 ("southern rivers"), 26 ("water power companies" and "labor"). Whitner's activities have been reconstructed from many sources: Anderson Water, Light & Power Company, *First Annual Report* (n.p., n.d.), and *Wm. C. Whitner & Co., Inc., Consulting and Construction Engineers* (Richmond, n.d.), are located in William Church Whitner (1864–1940) Papers, R69 Mss(R), Manuscripts Division, South Caroliniana Library, University of South Carolina, Columbia. See also Kohn, *Water Powers of South Carolina*, 37–39; Robert F. Durden, *Electrifying the Piedmont Carolinas: The Duke Power Company, 1904–1997* (Durham, N.C.: Carolina Academic Press, 2001), 3–11; and "Generators at Portman to Be Silenced Forever," *Anderson (S.C.) Independent*, December 9, 1960, clipping in folder 3, "Clark's Hill News Clippings," box 3, LMC, 2002.036.

62. At nearly the same moment, private investors developed similar systems in other southern states. In 1896 the Pelzer Manufacturing Company built a hydropower facility on the Saluda River in South Carolina to electrify a mill three miles away. And in April 1898 the Fries Manufacturing and Power Company installed the "first power-transmission plant in North Carolina" on the Yadkin River in Forsyth County. Electricity was transmitted about thirteen miles to five mills and factories and the railway company in Winston and Salem. See Swain, Holmes, and Myers, *Papers on the Waterpower in North Carolina*, 348–50, and Beth Ann Klosky, *"Six Miles That Changed the Course of the South": The Story of the Electric City, Anderson, South Carolina* (Anderson, S.C.: The Electric City Centennial Committee, in cooperation with the City of Anderson and Anderson Heritage, Inc., 1995), 46–47, 55–56.

63. On Whitner's life and work, see n. 61.

64. James C. Cobb, "Beyond Planters and Industrialists: A New Perspective on the New South," *Journal of Southern History* 54, no. 1 (February 1988): 45–68.

65. Carlton, *Mill and Town in South Carolina*, 8 ("town people"), 39 ("new world" and "embryonic"). The new industrial-social order is best described in Bryant Simon, *A Fabric of Defeat: The Politics of South Carolina Millhands, 1910–1948* (Chapel Hill: University of North Carolina Press, 1998).

66. *Descriptive Index of Current Engineering Literature*, Vol. 1, *1884–1891 (Inclusive)* (Chicago, 1892); *The Engineering Index: Five Years—1896–1900* (New York, 1901); *The Engineering Index Annual for 1906* (New York, 1907); *The Engineering Index Annual for 1907* (New York, 1908).

67. Durden, *Electrifying the Piedmont Carolinas*, 6.

68. James Mitchell's biography has been reconstructed from many sources: "James Mitchell Dies of Paralysis at 54," *New York Times*, July 24, 1920, 9, and Alabama Power Company, *Alabama Power Company, Golden Anniversary, December 4, 1956* (n.p.: The Company, 1956), 3. For Alabama Power's history, see Jackson, *Rivers of History*; Harvey H. Jackson III, *Putting "Loafing Streams" to Work: The Building of Lay, Mitchell, Martin, and Jordan Dams, 1910–1929* (Tuscaloosa: University of Alabama Press, 1997);

Leah Rawls Atkins, *"Developed for the Service of Alabama": The Centennial History of the Alabama Power Company, 1906-2006* (Birmingham: Alabama Power Co., 2006), 17-18; and Dub Taft and Sam Heys, *Big Bets: Decisions and Leaders That Shaped Southern Company* (Atlanta: Southern Company, 2011).

69. Duncan McDowall, *The Light: Brazilian Traction, Light, and Power Company Limited, 1899-1945* (Toronto: University of Toronto Press, 1988), 34.

70. Ibid., 92; Atkins, *"Developed for the Service of Alabama,"* 18.

71. Atkins, *"Developed for the Service of Alabama,"* 18.

72. Two other prominent transnational engineers include Massachusetts-born William E. Mitchell (1882-1960) and German-born Richard Pfaehler (1882-[1976?]). See Harllee Branch Jr., *Georgia and the Georgia Power Company: A Century of Free Enterprise!* (New York: Newcomen Society in North America, 1957), 24; Wade H. Wright, *History of the Georgia Power Company, 1855-1956* (Atlanta: Georgia Power Company, 1957), 235; Atkins, *"Developed for the Service of Alabama,"* 38; and "Biographical and Professional Record of Richard Pfaehler, N.C.," scrapbook, box 54, General Subseries, Miscellaneous Series, James Buchanan Duke Papers, David M. Rubenstein Rare Book and Manuscript Library, Duke University, Durham, N.C.

73. See *Electrical World* 91, no. 21 (May 26, 1928), for reports on regional development around the United States. The Rhine River's alpine headwaters were sites for hydroelectric development primarily after 1892. See Mark Cioc, *The Rhine: An Eco-Biography, 1815-2000* (Seattle: University of Washington Press, 2002), 62-64, 131-32, and David Blackbourn, "Dam-Building and Modern Times," in Blackbourn, *The Conquest of Nature: Water, Landscape, and the Making of Modern Germany* (New York: Norton, 2006). In 1895, the Folsom project on California's American River set new standards for generation and transmission; see Williams, *Energy and the Making of Modern California*, 176. British Columbia's development began in 1903. See Matthew D. Evenden, *Fish versus Power: An Environmental History of the Fraser River* (New York: Cambridge University Press, 2004), 56-69.

CHAPTER 2

1. Rupert B. Vance, *Human Geography of the South: A Study in Regional Resources and Human Adequacy* (Chapel Hill: University of North Carolina Press, 1932), 16-17 ("economic complexes"), 285 ("harnessed"), chap. 12 ("Piedmont Crescent of Industry"); William Cronon, *Nature's Metropolis: Chicago and the Great West* (New York: Norton, 1991); Edward Ayers, *The Promise of the New South: Life after Reconstruction* (New York: Oxford University Press, 1992).

2. Robert F. Durden, *Electrifying the Piedmont Carolinas: The Duke Power Company, 1904-1997* (Durham, N.C.: Carolina Academic Press, 2001), 64. The companies I will call Alabama Power, Duke Power, and Georgia Power throughout this chapter changed names though consolidation, new ownership, incorporation, or holding company transfers throughout the twentieth century. These names will be used for simplicity and to illustrate the current corporations' histories. Today, Georgia Power is one of four companies—including Alabama Power, Gulf Power, and Mississippi Power—under the umbrella of the Southern Company (established in 1945). Duke Power was initially known as the

Southern Power Company (established in 1904 and having no affiliation with the current Southern Company), became Duke Power in 1924, merged with Progress Energy in 2012, and is currently known as Duke Energy. For corporate histories, see Wade H. Wright, *History of the Georgia Power Company, 1855–1956* (Atlanta: Georgia Power Company, 1957); Jack Riley, *Carolina Power and Light Company, 1908–1958: A Corporate Biography, Tracing the Origin and Development of Electric Service in Much of the Carolinas* (Raleigh, N.C.: Edwards and Broughton, 1958); Durden, *Electrifying the Piedmont Carolinas*; Martha Elrod and Julie Groce, *Energizing Georgia: The History of Georgia Power, 1883–2004* (Macon, Ga.: Indigo Custom Publishing, 2004); Leah Rawls Atkins, *"Developed for the Service of Alabama": The Centennial History of the Alabama Power Company, 1906–2006* (Birmingham: Alabama Power Co., 2006); and Dub Taft and Sam Heys, *Big Bets: Decisions and Leaders That Shaped Southern Company* (Atlanta: Southern Company, 2011). Duke did not invent the term "white coal," which was already in global circulation. David Blackbourn charts a history of water, energy, and nationalism in Germany during the 1890s, where "'white coal' was cheap, clean, hygienic, and modern, not like smoky, sooty coal." See chapter 4, "Dam-Building and Modern Times," in Blackbourn, *The Conquest of Nature: Water, Landscape, and the Making of Modern Germany* (New York: Norton, 2006), esp. 201 and 219.

3. Vance, *Human Geography*, chap. 12, esp. 281.

4. Robert F. Durden, *The Dukes of Durham, 1865–1929* (Durham, N.C.: Duke University Press, 1975), 177–83.

5. "A Hydro-electric Power Development on the Catawba River, near Rock Hill, S.C.," *Electrical World and Engineer* 44, no. 4 (July 23, 1904): 129–32; Augustus Kohn, *The Water Powers of South Carolina* (Charleston, S.C.: Walker, Evans, and Cogswell, 1911), 82–83.

6. Durden, *Electrifying the Piedmont Carolinas*, ix–x, chap. 1.

7. C. A. Mees, "Development of the Rocky Creek Station of the Southern Power Company," *Engineering Record, Building Record, and Sanitary Engineer* 59, no. 14 (April 3, 1909): 462–69, esp. 462.

8. Durden, *Electrifying the Piedmont Carolinas*, 20, 33; Harriet L. Herring, [J. Herman Johnson,] Rupert B. Vance, and T. J. Woofter Jr., *A Survey of the Catawba Valley: A Study Made by the Institute for Research in Social Science for the Tennessee Valley Authority*, 2 vols. (Chapel Hill: Institute for Research in Social Justice at the University of North Carolina, 1935), 1:1, in the North Carolina Collection, University of North Carolina, Chapel Hill. See also Thorndike Saville, "The Power Situation in the South Appalachian States: The Development of Power Systems of the Southern Province," *Manufacturers' Record* 91, no. 16 (April 21, 1927): 68–77, esp. 68. Alabama Power also "manufactured" the company's initial industrial and commercial customer; see Taft and Heys, *Big Bets*, 20–22. Georgia Power also expressed little interest in rural lines because the investment could not be recouped from farmers; see Henry M. Atkinson, "The Relation of Electric Power to Farm Progress: Georgia's Need—More Industries and Less Politics," address before the Eighteenth Annual Farmers' Week Conference, Athens, Ga., January 28, 1925, 19.

9. Recent energy histories focus on coal as a critical fuel in Colorado and the mid-Atlantic; see Thomas G. Andrews, *Killing for Coal: America's Deadliest Labor War* (Cambridge: Harvard University Press, 2008), and Christopher F. Jones, "A Landscape

of Energy Abundance: Anthracite Coal Canals and the Roots of American Fossil Fuel Dependence, 1820–1860," *Environmental History* 15, no. 3 (July 2010): 449–84. David Nye offers the best synthetic treatment of U.S. energy history: *Consuming Power: A Social History of American Energies* (Cambridge: MIT Press, 1998).

10. James C. Williams, *Energy and the Making of Modern California* (Akron: University of Akron Press, 1997); Joseph A. Pratt, "The Ascent of Oil: The Transition from Coal to Oil in Early Twentieth-Century America," in *Energy Transitions: Long-Term Perspectives*, ed. Lewis J. Perelman, August W. Giebelhaus, and Michael D. Yokell (Boulder, Colo.: American Association for the Advancement of Science and Westview Press, 1981), 9–34, esp. 21; Joseph A. Pratt, "A Mixed Blessing: Energy, Economic Growth, and Houston's Environment," in *Energy Metropolis: An Environmental History of Houston and the Gulf Coast*, ed. Martin V. Melosi and Joseph A. Pratt (Pittsburgh: University of Pittsburgh Press, 2007), 21–51, esp. 26–33.

11. "What About 'Old King Coal'? Is He 'On the Way Out'?" *Right Way Magazine*, October 1936, 4–5.

12. Vance, *Human Geography*, 307.

13. Edward L. Doheny, a U.S. investor in the Mexican Central Railway, began exploring Mexican oil fields in 1900 looking for better fuel to replace poor quality Alabama coal; see Jonathan C. Brown, "Jersey Standard and the Politics of Latin American Oil Production, 1911–30," in *Latin American Oil Companies and the Politics of Energy*, ed. John D. Wirth (Lincoln: University of Nebraska Press, 1985), 8.

14. W. A. Kline, "Hooverize the Coal Pile," *Right Way Magazine*, August 1920, 25, 29.

15. Wayne Flynt, *Poor but Proud: Alabama's Poor Whites* (Tuscaloosa: University of Alabama Press, 1989); W. David Lewis, *Sloss Furnaces and the Rise of the Birmingham District: An Industrial Epic* (Tuscaloosa: University of Alabama Press, 1994); Andrews, *Killing for Coal*, 179.

16. J. A. Switzer, "Water-Power Development in the South," pt. 2, *Cassier's Magazine: An Engineering Monthly* [New York ed.] 42, no. 1 (July 1912): 90–96, esp. 96.

17. Thorndike Saville, "The Power Situation in North Carolina," *Manufacturers' Record* 86, no. 26 (December 25, 1924): 68–70, esp. 69.

18. Jacquelyn Dowd Hall, James Leloudis, Robert Korstad, Mary Murphy, Lu Ann Jones, and Christopher B. Daly, *Like a Family: The Making of a Southern Cotton Mill World* (Chapel Hill: University of North Carolina Press, 1987), 197.

19. J. A. Switzer, "Water-Power Development in the South," pt. 1, *Cassier's Magazine: An Engineering Monthly* [New York ed.] 41, no. 6 (June 1912): 561–76, esp. 561.

20. Ralph G. Macy, "The Southward Trend of Manufacturing: The Piedmont Section of the Carolinas," pt. 1, *Management and Administration* 7, no. 5 (May 1924): 517–22, esp. 520; Ralph G. Macy, "The Construction and Costs of Southern Cotton Mills and Equipment: The Piedmont Section of the Carolinas," pt. 3, *Management and Administration* 8, no. 1 (July 1924): 47–52, esp. 51.

21. L. W. W. Morrow, "The Interconnected South," *Electrical World* 91, no. 21 (May 26, 1928): 1077–84.

22. Vance, *Human Geography*, 284.

23. Switzer, "Water-Power Development in the South," pt. 1, 564.

24. Hales Bar may have been the first southeastern multiple-purpose project of its kind,

but other investors were working on similar projects in Alabama, Georgia, and Iowa. See "Hydroelectric Development on the Tennessee River," *Electrical Review and Western Electrician* 63, no. 21 (November 22, 1913): 1005–9, esp. 1005. For reference, the Bureau of Reclamation completed the Salt River and Roosevelt Dam project in Arizona in 1911, which was the bureau's first multiple-purpose reclamation (i.e., irrigation) and power project. See David P. Billington and Donald C. Jackson, *Big Dams of the New Deal Era: A Confluence of Engineering and Politics* (Norman: University of Oklahoma Press, 2006), 26–46. For more information regarding the Savannah River's Stevens Creek hydroelectric and navigation project, see "Great Hydro-Electric Power Development at Stevens Creek Attracting Attention of Many," *Augusta Chronicle*, November 17, 1912, 8; George G. Shedd, "Two Recent Southern Hydro-Electric Developments," *Power* 39, no. 3 (January 20, 1914): 83–86; and South Carolina Electric and Gas, *Stevens Creek Hydroelectric Project: Significant Historic and Archeological Resources* (n.p., n.d. [1999?]), http://www.sceg.com/NR/rdonlyres/25DD5351-2826-478B-9691-BE26A3F1CEB3/0/StevensCreekReport.pdf (February 15, 2013).

25. Thomas E. Murray, "The Improvement of the Tennessee River and Power Installation of the Chattanooga and Tennessee River Power Company at Hale's Bar, Tenn.," *Transactions of the American Society of Mechanical Engineers* 27 (May 1906): 521–55, esp. 534, copy in the Hales Bar Dam Collection, 1905–1968, Archives Center, NMAH. On the responsibilities of the Corps of Engineers, see also John W. Frink, "The Foundation of Hales Bar Dam," *Economic Geology* 41, no. 6 (1946): 576–97, esp. 579.

26. Jeffrey K. Stine, "United States Army Corps of Engineers," in *Government Agencies*, ed. Donald R. Whitnah, Greenwood Encyclopedia of American Institutions (Westport, Conn.: Greenwood Press, 1983), 513–16; Martin Melosi, *Precious Commodity: Providing Water for America's Cities* (Pittsburgh: University of Pittsburgh Press, 2011), 12–20.

27. Leland R. Johnson, *Engineers of the Twin Rivers: A History of the Nashville District Corps of Engineers, United States Army* (Nashville, Tenn.: United States Army Engineer District, 1978), 166–68.

28. "Hydroelectric Development on the Tennessee River" (November 22, 1913), 1005–9, esp. 1006 ("soluble") and 1007 ("solid rock"). See also Tennessee Valley Authority, "History of Leakage at the Hales Bar Dam," in *Proposed Improvements to the Hales Bar Project*, TVA Report No. 11–100 (November 1941), 1–4 (for discussion of "boils"), copy in Hales Bar Dam Collection, Archives Center, NMAH. The TVA eventually abandoned the Hales Bar project and buried the dam under Nickajack Lake in 1967.

29. Frink, "Foundation of Hales Bar Dam," 578; "Hydroelectric Development on the Tennessee River," *Electrical World* 62, no. 20 (November 15, 1913): 997–1000, esp. 997.

30. J. A. Switzer, "The Power Development at Hale's Bar," *Resources of Tennessee* 2 (March 1912): 86–99, esp. 98, copy in the Hales Bar Dam Collection, Archives Center, NMAH.

31. Norman Wengert, "The Antecedents of TVA: The Legislative History of Muscle Shoals," *Agricultural History* 26, no. 4 (October 1952): 141–47; Johnson, *Engineers of the Twin Rivers*, 169.

32. Preston J. Hubbard, *Origins of the TVA: The Muscle Shoals Controversy, 1920–1932* (Nashville: Vanderbilt University Press, 1961), 145.

33. Thomas K. McCraw, *TVA and the Power Fight, 1933–1939* (Philadelphia: Lippin-

cott, 1971), chap. 1; Billington and Jackson, *Big Dams of the New Deal Era*, chap. 2 and esp. 72.

34. Robert Ernest McFarland Jr., "Of Time and the River: Economy, People, and the Environment in the Tennessee River Valley, 1500–1990" (Ph.D. diss., University of Alabama, 1997), 240; Switzer, "Water-Power Development in the South," pt. 2, 93–94. Alcoa managed investments in at least two subsidiaries: Tallassee Power Company (Tapoco) and Nantahala Power and Light Company; see Charles C. Carr, *ALCOA: An American Enterprise* (New York: Rinehart, 1952), 94–95; Stephen Wallace Taylor, *The New South's New Frontier: A Social History of Economic Development in Southwestern North Carolina* (Gainesville: University Press of Florida, 2001), 30, 60–62; Mountain Heritage Center, Western Carolina University, "NP&L Company Timeline," http://www.wcu.edu/mhc/exhibits/NPL/Index.htm (accessed February 15, 2013); and J. S. Barrett, "History of Tapoco, North Carolina," in *Graham County Centennial, 1872–1972* (Robbinsville, N.C.: Graham County Centennial 1972, Inc., 1972), http://www.grahamcounty.net/GCHistory/06-tapoco/tapoco.htm (accessed February 15, 2013). The Tallassee Power Company also invested in hydroelectric facilities (1918) on the Yadkin River in Badin, N.C., to supply energy to an aluminum smelter originally owned by the Southern Aluminum Company; see Saville, "Power Situation in the South Appalachian States," 73–74, and Carr, *ALCOA*, 93.

35. Eric A. Lof, "The Hydro-electric Development of the Georgia Railway and Power Company at Tallulah Falls, Georgia," pt. 1, *General Electric Review* 17, no. 6 (June 1914): 608–21, esp. 608.

36. John Birkinbine, "Hydroelectric Development on the Tallulah River, Georgia," paper delivered to the Engineer's Club of Philadelphia (1914), 27–28, folder "Power Dam at Gregg Shoals," box 79, RG 77, NAS; Williams, *Energy and the Making of Modern California*, chap. 9.

37. Wright, *History of the Georgia Power Company*, 183.

38. H. M. Atkinson, "Georgia Railway and Power Company: Power Development on Tallulah and Chattooga Rivers," *Manufacturers' Record* 82 (November 2, 1922): 99–104, esp. 99.

39. "P. S. Arkwright, 75, Head of Utility," *New York Times*, December 3, 1946, 31; Preston S. Arkwright Sr., "Some of the Marvels of Electricity," *Manufacturers' Record* 86, no. 23 (December 4, 1924): 88.

40. J. A. Morris, "Scientific and Industrial," *Atlanta Constitution*, April 26, 1896, 5; "Elevators in Skyscraper Stop for Thirty Minutes," *Atlanta Constitution*, February 4, 1910, 6; Campbell Gibson, *Population of the 100 Largest Cities and Other Urban Places in the United States: 1790 To 1990*, Population Division Working Paper No. 27 (Washington, D.C.: U.S. Bureau of the Census, June 1998), table 12, http://www.census.gov/population/www/documentation/twps0027/twps0027.html.

41. "Thomson-Houston," *Atlanta Journal-Constitution*, February 10, 1889, 19.

42. Kohn, *Water Powers of South Carolina*, 45, 53. On manufacture and natural gas lighting, see Nye, *Consuming Power*, 83–84, 95, 121. See also "Atlanta Gas Part of Rome History," *Rome News-Tribune*, March 2, 1982.

43. J. H. Reed, "Atlanta: An Inspiring Story of Growth in Trade, Industry, Finance, Education, and Music," *Manufacturers' Record* 85, no. 9 (February 28, 1924): 76–84, esp.

79. For population estimation, see Gibson, *Population of the 100 Largest Cities*, tables 15 and 16.

44. W. S. Murray et al., *A Superpower System for the Region between Boston and Washington*, Department of the Interior, U. S. Geological Survey, Professional Paper 123 (Washington, D.C.: Government Printing Office, 1921), 13. For a primer on Giant Power and Super Power, see Sarah T. Phillips, *This Land, This Nation: Conservation, Rural America, and the New Deal* (New York: Cambridge University Press, 2007), 25–36.

45. "Hydro-Electric Developments 'Unparalleled in the World,'" *Manufacturers' Record* 65, no. 21 (May 28, 1914): 41–42; Thorndike Saville, "The Power Situation in the Southern Power Province," *Annals of the American Academy of Political and Social Science* 153, Coming of Industry to the South edition (January 1931): 94–123, esp. 116. See also the articles on regional electric generation, distribution, and service in *Electrical World* 91, no. 21 (May 26, 1928), esp. Morrow, "Interconnected South."

46. Wright, *History of the Georgia Power Company*, 213–16; Atkins, *"Developed for the Service of Alabama,"* 141–48, 162; Taft and Heys, *Big Bets*, esp. 39–55, 75–92.

47. Durden, *Electrifying the Piedmont Carolinas*, 4.

48. Thomas W. Martin, "Hydroelectric Development in the South," in *The South's Development: Fifty Years of Southern Progress, a Glimpse of the Past, the Facts of the Present, a Forecast of the Future*, special issue of the *Manufacturers' Record* 86, no. 24, pt. 2 (December 11, 1924), 242–62, esp. 257.

49. Joseph Hyde Pratt, "The Southeastern Power System and Its Tremendous Industrial Value to the States It Serves," *Manufacturers' Record* 86 (July 24, 1924): 83–84.

50. Phillips, *This Land, This Nation*, 30.

51. Philip J. Funigiello, *Toward a National Power Policy: The New Deal and the Electric Utility Industry, 1933–1941* (Pittsburgh: University of Pittsburgh Press, 1973), 6–29.

52. U.S. Congress, Senate, *Electric Power Development in the United States: Letter from the Secretary of Agriculture Transmitting a Report, in Response to a Senate Resolution of February 13, 1915, as to the Ownership and Control of the Water-Power Sites in the United States* (3 vols.), 64th Cong., 1st sess. (Washington, D.C.: Government Printing Office, 1916), 1:53, 2:74.

53. Image from *Southern Farming* (January 4, 1913) found in Atkins, *"Developed for the Service of Alabama,"* 54.

54. W. S. Murray, "The Superpower System as an Answer to a National Power Policy," *General Electric Review* 25, no. 2 (February 1922): 72–76, esp. 72.

55. Jean Christie, *Morris Llewellyn Cooke, Progressive Engineer* (New York: Garland, 1983), 79; Phillips, *This Land, This Nation*, 25.

56. Morrow, "Interconnected South," 1079–81, esp. 1081.

57. The interconnected companies included Southeastern Power and Light Co. (Alabama Power, Georgia Power, and Mississippi Power Companies); Carolina Power and Light Company; Duke Power Company; Florida Power and Light Company; Tennessee Electric Power Company; Appalachian Power Company; and Virginia Public Service Company. See ibid., 1079–81.

58. On interconnection and droughts, see Durden, *Electrifying the Piedmont Carolinas*, 62–63, and Saville, "Power Situation in North Carolina," 70. On interconnection, see Martin, "Hydroelectric Development in the South," 255–57.

59. Atkinson, "Georgia Railway and Power Company," 99.

60. "Alabama Sending Power to Georgia Because of Drouht [sic]," *Atlanta Constitution*, August 23, 1925, 9, 13.

61. Jacquelyn Dowd Hall, Robert Korstad, and James Leloudis, "Cotton Mill People: Work, Community, and Protest in the Textile South, 1880–1940," *American Historical Review* 91, no. 2 (April 1986): 245–86, esp. 258; Hall et al., *Like a Family*, 47–48; Allen Tullos, *Habits of Industry: White Culture and the Transformation of the Carolina Piedmont* (Chapel Hill: University of North Carolina Press, 1989), 16–17.

62. "Mills Close Down Today Due to Low Water in the Canal," *Augusta Chronicle*, September 19, 1918, 3.

63. David E. Ney brilliantly demonstrates how the "blackout" evolved as a cultural construction during the twentieth century. However, Nye's broad synthesis missed the complex relationship of droughts and electrical supply in the Southeast; see *When the Lights Went Out: A History of Blackouts in America* (Cambridge: MIT Press, 2010), esp. 39–40.

64. "New Dam to Protect Industries against Drought," *Atlanta Constitution*, May 23, 1920, K17.

65. "Alabama Sending Power to Georgia Because of Drouht," 9.

66. Wright, *History of the Georgia Power Company*, 212.

67. "Alabama Sending Power to Georgia Because of Drouht," 9, 13.

68. Atkinson, "Georgia Railway and Power Company," 99; Pratt, "Southeastern Power System," 84; Saville, "Power Situation in North Carolina," 70; "Alabama Sending Power to Georgia Because of Drouht," 9, 13; "Atlanta Gets Power as First Water Pours into Shoals Turbine," *Atlanta (Ga.) Constitution*, August 30, 1925, 1, 3; Taft and Heys, *Big Bets*, esp. 21 ("coal by wire").

69. Durden, *Electrifying the Piedmont Carolinas*, 64.

70. Ibid., 96–99.

71. Wright, *History of the Georgia Power Company*, 212, 247, 324–25. Georgia Power began operating Plant Atkinson upstream of Atlanta on the Chattahoochee River in 1930, and in 1941 the company began operating Plant Arkwright near Macon on the Ocmulgee River. The company retired and began dismantling both plants in 2003 to save money and reduce sulfur dioxide, carbon dioxide, and nitrogen oxide emissions; see "Ga. Power Retiring Old Plants," *Atlanta Journal-Constitution*, May 16, 2002, A1. Congress designated the Wild and Scenic Chattooga River in 1974.

72. C. B. Hawkins and W. W. Eberhardt, "Method of Handling Interconnected Operation," *Electrical World* 92, no. 15 (October 13, 1928): 725–31, esp. 727.

73. "Power Possibilities of Catawba River Highly Developed through Stream Control," *Engineering News-Record* 104, no. 25 (June 19, 1930): 1007–12, esp. 1008.

74. It is worth noting that droughts in 1918–19 and 1920–21 in California reduced hydroelectric generation capacity, and utilities responded by investing heavily in natural gas and steam to generate electricity; see Williams, *Energy and the Making of Modern California*, 277–79.

75. The TVA also acquired private electric companies and their management staff outright, according to Lynn Nelson, "'Harassed by the Floods and Storms of Nature': Remembering Private Hydro-Power and Rural Communities in Tennessee," paper read at

the American Society for Environmental History Conference, Tallahassee, Florida, February 2009.

76. Rupert Vance, "The Consumption of Coal in Relation to the Development of Hydroelectric Power in the Carolinas," in Herring et al., *Survey of the Catawba Valley*, vol. 2, Appendix D, 399 ("tremendous"), 408 ("hydro power or nothing"); Herring et al., *Survey of the Catawba Valley*, 1:3 ("hydro-industrial empire").

77. Murray, "Superpower System as an Answer to a National Power Policy," 72. Murray circulated within the transnational community of engineers, and in South Carolina in 1927 one of his companies eventually completed the massive Saluda River Hydroelectric Project dam and lake named in his honor: Lake Murray. Murray's project produced wholesale electricity that was transmitted directly into the southern Super Power system and distributed to Duke Power, Carolina Power and Light Company, and Broad River Power Company customers. Lake Murray is currently owned and operated by the South Carolina Electric and Gas Company. See *Saluda Hydroelectric Project, FERC Project No. 516: Construction History, Exhibit C*, prepared by Kleinschmidt Energy and Water Resources Consultants, December 2007, http://www.saludahydrorelicense.com/documents/EXHIBITC.pdf (February 15, 2013).

78. On one important technology, see Raymond Arsenault, "The End of the Long Hot Summer: The Air Conditioner and Southern Culture," *Journal of Southern History* 50, no. 4 (November 1984): 597–628.

79. Murray, "Improvement of the Tennessee," 531.

CHAPTER 3

1. On Augusta's drought, see *Mayors Message and Official Reports of the Department of the City of Augusta, for the Year 1907* (Augusta, Ga.: Phoenix Printing Co., 1908), 62–63. On valley flooding, see A. L. Dabney, "Report on Flood Protection for the City of Augusta, GA" (April 30, 1912), and H. T. Cory, "Report on Flood Protection at Augusta, Georgia" (May 20, 1912), folder SR 824.02, box 80, accession 76E342, RG 77, NAS.

2. The storm and flooding events have been reconstructed from multiple sources, including telephone conversation notes, October 2, 1929, folder DR 362.08, Georgia–South Carolina Flood, 9 & 10/29, box 760, Records of the American National Red Cross, 1917–1934, RG 200, NAII; "Two Georgia Towns Imperiled as Dams Loose Torrents into Valley; Battle of Workers to Save Augusta Levee Is Believed Successful," *Atlanta Constitution*, October 3, 1929, 1; E. D. Emigh, USDA Weather Bureau, *Report of the Floods in the Savannah River, September and October, 1929* (October 18, 1929), Mis. 10059/43.30, box 75, accession 76E342, RG 77, NAS; Ralph Howard, U.S. Army Corps of Engineers, *Augusta Flood 1929, Report of Emergency Work*, n.d. [possibly December 12, 1929], 5–6, Mis. 10059/43–62, box 75, accession 76E342, RG 77, NAS; U.S. Army Corps of Engineers and Secretary of War, *Savannah River Georgia, South Carolina, and North Carolina* (Washington, D.C.: Government Printing Office, 1935), 36–47.

3. Edward J. Cashin, *The Story of Augusta* (Augusta, Ga.: Richmond County Board of Education, 1980), 72.

4. Kathleen Ann Clark, *Defining Moments: African American Commemoration and*

Political Culture in the South, 1863-1913 (Chapel Hill: University of North Carolina Press, 2005), 126-30.

5. Emigh, *Report of the Floods in the Savannah River*, 8 ("many of the houses"); "Augusta Levee Breaks; Six Cities Isolated," *Atlanta Constitution*, September 28, 1929, 1 ("negro settlement"); Charles W. Carr, *Proposed Plans for Rehabilitation in Hamburg, S.C.* (November 18, 1929), folder DR 326, Georgia–South Carolina Flood, 9 & 10/29, box 760, RG 200, NAII. See also Timothy Cox, "Residents Recall Life in Black Community," *Augusta Chronicle*, November 10, 2002. For hurricane and tropical storm histories, see National Oceanic and Atmospheric Administration Historical Hurricane Tracking, http://maps.csc.noaa.gov/hurricanes/index.html#.

6. Philip J. Funigiello, *Toward a National Power Policy: The New Deal and the Electric Utility Industry, 1933-1941* (Pittsburgh: University of Pittsburgh Press, 1973). Karl B. Brooks argues that private energy companies "un-plugged" the New Deal's (and the Corps') water and energy program in the 1950s in the American West; see *Public Power, Private Dams: The Hells Canyon High Dam Controversy* (Seattle: University of Washington Press, 2006).

7. Bruce J. Schulman, *From Cotton Belt to Sunbelt: Federal Policy, Economic Development, and the Transformation of the South, 1938-1980* (Durham, N.C.: Duke University Press, 1994); Alan Brinkley, *End of Reform: New Deal Liberalism in Recession and War* (New York: Knopf, 1995); Jason Scott Smith, *Building New Deal Liberalism: The Political Economy of Public Works, 1933-1956* (New York: Cambridge University Press, 2006); Sarah T. Phillips, *This Land, This Nation: Conservation, Rural America, and the New Deal* (New York: Cambridge University Press, 2007).

8. Ted Steinberg, *Acts of God: The Unnatural History of Natural Disaster in America* (New York: Oxford University Press, 2006), xxii.

9. Jeffrey K. Stine, "United States Army Corps of Engineers," in *Government Agencies*, ed. Donald R. Whitnah, Greenwood Encyclopedia of American Institutions (Westport, Conn.: Greenwood Press, 1983), 513-16.

10. U.S. Congress, House, *Survey of the Savannah River above Augusta*, 51st Cong., 1st sess., February 18, 1890, House Executive Document 213, pp. 5, 11.

11. Col. Dan Kingman, Savannah, Ga., to Chief of Engineers, Washington, D.C., September 9, 1908, 5, folder Mis. 10059/1 to 10059/42, box 75, accession 76E342, RG 77, NAS.

12. The 1908 flood claimed sixteen lives; see *Mayors Message and Official Reports of the Department of the City of Augusta, for 1908* (Augusta, Ga.: Phoenix Printing Co., 1909), 16, 42.

13. *The City Council of Augusta, Ga., Yearbook 1910* (Augusta, Ga.: Williams Printing Co., 1911), 25, 41; *Nineteen Eleven Year Book of the City Council of Augusta, Ga.* (Augusta, Ga.: Phoenix Printing Co., 1912), 97-99.

14. John M. Barry, *Rising Tide: The Great Mississippi Flood of 1927 and How It Changed America* (New York: Simon and Schuster, 1997); Karen M. O'Neill, *Rivers by Design: State Power and the Origins of U.S. Flood Control* (Durham, N.C.: Duke University Press, 2006); David P. Billington and Donald C. Jackson, *Big Dams of the New Deal Era: A Confluence of Engineering and Politics* (Norman: University of Oklahoma Press, 2006).

15. Col. W. M. Black, Board of Engineers for Rivers and Harbors, *Savannah River at Augusta, Ga.*, December 7, 1915, 1-4, box 76, project 803025, RG 77, NAII; Major

D. Weart, "Report of Flood Study on Savannah River at Augusta, Georgia, Savannah, Georgia, District," December 18, 1929, p. 37, box 1111, project 803017, RG 77, NAII.

16. Martin Melosi, *Precious Commodity: Providing Water for America's Cities* (Pittsburgh: University of Pittsburgh Press, 2011), 16–20. See *Electrical World* 91, no. 21 (May 26, 1928), for reports on regional development around the United States.

17. U.S. Army Corps of Engineers, *Mississippi River Headwaters Reservoir Operating Plan Evaluation (ROPE): Upper Mississippi River Headwaters Bemidji to St. Paul, Minnesota, DRAFT Integrated Reservoir Operating Plan Evaluation and Environmental Impact Statement* (St. Paul, Minn.: United States Army Corps of Engineers, St. Paul District, August 2008), chap. 4, 20–32, http://www.co.aitkin.mn.us/ROPE/CHAPTER%204 .%20AFFECTED%20ENVIRONMENT.pdf (February 16, 2013).

18. "Dayton Flood-Protection Ready for Adoption," *Engineering News* 75, no. 10 (March 9, 1916): 485–86; "Final Flood-Protection Plan for Miami Valley," *Engineering News* 75, no. 14 (April 6, 1916): 674–75; Arthur Ernest Morgan, *The Miami Conservancy District* (New York: McGraw-Hill, 1951).

19. For more on Georgia Power's and Duke Power's projects, see chap. 2.

20. Billington and Jackson, *Big Dams of the New Deal Era*, 28–46.

21. For more on Hales Bar, see chap. 2. The Mississippi River Power Company completed the Keokuk (Iowa) dam, hydroelectric facilities, and navigation lock in 1913 soon after Hales Bar and delivered power to St. Louis 144 miles away; see Eric A. Lof, "The Mississippi River Hydro-electric Development at Keokuk, Iowa," pt. 1, *General Electric Review* 17, no. 2 (February 1914): 85–98. The Stevens Creek dam, hydroelectric facility, and navigation lock (completed in 1914) is located thirteen miles upstream from Augusta; see "Georgia-Carolina Power Company: Its Birth and Development," *Augusta Chronicle*, February 15, 1914, 4, and South Carolina Electric and Gas, *Stevens Creek Hydroelectric Project: Significant Historic and Archeological Resources* (n.p., n.d. [possibly 1999]), http://www.sceg.com/NR/rdonlyres/25DD5351-2826-478B-9691-BE26A3F1CEB3/0/ StevensCreekReport.pdf (February 15, 2013).

22. Samuel P. Hays, *Conservation and the Gospel of Efficiency: The Progressive Conservation Movement, 1890–1920* (Cambridge: Harvard University Press, 1959); James Scott, *Seeing Like a State: How Certain Schemes to Improve the Human Condition Have Failed* (New Haven: Yale University Press, 1998). For example, see Benjamin Mortimer Hall and Max R. Hall, *Third Report on the Water-Powers of Georgia*, Geological Survey of Georgia, Bulletin No. 38 (Atlanta: Byrd Printing Company, 1921).

23. Funigiello, *Toward a National Power Policy*, 6–29.

24. U.S. Congress, House, *Estimate of Cost of Examinations, Etc., of Streams Where Power Development Appears Feasible*, 69th Cong., 1st sess., April 13, 1926, House Document 308.

25. Correspondence between Major D. L. Weart and William States Lee, July 29 and 31, 1930, folder Copy of Savannah River 308 Report, Mis. 500/31–82–250, box 53, accession 76E342, RG 77, NAS.

26. For data sharing, see boxes 53 and 57, accession 76E342, RG 77, NAS, for correspondence between C. James (Allied Engineers) and Ralph Rhodes (Senior Engineer, Savannah District), July 23, 1930; Ralph S. Howard (Associate Engineer) and Major D. L. Weart (Savannah District), March 31, 1930; J. E. Parker (Allied Engineers, Inc.) and Major

D. L. Weart, August 18, September 5, and October 7, 1931; Ralph Rhodes, W. E. Sanford, and C. James, July 18 and 23, 1930; Elroy G. Smith and Major D. L. Weart, August 1, 1930.

27. Savannah River Electric Company Application for License, Federal Power Commission, November 5, 1926, and Savannah District, "Report on application for license by Savannah River Electric Co. of Edgefield, S.C., Project No. 798" (July 27, 1927), box 78, accession 76E342, RG 77, NAS.

28. Correspondence between J. E. Parker, Assistant Engineer, Commonwealth & Southern Corporation of New York, and Major C. Garlington, U.S. Army Corps of Engineers, Savannah District, March 18 and 27, 1933, box 53, accession 76E342, RG 77, NAS.

29. The TVA scholarship is extensive and the recommended sources include Preston J. Hubbard, *Origins of the TVA: The Muscle Shoals Controversy, 1920–1932* (Nashville: Vanderbilt University Press, 1961); Thomas K. McCraw, *Morgan vs. Lilienthal: The Feud within the TVA* (Chicago: Loyola University Press, 1970); Thomas K. McCraw, *TVA and the Power Fight, 1933–1939* (Philadelphia: Lippincott, 1971); Philip Selznick, *TVA and the Grass Roots: A Study of Politics and Organization* (New York: Harper and Row, 1980); Michael J. McDonald and John Muldowny, *TVA and the Dispossessed: The Resettlement of Population in the Norris Dam Area* (Knoxville: University of Tennessee Press, 1982); and Erwin C. Hargrove and Paul K. Conkin, eds., *TVA: Fifty Years of Grass-Roots Bureaucracy* (Chicago: University of Illinois Press, 1983).

30. T. Robert Hart has compiled the best interpretation of Santee-Cooper; see "The Lowcountry Landscape: Politics, Preservation, and the Santee-Cooper Project," *Environmental History* 18, no. 1 (January 2013): 127–56.

31. The Wheeler, Norris, Pickiwick, and Guntersville multiple-purpose projects were either completed or under construction in 1935.

32. Major D. L. Weart, Savannah District, "Report of Flood Study on Savannah River at Augusta, Georgia, Savannah, Georgia, District," December 18, 1929, box 1111, project #803017, RG 77, NAII.

33. U.S. Army Corps of Engineers and Secretary of War, *Savannah River Georgia, South Carolina, and North Carolina*, 2, 19–40, 50–51, 71–72, 103, 132–34.

34. Kay Dockins, "River Basin Development Team Is Set," *Augusta Chronicle*, January 19, 1966, 1; Paul Garber, "City Booster's Influence Felt in Many Areas," *Augusta Chronicle*, June 21, 1996; Mary Beth Reed, Barbara Smith Strack, and U.S. Department of Energy, *Savannah River Site at Fifty* (Washington, D.C.: U.S. Department of Energy and Government Printing Office, 2002), 101; Cashin, *Story of Augusta*, 236.

35. Copy of letter, Lester Moody, Augusta Chamber of Commerce, to President Franklin D. Roosevelt, August 8, 1935, folder 1, box 3, LMC, 2002.036.

36. For a parallel case study in the American West, see Brooks, *Public Power, Private Dams*, 34.

37. "Vast Plant Atkinson, Peerless in U.S., Shown as Place of Engineering Marvels," *Snap Shots* 3, no. 8 (August 1929): 1. On natural gas, see Wade H. Wright, *History of the Georgia Power Company, 1855–1956* (Atlanta: Georgia Power Company, 1957), 248.

38. Dub Taft and Sam Heys, *Big Bets: Decisions and Leaders That Shaped Southern Company* (Atlanta: Southern Company, 2011), 95–97; Robert F. Durden, *Electrifying the Piedmont Carolinas: The Duke Power Company, 1904–1997* (Durham, N.C.: Carolina Academic Press, 2001), 110–12.

39. *Georgia Power Company to United States, Warranty Deed*, Deed Record E-4, 109–20, Rabun County Courthouse, Clayton, Ga.

40. "Huge Hydro Plant Planned," *Snap Shots* 3, no. 9 (September 1929): 3.

41. "Harnessing Oconee for Georgia's Progress," *Snap Shots* 3, no. 11 (November 1929): 1; "550 Dixie Men Will Begin Dam in Icy Oconee," *Snap Shots* 3, no. 12 (December 1929): 3.

42. "Power Company Plans $16,000,000 Building Program," *Atlanta Constitution*, December 8, 1929, 11; "$16,000,000 Program Sets State Record," *Snap Shots* 3, no. 12 (December 1929): 1.

43. "Concrete Is Placed at Furman Shoals; Begin Vast Wall," *Snap Shots* 4, no. 4 (April 1930): 5; "Georgia Power Will Complete Oconee Plant," *Atlanta (Ga.) Constitution*, July 20, 1942, 3; Wright, *History of the Georgia Power Company*, 250, 332. The company eventually restarted construction in 1949 and began dam operations in 1952.

44. Savannah River Special Board, *Clark Hill Navigation–Flood Control–Power Project, Savannah River, Georgia–South Carolina, Report to the President* (Washington, D.C.: n.p, February 29, 1936), 6, project 803017, box 1109, RG77, NAII.

45. Ibid., 44–48. Construction on a similar southern energy and water scheme—the Santee Cooper Hydroelectric and Navigation Project—began in 1934 during the New Deal (funded by the PWA) and was operational by 1942. The South Carolina Public Service Authority oversees the state-owned water and electrical utility's operations today.

46. Preston S. Arkwright Sr.'s statement was provided via correspondence from Lester S. Moody, Chamber of Commerce Secretary, Augusta, Georgia, to Senator Richard B. Russell, November 25, 1936, Series XI, Rivers and Harbors, box 13, folder 6, RRC.

47. Henry M. Atkinson, "The Relation of Electric Power to Farm Progress: Georgia's Need—More Industries and Less Politics," address before the Eighteenth Annual Farmers' Week Conference, Athens, Ga., January 28, 1925, 19. See also D. Clayton Brown, *Electricity for Rural America: The Fight for the REA* (Westport, Conn.: Greenwood Press, 1980), 73.

48. "G.P.C. Makes Bid for Clarks Hill," *Augusta Chronicle*, October 9, 1939, 1.

49. The question was explicitly raised a few years later: John E. Stoddard, "Who Should Build the Clark Hill Dam?" *News-Reporter*, April 24, 1947.

50. Phillips, *This Land, This Nation*, chaps. 1 and 2.

51. McCraw, *TVA and the Power Fight*, chaps. 6 and 7.

52. Ibid., 63–65; Leah Rawls Atkins, *"Developed for the Service of Alabama": The Centennial History of the Alabama Power Company, 1906–2006* (Birmingham: Alabama Power Co., 2006), 80–84, 93–103, 175–89, 193–95.

53. Karen M. O'Neill, "Why the TVA Remains Unique: Interest Groups and the Defeat of New Deal River Planning," *Rural Sociology* 67, no. 2 (2002): 163–82; O'Neill, *Rivers by Design*.

54. O'Neill, *Rivers By Design*, 146–47, 164–65.

55. For a recent interpretation of the TVA and the global modernization projects New Deal regional planning inspired, see David Ekbladh, *The Great American Mission: Modernization and the Construction of an American World Order* (Princeton: Princeton University Press, 2010).

56. Schulman, *From Cotton Belt to Sunbelt*, 15–31.

57. David L. Carlton and Peter A. Coclanis, eds., *Confronting Poverty in the Great De-*

pression: The Report on the Economic Conditions of the South *with Related Documents* (Boston: Bedford Books of St. Martin's Press, 1996), 47, 50–52.

58. Schulman, *From Cotton Belt to Sunbelt*, 52.

59. Kari Frederickson, *The Dixiecrat Revolt and the End of the Solid South, 1932–1968* (Chapel Hill: University of North Carolina Press, 2001), 13–27.

60. "An Inspiring Project," *Atlanta Journal*, March 15, 1945; "Fortson Lauds Benefits of Savannah River Project," *Atlanta Constitution*, March 15, 1945; U.S. Congress, Senate, *Savannah Valley Authority*, 79th Cong., 1st sess., S. 737, *Congressional Record*, March 14, 1945, 2168; "Bill Is Offered for Huge SRA," *Augusta Chronicle*, March 15, 1945, 1; U.S. Congress, Senate, *Savannah Valley Authority*, 80th Cong., 1st sess., S. 1534, *Congressional Record*, June 30, 1947, 7876.

61. John T. McMullen, Liaison Representative, American Red Cross, Atlanta (Ga.) Regional Office, to Colin Herrle, Assistant Director, Disaster Relief, American Red Cross, March 12, 1929, folder DR 305, South Carolina, Hamburg Flood, 2/28/29, box 756, RG 200, NAII.

62. Howard, *Augusta Flood 1929*, 10.

63. Charles W. Carr, Disaster Relief Representative, American National Red Cross, Washington, D.C., to Colin Herrle, Assistant Director, Disaster Relief, American Red Cross, November 12, 1929, folder DR 305, South Carolina, Hamburg Flood, 2/28/29, box 757, RG 200, NAII.

64. $350 per acre would have been an exorbitant price, and it is possible this proposal contained computational or other errors; see Carr, *Proposed Plans for Rehabilitation in Hamburg.*

65. Charles W. Carr, *The Georgia–South Carolina Flood of 1929: Narrative Report*, February 11, 1930, folder DR 362, Georgia–South Carolina Flood, 9 & 10/29, box 760, RG 200, NAII.

66. John F. Battle, "New Hamburg, Now on a Hill, Rises From Ruins of the Old," *Augusta Chronicle*, January 20, 1930, 3; "Hamburg 'On Heights,'" *Augusta Chronicle*, January 27, 1930, newspaper clipping, folder DR 362, Georgia–South Carolina Flood, 9 & 10/29, box 760, RG 200, NAII.

67. Carr, *Georgia–South Carolina Flood of 1929*; "Insurance Firm Pays Tribute to Dr. Stoney," *Augusta Chronicle*, October 13, 1926, 8; editorial, "A Negro Bank For Augusta," *Augusta Chronicle*, February 23, 1928, 4. A likely picture of Carpenter's insurance staff and grocery storefront can be found in Walter B. Ware, *Black Business in the New South: A Social History of the North Carolina Mutual Life Insurance Company* (Urbana: University of Illinois Press, 1973).

68. Charles W. Carr, Disaster Relief Representative, American National Red Cross, Augusta, Ga., to J. C. Whatley, Purchasing Officer, Aiken County Chapter Flood Relief, North Augusta, S.C., December 17, 1929, folder DR 362, Georgia–South Carolina Flood, 9 & 10/29, box 760, RG 200, NAII.

69. "Southern Realty Company" source: advertisement, Augusta *Chronicle*, June 2, 1929, D-5. Carpenter's land ownership: Charles W. Carr, Disaster Relief Representative, American National Red Cross, Washington, D.C., to Colin Herrle, Assistant Director, Disaster Relief, American Red Cross, November 12, 1929, folder DR-305, South Carolina, Hamburg Flood, 2/28/29, box 757, RG 200, NAII, and "Plat Showing Property Located

in Schultz's (66) Township, Aiken County, South Carolina, Surveyed for O. M. Blount," December 1929, folder DR 362, Georgia–South Carolina Flood, 9 & 10/29, box 760, RG 200, NAII.

70. Robert D. Bullard, *Dumping in Dixie: Race, Class, and Environmental Quality* (Boulder, Colo.: Westview Press, 1990); Andrew Hurley, *Environmental Inequalities: Class, Race, and Industrial Pollution in Gary, Indiana, 1945–1980* (Chapel Hill: University of North Carolina Press, 1995); Eileen Maura McGurty, "From NIMBY to Civil Rights: The Origins of the Environmental Justice Movement," *Environmental History* 2, no. 3 (July 1997): 301–23; Ellen Stroud, "Troubled Waters in Ecotopia: Environmental Racism in Portland, Oregon," *Radical History Review* 74 (Spring 1999): 65–95; Robert Bullard and Beverly Wright, *The Wrong Complexion for Protection: How the Government Response to Disasters Endangers African American Communities* (New York: New York University Press, 2012), chap. 3.

71. Smith, *Building New Deal Liberalism*, 195–97.

CHAPTER 4

1. "Sacrifices Being Made by Augustans to Avert Threatened Power Shortage," *Augusta Chronicle*, May 30, 1941, 3.

2. Weather Bureau statement: "U.S. Forester Warns of Fires," *Atlanta Constitution*, May 18, 1941, 2D; advertisement, "An Appeal to All Users of Electric Light, Heat and Power," *Atlanta Constitution*, May 25, 1941, 10C.

3. Display ad, "Public Welfare Demands GREATER Power Savings," *Atlanta Constitution*, June 13, 1941, 8.

4. "Sacrifices Being Made by Augustans," emphasis in original.

5. *Augusta Chronicle*, June 26, 1941, 2.

6. Display ad, "Monday's the Deadline," *Augusta Chronicle*, June 15, 1941, 10.

7. "The Artistry in the Waterworks Lawn," *Atlanta Constitution*, May 11, 1941, 5; U.S. Congress, House, *Apalachicola, Chattahoochee, and Flint Rivers, Ga. and Fla.*, 80th Cong., 1st sess., House Document no. 300, June 6, 1947, 34.

8. Campbell Gibson, *Population of the 100 Largest Cities and Other Urban Places in the United States: 1790 To 1990*, Population Division Working Paper No. 27 (Washington, D.C.: U.S. Bureau of the Census, June 1998), table 17, http://www.census.gov/population/www/documentation/twps0027/twps0027.html.

9. Display ad, "How Power Pooling Helps Relieve Shortage," *Atlanta Constitution*, November 16, 1941, 10A; "Trout Streams Likely to Reopen This Week," *Atlanta Constitution*, May 6, 1942, 15. Annual average precipitation data from the Southeast Regional Climate Center, http://www.sercc.com/climateinfo/monthly_seasonal.html. See also Nancy L. Barber and Timothy C. Stamey, *Droughts in Georgia*, U.S. Geological Survey Report 00-380, October 2000, 1.

10. For detailed treatments of two major Sun Belt navigation projects, see Jeffrey K. Stine, *Mixing the Waters: Environment, Politics, and the Building of the Tennessee-Tombigbee Waterway* (Akron: University of Akron Press, 1993), and Steven Noll and David Tegeder, *Ditch of Dreams: The Cross Florida Barge Canal and the Struggle for Florida's Future* (Gainesville: University of Florida Press, 2009).

11. The dam and lake project that I will refer to as Clarks Hill throughout this book has a storied "name" history. The waterpower site was known as Clarks Hill throughout the nineteenth century as a reference to an adjacent South Carolina rural community. Due to a stenographer's mistake in the initial congressional authorization legislation, the Corps' project became Clark Hill Dam and Lake. Between the 1950s and 1980s, the project was referred to as Clark Hill and Clarks Hill. In 1988, Congress changed the name to J. Strom Thurmond Dam and Lake at Clarks Hill.

12. Kari Frederickson provides one of the best interpretations of disintegration of "the Solid South" in her book *The Dixiecrat Revolt and the End of the Solid South, 1932–1968* (Chapel Hill: University of North Carolina Press, 2001).

13. U.S. Congress, Senate, *Savannah River and Clark Hill Reservoir*, 76th Cong., 1st sess., Senate Document 66 [1939], 1, 33.

14. U.S. Army Corps of Engineers and Secretary of War, *Savannah River Georgia, South Carolina, and North Carolina* (Washington, D.C.: Government Printing Office, 1935).

15. U.S. Congress, House, *Savannah River, GA*, 78th Cong., 2nd sess., June 9, 1944, House Document 657.

16. John M. Clark Jr., "John Mulford Clark, October 8, 1813–January 8, 1880," March 25, 1952, 1–5, folder Legislation, 1952, Clarks Hill Project, box 29, OJP.

17. U.S. Congress, House, *Savannah River, GA*, 47–50. See also Edward B. Burwell Jr., *Report on Geology of Dam and Reservoir Sites in the Savannah River Basin, Georgia and South Carolina* (Cincinnati: War Department, Office of the Division Engineer, Ohio River Division, October 1, 1942), box 66, accession 76E342, RG 77, NAS.

18. U.S. Congress, House, Committee on Rivers and Harbors, *Hearings before the Committee on Rivers and Harbors, House of Representatives: On the Subject of the Improvement of the Savannah River, GA & Savannah River and Clarks Hill Reservoir*, 78th Cong., October 27, 1943, 2–3.

19. Frederickson, *Dixiecrat Revolt*, 2.

20. Josephine Mellinchamp, *Senators from Georgia* (Huntsville, Ala.: Strode Publishers, 1976); "Walter Franklin George," *The Biographical Directory of the U.S. Congress*, http://bioguide.congress.gov/scripts/biodisplay.pl?index=g000131.

21. "George Is Asked by Camp to Show 'Letter' To FDR," *Atlanta Constitution*, September 2, 1938, 1; "Arkwright Denies Company Participated in George Campaign," *Atlanta Constitution*, April 17, 1940, 1.

22. "Senator George Discusses Clark Hill," *Augusta Herald*, October 24, 1944, 1, RRC clipping.

23. Alan Brinkley, *End of Reform: New Deal Liberalism in Recession and War* (New York: Knopf, 1995); Jason Scott Smith, *Building New Deal Liberalism: The Political Economy of Public Works, 1933–1956* (New York: Cambridge University Press, 2006), 263 for terminology citations.

24. *Flood Control Act of 1944*, Public Law 534, 78th Cong., 2nd Sess., Chapter 665, HR 4485 (December 22, 1944), 8. Of the eleven dams recommend by *Savannah River, GA*, House Document 657, 78th Cong., 2nd sess., and approved by the Flood Control Act (1944), the federal government (Corps) built three between 1954 and 1985. Among the four dams Duke Power Company constructed in the upper Savannah River valley after 1970,

the company built two dams at sites originally recommended in these documents, using the two adjacent Newry–Old Pickens sites to create the giant Lake Keowee.

25. *Flood Control Act 1944.*

26. "Clarks Hill Project Would Mean Enormous Benefits for This Section of Two States," *Augusta Herald*, January 21, 1944, RRC.

27. U.S. Congress, House, *Savannah River, GA*, 3.

28. For "keystone" quote, see Hillary H. Mangum, "Interstate Cooperation Shown in Clark's Hill Development," *South Carolina Magazine* 10, no. 1 (January 1947): 28.

29. Savannah River Special Board, *Clark Hill Navigation-Flood Control-Power Project, Savannah River, Georgia–South Carolina, Report to the President* (Washington, D.C.: n.p.; February 29, 1936), 6, box 1109, project 803017, RG 77, NAII.

30. "G.P.C. Makes Bid for Clarks Hill," *Augusta Chronicle*, October 9, 1939, RRC clipping.

31. In Idaho, for example, see Karl Boyd Brooks, *Public Power, Private Dams: The Hells Canyon High Dam Controversy* (Seattle: University of Washington Press, 2006).

32. "All Citizens Are Concerned with Clark Hill Project," *Claxton Enterprise*, September 5, 1946, sent to Russell from Georgia Power Company, Clark Hill Correspondence Materials, Rivers and Harbors Series, RRC.

33. "The Clark Hill Power Development," *Milledgeville Union-Recorder*, September 5, 1946, 2, RRC clipping; "Georgia Power Will Complete Oconee Plan," *Atlanta Constitution*, July 20, 1942, 3, RRC clipping; Wade H. Wright, *History of the Georgia Power Company, 1855–1956* (Atlanta: Georgia Power Company, 1957), 250, 332. See also Federal Energy Regulatory Commission, Georgia Power Company Project No. 1951–037 License (issued March 19, 1996), http://www.hydroreform.org/.

34. "Trade Groups Decline to Back Power Firm's Plan for Clarks Hill," *Augusta Herald*, September 14, 1946, RRC clipping.

35. "L. S. Moody Traces History of Clarks Hill Development," *Augusta Herald*, September 15, 1946, 12, folder 3, "Clark's Hill News Clippings," box 3, LMC.

36. "Let the Government Build Clark Hill," *Augusta Chronicle*, September 14, 1946, 4.

37. "Will Our Hopes and Aspirations for Clark Hill Be Met?" *Edgefield Advertiser*, May 3, 1950, folder 3, "Clark's Hill News Clippings," box 3, LMC.

38. Paul S. Sutter, *Driven Wild: How the Fight against Automobiles Launched the Modern Wilderness Movement* (Seattle: University of Washington Press, 2002), 41–48 and chap. 2.

39. "State Parks in Georgia," in Department of Natural Resources and State Department of Education, *Natural Resources of Georgia: Georgia Program for the Improvement of Instruction in the Public Schools* (Atlanta: State Department of Education, 1938), 11, 13–16.

40. *Natural Resources: Georgia's Vast Undeveloped Wealth* (n.d. [likely 1941 or 1942]), Publications, Bulletins, and Circulars, Commissioner's Office, Department of Game and Fish (025-01-002), GAA.

41. State Planning Board and the National Park Service, *Report on Outdoor Recreation in Georgia* (Atlanta: n.p., February 1939), 4, 57, Department of the Interior Library, Washington, D.C.

42. Russ Rymer, *American Beach: How "Progress" Robbed a Black Town—and Nation—of History, Wealth, and Power* (New York: Harper Perennial, Harper Collins, 1998); Jeff Wiltse, *Contested Waters: A Social History of Swimming Pools in America* (Chapel Hill: University of North Carolina Press, 2007); Andrew W. Kahrl, "The Political Work of Leisure: Class, Recreation, and African American Commemoration at Harpers Ferry, West Virginia, 1881–1931," *Journal of Social History* 42, no. 1 (2008): 57–77; Andrew W. Kahrl, "'The Slightest Semblance of Unruliness': Steamboat Excursions, Pleasure Resorts, and the Emergence of Segregation Culture on the Potomac River," *Journal of American History* 94, no. 4 (March 2008): 1108–36; Terence Young, "'A Contradiction in Democratic Government': W. J. Trent, Jr., and the Struggle to Desegregate National Park Campgrounds," *Environmental History* 14, no. 4 (October 2009): 651–82.

43. North Carolina State Parks, "Jones Lake State Park History," http://www.ncparks.gov/Visit/parks/jone/history.php (February 16, 2013); North Carolina Department of Environment and Natural Resources, Division of State Parks and Recreation, "Lake Waccamaw State Park General Management Plan," March 19, 2007, I-9–I-10, http://www.ncparks.gov/About/plans/gmp/lawa/2007/desc.pdf (February 16, 2013).

44. Andrew W. Kahrl, *The Land Was Ours: African American Beaches from Jim Crow to the Sunbelt South* (Cambridge: Harvard University Press, 2012); Andrew W. Kahrl, "The 'Negro Park' Question: Land, Labor, and Leisure in Pitt County, North Carolina, 1920–1930," *Journal of Southern History* 79, no. 1 (February 2013): 113–42.

45. State Planning Board and the National Park Service, *Report on Outdoor Recreation in Georgia*, 4–5, 22–23. For other interpretations at the intersection of race, class, and gender, see Colin Fisher, "Race and US Environmental History," in *A Companion to American Environmental History*, ed. Douglas Cazaux Sackman (Chichester, West Sussex: Wiley-Blackwell, 2010), 108–9; Harvey H. Jackson III, *The Rise and Decline of the Redneck Riviera: An Insider's History of the Florida-Alabama Coast* (Athens: University of Georgia Press, 2012).

46. "L.S. Moody Traces History of Clarks Hill Development," *Augusta Herald*, September 15, 1946, 12, folder 3, "Clark's Hill News Clippings," box 3, LMC; Lester Moody, "An Address Before the Georgia Recreation Workers Association," Augusta, Georgia, March 7, 1946, 6, folder 4, "Local News," box 2, LMC.

47. *The Truth about the Clark's Hill Project* (n.p.: Clark's Hill Authority of South Carolina, [1946?]), 17–18, Reese Library Special Collections, Augusta State University, Augusta, Ga. See also Joe Mulieri, "Funds Will Be Granted for Clark Hill Thurmond Tells Audience at Orangeburg," news clipping (June 17, 1947), and "S.C. Governor Warns That Power Interests Still Seek to Gain Control of Clark Hill," *Augusta Herald*, February 7, 1947, both in folder 3, "Clark's Hill News Clippings," box 3, LMC.

48. Thurmond's speech can be found in *Truth about the Clark's Hill Project*, 17; Allyn P. Bursley and the National Park Service, *Exhibit II, Recreation, Exhibit A: Memorandum Report: Recreational Resources of the Clark Hill Reservoir, Savannah River, Georgia and South Carolina, Prepared August 22, 1945*, in *Definite Project Report on Savannah River Basin, Georgia and South Carolina, Clark Hill Project*, Appendix XI, Recreation, complied by the Department of the Interior, National Park Service for the War Department, Corps of Engineers, South Atlantic Division (February 20, 1946), XI-A9, box 141, entry 53a114, RG 77, NAII.

49. White visitors had shared facilities in the past and expressed preference for segregated facilities; see Stephen Lewis Cox, "The History of Negro State Parks in South Carolina, 1940–1965" (M.A. thesis, University of South Carolina, 1992), 22–23, 25–26, and Pete Daniel, *Lost Revolutions: The South in the 1950s* (Chapel Hill and Washington, D.C.: University of North Carolina Press for the Smithsonian National Museum of American History, Washington, D.C., 2000), 243.

50. U.S. Army Corps of Engineers, *Clark Hill Reservoir, Savannah River Basin, Georgia and South Carolina: General Information Proposed Recreational Development*, Savannah District (October 1948), 4–5, box 3, LMC; "Clark Hill Dam Area Recreational Plans Announced by Army Corps of Engineers," *Augusta Chronicle*, October 31, 1948, 4-B. In 1945, an NPS study recommended the Corps consider placing one African American state park at Hicks Creek between today's Mistletoe State Park and Leah, Ga., before suggesting the Keg Creek location in 1948, and the NPS originally suggested the Hawe Creek (S.C.) site for an African American park (today this is a Corps campground) before recommending the Hickory Knob location.

51. The idea for 345-acre Carver State Park was hatched by former Tuskegee airman and Atlanta resident John Loyd Atkinson Sr. He originally wanted to build a private lake resort and replicate the American Beach (Amelia Island, Fla.) African American resort community assembled between 1935 and 1946 by Afro-American Industrial & Benefit Association founder and millionaire Abraham Lincoln Lewis. Though the private resort plans fell through, with Governor Herman Talmadge's assistance in 1950 the state leased additional land from the Corps at Lake Allatoona, and Atkinson served as the park's first superintendent until 1958. See Charles Atkinson (John Atkinson's son) and Greg Germani, "State Parks (Segregated)," *The Atlanta Time Machine*, which includes images of four "Georgia State Parks for Negroes," http://www.atlantatimemachine.com/misc/state_parks.htm (February 16, 2013); Billy Townsend, Georgia Department of Natural Resources, *History of the Georgia State Parks and Historic Sites Division* (October 2001), http://gastateparks .org/content/georgia/parks/georgia-parks-history.pdf (February 16, 2013); and Southern Regional Council, "State Parks for Negroes—New Tests of Equality," *New South* 9, nos. 4 & 5 (April–May 1954): 7. George Washington Carver State Park was eventually consolidated with other state park property and renamed Red Top Mountain State Park, only to be divided again in 1975 when the old Carver portion of the park was transferred to the Bartow County park system to create Bartow Carver Park.

52. Cox, "History of Negro State Parks in South Carolina," 12, 19.

53. Robert F. Durden, *Electrifying the Piedmont Carolinas: The Duke Power Company, 1904–1997* (Durham, N.C.: Carolina Academic Press, 2001), 107–9; Jack I. Hayes, *South Carolina and the New Deal* (Columbia: University of South Carolina Press, 2001), 75–84. After fighting this project in the 1930s, Duke Power eventually acquired the Greenwood Electrical Power Commission's properties in 1966; see Duke Energy Carolinas, LLC, "South Carolina Only, Index of Rate Schedules," October 5, 2009, 2, http://www.duke-energy.com/pdfs/SCMasterIndex.pdf (February 16, 2013).

54. Robert A. Waller, "The Civilian Conservation Corps and the Emergence of South Carolina's State Park System, 1933–1942," *South Carolina Historical Magazine* 104, no. 2 (April 2003): 112–13.

55. *Brown v. Board of Education*, 347 U.S. 483 (1954).

56. Southern Regional Council, "A Court Rules That Parks Are for All" and "Text of The Park Decision," *New South* 10, no. 4 (April 1955): 1, 3–4.

57. Southern Regional Council, "Court Rules That Parks Are for All," 1. See also "History of Virginia State Parks," Virginia Department of Conservation and Recreation, http://www.dcr.virginia.gov/state_parks/his_parx.shtml (February 16, 2013).

58. U. S. Army Corps of Engineers, *The Master Plan for Development and Management, Clark Hill Reservoir, Savannah River, Georgia and South Carolina* (Savannah District, December 1950), 62–66.

59. Charles H. Flory, South Carolina State Forester, to Col. W. E. Wilhoyt Jr., Savannah District, April 23, 1953, folder Legislation, 1953 Clarks Hill Project, box 35, OJP.

60. C. West Jacocks, "State Parks and Segregation," *South Carolina Magazine* 20, no. 1 (January 1956): 3.

61. Southern Regional Council, "State Parks for Negroes," 4.

62. Cox, "History of Negro State Parks in South Carolina," chaps. 5 and 6.

63. Andrew Sparks, "Mile-Wide Dam for the Savannah," *Atlanta Journal Magazine*, January 12, 1947, 8–9, folder 3, box 3, LMC.

64. "Government Increases Estimated Cost of Clark Hill to Nearly $50,000,000," *Augusta Chronicle*, January 29, 1947, 4; J. S. Durant and B. H. Grant, *Real Estate Planning Report for Clark Hill Reservoir, Savannah River Basin, Georgia and South Carolina* (Atlanta: War Department, U.S. Division Engineer, Real Estate Branch, October 1942), box 66, accession 76E342, RG 77, NAS; *Appendix IX, Real Estate*, in *Definite Project Report on Savannah River Basin, Georgia and South Carolina, Clark Hill Project*, Corps of Engineers, South Atlantic Division (revised May 1, 1946), IX-3, folder 821.2, "Clark Hill Dam," box 141, entry 53a114, RG 77, NAII.

65. Robert W. Benson, *Cultural Resources Overview of the Sumter National Forest*, prepared for Francis Marion and Sumter National Forests by Southeastern Archeological Services, Inc. (April 2006), 79.

66. Jesse D. Jennings, "River Basin Surveys: Origins, Operations, and Results, 1945–1969," *American Antiquity* 50, no. 2 (April 1985): 281–96.

67. Clark Hill Field Notebooks, bk. 1, pp. 96, 99, 127, 139, box 595, CFM.

68. Eugene P. Odum, "Ecology and the Atomic Age," *Association of Southeastern Biologists Bulletin* 4, no. 2 (1957): 27–29; Joel B. Hagen, *An Entangled Bank: The Origins of Ecosystem Ecology* (New Brunswick: Rutgers University Press, 1992), chap. 6; Betty Jean Craige, *Eugene Odum: Ecosystem Ecologist and Environmentalist* (Athens: University of Georgia Press, 2001), chap. 3; Mary Beth Reed, Barbara Smith Strack, and U.S. Department of Energy, *Savannah River Site at Fifty* (Washington, D.C.: U.S. Department of Energy and Government Printing Office, 2002), chap. 17.

69. Clark Hill Field Notebooks, bk. 1, p. 139, box 595, CFM.

70. Site No. 65, 38MC17, River Basin Survey Site Files, box 598, folder "38 MC McCormick County, SC 1948," CFM.

71. Clark Hill Field Notebooks, bk. 1, pp. 137, 150, box 595, CFM.

72. Ibid., pp. 55, 61.

73. Site No. 56, 9LC67, River Basin Survey Site Files, box 598, folder "9 LC 1–98 (Lincoln County, GA) s.d.," CFM.

74. Edward M. Riley, *The Survey of the Historic Sites of the Clark Hill Reservoir Area, South Carolina and Georgia* (Richmond, Va.: National Park Service, June 1949), 12–15, 17, 27–28, U.S. Army Corps of Engineers, Savannah District Library, Savannah, Ga.

75. Sparks, "Mile-Wide Dam for the Savannah."

76. Riley, *Survey of the Historic Sites of the Clark Hill Reservoir Area*, 15.

77. "Power Company Seeks to Halt Clark Hill Work," *Augusta Chronicle*, April, 19, 1947, folder 3, "Clarks Hill News Clippings," box 3, LMC; Savannah River Special Board, *Clark Hill Navigation–Flood Control–Power Project*, 6, 46; Henry E. Barber and Allen R. Gann, *A History of the Savannah District, U.S. Army Corps of Engineers* (Savannah, Ga.: U.S. Army Corps of Engineers, 1989), 427. Historians have evaluated other land acquisition processes in the Tennessee Valley and reached similar conclusions; see Michael J. McDonald and John Muldowny, *TVA and the Dispossessed: The Resettlement of Population in the Norris Dam Area* (Knoxville: University of Tennessee Press, 1982), 154, and Darren Anthony Shuler, "On Our Land: Progress, Destruction, and the Tennessee Valley Authority's Tellico Dam Project" (M.A. thesis, University of Georgia, 2000). Most recently, Robert P. Shapard also reached this conclusion based on analysis of oral histories, real estate files, and condemnation cases associated with the Clarks Hill project; see "Building an Inland Sea: Clarks Hill Lake on the Upper Savannah and the Twentieth-Century Lives, Land, and River Hidden by Its Waters" (M.A. thesis, North Carolina State University, 2009), chaps. 3 and 4. The history behind the Lexington Water Power Company's Lake Murray (1927; 5,000 people removed) and the New Deal's Santee-Cooper (1938; 900 families removed) signifies the need for greater scrutiny of project histories. See Coy Bayne, *Lake Murray: Legend and Leisure*, 3rd ed., rev. (n.p.: Bayne Publishing Co., 1999), and T. Robert Hart, "The Lowcountry Landscape: Politics, Preservation, and the Santee-Cooper Project," *Environmental History* 18, no. 1 (January 2013): 127–56.

78. Barber and Gann, *History of the Savannah District*, 422–26.

79. Andrew Sparks, "Georgia's New Ocean: Builds Up behind Clark Hill Dam," *Atlanta Journal and Constitution Magazine*, September 7, 1952, 28–30, folder 3, box 3, LMC.

80. "Lincoln, Columbia Counties Opposed Rerouting of Road," *Augusta Chronicle*, June 27, 1948, 1; Durant and Grant, *Real Estate Planning Report for Clark Hill Reservoir*, 1–2; *Appendix VII, Relocations*, in *Definite Project Report on Savannah River Basin, Georgia and South Carolina, Clark Hill Project*, VII-20; *Appendix X, Malaria Control*, in *Definite Project Report on Savannah River Basin, Georgia and South Carolina, Clark Hill Project*, X-1 through X-2, and X-A2 through X-A4; "Contracts Awarded for Clearing in the Clark Hill Reservoir," [unknown clipping], April 13, 1950, folder 3, Hartwell Reservoir, box 4, LMC; Mary Carter Winter, "Strong Call Is Made for Total Clearing of Clark Hill Basin," *Augusta Chronicle*, April 26, 1950, 1, box 3, LMC.

81. Editors, "Clark's Hill," *Atlanta Journal*, May 29, 1947, LMC.

82. "S.C. Governor Warns That Power Interests Still Seek to Gain Control of Clark Hill," *Augusta Herald*, February, 7, 1947, 1, LMC.

83. "Thurmond Sees Development of Water Resources as Key to Continued US Progress," *Columbia State*, May 4, 1947, 10-B, LMC.

84. *Truth about the Clark's Hill Project*, 20.

85. William Faulkner, *Big Woods* (New York: Random House, 1955), 170.

1. "Georgians Pray for Rain," *Augusta Chronicle*, October 11, 1954, 2; "Georgia Drought Rated with Worst," *Augusta Chronicle*, December 28, 1954, 1.

2. "Atlanta May Ration Water," *Augusta Chronicle*, October 14, 1954, 1.

3. "Emergency Water Shortages Hit Six Georgia Communities; Bremen Situation Is Critical," *Augusta Chronicle*, October 6, 1954, 1.

4. "Drought Devastating Crops; Losses Already Top Million," *Augusta Chronicle*, June 30, 1954, 1; "Disaster Aid Sought in 16 Area Counties," *Augusta Chronicle*, August 12, 1954, 3-A.

5. "State Nurses $100,000,000 Bruise from 1954 Drought," *Augusta Chronicle*, November 7, 1954, 4A, originally published in the *Atlanta Journal*.

6. T. M. Forbes, Executive Vice President, Cotton Manufactures Association of Georgia, "Cooperation in the Use and Conservation of Georgia's Water Resources," speech, Atlanta, Ga., December 5, 1955, 4, Georgia Water Use & Conservation Files, Department of Agriculture, Commissioner's Office, Commissioner's Subject Files, 1955–1958, 13-1-2, GAA.

7. Karl Boyd Brooks, *Public Power, Private Dams: The Hells Canyon High Dam Controversy* (Seattle: University of Washington Press, 2006), esp. 222 and chap. 7, "Unplugging the New Deal: Hells Canyon High Dam and the Postwar Public-Power Debate."

8. Mark W. T. Harvey provides the best interpretation of the Echo Park story; see *A Symbol of Wilderness: Echo Park and the American Conservation Movement* (Albuquerque: University of New Mexico Press, 1994). See also Marc Reisner, *Cadillac Desert: The American West and Its Disappearing Water* (New York: Penguin, 1986; rev. and updated ed., 1993).

9. James Cobb, *The Selling of the South: The Southern Crusade for Industrial Development, 1936–1990* (Urbana: University of Illinois Press, 1993); Bruce J. Schulman, *From Cotton Belt to Sunbelt: Federal Policy, Economic Development, and the Transformation of the South, 1938–1980* (Durham, N.C.: Duke University Press, 1994).

10. Alan Brinkley, *End of Reform: New Deal Liberalism in Recession and War* (New York: Knopf, 1995).

11. Major Corps projects completed between 1950 and 1985 in Mississippi, Alabama, Georgia, and North Carolina include the following twenty-two developments: Allatoona, J. Strom Thurmond Dam and Lake, Philpott, John H. Kerr Dam and Reservoir, Buford Dam and Lake Lanier, Jim Woodruff Dam and Lake Seminole, Smith Reservoir and Lock & Dam, Hartwell, Walter F. Georgia, George W. Andrews Lock and Dam, W. Kerr Scott Dam and Reservoir, Holt Lock & Dam, R. E. "Bob" Woodruff Lake and Robert F. Henry Lock & Dam, William "Bill" Dannelly Reservoir and Millers Ferry Lock & Dam, B. Everett Jordan Lake and Dam, West Point, Claiborne Lake Lock & Dam, Carters Lake, Falls Lake, Richard B. Russell, Yazoo Headwaters Project, and the Tenn-Tom Waterway.

12. On the New Right and "the Rise of Modern Conservatism," see Dan Carter, *The Politics of Rage: George Wallace, the Origins of the New Conservatism, and the Transformation of American Politics* (New York: Simon and Schuster, 1995); Lisa McGirr, *Suburban Warriors: The Origins of the New American Right* (Princeton: Princeton University Press, 2001); Kevin M. Kruse, *White Flight: Atlanta and the Making of Modern Conservatism* (Princeton: Princeton University Press, 2005); Matthew D. Lassiter, *The Silent Majority:*

Suburban Politics in the Sunbelt South (Princeton: Princeton University Press, 2006); James M. Turner, "'The Specter of Environmentalism': Wilderness, Environmental Politics, and the Evolution of the New Right," *Journal of American History* 96, no. 1 (June 2009): 123–48; and Brian Allen Drake, "The Skeptical Environmentalist: Barry Goldwater and the Environmental Management State," *Environmental History* 15, no. 4 (October 2010): 587–611.

13. *Report on Savannah River*, House Document 64, 74th Cong., 1st sess., January 3, 1935, 102; *Savannah River, Ga.*, House Document 657, 78th Cong., 2nd sess., 43.

14. *Definite Project Report: Hartwell Reservoir, Savannah River, Georgia and South Carolina*, vol. 1, Corps of Engineers, Savannah District (December 15, 1952), VIII, Department of the Interior Library, Washington, D.C.

15. "Clarks Hill Power May Be Increased," *Augusta Chronicle*, February 25, 1949, 1.

16. *Flood Control Act of 1950*, Public Law No. 516, 81st Cong., 2nd sess., May 17, 1950.

17. "$60,000,000 Hartwell Dam Project Launched by Clarks Hill Authority," *Anderson Independent*, November 23, 1948, Correspondence and Materials, 1949, Rivers and Harbors Series, RRC.

18. Wilton E. Hall, Butler B. Hare, Louie B. Morris, and L. S. Moody, *The Hartwell Project . . . Now: Presented to the Congress of the United States by the People of South Carolina and Georgia* (Anderson, S.C.: Hartwell Steering Committee, January 15, 1949), 23, Correspondence and Materials, 1949, Rivers and Harbors Series, RRC.

19. Jason Scott Smith, *Building New Deal Liberalism: The Political Economy of Public Works, 1933–1956* (New York: Cambridge University Press, 2006), 191.

20. Kari Frederickson, *The Dixiecrat Revolt and the End of the Solid South, 1932–1968* (Chapel Hill: University of North Carolina Press, 2001), 26.

21. Gilbert C. Fite, *Richard B. Russell, Jr., Senator from Georgia* (Chapel Hill: University of North Carolina Press, 1991), 318. See also Josephine Mellinchamp, *Senators from Georgia* (Huntsville, Ala.: Strode Publishers, 1976), 245–60.

22. Harold D. Lasswell, "The Garrison State," *American Journal of Sociology* 46, no. 4 (January 1941): 455–69; Kari Frederickson, "Confronting the Garrison State: South Carolina in the Early Cold War Era," *Journal of Southern History* 72, no. 3 (May 2006): 349–78.

23. For information on NSC-68, see Schulman, *From Cotton Belt to Sunbelt*, 109; Walter LaFeber, *America, Russia, and the Cold War, 1945–2000* (Boston: McGraw-Hill, 2002), 101–3; Granville M. Read, Savannah River Plant (E. I. Du Pont de Nemours & Company), and Rotary Club (Wilmington, Del.), *"The Savannah River Project": A Speech by Granville M. Read, Chief Engineer, E.I. Du Pont de Nemours & Company, before the Rotary Club, Wilmington, Delaware*, November 18, 1954; Mary Beth Reed, Barbara Smith Strack, and U.S. Department of Energy, *Savannah River Site at Fifty* (Washington, D.C.: U.S. Department of Energy and Government Printing Office, 2002).

24. *Definite Project Report: Hartwell Reservoir*, 70–71.

25. Rep. W. J. Bryan Dorn, Washington, D.C., to Rep. Gerald Ford Jr., Washington, D.C., May 28, 1951, folder Topical Files, 1951–1952, Public Works, Dams, Hartwell, box 39, WDP; Senator Olin D. Johnston, before House Appropriations Committee on Hartwell Dam Funding, Legislation, February 7, 1952, Public Works, Dams, Hartwell, box 32, OJP; Senator Richard B. Russell Jr., Washington, D.C., to E. B. Woodward, April 9, 1952, Correspondence, 1949–1958, Rivers and Harbors Series, RRC.

26. Correspondence between E. M. Lander Jr., Professor, Clemson, S.C., to Rep. William J. Bryan Dorn, Washington, D.C., June 14 and 20, 1953, folder Topical Files, 1953–1954, Public Works, Dams, Hartwell, box 41, WDP; Savannah River Operations Office, Atomic Energy Commission, "Comments on Hartwell Dam," 1956, folder Topical Files, 1955–1956, Public Works, Dams, Hartwell, box 43, WDP; Major General E. C. Itschner, Chief of Engineers, Washington, D.C., to Senator J. Strom Thurmond, Washington, D.C., December 21, 1956, J. Strom Thurmond, Mss 100, folder Hartwell Dam, November 23–December 29, 1956, box 3, Subject Correspondence, 1956, STP.

27. C. T. Wyche, Greenville, S.C., to Senator J. Strom Thurmond, Washington, D.C., April 9, 1958, box 23, Subject Correspondence Series, 1958, STP.

28. Savannah District's Shoreline Management Program, http://www.sas.usace.army.mil/About/DivisionsandOffices/OperationsDivision/HartwellDamandLake/ShorelineManagement.aspx (August 1, 2013); "Shoreline Management on Civil Works Projects," in Title 36 Code of Federal Regulations, Part 327.30, http://www.gpo.gov/fdsys/pkg/CFR-2001-title36-vol3/xml/CFR-2001-title36-vol3-chapIII.xml#seqnum327.30 (August 1, 2013).

29. C. T. Wyche, Greenville, S.C., to Senator J. Strom Thurmond, Washington, D.C., October 22, 1959, folder Rivers and Harbors 3-1 (Hartwell Dam) February 21–November 25, 1959, box 22, Subject Correspondence Series, 1959, STP; Robert L. Small, Greenville, S.C., to Senator J. Strom Thurmond, Washington, D.C., September 25, 1961, folder Rivers and Harbors 3-1 (Hartwell Dam) March 17, 1961–November 3, 1961, box 30, Subject Correspondence 1961, STP.

30. Major General W. K. Wilson Jr., Deputy Chief of Engineers for Construction, to Senator J. Strom Thurmond, Washington, D.C., November 25, 1959, folder Rivers and Harbors 3-1 (Hartwell Dam) February 21–November 25, 1959, box 22, Subject Correspondence Series, 1959, STP; Col. W. A. Stevens, Savannah District Engineer, to Senator J. Strom Thurmond, Washington, D.C., October 3, 1961, folder Rivers and Harbors 3-1 (Hartwell Dam) March 17, 1961–November 3, 1961, box 30, Subject Correspondence Series, 1961, STP.

31. Some of the potential real estate investors included C. T. Wyche (Greenville attorney); Charlie Ballenger (Ballenger Paving Company, founded 1927); Buck Mickel (Daniel Construction Company, a firm that landed industrial and federal agency contracts); and Francis Hipp (The Liberty Corporation; his father founded Liberty Life Insurance). See Knowitall.org and ETV Creative Services, "Legacy of Leadership" (Columbia, S.C.), http://www.knowitall.org/legacy/index.html (August 1, 2013), and "Charlie Daniel of Daniel Construction Company," *South Carolina Magazine* 15, no. 10 (October 1951): 12.

32. See "Robert's Firm to Supervise Army Project," *Atlanta Constitution*, December 12, 1940, 15; "Robert Firm Consultant in Port Survey," *Atlanta Constitution*, October 6, 1945, 6; and Robert and Company, http://www.robertandcompany.com/History.html (August 1, 2013).

33. Clemson Alumni Corporation, *Preliminary Report on the Damage to the Property of Clemson College by the Proposed Hartwell Dam Development*, April 1951, provided by A. G. Stanford, V.P., Robert and Company Associates, Atlanta, Ga., to Senator J. Strom Thurmond, Washington, D.C., April 12, 1957, folder Hartwell Dam, November 29, 1956–October 18, 1957, box 19, Subject Correspondence Series, 1957, STP.

34. Cecil L. Reid, Al G. Stanford, and Ed D. Sloan, *The Truth about "Hartwell"* (Fredericksburg, Va.: January 7, 1952), pamphlet, Correspondence—Hartwell Dam Material, 1949–1957, Rivers and Harbors Series, RRC.

35. Ibid., 5, 24–25.

36. J. C. Turner et al. to Senator Olin D. Johnston, Washington, D.C., February 25, 1957, box 61, folder Legislation, 1957, Public Works, Dams, Hartwell, OJP; Editors, "Remember These 'Predictions'?" *Anderson Independent*, April 26, 1963, OJP; Senator J. Strom Thurmond, Aiken, S.C., to Alex McCullough, Washington, D.C., November 26, 1956, Subject Correspondence 1956, box 3, folder Hartwell Dam, November 23–December 29, 1956, STP.

37. Rep. William J. Bryan Dorn to E. M. Lander Jr., Professor, Clemson, S.C., June 20, 1953, folder Topical Files, 1953–1954, Public Works, Dams, Hartwell, box 41, WDP.

38. Harriet L. Herring, [J. Herman Johnson,] Rupert B. Vance, and T. J. Woofter Jr., *A Survey of the Catawba Valley: A Study Made by the Institute for Research in Social Science for the Tennessee Valley Authority*, 2 vols. (Chapel Hill: Institute for Research in Social Justice at the University of North Carolina, 1935), 1:3 ("hydro-industrial empire").

39. D. Nabow, "Statement of Duke Power Company," before the Commission on Organization of the Executive Branch of the Government: Task Force of Water Resources and Power, June 2, 1954, 9, folder Topical Files, 1953–1954, Public Works, Dams, Hartwell, box 41, WDP.

40. S. Maner Martin, Clemson, S.C., to Rep. W. J. B. Dorn, Washington, D.C., December 4, 1956, folder Topical Files, 1955–1956, Public Works, Dams, Hartwell, box 43, WDP.

41. Lucile Buriss Watson, Clemson, S.C., to Senator (elect) J. Strom Thurmond, Washington, D.C., November 30, 1954, folder Hartwell, box 10, Subject Correspondence Series, 1955, STP.

42. Bill Allen, "State Hooks Title: 'Paradise o' Ponds,'" *Atlanta Journal*, September 13, 1953, 12. Allen claimed 15,000 irrigated acres, and another source cited 27,700 acres: Georgia Water Use and Conservation Committee, *Water in Georgia: A Report on the Historical, Physical, and Legal Aspects of Water in Georgia, Prepared and Submitted to the Governor, the General Assembly, and the People of Georgia* ([Atlanta]: Georgia Water Law Revision Commission, 1955), 55.

43. Georgia Water Use and Conservation Committee, *Water in Georgia*, 18–23.

44. Frank K. Meyers, "Washington Residents Facing Possible 14-day Water Supply," *Augusta Chronicle*, August 12, 1954, 1D.

45. "East Point Buys Water from Lake," *Rome News-Tribune*, October 3, 1954, 2.

46. W. D. Workman Jr., "South Carolina Legislators Are Facing Problem of Protecting State's Water," *Augusta Chronicle*, January 3, 1954, 1.

47. Georgia Water Use and Conservation Committee, *Water in Georgia*, 4, 7.

48. Ibid., 4.

49. "Half of Georgia's Lost Crops within 500 Feet of Water," *Atlanta Journal*, October 20, 1954, 4; Lynn Willoughby, *Flowing through Time: A History of the Lower Chattahoochee River* (Tuscaloosa: University of Alabama Press, 1999), 167–73.

50. Benjamin Mortimer Hall and Max R. Hall, *Second Report on the Water-Powers of Georgia*, Geological Survey of Georgia, Bulletin No. 16 (Atlanta: Franklin-Turner Co., 1908), 21.

51. "Drought Spotlights Need for Irrigation Planning," *Rome News-Tribune*, October 7, 1954, 14.

52. "Farm Irrigation Is Useless without Ample Water Supply, Georgia Authority Points Out," *Augusta Chronicle*, October 16, 1954, 3.

53. U.S. Department of Labor, Bureau of Labor Statistics, CPI Inflation Calculator, http://www.bls.gov/data/inflation_calculator.htm.

54. Allen, "State Hooks Title," 12. Allen claimed 15,000 irrigated acres, and another source claimed 27,700 acres: Georgia Water Use and Conservation Committee, *Water in Georgia*, 55. For irrigation loan sources, see display ad, Georgia Railroad Bank, *Augusta Chronicle*, August 8, 1954, 6A; "Southeast's Irrigation Need Pointed Up by Long Drought, Georgia Agriculturalist Says," *Augusta Chronicle*, September 30, 1954, 5C; "C. and S. Bank Announces Plan for Farm Irrigation," *Augusta Chronicle*, October 2, 1954, 9; "Cheaper Loans for Irrigation Announced," *Augusta Chronicle*, October 24, 1954, 13B; and "Tifton Farmer Gets Loan for Irrigation of His Land," *Augusta Chronicle*, December 3, 1954, 8C.

55. Leila B. Watson, Clemson, S.C., to Senator Olin D. Johnston, Washington, D.C., April 1, 1954, folder Legislation, 1954, Public Works, Dams, Hartwell, box 43, OJP.

56. On the Water Facilities Act (1937), see *A Brief History of the Farmers Home Administration* (Washington, D.C.: USDA, Farmers Home Administration, 1989), 4, http://www.rurdev.usda.gov/rd/70th/History%20of%20Farmers%20Home.pdf (August 1, 2013), and Eugene C. Buie, *A History of United States Department of Agriculture Water Resource Activities* (Washington, D.C.: USDA, SCS, September 1979), 25, http://www.nrcs.usda.gov/Internet/FSE_DOCUMENTS/nrcs143_021271.pdf (August 1, 2013).

57. Buie, *History of United States Department of Agriculture Water Resource Activities*, 25.

58. Luna B. Leopold and Thomas Maddock Jr., *The Flood Control Controversy: Big Dams, Little Dams, and Land Management* (New York: Ronald Press Co., 1954), ix.

59. Elmer T. Peterson, *Big Dam Foolishness: The Problem of Modern Flood Control and Water Storage* (New York: Devin-Adair Co., 1954).

60. David A. Tillinghast, "Twelve Mile Creek Waters Begin to Yield," [*Greenville Piedmont*, May ?, 1955], newspaper clipping included with Lucile Watson, Clemson, S.C., to Senator (elect) J. Strom Thurmond, Washington, D.C., May 19, 1955, folder Hartwell, box 10, Subject Correspondence Series, 1955, STP.

61. T. R. Waring, editor, *Charleston News and Courier*, to Senator J. Strom Thurmond, Washington, D.C., June 4, 1955, folder Hartwell, box 10, Subject Correspondence Series, 1955, STP.

62. "'Stop, Look and Listen' Notes on Hartwell Dam Construction," *Charleston News and Courier*, June 12, 1955, 16B, folder Hartwell, box 10, Subject Correspondence Series, 1955, STP.

63. T. Wilbur Thornhill, Charleston Oil Company, Charleston, S.C., to Senator Olin D. Johnston, Washington, D.C., December 11, 1956, box 61, folder Legislation, 1957, Public Works, Dams, Hartwell, OJP.

64. Donald J. Pisani, *To Reclaim a Divided West: Water, Law, and Public Policy, 1848–1902* (Albuquerque: University of New Mexico Press, 1992), 31.

65. Georgia Water Use and Conservation Committee, *Water in Georgia*, 62.

66. "Summary Notes of Conference Held in Office of District Engineer," Col. T. Def.

Rogers, District Engineer, Savannah, Ga., February, 21, 1955, folder Clarks Hill, box 5, Subject Correspondence Series, 1955, STP.

67. *Water Supply Act of 1958* (Public Law 85-500).

68. Sara V. Liverance, "McCormick County Citizens Disappointed with Dam," *Greenville News*, [January 6, 1955?], folder Hartwell, box 10, Subject Correspondence Series, 1955, STP.

69. Brigadier General William F. Cassidy, Assistant Chief of Engineers for Civil Works, Washington, D.C., to Senator J. Strom Thurmond, November 2, 1959, folder Rivers and Harbors 3-1 (Hartwell Dam) February 21–November 25, 1959, box 22, Subject Correspondence Series, 1959, STP. At least five communities withdraw water from the Clarks Hill reservoir via water contract and storage reallocation mechanisms; see H. Al Pless, "Reallocation of Water Storage in Federal Water Projects," *Proceedings of 1991 Georgia Water Resources Conference*, held March 19–20, 1991, at the University of Georgia, edited by Kathryn J. Hatcher, 129–30. For an excellent summary of the Water Supply Act, see Cynthia Brougher and Nicole T. Cater, *Reallocation of Water Storage at Federal Water Projects for Municipal and Industrial Water Supply* (Washington, D.C.: Congressional Research Service, October 31, 2012).

70. "McCormick Wants Gov't. Restrictions Removed," *Anderson Free Press*, November 19, 1959, 1.

71. *Flood Control Act of 1950*; Maj. General William F. Cassidy, Assistant Chief of Engineers for Civil Works, Washington, D.C., to Senator Olin D. Johnston, Washington, D.C., February 25, 1960, folder Legislation, 1960, Persons, Hall, Wilton E., box 78, OJP.

72. Ernest B. Rogers Jr., *An Evaluation of Carters Island and Goat Island Reservoirs Proposed to be Built by the U.S. Army Corps of Engineers on the Savannah River*, for the McCormick (S.C.) Chamber of Commerce and the Abbeville County (S.C.) Planning and Development Board (February 17, 1960), folder Rivers and Harbors 4 (Rivers) January 8–May 24, 1960, box 31, Subject Correspondence Series, 1960, STP.

73. Frank E. Harrison, before the Board of Engineers, Savannah (Ga.) District, February 17, 1960, folder Rivers and Harbors 4 (Rivers) January 8–May 24, 1960, box 31, Subject Correspondence Series, 1960, STP.

74. Tracy Robillard, Public Affairs Specialist for the Savannah District, "The Significance of Water Supply in the SRB," *Balancing the Basin* (August 21, 2013), http://balancingthe basin.armylive.dodlive.mil/2013/08/21/the-significance-of-water-supply-in-the-srb/ (March 30, 2014); personal communication with Paula Feldmeier, Assistant District Counsel, Savannah District, U.S. Army Corps of Engineers, November 5, 2013.

75. Robert T. Sorrells, *Clemson Experimental Forest: Its First Fifty Years* (Clemson, S.C.: Clemson University, College of Forest and Recreation Resources, 1984), 21–23; Jerome V. Reel, *The High Seminary*, vol. 1, *A History of the Clemson Agricultural College of South Carolina, 1889–1964* (Clemson: Clemson University Digital Press, 2011), http://www.clemson.edu/cedp/cudp/pubs/ths-v1/ (August 1, 2013), 451–54.

76. *Definite Project Report: Hartwell Reservoir*, 41–42.

77. Harold Timms, Seneca, S.C., to Senator J. Strom Thurmond, Washington, D.C., November 21, 1955, folder Clarks Hill, February 15–April 4, 1956, box 2, Subject Correspondence Series, 1956, STP.

78. Darren Anthony Shuler, "On Our Land: Progress, Destruction, and the Tennes-

see Valley Authority's Tellico Dam Project" (M.A. thesis, University of Georgia, 2000); Robert P. Shapard, "Building an Inland Sea: Clarks Hill Lake on the Upper Savannah and the Twentieth-Century Lives, Land, and River Hidden by Its Waters" (M.A. thesis, North Carolina State University, 2009). The Hartwell project required the removal of more people than did Clarks Hill, but apparently far fewer than relocated for two South Carolina hydroelectric projects: the Lexington Water Power Company's Lake Murray (1927, 5,000 people) and the New Deal's Santee-Cooper (1938, 900 families). See Coy Bayne, *Lake Murray: Legend and Leisure*, 3rd ed., rev. (n.p.: Bayne Publishing Co., 1999), and T. Robert Hart, "The Lowcountry Landscape: Politics, Preservation, and the Santee-Cooper Project," *Environmental History* 18, no. 1 (January 2013): 127–56.

79. NAII, RG21, contains the U.S. District Court's Western District of South Carolina civil case files pertaining to the Hartwell condemnation proceedings; for example, see boxes 254, 257–60.

80. Henry E. Barber and Allen R. Gann, *A History of the Savannah District, U.S. Army Corps of Engineers* (Savannah, Ga.: U.S. Army Corps of Engineers, 1989), 441.

81. Senate Bill 3172, 87th Cong., 2nd sess., April 16, 1962, folder Legislation 1962, box 167, Public Works, Dams, Hartwell, OJP.

82. U.S. Department of Labor, Bureau of Labor Statistics, CPI Inflation Calculator, http://www.bls.gov/data/inflation_calculator.htm.

83. Barber and Gann, *History of the Savannah District*, 434–44; Jeffrey S. Allen, Robert T. Carey, Lori A. Dickes, Ellen W. Saltzman, and Corey N. Allen for the U.S. Army Corps of Engineers, Savannah District, *An Economic Analysis of Lower Water Levels in Hartwell Lake: Final Report*, November 8, 2010, 13.

84. Medford Theodore Thomson and R. F. Carter, *Effect of a Severe Drought (1954) on Streamflow in Georgia*, The Geological Survey, Bulletin Number 73 (Atlanta, 1963), 1; U.S. Army Corps of Engineers National Inventory of Dams (2013), http://geo.usace.army .mil/pgis/f?p=397:1:0; Georgia Soil and Water Conservation Commission, http://gaswcc .georgia.gov/watershed-dams.

CHAPTER 6

1. Ron Rash, *One Foot in Eden* (New York: Henry Holt, 2002), 4, 214.

2. In 1973, Congress renamed Trotters Shoals the Richard B. Russell Dam and Lake, but I refer to the project as Trotters Shoals throughout this chapter.

3. Craig E. Colten makes a similar argument in "Southern Pollution Permissiveness: Another Regional Myth?" *Southeastern Geographer* 48, no. 1 (May 2008): 75–96.

4. Samuel P. Hays, *Conservation and the Gospel of Efficiency: The Progressive Conservation Movement, 1890–1920* (Cambridge: Harvard University Press, 1959); Samuel P. Hays and Barbara D. Hays, *Beauty, Health, and Permanence: Environmental Politics in the United States, 1955–1985* (New York: Cambridge University Press, 1987), chap. 5 and p. 43 for quote; Samuel P. Hays, *A History of Environmental Politics since 1945* (Pittsburgh: University of Pittsburgh Press, 2000), 185–88. See also Adam W. Rome, *The Bulldozer in the Countryside: Suburban Sprawl and the Rise of American Environmentalism* (New York: Cambridge University Press, 2001); Adam W. Rome, "'Give Earth a Chance': The Environmental Movement and the Sixties," *Journal of American History* 90, no. 2

(September 2003): 525–54; and Christopher Sellers, "Nature and Blackness in Suburban Passage," in *"To Love the Wind and the Rain": African Americans and Environmental History*, ed. Diane D. Glave and Mark Stoll (Pittsburgh: University of Pittsburgh Press, 2006), 93–119.

5. Andrew Beecher McCallister, "'A Source of Pleasure, Profit, and Pride': Tourism, Industrialization, and Conservation at Tallulah Falls, Georgia, 1820–1915" (M.A. thesis, University of Georgia, 2002).

6. Frank Wright, "Anchor of the Deep South," *AT Journeys: The Magazine of the Appalachian-Trial Conservancy* 1, no. 3 (November–December 2005): 24–28; Paul S. Sutter, *Driven Wild: How the Fight against Automobiles Launched the Modern Wilderness Movement* (Seattle: University of Washington Press, 2002), 3–4.

7. Jack E. Davis, *An Everglades Providence: Marjory Stoneman Douglas and the American Environmental Century* (Athens: University of Georgia Press, 2009); Albert G. Way, *Conserving Longleaf: Herbert Stoddard and the Rise of Ecological Land Management* (Athens: University of Georgia Press, 2011); Frederick R. Davis, "A Naturalist's Place: Archie Carr and the Nature of Florida," in *Paradise Lost? The Environmental History of Florida*, ed. Jack E. Davis and Raymond Arsenault (Gainesville: University Press of Florida, 2005), 72–91; Steven Noll and David Tegeder, *Ditch of Dreams: The Cross Florida Barge Canal and the Struggle for Florida's Future* (Gainesville: University of Florida Press, 2009).

8. Betty Jean Craige, *Eugene Odum: Ecosystem Ecologist and Environmentalist* (Athens: University of Georgia Press, 2001).

9. Paul Charles Milazzo, *Unlikely Environmentalists: Congress and Clean Water, 1945–1972* (Lawrence: University of Kansas Press, 2006); Craig Colten, "Contesting Pollution in Dixie: The Case of Corney Creek," *Journal of Southern History* 72, no. 3 (August 2006): 605–34.

10. Hays and Hays, *Beauty, Health, and Permanence*, 43.

11. Duke Power, "Keowee-Toxaway Timeline," folder Topical Files, 1965, Keowee-Toxaway, box 72, WDP. Robert F. Durden noted that Duke began acquiring this property before the Catawba River's 1916 flood; see *Electrifying the Piedmont Carolinas: The Duke Power Company, 1904–1997* (Durham, N.C.: Carolina Academic Press, 2001), 141. Also see "Tax Facts about Hart Dam," *South Carolina Farmer*, March 1957; Old Calhoun Estate: James P. Nickles, Attorney, Abbeville, S.C., to Rep. W. J. B. Dorn, Washington, D.C., September 21, 1959, folder Topical Files, 1962, Trotters Shoals, box 63, WDP; James P. Nickles to Senator Richard Russell, October 9, 1962, folder Legislation 1962, Public Works, Dams, Trotters Shoals, box 167, OJP; The History Group, Inc., *Historical Investigations of the Richard B. Russell Multiple Resource Area* (Atlanta: History Group, 1981), prepared for the Archeological Services Division, National Park Service, and funded by the Savannah District, U.S. Army Corps of Engineers, 177, 189; and Sharyn Kane and Richard Keeton, *Beneath These Waters: Archeological and Historical Studies of 11,500 Years along the Savannah River* (Savannah, Ga.: U.S. Army Corps of Engineers and the Interagency Archeological Services Division, National Park Service, 1993), 268.

12. Marko Maunula, "Another Southern Paradox: The Arrival of Foreign Corporations: Change and Continuity in Spartanburg, South Carolina," in *Globalization and the American South*, ed. James C. Cobb and William Stueck (Athens: University of Georgia Press, 2005), 164–84.

13. Duke Power Company, "Presentation for 1959 Edison Award," 1960, folder Topical Files, 1962, Duke Power Co., box 61, WDP.

14. Duke Power Company, "The Catawba River Story," n.d. [probably 1961], folder Legislation 1961, Duke Power, box 81, OJP.

15. The Catawba-Wateree River merges with the Congaree River to form the Santee River in South Carolina. New Dealers built the Santee Cooper Hydroelectric and Navigation Project—located downstream of this confluence—beginning in 1938, and it was operational by 1942. The South Carolina Public Service Authority oversees the state-owned water and electrical utility's operations today. See T. Robert Hart, "The Lowcountry Landscape: Politics, Preservation, and the Santee-Cooper Project," *Environmental History* 18, no. 1 (January 2013): 127–56.

16. "Greenwood, Calhoun Falls Opposed to New Dams," *Anderson Independent*, November 18, 1959; "Elberton and Augusta Favor New Dams on Savannah," *Anderson Independent*, November 18, 1959; "Savannah Development Debated at Hearing," *Anderson Independent*, November 20, 1959, clippings in Rivers and Harbors Series, RRC.

17. Correspondence, W. Harper Welborn, Attorney, Anderson, S.C., to Rep. W. J. B. Dorn, Washington, D.C., December 28, 1956, and January 3, 1957, folder Topical Files, 1957–1958, Public Works, Dams, Hartwell, box 43, WDP.

18. "Duke Power President Promises Huge Plant," *Anderson Independent*, November 20, 1959, 16, clipping, folder Rivers and Harbors 4 (Rivers) January 21–December 29, 1959, box 23, Subject Correspondence Series, 1959, STP.

19. "Why Leave the Job Half Done?" editorial originally published in the *Athens Banner-Herald* and reprinted in the *Anderson Independent*, November 26, 1959, clipping in RRC.

20. Minutes from a meeting held in Senator Richard B. Russell's office, April 13, 1961, folder Legislation 1961, Duke Power, box 81, OJP.

21. "Hollings Blocks 2 New Dams," *Anderson Independent*, May 14, 1960, clipping in RRC.

22. "We Oppose Trotters Shoals," *Augusta Chronicle Herald*, April 28, 1963.

23. L. S. Moody, Augusta Chamber of Commerce, to Peyton S. Hawes, Elberton, Ga., August 24, 1961, and *Notice of Report on Savannah River, Georgia and South Carolina Trotters Shoals Reservoir*, February 19, 1962, Trotters Shoals Dam—Material, 1961–1965, Rivers and Harbors Series, RRC.

24. Major General Keith R. Barney, Chairman, Board of Engineers for Rivers and Harbors, to Chief of Engineers, Department of the Army, March 22, 1962, folder Rivers and Harbors 3 (Dams and Reservoirs) March 2–December 18, 1962, box 28, Subject Correspondence Series, 1962, STP.

25. Draft statement, Rep. W. J. B. Dorn, to Governor Donald S. Russell, Columbia, S.C., March 18, 1963, Rivers and Harbors 3 (Dams and Reservoirs), folder 1, February 18–March 29, 1963, Subject Correspondence Series, 1962, box 32, STP.

26. Guest list, folder Topical Files, 1955–1956, Mead Corporation, box 43, WDP.

27. R. M. Cooper, Columbia, S.C., to Rep. W. J. B. Dorn, Washington, D.C., July 31, 1956, folder Topical Files, 1955–1956, Mead Corporation, box 43, WDP.

28. Allatoona (1950), Clarks Hill (1952), Lanier (1956), Woodruff/Seminole (1957), Walter F. George (1963), George W. Andrews (1963), and Hartwell (1963).

29. James P. Nickles, Attorney, Abbeville, S.C., to Rep. W. J. B. Dorn, Washington, D.C., March 19, 1962, folder Topical Files, 1962, Trotters Shoals, box 63, WDP.

30. "Free Enterprise and Trotters Shoals," *Crawfordville Advocate-Democrat*, May 3, 1963, clipping, folder Topical Files, 1963, Trotters Shoals, box 65, WDP; "Does Georgia Want Industry?" *Macon (Ga.) News*, May 6, 1963, clipping, folder Topical Files, 1963, Trotters Shoals, box 66, WDP; "Private Enterprise Best," *Savannah (Ga.) Morning News*, June 1, 1963, clipping, folder Topical Files, 1963, Trotters Shoals, box 65, WDP; Gov. Carl E. Sanders, Atlanta, Ga., to Scott Nixon, Atlanta, Ga., June 14, 1963, folder Topical Files, 1963, Trotters Shoals, box 65, WDP.

31. Durden, *Electrifying the Piedmont Carolinas*, 131–34, 134 (Dorn quote); "Duke Plans $700 Million Oconee, Pickens Projects," *Anderson Mail*, January 2, 1965, folder Legislation Clippings, Industry, box 158, OJP.

32. "Duke Tells Long Range Power Plans," unknown newspaper clipping, January 2, 1965, News clippings 1965, Pre-Authorization Series, RWC.

33. "Project Pushed for Duke Power," *New York Times*, January 11, 1965, 39.

34. Statement, Rep. W. J. B. Dorn, "Trotters Shoals, Middleton Shoals, and Keowee-Toxaway," July 19, 1966, folder Topical Files, 1965, Trotters Shoals, box 74, WDP.

35. "Switches Position on Trotters Shoals: Dorn Says Now Backing Both River Projects," *Anderson Independent*, June 20, 1966, clipping in RWC; *Rivers and Harbors Act of 1966*, Public Law 89-789, 89th Cong., H.R. 18233, November 7, 1966, 16.

36. Peyton S. Hawes, Chairman, Trotters Shoals Steering Committee, *Brief . . . In Support of the Trotters Shoals Project, Savannah River, Georgia and South Carolina*, May 27, 1963, Rivers and Harbors 3 (Dams and Reservoirs), folder III, May 20–June 28, 1963, box 32, Subject Correspondence Series, 1962, STP.

37. James M. Fallows and Ralph Nader, *The Water Lords: Ralph Nader's Study Group Report on Industry and Environmental Crisis in Savannah, Georgia* (New York: Grossman, 1971).

38. James Silver, *A Report of the Fish and Wildlife Resources in Relation to the Water Development Plan for the Clark Hill Reservoir, Savannah River Basin, Georgia and South Carolina for the U.S. Army Corps of Engineers* (Atlanta, Ga.: U.S. Department of the Interior, Fish and Wildlife Service, July 1946), folder 821.2, "Clark Hill Dam," box 140, entry 53a114, RG 77 NAII; "Appendix X, Malaria Control," in *Definite Project Report on Savannah River Basin, Georgia and South Carolina, Clark Hill Project*, Corps of Engineers, South Atlantic Division (revised May 1, 1946), folder 821.2, "Clark Hill Dam," box 141, entry 53a114, RG 77, NAII.

39. Colten, "Southern Pollution Permissiveness."

40. Daniel Schaffer, "Managing Water in the Tennessee Valley in the Post-War Period," *Environmental Review* 13, no. 2 (Summer 1989): 1–16, esp. 7. For more on one of the Tennessee River's polluters, see Richard A. Bartlett, *Troubled Waters: Champion International and the Pigeon River Controversy* (Knoxville: University of Tennessee Press, 1995).

41. The Corps' *Savannah River, Georgia Review Report* (July 1, 1959) was quoted extensively in Ernest B. Rogers Jr., *An Evaluation of Carters Island and Goat Island Reservoirs Proposed to Be Built by the U.S. Army Corps of Engineers on the Savannah River*, for the McCormick (S.C.) Chamber of Commerce and the Abbeville County (S.C.) Planning and

Development Board (February 17, 1960), 1–2, folder Rivers and Harbors 4 (Rivers) January 8–May 24, 1960, box 31, Subject Correspondence Series, 1960, STP.

42. Milazzo, *Unlikely Environmentalists*, 33–34.

43. James P. Nickles to Senator Richard Russell, October 9, 1962, folder Legislation 1962, Public Works, Dams, Trotters Shoals, box 167, OJP.

44. Abbeville County Citizens for Trotters Shoals advert, "Why Mead Will Not Locate at Calhoun Falls," *Anderson Independent*, February 16, 1963, 5, folder Legislation Clippings, Industry, box 158, OJP.

45. Carol Speight, "Trotters Shoals: The Big Boondoggle," *South Carolina Wildlife* (July–August 1976): 18–39, esp. 20.

46. Hays, *History of Environmental Politics*, 126; Robert Gottlieb, *Forcing the Spring: The Transformation of the American Environmental Movement* (Washington, D.C.: Island Press, 2005), 175–77, 180–81.

47. Jeffrey K. Stine, *Mixing the Waters: Environment, Politics, and the Building of the Tennessee-Tombigbee Waterway* (Akron: University of Akron Press, 1993), 85–86. The Corps lost another navigation project in part due to NEPA; see also Noll and Tegeder, *Ditch of Dreams*, 262.

48. U.S. Corps of Engineers, *PRELIMINARY Environmental Impact Statement, Trotters Shoals Dam and Lake, Savannah River, Georgia and South Carolina* (Savannah, Ga.: U.S. Army Engineer, Savannah District, November 1970), 23–28, series II, box 1, folder "Correspondence, 1971," RWC. See also Thomas L. Crisman, "Natural Lakes of the Southeastern United States: Origin, Structure, and Function," in *Biodiversity of the Southeastern United States: Aquatic Communities*, ed. Courtney Thomas Hackney, S. Marshall Adams, and William Haywood Martin (New York: Wiley, 1992), 475–538; John J. Hains, William E. Jabour, Robert H. Kennedy, William Boyd, James M. Satterfield, and Patrick K. Howle, *Water Quality in Richard B. Russell and J. Strom Thurmond Lakes: Interim Report for the Period 1997–1998*, Technical Report EL-99-13 (Calhoun Falls, S.C.: U.S. Army Engineers Research and Development Center, November 1999); and John J. Hains, "Southeastern Lakes: Changing Impacts, Issues, Demands," *LakeLine* (Winter 2001/2002): 23–28.

49. U.S. Corps of Engineers, *Final Environmental Impact Statement: Richard B. Russell Dam and Lake (Formerly Trotters Shoals Lake), Savannah River, Georgia and South Carolina* (Savannah, Ga.: U.S. Army Engineer, Savannah District, May 1979), 46, Environmental Impact 5/74 Report folder, Construction Series, 1974–1993, RWC.

50. James R. Young, Associate Editor [*Elberton Star*], to "Brownie," October 18, 1971, Correspondence, 1971, Planning and Funding Series, RWC.

51. Rep. William Jennings Bryan Dorn, Washington, D.C., to Wilbur H. Hoover, November 1, 1971, Correspondence, 1971, Planning and Funding Series, RWC.

52. Robert Williford to Waldo "Bo" McLeod, Editor, *Donaldsonville News*, November 24, 1971, Correspondence, 1971, Planning and Funding Series, RWC.

53. Frank Harrison, Attorney, McCormick, S.C., to Senator Olin D. Johnston, Washington, D.C., May 26, 1954, folder Legislation, 1954, Public Works, Dams, Hartwell, box 43, OJP.

54. Ibid.

55. "More Than 1,000 to Attend Annual Farm Bureau Meet," *Augusta Chronicle*, November 1, 1954, 11.

56. Lisa McGirr, *Suburban Warriors: The Origins of the New American Right* (Princeton: Princeton University Press, 2001); Kevin M. Kruse, *White Flight: Atlanta and the Making of Modern Conservatism* (Princeton: Princeton University Press, 2005); Matthew D. Lassiter, *The Silent Majority: Suburban Politics in the Sunbelt South* (Princeton: Princeton University Press, 2006).

57. Both letters can be found in folder Legislation 1963, Public Works, Dams, Trotters Shoals, box 89, OJP; see B. H. Tucker et al. to Sen. Johnston, September 30, 1963, and Jack H. Gunnells, Greenville, S.C., to Sen. Johnston, July 22, 1963.

58. Multiple letters can be found in folder Legislation 1963, Public Works, Dams, Trotters Shoals, box 89, OJP; see Robert G. Heller to Sen. Johnston, Washington, D.C., [n.d.], 1963; N. R. Marr to Sen. Johnston, Washington, D.C., May 25, 1963; and Ralph L. Brewer, to Sen. Johnston, Washington, D.C., May 26, 1963.

59. U.S. Corps of Engineers, *Final Environmental Impact Statement*, 14. On landowner opposition to the project in Georgia, see Steve Oney, "A Story of Rage," *Atlanta Journal-Constitution Magazine*, September 18, 1977, 14, and Steve Oney, "How the Corps Buys the Land," *Atlanta Journal-Constitution Magazine*, September 18, 1977, 14, clippings in 86-01-12 Natural Resources, Commissioner's Office—Special Projects and Issues and Areas Files, box 18, folder Richard Russell Reservoir 7/76–12/77, GAA.

60. A copy of a letter from Peyton S. Hawes to Senator Herman E. Talmadge, January 26, 1971, folder Correspondence, 1971, Planning and Funding Series, RWC; *Designating the Trotters Shoals Dam and Lake, Ga. and S.C., as the Richard B. Russell Dam and Lake*, 93rd Cong., 1st sess., S. Report 454, October 9, 1973.

61. Henry E. Barber and Allen R. Gann, *A History of the Savannah District, U.S. Army Corps of Engineers* (Savannah, Ga.: U.S. Army Corps of Engineers, 1989), 442–52.

62. The Russell project is one of about a dozen "pump-storage" facilities found in the United States. Water is released downstream into Clarks Hill reservoir during periods of peak demand to generate hydroelectricity, and the turbines can also be used to pump water back into Russell's reservoir from Clarks Hill during off-peak periods. After decades of environmental studies and mitigation planning, the Corps announced in June 2013 they would begin operating all four reversible turbines at once when necessary; see "Corps Cleared to Use All Four Russell Pumpback Turbines," *Augusta Chronicle*, June 3, 2013, http://chronicle.augusta.com/news/metro/2013-06-03/corps-cleared-use-all-four-russell-pumpback-turbines.

63. A. Stephen Johnson, *Georgia Scenic Rivers Report*, prepared for the Georgia Natural Areas Council (1971).

64. "Carter Stands Barefooted, Promises to Fight Pollution," *Atlanta Journal*, August 5, 1970.

65. "Georgia Governor Dunked by Canoe," *Clayton Tribune*, August 2, 1972, 6; Marc Reisner, *Cadillac Desert: The American West and Its Disappearing Water* (New York: Penguin, 1986; rev. and updated ed., 1993), 307.

66. For Carter quote, see "Cost of Flint Dam Project Gives Carter 2nd Thought," *Atlanta Journal*, February 25, 1973, 2A. For Carter's claim on Flint River correspondence, see "Carter Will Await Dam Impact Report," *Atlanta Journal*, June 1, 1973, 2A. The letters supporting and opposing the Flint River project can be found in Governor, Executive Dept., Governor's Subject Files (aka Incoming Correspondence), 1781–2008, Gov. James

Earl Carter (1971–1974), Subject Files, Flint River, Letters, boxes RCB 31376 and RCB 31379, 001-08-045, GAA.

67. "Carter Rejects Dam on Flint," *Atlanta Journal*, October 1, 1973, 1A. In an age of fiscal conservatism and mushrooming Cold War deficits, Congress finished what Carter started and officially de-authorized the Corps' proposed Flint River dam plans during the Ronald Reagan administration via the Water Resources Development Act of 1986 (Section 1002).

68. "Busbee Hails Proposals for 2 Dams," *Augusta Chronicle*, February 3, 1975, 1; "Rep. Derrick Defies Conventional Wisdom on Dam," *Washington Post*, April 3, 1977, 4.

69. "Carter's Opposition to Water Projects Linked to '73 Veto of Georgia Dam," *New York Times*, June 13, 1977, 14; Scott A. Frisch and Sean Q. Kelly, *Jimmy Carter and the Water Wars: Presidential Influence and the Politics of Pork* (Amherst, N.Y.: Cambria Press, 2008), 40 n. 8.

70. For a synthesis of Carter's hit list, see Reisner, *Cadillac Desert*, chap. 9, "The Peanut Farmer and the Pork Barrel," and p. 330 for Martin quote. For more on Carter's environmental presidency, see Jeffrey K. Stine, "Environmental Policy during the Carter Presidency," in *The Carter Presidency: Policy Choices in the Post-New Deal Era*, ed. Gary M. Fink and Hugh Davis Graham ([Lawrence]: University Press of Kansas, 1998), 179–201.

CHAPTER 7

1. "Blazes Blamed on Mountaineers," *Atlanta Constitution*, March 2, 1976, 2-A; "Arsonists Fire NE Georgia Woodlands," *Clayton Tribune*, March 4, 1976, 1 (quote); Jack Temple Kirby, "Retro Frontiersmen," in *The Countercultural South*, Mercer University Lamar Memorial Lectures No. 38 (Athens: University of Georgia Press, 1995), 33–56.

2. The Wild and Scenic Rivers Act (1968) named eight "instant" rivers to this protection category and identified twenty-seven additional study rivers. Southeastern study rivers included the Chattooga (Ga. and S.C.), Suwannee (Ga. and Fla.), Obed (Tenn.), and Buffalo (Tenn.). Of these four southern study rivers, only the Chattooga (1974) and Obed (1976) were granted federal wild and scenic status. A complete listing of Wild and Scenic Rivers and a legislative timeline can be found at http://www.rivers.gov/.

3. Mark W. T. Harvey, *A Symbol of Wilderness: Echo Park and the American Conservation Movement* (Albuquerque: University of New Mexico Press, 1994).

4. Nationally: Louis Warren, *The Hunter's Game: Poachers and Conservationists in Twentieth-Century America* (New Haven: Yale University Press, 1997); Richard W. Judd, *Common Lands, Common People: The Origins of Conservation in Northern New England* (Cambridge: Harvard University Press, 1997); Karl Jacoby, *Crimes against Nature: Squatters, Poachers, Thieves, and the Hidden History of American Conservation* (Berkeley: University of California Press, 2001). In Appalachia: Stephen L. Fisher, ed., *Fighting Back in Appalachia: Traditions of Resistance and Change* (Philadelphia: Temple University Press, 1993); Suzanne Marshall, *"Lord, We're Just Trying to Save Your Water": Environmental Activism and Dissent in the Appalachian South* (Gainesville: University Press of Florida, 2002); Kathryn Newfont, *Blue Ridge Commons: Environmental Activism and Forest History in Western North Carolina* (Athens: University of Georgia Press, 2012).

5. David L. Carlton and Peter A. Coclanis, eds., *Confronting Poverty in the Great Depression: The Report on the Economic Conditions of the South with Related Documents* (Boston: Bedford Books of St. Martin's Press, 1996).

6. Harvey, *Symbol of Wilderness*, xvi; Karl Boyd Brooks, *Public Power, Private Dams: The Hells Canyon High Dam Controversy* (Seattle: University of Washington Press, 2006).

7. Vicki Constantine Croke, "The Brothers Wild," *Washington Post Magazine*, November 11, 2007.

8. U.S. Congress, Senate, Select Committee on National Water Resources, *Water Resources Hearing*, 86th Cong., 1st sess., October 9, 12, 1959, 460.

9. John J. Craighead, "Wild Rivers," *Naturalist* 16, 3 (Autumn 1965): 1–5, esp. 5.

10. U.S. Congress, Senate, Select Committee on National Water Resources, *Water Resources Hearing*, 457–63.

11. U.S. Outdoor Recreation Resources Review Commission, *Outdoor Recreation for America, a Report to the President and to the Congress* (Washington, D.C.: Government Printing Office, 1962), 173.

12. Tim Palmer has made significant contributions to the national history of wild and scenic rivers, and the best books are *The Wild and Scenic Rivers of America* (Washington, D.C.: Island Press, 1993) and *Endangered Rivers and the Conservation Movement*, 2nd ed. (Lanham, Md.: Rowman and Littlefield, 2004), 155–56 (Craighead quote).

13. President Lyndon Baines Johnson, *Special Message to the Congress on Conservation and Restoration of Natural Beauty*, February 8, 1965, http://www.lbjlib.utexas.edu/johnson/archives.hom/speeches.hom/650208.asp (March 10, 2013).

14. U.S. Congress, House, Committee on Interior and Insular Affairs, *Amending the Wild and Scenic Rivers Act by Designating the Chattooga River, North Carolina, South Carolina, and Georgia as a Component of the National Wild and Scenic Rivers System, submitted by the Committee on Interior and Insular Affairs*, 93rd Cong., 1st sess., November 29, 1973, House Report 675, 2; Palmer, *Wild and Scenic Rivers of America*, 25–26.

15. U.S. Department of the Interior, news release, "Wild Rivers Team Selects Twelve Rivers for Detailed Study," August 5, 1964, folder Topical Files, 1964, Duke Power, box 68, WDP.

16. "Duke Plans $700 Million Oconee, Pickens Projects," *Anderson Mail*, January 2, 1965, folder Legislation Clippings, Industry, box 158, OJP.

17. Stewart L. Udall, Secretary of the Interior, to Joseph C. Swidler, Chairman, Federal Power Commission, July 28, 1965, 3, folder Topical Files, 1965, Keowee-Toxaway, box 72, WDP.

18. Jack L. Brown, Postmaster, Mountain Rest, S.C., to Rep. W. J. B. Dorn, Washington, D.C., May 25, 1966, folder Topical Files, 1966, Savannah River, box 77, WDP.

19. Ramone Eaton, Vice President, American Red Cross, Washington, D.C., to C. Thomas Wyche, Greenville, S.C., December 18, 1967, Chattooga Conservancy Files, Clayton, Ga.; Henry Wallace, "Ramone Eaton—A Tribute," *American Whitewater* 25, no. 3 (May–June 1980): 15–19; Payson Kennedy, "River Exploration in the Southern Appalachians," in *First Descents: In Search of Wild Rivers*, ed. Cameron O'Connor and John Lazenby (Birmingham, Ala.: Menasha Ridge Press, 1989), 146–54.

20. C. Thomas Wyche, Greenville, S.C., to Senator Ernest Hollings (August 10, 1967)

and to Rep. W. J. B. Dorn (August 10, 1967), both in Chattooga Conservancy Files, Clayton, Ga. See also John Lane, *Chattooga: Descending into the Myth of Deliverance River* (Athens: University of Georgia Press, 2004), 35–37.

21. John McPhee, *Encounters with the Archdruid* (New York: Farrar, Straus, and Giroux, 1971), 159.

22. State Council for the Preservation of Natural Areas Act (March 10, 1966), Ga. L. 1966, 330; Georgia Council for the Preservation of Natural Areas, *Report of the First Year of Operation, 1967–69* (Decatur: n.p., n.d.).

23. Marshall, *"Lord, We're Just Trying to Save Your Water,"* 111–13; Jerry L. McCollum, "President's Column: Charles Wharton—Champion of Georgia's Unspoiled Places," *The Call* 14, no. 1 (Winter 2004).

24. Georgia was among a half-dozen states that did, or attempted to, establish state-level river protection acts before 1970. See Palmer, *Endangered Rivers*, 158; *Georgia Scenic Rivers Act of 1969* (April 28, 1969), Ga. L. 1969, 933; "Georgia Scenic Rivers Bill in Senate, Has Chattooga," *Clayton (Ga.) Tribune*, February 13, 1969; A. Stephen Johnson, *Georgia Scenic Rivers Report*, prepared for the Georgia Natural Areas Council (1971); Phil Garner, "The Master Grantsman," *Atlanta Journal-Constitution Magazine*, May 14, 1978, 12.

25. Robert E. Hanie to Dr. H. S. Alden, Atlanta, Georgia, May 13, 1967, folder History of the Conservancy, box 7, GNAC, 1966–73, State Parks and Historical Sites (of the Georgia Dept. of Natural Resources collection), 30-8-43, GAA; "Georgia Conservancy Receives Charter; Officers, Committees Named," *Georgia Conservancy Quarterly*, Winter 1968, box 22, folder "Miscellaneous re Various Civic Activities," JMP.

26. Frustrated members left the conservancy and formed Save America's Vital Environment to "attack environmental problems from a non-tax-exempt platform"; see Merle Schlesinger Lefkoff, "The Voluntary Citizens' Group as a Public Policy Alternative to the Political Party: A Case Study of the Georgia Conservancy" (Ph.D. diss., Emory University, 1975), 25–34, 156–59.

27. "Georgia Conservancy Receives Charter"; Lefkoff, "Voluntary Citizens' Group," 156.

28. "Field Trips—Rare Good Fun," *Georgia Conservancy Quarterly*, Winter 1968, folder "Miscellaneous re Various Civic Activities," box 22, JMP.

29. Doug Woodward, *Wherever Waters Flow: A Lifelong Love Affair with Wild Rivers* (Franklin, N.C.: Headwaters Publishing, 2006), 106 n. 25; William Dunlap, telephone conversation with author, September 1, 2005, notes in author's possession.

30. Andrew Sparks, "Can We Keep the Chattooga Wild?" *Atlanta Journal and Constitution Magazine*, September 22, 1968, 12; "Group Discusses Development and Objectives for Chattooga River," *Clayton Tribune*, November 28, 1968; "Chattooga Has Friends," *Atlanta Journal-Constitution*, December 8, 1968. See also a sample letter sent to the Dillard meeting invitees, Robert Hanie, Executive Director, Georgia Council for the Preservation of Natural Areas, October 22, 1968, GNAC, folder Chattooga Seminar, Nov. 20–21, box 10, GAA.

31. The watershed drains approximately 180,000 acres. Today, the Forest Service manages about 122,000 acres, with 14,000 acres making up the Wild and Scenic River Corridor. U.S. Department of Agriculture, Forest Service, Southern Region, *Wild and Scenic River Study Report: Chattooga River*, June 15, 1971, 31; U.S. Congress, House, Subcommittee on Interior and Insular Affairs, *Wild and Scenic Rivers Act Amendments*, pt. 2, 93rd Cong., 1st sess., October 29–30, 1973, 11; U.S. Department of Agriculture, Forest

Service, Southern Region, *Revised Land and Management Plan: Sumner National Forest*, Management Bulletin R8-MB 116A, January 2004, 4–5 and chapter 4, "Management Area 2—Chattooga River."

32. Wade H. Wright, *History of the Georgia Power Company, 1855–1956* (Atlanta: Georgia Power Company, 1957), 212.

33. "Atom Site Chosen by Georgia Power," *Atlanta Journal*, November 2, 1967, 22-A; "Power Firm Nets 5.2 PCT," *Atlanta Journal*, October 18, 1968, 21-A; "Georgia Power Company Faces Job Bias Suit," *Atlanta Journal*, January 10, 1969, 2-A. See also Jeff Goodell, *Big Coal: The Dirty Secret behind America's Energy Future* (Boston: Houghton Mifflin, 2006), 155–57.

34. For quotes: Sparks, "Can We Keep the Chattooga Wild?" 17; U.S. Department of Agriculture, Forest Service, Southern Region, *Wild and Scenic River Study Report*, 117–18. See also Buzz Williams, "The Wild and Scenic Chattooga River," *Chattooga Quarterly*, Spring 2004, 3–4.

35. Del W. Thorsen, Forest Supervisor, Columbia, S.C., to Rep. W. J. B. Dorn, Washington, D.C., March 10, 1971, folder Topical Files, 1971–1972, Rivers and Harbors, Chattooga River, box 97, WDP.

36. Rabun County, Georgia, and Oconee County, South Carolina: U.S. Department of Commerce, Bureau of the Census, *Eighteenth U.S. Census, 1960: Characteristics of the Population*, and *Nineteenth U.S. Census, 1970: Characteristics of the Population*.

37. John D. Ridley, telephone conversation with the author, March 27, 2006, notes in author's possession.

38. The Forest Service has since turned the Russell property into an interpretive site highlighting the property's nineteenth-century use. An arsonist targeted one structure in 1988; see Ray Chandler, "Forest Service to Allow More Public Comment on Proposed Oconee Pioneer Farmstead," *Anderson Independent Mail*, September 4, 2009, http://www.independentmail.com/news/2009/sep/04/forest-service-allow-more-public-comment-proposed-/ (March 10, 2013).

39. Nicole Hayler, *Sound Wormy: Memoir of Andrew Gennett, Lumberman* (Athens: University of Georgia Press, 2002), 101–6, 112–13, 209 n. 8; Susan Lewis Koyle, *Genealogy Extracted from Forest Service Court Cases in Rabun County, Georgia* (Bowie, Md.: Heritage Books, 2001); R. C. Nicholson, "The Federal Forestry Service," in *Sketches of Rabun County History, 1819–1948*, ed. Andrew Jackson Ritchie (Chelsea, Mich.: Rabun County, Georgia, Historical Society, 1995), 358–66.

40. Handwritten notes on map, U.S. Forest Service, *Chattooga River: As a Wild and Scenic River* (1971), folder Chattooga River, box 28, Special Projects and Issues and Areas Files, Commissioner's Office, Georgia Department of Natural Resources (86-01-12), GAA.

41. Ridley telephone conversation with the author.

42. "Chattooga's Role under Rivers Act Discussed," *Keowee Courier*, December 4, 1968, 3; "Proposals Outlined to Make Wild, Scenic Site of Area along Chattooga River," *Greenville News*, April 16, 1969, 10; "Hearing on Chattooga River Project Set for December 5," *Clayton Tribune*, December 4, 1969, 1; "Group Studies Chattooga Wild River; To Have Camping Facilities," *Clayton Tribune*, March 26, 1970, 1 (quote).

43. Sparks, "Can We Keep the Chattooga Wild?" 18; "Proposals Outlined to Make Wild, Scenic Site of Area along Chattooga River," 10.

44. "Proceeding of Chattooga River Study Meeting," Clemson House, Clemson, S.C., April 15, 1969, GNAC, folder Chattooga Seminar, Nov. 20–21, box 10, GAA.

45. "Opinions on Developing Chattooga River Differ," *Greenville News*, September 1, 1971.

46. Louis Warren articulates the difference between locals and elites, as well as their residence status, to illustrate how local and state authorities negotiated access to, and protection of, resources. See *Hunter's Game*, 23–27, 177.

47. U.S. Congress, House, Subcommittee on Interior and Insular Affairs, *Wild and Scenic Rivers Act Amendments*, 54.

48. Sparks, "Can We Keep the Chattooga Wild?" 17; Kennedy, "River Exploration in the Southern Appalachians," 146–54.

49. "Chattooga Well Worth Effort," *Keowee Courier*, April 23, 1969; U.S. Congress, House, Subcommittee on Interior and Insular Affairs, *Wild and Scenic Rivers Act Amendments*, 59–60.

50. "Bill Would Add Chattooga River to Wild, Scenic Rivers System," *Sylva Herald and Ruralite*, July 26, 1973, 6; U.S. Congress, House, Subcommittee on Interior and Insular Affairs, *Wild and Scenic Rivers Act Amendments*.

51. U.S. Department of Agriculture, Forest Service, *A Proposal: The Chattooga, "A Wild and Scenic River,"* March 3, 1970; Jim Morrison, "Chattooga Wild River Study Release: Is It Strong Enough to Save River?" *Newsletter of the Georgia Conservancy, Inc.*, March 18, 1970; "March 17 Meeting to Hear Forest Service Proposal," *Clayton Tribune*, March 12, 1970, 1.

52. Dr. Claude Terry, Watershed Development Subcommittee of the House Public Works Committee, Macon, Georgia, October 12, [1969?], folder Georgia Conservancy, 1969–1970, box 9, Department of Game and Fish (25-01-008), GAA; Dr. Claude Terry, "What Is a Floodplain?" *Georgia Conservancy Quarterly Magazine: The Rivers and Streams of Georgia*, August 1972, Georgia Room, Hargrett Rare Book and Manuscript Library, University of Georgia, Athens; U.S. Congress, Senate, Subcommittee on Public Lands of the Committee on Interior and Insular Affairs, *Proposed Wild and Scenic Chattooga River and the Conveyance of Certain Public Lands*, 93rd Congress, 1st sess., October 10, 1973, 81.

53. U.S. Congress, Senate, Subcommittee on Public Lands of the Committee on Interior and Insular Affairs, *Proposed Wild and Scenic Chattooga River*, 89.

54. Doug Woodward, "Ship of State," in *Wherever Waters Flow*, 193–201.

55. U.S. Congress, Senate, Subcommittee on Public Lands of the Committee on Interior and Insular Affairs, *Proposed Wild and Scenic Chattooga River*, 46, 57–58.

56. *Wild and Scenic Rivers Act*, P.L. 90–542, October 2, 1968, Section 10(a), emphasis added.

57. John Craighead, "Wild River," *Montana Wildlife*, June 1957, 15–20; U.S. Congress, Senate, Select Committee on National Water Resources, *Water Resources Hearing*, 457–63.

58. John Boorman, *Deliverance* (1974), DVD.

59. John C. Inscoe, "Appalachian Otherness, Real and Perceived," in *The New Georgia Guide* (Athens: University of Georgia Press, 1996), 165–70.

60. Claude E. Hastings, Environmental Protection Coordinator, Georgia State Game

and Fish Commission, to Jack Crockford, Assistant Director, Georgia State Game and Fish Commission, Atlanta, Ga., September 10, 1971, 25-01-008 Department of Game and Fish Records, box 3, folder Chattooga River, Wild and Scenic River Study, 1971, GAA.

61. Phil Garner, "Shooting Georgia's Wildest Rapids," *Atlanta Journal and Constitution Magazine*, September 19, 1971, 20; Phil Garner, "The Deliverance Syndrome," *Atlanta Journal and Constitution Magazine*, November 18, 1973, 16; *American Whitewater*, archived online, http://www.americanwhitewater.org/journal/archive/, specifically see Donal R. Mayrick, "Spelunkers on the Chattooga River," *American Whitewater* 17, no. 4 (Winter 1972): 142–47, and Donald H. Wilson, "Chattooga!" *American Whitewater* 18, no. 3 (Autumn 1973): 113–17.

62. Kennedy, "River Exploration in the Southern Appalachians"; Woodward, *Wherever Waters Flow*, 177–91.

63. Woodward, *Wherever Waters Flow*, 162–70. For visitor statistics, see Don Belt, "Chattooga River Country: Wild Water, Proud People," *National Geographic* 163, no. 4 (April 1983): 458–76, esp. 471. Since 1970 the Forest Service has recorded forty fatalities on the Chattooga River; see "Fatalities or Near Fatalities," http://www.fs.usda.gov/Internet/FSE_DOCUMENTS/stelprdb5392005.pdf (August 14, 2013).

64. "River Bill Backed without a Ripple," *Atlanta Journal*, October 10, 1973, 10-C.

65. T. Craig Martin, "Chattooga," *Outdoors in Georgia* 2, no. 7 (July 1973): 15–23, esp. 20 (quotes).

66. "No Place for Amateur: The Chattooga Is Dangerous," *Atlanta Constitution*, May 4, 1973, 9-A; "Many Try to Beat the River," *Atlanta Constitution*, August 26, 1973, 8-F; U.S. Congress, Senate, Subcommittee on Public Lands of the Committee on Interior and Insular Affairs, *Proposed Wild and Scenic Chattooga River*, 71; *An Act to Amend Wild and Scenic Rivers*, P.L. 93-279, May 10, 1974.

67. "Proposals Outlined to Make Wild, Scenic Site of Area along Chattooga River," 10; "Hearing on Chattooga River Project Set for December 5," 1; "March 17 Meeting To Hear Forest Service Proposal, Chattooga River," 1; "Chattooga Listening Sessions," *Clayton Tribune*, January 24, 1974, 4.

68. Williams, "Wild and Scenic Chattooga River," 4; U.S. Department of Agriculture, Forest Service, Southern Region, *Wild and Scenic River Study Report*. I have attempted to locate these comments without success.

69. Max Gates, telephone conversation with author, February 21, 2006, notes in author's possession.

70. Paul W. Hirt, *A Conspiracy of Optimism: Management of the National Forests since World War II* (Lincoln: University of Nebraska Press, 1994), 183.

71. "Forest Service Lists Sites for Fuelwood without Permit," *Clayton Tribune*, September 12, 1974; "Free Firewood Areas Prove to Be Successful," *Clayton Tribune*, January 29, 1976, 11.

72. Gates telephone conversation with author. See also "News from the US Forest Service," *Clayton Tribune*, December 11, 1975, A12; "News from the Forest Service," *Clayton Tribune*, January 8, 1976.

73. Kathryn Newfont, "Grassroots Environmentalism: Origins of the Western North Carolina Alliance," *Appalachian Journal* 27, no. 1 (Fall 1999): 46–61, esp. 57. See also Newfont, *Blue Ridge Commons*, and Belt, "Chattooga River Country," 471.

74. "Public vs. Private Land Use," *Clayton Tribune*, March 11, 1976, 4; Shelley Smith Mastran and Nan Lowerre, *Mountaineers and Rangers: A History of Federal Forest Management in the Southern Appalachians, 1900–81*, FS-380 (Washington, D.C.: USDA, Forest Service, April 1983), esp. chap. 8.

75. "Opinions on Developing Chattooga River Differ."

76. U.S. Forest Service, "For Immediate Release" (copy), Rivers and Harbors 4 (Rivers), May 13–October 1, 1974, box 34, Subject Correspondence Series, 1954–1976, J. Strom Thurmond, Mss 100, Special Collections Unit, Clemson University Libraries, Clemson, S.C.

77. *Wild and Scenic Rivers Act*, Section 2(b), emphasis in original.

78. *Proceedings of Chattooga River Study Meeting*, Clemson House, Clemson, S.C., April 15, 1969, folder Natural Areas Council, Georgia, Scenic Rivers, Chattooga River, 1969, box 12, Department of Game and Fish (25-01-008), GAA; U.S. Department of Agriculture, Forest Service, Southern Region, *Wild and Scenic River Study Report*, 159.

79. Rabun County (Ga.) Board of Commissioners—Monthly Board Meeting, October 2, 1972, 2, available online through MCCi Online Library: http://www.mccinnovations.com/weblink/login.aspx (March 10, 2013).

80. "Corridor of Chattooga Closed to Vehicles," *Clayton Tribune*, October 10, 1974, 1; Senator Herman E. Talmadge, Washington, D.C., to Brian Webb, Blairsville, Ga., May 20, 1976, letter reprinted in the *Clayton Tribune*, June 3, 1976, 4.

81. Charlie Huppuch, interview notes in Tetra Tech EC, Inc., *Chattooga River History Project: Literature Review and Interview Summary*, prepared for USDA, Forest Service, Atlanta, Georgia, August 25, 2006, http://www.fs.usda.gov/Internet/FSE_DOCUMENTS/fsbdev3_037030.pdf (August 14, 2013).

82. "Chattooga Included in Wild Rivers Act," *Clayton Tribune*, June 6, 1974, 1; "Chattooga Access to Be Limited," *Clayton Tribune*, June 6, 1974, 1.

83. Kirby, "Retro Frontiersmen," 33–56; Paul M. Kankula, "Environmental Legislation," *Mountain Rest Community Club: US Forest Service* (Seneca, Oconee County, S.C., April, 2003), http://files.usgwarchives.net/sc/oconee/history/MR-02.txt (August 14, 2013).

84. "Suspected Arsonist Captured; Charged with Shooting Ranger," *Clayton Tribune*, March 16, 1972, 1.

85. "Mountain Men Rekindle Feud with Government," *Sumter Daily Item*, March 1, 1976, 16; "Blazes Blamed on Mountaineers," "Forests Burned in Timber Feud," *Ocala (Fla.) Star-Banner*, March 2, 1976, 6; "Arsonists Fire NE Georgia Woodlands," *Clayton Tribune*, March 3, 1976, 1.

86. Kankula, "Environmental Legislation." A search in the *Clayton Tribune* between March 1976 and May 1978 did not reveal if anybody was ever caught or charged in connection with these fires.

87. Smith and Lowerre, *Mountaineers and Rangers*, 169.

88. U.S. Congress, House, Subcommittee on Interior and Insular Affairs, *Wild and Scenic Rivers Act Amendments*, 11.

89. Congress eventually designated other wild, scenic, and recreational rivers in the southeastern United States after 1974, but the Chattooga remains the longest Appalachian and southern mountain river with segments in all three categories. See the National Park

Service's "National Wild and Scenic Rivers System" for statistics: http://www.rivers.gov/rivers/ (August 14, 2013).

90. Lane, *Chattooga*, 97.

EPILOGUE

1. U.S. Drought Monitor Archive, http://droughtmonitor.unl.edu/archive.html; Andrew Freedman, "Heat Wave Leads to 'Weather Whiplash,'" Capital Weather Gang, *Washington Post*, April 27, 2009, http://voices.washingtonpost.com/capitalweather gang/2009/04/in_light_of_last_weeks.html (August 24, 2013); "How Wet Has It Been?" *Atlanta Journal-Constitution*, June 25, 2013, http://www.ajc.com/news/news/local/how-wet-has-it-been-atlantas-rainfall-in-first-hal/nYTdh/ (August 24, 2013); "Not Much Impact near Savannah after Dam Bursts in Screven County," *Savannah Morning News*, July 14, 2013, http://savannahnow.com/news/2013-07-14/not-much-impact-near-savannah-after-dam-bursts-screven-county#.UhkPF9Jwp9k (August 24, 2013); "Lake Alice Remedy in Place," NorhtFulton.com, June 10, 2013, http://www.northfulton.com/Articles-NEWS-c-2013-06-10-199218.114126-sub-Lake-Alice-remedy-in-place.html (August 24, 2013); "Torrential Rains Take a Toll on S.C. Crops," *Charlotte Observer*, August 24, 2013, http://www.charlotteobserver.com/2013/08/19/4248757/torrential-rains-take-toll-on.html (24, 2013); "Augusta Closes Parks, Cancels Events as Savannah River Rises from Upstream Flooding," *Florida Times Union*, July 11, 2013, http://jacksonville.com/news/georgia/2013-07-11/story/augusta-closes-parks-cancels-events-savannah-river-rises-upstream (August 24, 2013).

2. "Carolinas Reach Deal on Catawba," *Charlotte Observer*, November 13, 2010, http://www.charlotteobserver.com/2010/11/13/1834088/carolinas-reach-deal-on-catawba.html (July 23, 2011); "McMaster Says SC-NC Water Case Is Over," *Columbia State*, December 21, 2010, http://www.thestate.com/2010/12/21/1615297/mcmaster-says-sc-nc-water-case.html (July 23, 2011); "Water War's Welcome End," *Charleston Post and Courier*, December 31, 2010, http://www.postandcourier.com/news/2010/dec/31/water-wars-welcome-end/ (July 23, 2011).

3. E-mail announcement, attendee list and agenda minutes, "Southeastern Drought & Reliability Meeting" (November 16, 2007), provided to the author by Southeastern Power Administration (SEPA), Freedom of Information Act Request #2011-0032. A single sentence in one media story did result; see "Georgia's Water Crisis: The Power of Water," *Atlanta Journal-Constitution*, November 18, 2007, A1.

4. Southern Company is the second-largest, based on market value, http://www.statista.com/statistics/237773/the-largest-electric-utilities-in-the-us-based-on-market-value/ (March 27, 2014); "Duke and Progress Energy Become Largest U.S. Utility," *New York Times*, July 3, 2012, http://www.nytimes.com/2012/07/04/business/energy-environment/duke-energy-merger-creates-largest-us-utility.html?_r=0 (August 24, 2013); Jeff Goodell, *Big Coal: The Dirty Secret behind America's Energy Future* (Boston: Houghton Mifflin, 2006), 149–55; "Barbour's Kemper Connection," *Mississippi Business Journal*, April 25, 2010, http://msbusiness.com/2010/04/barbour%E2%80%99s-kemper-connection/ (August 24, 2013); "Alabama's Cost of Power—I mean Influence—Is

High," Birmingham (Ala.), *al.com*, April 17, 2011, http://blog.al.com/archiblog/2011/04/alabamas_cost_of_power_—_i_me.html (August 24, 2013); "Southern Company, a Lobbying Powerhouse, Fights New Carbon Rules," *Atlanta Journal-Constitution*, September 1, 2013; "Lobbyist Spending Scaled Back 12 Percent in 2013," *International Business Times*, January 23, 2014, http://www.ibtimes.com/lobbyist-spending-scaled-back-12-percent-2013-1547081 (March 31, 2014).

5. "N.C. Pulls Deal with Duke on Coal Ash Pollution," Associated Press, March 21, 2014, http://bigstory.ap.org/article/nc-pulls-deal-duke-coal-ash-pollution (March 27, 2014); "Duke Energy Has the Power," *News and Observer*, March 8, 2014, http://www.newsobserver.com/2014/03/08/3685111/christensen-duke-energy-has-the.html (March 27, 2014).

6. Garrett retired, and Paul Bowers succeeded him not only as the new Georgia Power CEO but also as "the behind the scenes consultant" for Georgia, according to Governor Nathan Deal; see "Deal Taps Ga. Power's Bowers for Water Talks," *Atlanta Business Chronicle*, February 3, 2011, http://www.bizjournals.com/atlanta/print-edition/2011/02/04/Bowers.html (August 24, 2013). See also "Georgia Power Takes a Fresh Look at Nuclear Power," *Creative Loafing Atlanta*, August 22, 2007, http://clatl.com/atlanta/georgia-power-takes-a-fresh-look-at-nuclear-power/Content?oid=1269189 (August 24, 2013).

7. "Electricity Demand Guzzling State's Water," *Atlanta Journal-Constitution*, November 18, 2007; "Regulators Weigh Small Fish vs. Power Plants," *Charlotte Observer*, July 17, 2011, http://www.newsobserver.com/2011/07/17/1349621/small-fish-vs-power-plants.html (August 24, 2013); Joan F. Kenny et al., *Estimated Use of Water in the United States in 2005*, U.S. Geological Survey Circular 1344 (2009), 1.

8. Georgia Power, *Plant Bowen: One Team, One Future*, n.d., http://www.georgiapower.com/docs/about-us/Plant%20Bowen%20brochure.pdf (August 24, 2013); "Georgia Power to Set Up Water Research Center at Plant Bowen," SaportaReport.com, April 20, 2011, http://saportareport.com/blog/2011/04/georgia-power-to-set-up-water-research-center-at-plant-bowen/ (August 24, 2013); Georgia Power Press Release, "Georgia Power to Develop Water Research Center," April 20, 2011, http://www.georgiapower.com/news/iframe_pressroom.asp (July 22, 2011); Georgia Power Press Release via *Rome Tribune*, "New Technology Assists Plant Bowen in Water Usage Efficiency," May 31, 2011, http://rn-t.com/view/full_story/13501656/article-New-technology-assists-Plant-Bowen-in-water-usage-efficiency-?instance=home_news_lead_story (August 24, 2013); "Georgia Power Dedicated Research Center at Plant Bowen," *Daily Tribune News*, November 20, 2013, http://www.daily-tribune.com/view/full_story/24085712/article-Georgia-Power-dedicates-research-center-at-Plant-Bowen (March 27, 2014); "EPA Surveys Plant Bowen Coal Ash Pond as Part of National Study," *Rome News Tribune*, September 12, 2009, http://www.northwestgeorgianews.com/rome/news/epa-surveys-plant-bowen-coal-ash-pond-as-part-of/article_0a28775f-770a-5e72-aa76-689f40fc5ea7.html (March 31, 2014).

9. Georgia Power, "About Us: Our Promise to You," http://www.georgiapower.com/about-us/our-brand-promise.cshtml (August 24, 2013).

10. "Solar Groups Seek Tea-Party Support," *Wall Street Journal*, July 2, 2013, http://online.wsj.com/article/SB10001424127887323689204578573720128231396.html (September 3, 2013).

11. Kenny et al., *Estimated Use of Water in the United States in 2005*, 1.

12. Elias Fereres, David A. Goldhamer, and Larry R. Parsons, "Irrigation Water Management of Horticultural Crops," *HortScience* 38, no. 5 (August 2003): 1036–42, esp. 1037–38.

13. U.S. Study Commission, *Plan for the Development of the Land and Water Resources of the Southeast River Basins, Appendix 12, Planning* (Atlanta: n.p., 1963), 2-40 through 2-48. See also Bill Allen, "State Hooks Title: 'Paradise o' Ponds,'" *Atlanta Journal*, September 13, 1953, 12. Allen claimed 15,000 irrigated acres, and another source claimed 27,700 acres: Georgia Water Use and Conservation Committee, *Water in Georgia: A Report on the Historical, Physical, and Legal Aspects of Water in Georgia, Prepared and Submitted to the Governor, the General Assembly, and the People of Georgia* ([Atlanta]: Georgia Water Law Revision Commission, 1955), 55.

14. Robert R. Pierce, Nancy L. Barber, and Harold R. Stiles, *Georgia Irrigation, 1970–1980: A Decade of Growth*, Water-Resources Investigations Report 83-4177 (n.p.: U.S. Geological Survey and Georgia Department of Natural Resources, 1984), 1, 14, 24. For crop and irrigation data, see the National Environmentally Sound Production Agriculture Laboratory (NESPAL), a unit of the University of Georgia's College of Agricultural and Environmental Sciences, data online, http://www.nespal.org/sirp/agwateruse/facts/survey/default.asp (August 24, 2013).

15. Kerry Harrison, "2008 Irrigation Survey," January 16, 2009, http://www.nespal.org/sirp/agwateruse/facts/survey/. .%5C2009.0122.IrrSurvey08_misc_pub.pdf (August 24, 2013); Jim Hook and Kerry Harrison, "Agricultural Irrigation Development in Georgia" (2009), in "Agricultural Irrigation Water Demand: Georgia's Major and Minor Crops, 2011 through 2050," http://www.nespal.org/sirp/waterinfo/state/awd/Background/AgWaterDemand_GaIrrDevelopment.htm (August 24, 2013).

16. Kenny et al., *Estimated Use of Water in the United States in 2005*, 1.

17. "'We're Not Really Rooting for Ourselves Anymore,'" *Atlanta Journal-Constitution*, February 6, 2011, http://www.ajc.com/news/news/local/were-not-really-rooting-for-ourselves-anymore/nQqNk/ (July 23, 2011); "Atlanta's Reputation Is Sinking," *Atlanta Business Chronicle Blog: Real Talk*, June 20, 2011, http://www.bizjournals.com/atlanta/real_talk/2011/06/atlantas-reputation-is-sinking.html (July 23, 2011).

18. "Regulator: New Nuke Plant Now Wouldn't Make Sense," *Atlanta Journal-Constitution*, August 13, 2013; "Solar Has Bright Future in Georgia," *Savannah Morning News*, September 3, 2013.

19. For an excellent synthesis of the so-called water wars and the 2013 flare-up, see Neill Herring, "Water Wars Redux," *Creative Loafing Atlanta*, August 21, 2013, http://clatl.com/atlanta/water-wars-redux/Content?oid=9059308 (August 24, 2013), and Susannah Nesmith, "Return of the Water Wars," *Columbia Journalism Review*, August 27, 2013, http://www.cjr.org/united_states_project/water_wars_return_florida_to_sue_georgia_over_apalachicola_oysters.php?page=all (September 3, 2013).

20. "Ga., S.C. Stuck on Saltwater Intrusion," *Savannah Morning News*, May 12, 2013, http://savannahnow.com/news/2013-05-12/ga-sc-stuck-saltwater-intrusion#.UhjWT3_3N1o (August 24, 2013).

21. "Georgia's Offer to Settle a 195-Year-Old Border Fight with Tennessee," *Atlanta Journal-Constitution*, February 8, 2013, http://www.ajc.com/weblogs/political-insider/2013/feb/08/your-daily-jolt-georgias-offer-settle-195-year-old/ (August 24,

2013); Georgia Water Contingency Planning Task Force, Appendix III, December 2009, http://sonnyperdue.georgia.gov/vgn/images/portal/cit_1210/0/57/155134868Water %20Contingency%20Planning%20Task%20Force%20Report%20-%20Appendix%20 III%20-%20Complete%20set%20of%20options%20evaluated.pdf (August 24, 2013).

22. "Tussle over Plan to Supplement Flint River Streams," *Newnan Times Herald*, March 31, 2013, http://www.times-herald.com/local/BC-GA-XGR—Flint-River-Pumping-1st-Ld-Writethru-MOS (March 31, 2014); "Georgia's Water Negotiator's Role May Be Seen as Conflict," *Memphis (Tenn.) Commercial Appeal*, May 19, 2013, http://www.commercial appeal.com/news/2013/may/19/georgia-water-negotiators-role-may-be-seen-conflic/ (August 24, 2013).

23. John Brock, "Future of Metro Atlanta's Water Should Be a Balance between the Economy and the Environment," *SaportaReport*, February 21, 2011, http://saportareport .com/blog/2011/02/water-in-atlanta-region-should-be-a-balance-between-the-economy-and-the-environment/ (August 24, 2013).

24. Thomas P. Hughes, *Networks of Power: Electrification in Western Society, 1880–1930* (Baltimore: Johns Hopkins University Press, 1983).

25. Juliet Christian-Smith and Peter H. Glick, *A Twenty-First Century US Water Policy* (New York: Oxford University Press, 2012).

26. American Rivers—among other NGOs—has advocated on these issues for more than a decade. See *Hidden Reservoir: Why Water Efficiency Is the Best Solution for the Southeast* (2008), http://www.americanrivers.org/assets/pdfs/reports-and-publications/ SE_Water_Efficiency_Oct_2008_opt3534.pdf (September 1, 2013), and *Money Pit: The High Cost and High Risk of Water Supply Reservoirs in the Southeast* (July 2012), http:// www.americanrivers.org/assets/pdfs/reports-and-publications/money-pit-report.pdf (September 1, 2013).

27. L. M. Carter et al., "Southeast and the Caribbean," chap. 17 in *Climate Change Impacts in the United States: The Third National Climate Assessment*, ed. J. M. Melillo et al. (U.S. Global Change Research Program, 2014), 396–417; J. Rogers et al., *Water-Smart Power: Strengthening the U.S. Electricity System in a Warming World* (Cambridge, Mass.: Union of Concerned Scientists, July 2013).

Bibliography

ARCHIVAL COLLECTIONS, MANUSCRIPTS,
AND CORRESPONDENCE

Augusta Museum of History, Augusta, Ga.
  Lester S. Moody Collection
Chattooga Conservancy, Clayton, Ga.
Georgia Archives, Morrow
  Department of Game and Fish (025-01-002, 025-01-004, 25-01-008)
  Department of Natural Resources (086-01-12)
  Georgia Natural Areas Council Records (030-08-043)
  Governor's Subject Files, Gov. James Earl Carter (001-08-045)
Hargrett Rare Book and Manuscript Library, University of Georgia, Athens
  Alma Toevs Walker Collection (2696)
  Eugene P. Odum Papers, Institute of Ecology (97-045)
National Anthropological Archives, Smithsonian Institution, Suitland, Md.
  Carl F. Miller Files, River Basin Survey Collection
National Archives Records Administration, Southeast Region, Morrow, Ga.
  Records of the Corps of Engineers (RG 77)
National Archives Records Administration II, College Park, Md.
  Records of the American National Red Cross (RG 200)
  Records of the Corps of Engineers (RG 77)
  Records of the United States Fish and Wildlife Service (RG 22)
National Museum of American History, Smithsonian Institution, Washington, D.C.
  Hales Bar Dam, Tennessee River, TVA, 1910–1913 (1051)
Rabun County Courthouse, Clayton, Ga.
Rabun County Historical Society, Clayton, Ga.
  Georgia Power Company Files
  Lake Burton Files
David M. Rubenstein Rare Book and Manuscript Library, Duke University,
    Durham, N.C.
  James Buchanan Duke Papers
Richard B. Russell Library for Political Research and Studies, University of
    Georgia, Athens
  Richard B. Russell Jr. Collection
  Robert L. Williford Richard B. Russell Dam and Lake Project Files

South Carolina Political Collections, University of South Carolina, Columbia
  Olin DeWitt Talmadge Johnston Papers
  William Jennings Bryan Dorn Papers
South Caroliniana Library, University of South Carolina, Columbia
  Twin City Power Company
  William Church Whitner Papers
Southern Historical Collection, Manuscripts Department, University of North Carolina,
    Chapel Hill
  John Ewing Colhoun Papers
Strom Thurmond Institute, Clemson University, Clemson, S.C.
  James Edward Colhoun
  John Ewing Colhoun
  Strom Thurmond Collection
University of Alabama Office of Archaeological Research, Moundville
  Russell Papers
Robert W. Woodruff Library, Special Collections Department, Emory University,
    Atlanta, Ga.
  James A. Mackay Papers

NEWSPAPERS AND MEDIA OUTLETS

Anderson (S.C.) Free Press
Anderson (S.C.) Independent
Associated Press Wire
Athens-Banner (Ga.) Herald
Atlanta (Ga.) Business Chronicle
Atlanta (Ga.) Constitution
Atlanta (Ga.) Creative Loafing
Atlanta (Ga.) Journal
Atlanta (Ga.) Journal-Constitution
Atlanta Journal-Constitution
  Magazine
Augusta (Ga.) Chronicle
Augusta (Ga.) Chronicle and
  Constitutionalist
Augusta (Ga.) Chronicle and
  Sentinel
Augusta (Ga.) Daily Chronicle
  and Sentinel
Augusta (Ga.) Herald
Charleston (S.C.) Post and
  Courier
Charlotte (N.C.) Observer
Christian Science Monitor
Claxton (Ga.) Enterprise

Clayton (Ga.) Tribune
Columbia Journalism Review
Columbia (S.C.) State
Daily Mail (S.C.)
Edgefield (S.C.) Advertiser
Elberton (Ga.) Star
Flagpole Magazine (Ga.)
Greenville (S.C.) News
Hartwell (Ga.) Sun
Keowee (Walhalla, S.C.) Courier
Lincolnton (Ga.) Journal
Madisonian (Ga.)
Milledgeville (Ga.) Union-Recorder
Mississippi Business Journal
News and Reporter (Ga.)
New York Times
Rome (Ga.) News-Tribune
Saporta Report (Ga.)
Savannah (Ga.) Morning News
South Carolina Farmer
Sylva (N.C.) Herald and Ruralite
USA Today
Wall Street Journal
Washington Post

GOVERNMENT PUBLICATIONS AND DOCUMENTS

An Act to Amend Wild and Scenic Rivers. P.L. 93-279. May 10, 1974.

Ayers, Horace B., and William Willard Ashe. *The Southern Appalachian Forests.* Professional Paper No. 37, United States Geological Survey. Washington, D.C.: Government Printing Office, 1905.

Barber, Henry E., and Allen R. Gann. *A History of the Savannah District, U.S. Army Corps of Engineers.* Savannah, Ga.: United States Army Corps of Engineers Savannah District, 1989.

Barber, Nancy L., and Timothy C. Stamey. *Droughts in Georgia.* U.S. Geological Survey Report 00-380. October 2000.

Brougher, Cynthia, and Nicole T. Cater. *Reallocation of Water Storage at Federal Water Projects for Municipal and Industrial Water Supply.* Washington, D.C.: Congressional Research Service, October 31, 2012.

Buie, Eugene C. *A History of United States Department of Agriculture Water Resource Activities.* Washington, D.C.: U.S. Department of Agriculture, Soil Conservation Service, September 1979.

Bursley, Allyn P., and the National Park Service. *Appendix II, Recreation, Exhibit A: Memorandum Report: Recreational Resources of the Clark Hill Reservoir, Savannah River, Georgia and South Carolina, Prepared August 22, 1945.* In *Definite Project Report on Savannah River Basin, Georgia and South Carolina, Clark Hill Project.* U.S. Corps of Engineers, South Atlantic Division. February 20, 1946.

Burwell, Edward B., Jr. *Report on Geology of Dam and Reservoir Sites in the Savannah River Basin, Georgia and South Carolina.* Cincinnati, Ohio: War Department, Office of the Division Engineer, Ohio River Division, October 1, 1942.

Carter, L. M., et al. "Southeast and the Caribbean." Chapter 17 in *Climate Change Impacts in the United States: The Third National Climate Assessment,* edited by J. M. Melillo et al., 396–417. U.S. Global Change Research Program, 2014.

Collins, M. D., and State Superintendent of Schools. *Natural Resources of Georgia: Georgia Program for the Improvement of Instruction in the Public Schools.* Atlanta: State Department of Education, 1938.

Durant, J. S., and B. H. Grant. *Real Estate Planning Report for Clark Hill Reservoir, Savannah River Basin, Georgia and South Carolina.* Atlanta: War Department, U.S. Division Engineer, Real Estate Branch, October 1942.

Facey, Douglas E., and M. J. Van Den Avyle. *Species Profiles: Life Histories and Environmental Requirements of Coastal Fishes and Invertebrates (South Atlantic): American Shad.* United States Fish and Wildlife Service and United States Army Corps of Engineers, 1986.

Flood Control Act of 1944. Public Law 534, 78th Cong., 2nd sess. December 22, 1944.

Flood Control Act of 1950. Public Law 516, 81st Cong., 2nd sess. May 17, 1950.

Flood Control Act of 1966. Public Law 89, 89th Cong. November 7, 1966.

Geological Survey (U.S.). Division of Hydrography. *Water-Powers of North Carolina (a Supplement to Bulletin No. 8).* Raleigh: E. M. Uzzell & Co., 1911.

Georgia. Augusta. *The City Council of Augusta, Ga., Yearbook 1910.* Augusta, Ga.: Williams Printing Co., 1911.

————. *Mayors Message and Official Reports of the Department of the City of Augusta, for the Year 1907*. Augusta, Ga.: Phoenix Printing Co., 1908.

————. *Mayors Message and Official Reports of the Department of the City of Augusta, for 1908*. Augusta, Ga.: Phoenix Printing Co., 1909.

————. *Nineteen Eleven Year Book of the City Council of Augusta, Ga.* Augusta, Ga.: Phoenix Printing Co., 1912.

Georgia. State Planning Board and the National Park Service. *Report on Outdoor Recreation in Georgia*. Atlanta: n.p., February 1939.

Gibson, Campbell. *Population of the 100 Largest Cities and Other Urban Places in the United States: 1790 To 1990*. Population Division Working Paper No. 27. Washington, D.C.: U.S. Bureau of the Census, June 1998.

Granger, Mary, and United States Army Corps of Engineers. *Savannah Harbor: Its Origin and Development, 1733–1890*. Savannah, Ga.: U.S. Army Engineer District, Savannah Corps of Engineers, 1968.

Hains, John, William E. Jabour, Robert H. Kennedy, William Boyd, James M. Satterfield, and Patrick K. Howle. *Water Quality in Richard B. Russell and J. Strom Thurmond Lakes: Interim Report for the Period 1997–1998*. Technical Report EL-99-13. Calhoun Falls, S.C.: U.S. Army Engineers Research and Development Center, November 1999.

Hall, Benjamin Mortimer. *A Preliminary Report on a Part of the Water-Powers of Georgia*. Atlanta: G. W. Harrison, 1896.

Hall, Benjamin Mortimer, and Max R. Hall. *Second Report on the Water Powers of Georgia*. Geological Survey of Georgia, Bulletin No. 16. Atlanta: Franklin-Turner Co., 1908.

————. *Third Report on the Water Powers of Georgia*. Atlanta: Byrd Printing Co., 1921.

————. *Water Resources of Georgia*. Washington, D.C.: Government Printing Office, 1907.

History Group, Inc., and Darlene R. Roth. *Historical Investigations of the Richard B. Russell Multiple Resource Area*. United States Interagency Archaeological Services and the U.S. Army Corps of Engineers, Savannah District. Atlanta: History Group, 1981.

Johnson, John P. *Gregg Shoals Dam and Power Plant, Historic American Engineering Record (HAER), SC, 4-SAVRI*. Washington, D.C.: National Park Service, 1980.

Johnson, Leland R. *Engineers of the Twin Rivers: A History of the Nashville District Corps of Engineers, United States Army*. Nashville, Tenn.: United States Army Engineer District, 1978.

Kane, Sharyn, and Richard Keeton. *In Those Days: African-American Life near the Savannah River*. Atlanta: National Park Service, 1994.

Kane, Sharyn, and Richard Keeton in association with United States Army Corps of Engineers, Savannah District, and United States Interagency Archaeological Services, Atlanta. *Beneath These Waters: Archeological and Historical Studies of 11,500 Years along the Savannah River*. 2nd ed. Washington, D.C.: National Park Service, 1994.

Kenny, Joan F., et al. *Estimated Use of Water in the United States in 2005*. U.S. Geological Survey Circular 1344. 2009.

Leighton, Marshall O., M. R. Hall, and R. H. Bolster. *The Relation of the Southern Appalachian Mountains to the Development of Water Power*. Forest Service Circular 144. Washington, D.C.: Government Printing Office, 1908.

Mastran, Shelley Smith, and Nan Lowerre. *Mountaineers and Rangers: A History of Federal Forest Management in the Southern Appalachians, 1900–81.* FS-380. Washington, D.C.: USDA, Forest Service, April 1983.

McGuire, John R., Chief, Forest Service. "Chattooga Wild and Scenic River: Classifications, Boundaries, and Development Plan." *Federal Register* 41, no. 56 (March 22, 1976): 11847–57.

Murray, W. S., et al. *A Superpower System for the Region between Boston and Washington.* Department of the Interior, U.S. Geological Survey, Professional Paper 123. Washington, D.C.: Government Printing Office, 1921.

Orser, Charles E., Annette M. Nekola, and James L. Roark. *Exploring the Rustic Life: Multidisciplinary Research at Millwood Plantation.* 3 vols. Russell Papers. Atlanta: Archeological Services, National Park Service, 1987.

Perdue, Governor Sonny. *Water Contingency Task Force: Final Report.* Atlanta, December 21, 2009.

Pierce, Robert R., Nancy L. Barber, and Harold R. Stiles. *Georgia Irrigation, 1970–1980: A Decade of Growth.* Water-Resources Investigations Report 83-4177. N.p.: U.S. Geological Survey and Georgia Department of Natural Resources, 1984.

Rahn, Ruby A. *River Highway for Trade, the Savannah: Canoes, Indian Tradeboats, Flatboats, Steamers, Packets, and Barges.* Savannah, Ga.: U.S. Army Engineer District, Corps of Engineers, 1968.

Reed, Mary Beth, Barbara Smith Strack, and U.S. Department of Energy. *Savannah River Site at Fifty.* Washington, D.C.: U.S. Department of Energy and Government Printing Office, 2002.

Riley, Edward M. *The Survey of the Historic Sites of the Clark Hill Reservoir Area, South Carolina and Georgia.* Richmond, Va.: National Park Service, June 1949.

Roth, Darlene R., and History Group Inc., in association with United States Interagency Archaeological Services, Atlanta, and United States Army Corps of Engineers, Savannah District. *Historical Investigations of the Richard B. Russell Multiple Resource Area.* Atlanta: History Group Inc., 1981.

Savannah River Special Board. *Clark Hill Navigation–Flood Control–Power Project, Savannah River, Georgia–South Carolina, Report to the President.* Washington, D.C.: n.p., February 29, 1936.

Silver, James. *A Report of the Fish and Wildlife Resources in Relation to the Water Development Plan for the Clark Hill Reservoir, Savannah River Basin, Georgia and South Carolina for the U.S. Army Corps of Engineers.* Atlanta: U.S. Department of the Interior, Fish and Wildlife Service, July 1946.

Spude, Robert L. *Augusta Canal, Historic American Engineering Record (HAER), GA-5.* Washington, D.C.: Department of the Interior, 1977.

State Council for the Preservation of Natural Areas Act. March 10, 1966. Ga. L. 1966, 330.

Swain, George Fillmore, J. A. Holmes, and E. W. Myers. *Papers on the Waterpower in North Carolina: A Preliminary Report.* North Carolina Geological Survey, Bulletin No. 8. Raleigh: Guy V. Barnes, 1899.

Taylor, Richard, and Marion Smith. *The Report of the Intensive Survey of the Richard B. Russell Dam and Lake, Savannah River, Georgia and South Carolina.* Columbia: Institute of Archaeology and Anthropology, University of South Carolina, 1978.

Tennessee Valley Authority. "History of Leakage at the Hales Bar Dam." In *Proposed Improvements to the Hales Bar Project*. TVA Report No. 11–100. November 1941.

Tetra Tech EC, Inc. *Chattooga River History Project: Literature Review and Interview Summary*. Prepared for USDA Forest Service. Atlanta, August 25, 2006.

Thomson, Medford Theodore, and R. F. Carter. *Effect of A Severe Drought (1954) on Streamflow in Georgia*. The Geological Survey, Bulletin Number 73. Atlanta, 1963.

U.S. Army Corps of Engineers. *Clark Hill Reservoir, Savannah River Basin, Georgia and South Carolina: General Information, Proposed Recreational Development*. Savannah District, October 1948.

———. *Definite Project Report: Hartwell Reservoir, Savannah River, Georgia and South Carolina*. Corps of Engineers, Savannah District, December 15, 1952.

———. *Definite Project Report on Savannah River Basin, Georgia and South Carolina, Clark Hill Project*. South Atlantic Division, Revised, May 1, 1946.

———. *Final Environmental Impact Statement: Richard B. Russell Dam and Lake (Formerly Trotters Shoals Lake), Savannah River, Georgia and South Carolina*. Savannah, Ga., May 1979.

———. *The Master Plan for Development and Management, Clark Hill Reservoir, Savannah River, Georgia and South Carolina*. Savannah District, December 1950.

———. *Mississippi River Headwaters Reservoir Operating Plan Evaluation (ROPE): Upper Mississippi River Headwaters, Bemidji to St. Paul, Minnesota, DRAFT Integrated Reservoir Operating Plan Evaluation and Environmental Impact Statement*. St. Paul, Minn., August 2008.

———. *New Savannah Bluff Lock and Dam Project, Savannah River, Georgia and South Carolina, Section 216, Disposition Study, Final Report*. Savannah, Ga., September 8, 2000.

———. *PRELIMINARY Environmental Impact Statement, Trotters Shoals Dam and Lake, Savannah River, Georgia and South Carolina*. Savannah, Ga., 1970.

———. *Savannah River, Georgia, South Carolina, and North Carolina*. Washington, D.C.: Government Printing Office, 1935.

———. *Study of Death and Decay of Trees From Flooding*. Civil Works Investigations Program of Research on Clearing, Mosquito Control, and Flotage Removal, Clark Hill Reservoir, Georgia and South Carolina. Savannah, Ga., January 1961.

———. *Water Control Manual: Savannah River Basin Multiple Purpose Projects: Hartwell Dam and Lake, Richard B. Russell Dam and Lake, J. Strom Thurmond Dam and Lake, Georgia and South Carolina*. Savannah, Ga., 1996.

———. *Water Resources Development in Georgia*. South Atlantic Division, Atlanta, 1981.

U.S. Commission of Fish and Fisheries. *Report of the Commissioner for 1872 and 1873*. Washington, D.C.: Government Printing Office, 1874.

U.S. Congress. House. *Apalachicola, Chattahoochee, and Flint Rivers, Ga. and Fla.* 80th Cong., 1st sess., June 6, 1947. House Document no. 300.

———. *Estimate of Cost of Examinations, Etc., of Streams Where Power Development Appears Feasible*. 69th Cong., 1st sess., April 13, 1926. House Document 308.

———. *Report on the Savannah River*. 74th Cong., 1st sess., January 3, 1935. House Document 64.

———. *Savannah River, GA.* 78th Cong., 2nd sess., June 9, 1944. House Document 657.

———. *Savannah River, Georgia (between Augusta and Savannah).* 51st Cong., 2nd sess. House Executive Document 255.

———. *State of the Union.* 79th Cong., 1st sess. *Congressional Record,* January 6, 1945.

———. *Survey of the Savannah River above Augusta.* 51st Cong., 1st sess., 1890. House Executive Document 213.

———. Committee on Interior and Insular Affairs. *Amending the Wild and Scenic Rivers Act by Designating the Chattooga River, North Carolina, South Carolina, and Georgia as a Component of the National Wild and Scenic Rivers System.* 93rd Cong., 1st sess., November 29, 1973. House Report 675.

U.S. Congress. House. Committee on Interstate and Foreign Commerce. *Dam Across Savannah River at Cherokee Shoals.* 61st Cong., 3rd sess., January 7, 1911. House Report 1863.

U.S. Congress. House. Committee on Rivers and Harbors. *Hearings before the Committee on Rivers and Harbors, House of Representatives: On the Subject of the Improvement of the Savannah River, GA & Savannah River and Clarks Hill Reservoir.* 78th Cong., October 27, 1943.

U.S. Congress. House. Subcommittee on Interior and Insular Affairs. *Wild and Scenic Rivers Act Amendments.* Pt. 2. 93rd Cong., 1st sess., October 29–30, 1973.

U.S. Congress. Senate. *Designating the Trotters Shoals Dam and Lake, Ga. and S.C., as the Richard B. Russell Dam and Lake.* 93rd Cong., 1st sess., October 9, 1973. S. Report 454.

———. *Electric Power Development in the United States: Letter from the Secretary of Agriculture Transmitting a Report, in Response to a Senate Resolution of February 13, 1915, as to the Ownership and Control of the Water-Power Sites in the United States* (3 vols.). 64th Cong., 1st sess. Washington, D.C.: Government Printing Office, 1916.

———. *Savannah River and Clark Hill Reservoir.* 76th Cong., 1st sess., Senate Document 66 [1939].

———. *Savannah River Valley Authority.* 79th Cong., 1st sess., S. 737. *Congressional Record,* March 14, 1945.

———. *Savannah River Valley Authority.* 80th Cong., 1st sess., S. 1534. *Congressional Record,* June 30, 1947.

———. Committee on Interior and Insular Affairs. *Wild and Scenic Rivers, Hearings Before the Committee On Interior and Insular Affairs.* 90th Cong., 1st sess., April 13, 1967.

———. *Amending the Wild and Scenic Rivers Act.* 93rd Cong., 2nd sess., March 20, 1974. Senate Report 738.

U.S. Congress. Senate. Select Committee on National Water Resources. *Water Resources Hearing.* 86th Cong., 1st sess., October 9, 12, 1959.

U.S. Congress. Senate. Subcommittee on Public Lands of the Committee on Interior and Insular Affairs. *Proposed Wild and Scenic Chattooga River and the Conveyance of Certain Public Lands.* 93rd Cong., 1st sess., October 10, 1973.

U.S. Court of Appeals for the Eleventh Circuit. Re: MDL-1824 Tri-State Water Rights Litigation. No. 09-14657. D.C. Docket No. 07-00001. MD-J-PAM-JRK. June 28, 2011.

U.S. Department of Agriculture. *Electric Power Development in the United States. Letter from the Secretary of Agriculture Transmitting a Report, in Response to a Senate*

Resolution of February 13, 1915, as to the Ownership and Control of the Water-Power Sites in the United States. Pt. 1 (of 3). Washington, D.C., 1916.

U.S. Department of Agriculture. Farmers Home Administration. *A Brief History of the Farmers Home Administration*. Washington, D.C., 1989.

U.S. Department of Agriculture. Forest Service. *Chattooga Wild and Scenic River Management Plan*. [1979].

———. *A Proposal: The Chattooga, "A Wild and Scenic River."* March 3, 1970.

———.Southern Region. *Draft Environmental Impact Statement: Land and Resource Management Plan: Sumter National Forest*. Atlanta: USDA, Forest Service, Southern Region, n.d.

———. *Revised Land and Management Plan: Sumner National Forest*. Management Bulletin R8-MB 116A, January 2004.

———. *Wild and Scenic River Study Report: Chattooga River*. June 15, 1971.

U.S. Department of Commerce. Bureau of the Census. *Eighteenth U.S. Census, 1960: Characteristics of the Population*.

———. *Nineteenth U.S. Census, 1970: Characteristics of the Population*.

U.S. Department of Energy. *Energy Demands on Water Resources: Report to Congress of the Interdependency of Energy and Water*. December 2006.

U.S. Department of the Interior. *Statistics of Power and Machinery Employed in Manufactures, Prof. W.P. Trowbridge, Chief Special Agent. Reports on the Water Power of the United States*. Pt. 1. Edited by Walter G. Elliot, James L. Greenleaf, Dwight Porter, George F. Swain, and William Pettit Trowbridge. Washington, D.C.: U.S. Census Office, 1883.

U.S. District Court, Middle District of Florida. *Memorandum and Order, Re: Tri-State Water Rights Litigation*. Case No. 3:07-md-01 (PAM/JRK). Document 264. July 17, 2009.

U.S. Outdoor Recreation Resources Review Commission. *Outdoor Recreation for America, a Report to the President and to the Congress*. Washington, D.C.: Government Printing Office, 1962.

U.S. Study Commission. *Plan for the Development of the Land and Water Resources of the Southeast River Basins*. Atlanta: n.p., 1963.

Water Supply Act of 1958. Public Law 85-500. July 3, 1958.

Wild and Scenic Rivers Act. Public Law 90-542. October 2, 1968.

ARTICLES IN PERIODICALS AND TRADE JOURNALS

"550 Dixie Men Will Begin Dam in Icy Oconee." *Snap Shots* 3, no. 12 (December 1929): 3.

"$16,000,000 Program Sets State Record." *Snap Shots* 3, no. 12 (December 1929): 1.

Arkwright, Preston S., Sr. "Some of the Marvels of Electricity." *Manufacturers' Record* 86, no. 23 (December 4, 1924): 88.

Asdit, Charles G., and W. P. Hammon. "Construction Elements of the Tallulah Falls Development." Paper presented before the 313th Meeting of the American Institute of Electrical Engineers (October 11, 1915). *American Institute of Electrical Engineers Proceedings* 34 (July–December 1915): 2497–2546.

Atkinson, H. M. "Georgia Railway and Power Company: Power Development on
    Tallulah and Chattooga Rivers." *Manufacturers' Record* 82 (November 2, 1922):
    99–104.
Belt, Don. "Chattooga River Country: Wild Water, Proud People." *National Geographic*
    163, no. 4 (April 1983): 458–76.
"Charlie Daniel of Daniel Construction Company." *South Carolina Magazine* 15, no. 10
    (October 1951): 12.
"Concrete Is Placed at Furman Shoals; Begin Vast Wall." *Snap Shots* 4, no. 4 (April
    1930): 5.
"Construction Is Begun at Furman Shoals." *Snap Shots* 3, no. 10 (October 1929): 1.
Craighead, Frank. "Wild Rivers in Our Blood." *National Wildlife*, October 1972, 16–18.
Craighead, John J. "Wild River." *Montana Wildlife*, June 1957, 15–20.
———. "Wild Rivers." *Naturalist* 16, no. 3 (Autumn 1965): 1–5.
Creager, William P. "Developing Electric Power Under 250-Head in Tennessee."
    Engineering Record, Building Record, and Sanitary Engineer 69, no. 16 (April 18,
    1914): 454–56.
Croke, Vicki Constantine. "The Brothers Wild." *Washington Post Magazine*, November
    11, 2007.
"Dayton Flood-Protection Ready for Adoption." *Engineering News* 75, no. 10 (March 9,
    1916): 485–86.
Doble, Robert McF. "Hydro-Electric Power Development and Transmission in
    California." *Journal of the Association of Engineering Societies* 34, no. 3 (March 1905):
    75–99.
Doyle, Robert E. "Rivers Wild and Pure: A Priceless Legacy." *National Geographic* 152,
    no. 1 (July 1977): 2.
"Electric Railroad Development." *Engineering Record, Building Record, and Sanitary
    Engineer* 23 (May 9, 1891): 383.
"Final Flood-Protection Plan for Miami Valley." *Engineering News* 75, no. 14 (April 6,
    1916): 674–75.
Finkle, F. C. "Electrical Development of Hydraulic Power." *Engineering Magazine* 14,
    no. 6 (March 1898): 1011–26.
Frink, John W. "The Foundation of Hales Bar Dam." *Economic Geology* 41, no. 6 (1946):
    576–97.
"Further Details of the Failure of the Portman Shoals Dams, Near Anderson, S.C."
    Engineering News 47, no. 3 (January 16, 1902): 48.
Garner, Phil. "The Master Grantsman." *Atlanta Journal-Constitution Magazine*, May 14,
    1978.
"The Georgia Story—A Special Edition." *Manufacturers' Record* 117, no. 5 (May 1948).
Hardaway, B. H. "Failure of Dams near Anderson, S.C., and at Columbus, GA."
    Engineering News 47, no. 2 (January 9, 1902): 34.
———. "Remarks on the Recent Failures of Masonry Dams in the South." *Engineering
    News* 47, no. 6 (February 6, 1902): 107–9.
"Harnessing Oconee for Georgia's Progress." *Snap Shots* 3, no. 11 (November 1929): 1.
Hawkins, C. B., and W. W. Eberhardt. "Method of Handling Interconnected Operation."
    Electrical World 92, no. 15 (October 13, 1928): 725–31.

Holly, Byron. *The Enlarged Augusta Canal, Augusta, GA: Its Capacity and Advantages for the Manufacture of Cotton Goods, with Map of Location.* New York: Corlies Macy & Co. Stationers, 1875.

"How Power Dams Saved the Day in the Carolinas." *Electrical World* 92, no. 10 (September 8, 1928): 477.

"Huge Hydro Plant Planned." *Snap Shots* 3, no. 9 (September 1929): 3.

"Hydroelectric Development on the Tennessee River." *Electrical Review and Western Electrician* 63, no. 21 (November 22, 1913): 1005–9.

"Hydroelectric Development on the Tennessee River." *Electrical World* 62, no. 20 (November 15, 1913): 997–1000.

"Hydro-Electric Developments 'Unparalleled in the World.'" *Manufacturers' Record* 65, no. 21 (May 28, 1914): 41–42.

"Hydro-Electric Power Development of the Southern Appalachian Region." In *Blue Book of Southern Progress*, 131–33. 1924 ed. Baltimore: Manufacturers' Record, 1924.

"A Hydro-electric Power Development on the Catawba River, Near Rock Hill, S.C." *Electrical World and Engineer* 44, no. 4 (July 23, 1904): 129–32.

Jacobs, Jane. "Why TVA Failed." *New York Review of Books* 31, no. 8 (May 10, 1984): 41–47.

Jacocks, C. West. "State Parks and Segregation." *South Carolina Magazine* 20, no. 1 (January 1956): 3.

Jorgensen, Lars. "The Record of 100 Dam Failures." Pt. 1. *Journal of Electricity* 44, no. 6 (March 15, 1920): 274–76.

———. "The Record of 100 Dam Failures." Pt. 2. *Journal of Electricity* 44, no. 7 (April 1, 1920): 320–321.

Kline, W. A. "Hooverize the Coal Pile." *Right Way Magazine*, August 1920, 25.

Knowles, Morris. "Hydro-Electric Development and Water Conservation." *Electric Journal* 10, no. 7 (July 1913): 631–36.

Ladshaw, George E. *The Economics of the Flow of Rivers and the Development of Hydraulic Power: Water Power vs. Steam Power.* Spartanburg, S.C.: Jones and Co., 1889.

Lof, Eric A. "The Hydro-electric Development of the Georgia Railway and Power Company at Tallulah Falls, Georgia." Pt. 1. *General Electric Review* 17, no. 6 (June 1914): 608–21.

———. "The Mississippi River Hydro-electric Development at Keokuk, Iowa." Pt. 1. *General Electric Review* 17, no. 2 (February 1914): 85–98.

Macy, Ralph G. "The Construction and Costs of Southern Cotton Mills and Equipment: The Piedmont Section of the Carolinas." Pt. 3. *Management and Administration* 8, no. 1 (July 1924): 47–52.

———. "The Southward Trend of Manufacturing: The Piedmont Section of the Carolinas." Pt. 1. *Management and Administration* 7, no. 5 (May 1924): 517–22.

Mangum, Hillary H. "Interstate Cooperation Shown in Clark's Hill Development." *South Carolina Magazine* 10, no. 1 (January 1947): 28.

Martin, T. Craig. "Chattooga." *Georgia Outdoors* 2, no. 7 (July 1973): 16–23.

Martin, Thomas W. "Hydroelectric Development in the South." In *The South's Development: Fifty Years of Southern Progress, a Glimpse of the Past, the Facts of the*

Present, a Forecast for the Future. Special issue of the *Manufacturers' Record*, 86, no. 24, pt. 2. (December 11, 1924): 241–61.

Mayrick, Donal R. "Spelunkers on the Chattooga River." *American Whitewater* 17, no. 4 (Winter 1972): 142–47.

McCollum, Jerry L. "President's Column: Charles Wharton—Champion of Georgia's Unspoiled Places." *The Call* 14, no. 1 (Winter 2004).

McGuane, Thomas. "Wild Rivers." *Audubon* 95, no. 6 (1993): 60.

Mees, C. A. "Development of the Rocky Creek Station of the Southern Power Company." *Engineering Record, Building Record, and Sanitary Engineer* 59, no. 14 (April 3, 1909): 462–69.

Morrison, Jim. "Chattooga Wild River Study Release: Is It Strong Enough to Save River?" *Newsletter of the Georgia Conservancy, Inc.*, March 18, 1970.

Morrow, L. W. W. "The Interconnected South." *Electrical World* 91, no. 21 (May 26, 1928): 1077–82.

Murray, Thomas E. "The Improvement of the Tennessee River and Power Installation of the Chattanooga and Tennessee River Power Company at Hale's Bar, Tenn." *Transactions of the American Society of Mechanical Engineers* 27 (May 1906): 521–55.

Murray, W. S. "The Superpower System as an Answer to a National Power Policy." *General Electric Review* 25, no. 2 (February 1922): 72–76.

"Outstanding Electric Power Developments in the South." In *Blue Book of Southern Progress*, 84–88. Baltimore: Manufacturers' Record, 1927.

"Power Possibilities of Catawba River Highly Developed through Stream Control." *Engineering News-Record* 104, no. 25 (June 19, 1930): 1007–12.

Pratt, Joseph Hyde. "The Southeastern Power System and Its Tremendous Industrial Value to the States It Serves." *Manufacturers' Record* 86 (July 24, 1924): 83–84.

Reed, J. H. "Atlanta: An Inspiring Story of Growth in Trade, Industry, Finance, Education, and Music." *Manufacturers' Record* 85, no. 9 (February 28, 1924): 76–84.

Rogers, Warren O. "Tallulah Falls Hydro-Electric Development." *Power* 39, no. 4 (January 27, 1914): 114–19.

Saville, Thorndike. "The Power Situation in North Carolina." *Manufacturers' Record* 86, no. 26 (December 25, 1924): 68–70.

———. "The Power Situation in the Southern Appalachian States: The Development of Power Systems of the Southern Province." *Manufacturers' Record* 91, no. 16 (April 21, 1927): 68–77 plus fold-out map.

———. "The Power Situation in the Southern Power Province." *Annals of the American Academy of Political and Social Science* 153 (January 1931): 94–123. Coming of Industry to the South edition.

Shedd, George G. "Two Recent Southern Hydro-Electric Developments." *Power* 39, no. 3 (January 20, 1914): 83–86.

Smith, Frank E. "TVA and the Politics of Conservation." *New South* 21, no. 4 (1966): 78–87.

Southern Regional Council. "Court Rules That Parks Are for All." *New South* 10, no. 4 (April 1955): 1.

———. "State Parks for Negroes—New Tests of Equality." *New South* 9, no. 4–5 (April–May 1954): 1–7.

———. "Text of The Park Decision." *New South* 10, no. 4 (April 1955): 4.

Sparks, Andrew. "Can We Keep the Chattooga Wild?" *Atlanta Journal and Constitution Magazine*, September 22, 1968, 12.

———. "Georgia's New Ocean: Builds Up behind Clark Hill Dam." *Atlanta Journal and Constitution Magazine*, September 7, 1952, 28–30.

———. "Mile-Wide Dam for the Savannah." *Atlanta Journal Magazine*, January 12, 1947, 8–9.

Speight, Carol. "Trotters Shoals: The Big Boondoggle." *South Carolina Wildlife*, July–August 1976, 18–39.

Switzer, J. A. "The Power Development at Hale's Bar." *Resources of Tennessee* 2 (March 1912): 86–99.

———. "Water-Power Development in the South." Pt. 1. *Cassier's Magazine: An Engineering Monthly* 41, no. 6 (June 1912): 561–76. New York edition.

———. "Water-Power Development in the South." Pt. 2. *Cassier's Magazine: An Engineering Monthly* 42, no. 1 (July 1912): 90–96. New York ed.

Terry, Claude. "What Is a Floodplain?" *Georgia Conservancy Quarterly Magazine: The Rivers and Streams of Georgia*, August 1972.

"Vast Plant Atkinson, Peerless in U.S., Shown as Place of Engineering Marvels." *Snap Shots* 3, no. 8 (August 1929): 1.

Wallace, Henry. "Ramone Eaton—A Tribute." *American Whitewater* 25, no. 3 (May–June 1980): 15–19.

"Water-Power of the World." In *Blue Book of Southern Progress*, 129–31. Baltimore: Manufacturers' Record, 1924.

"What About 'Old King Coal'? Is He 'On the Way Out'?" *Right Way Magazine*, October 1936, 4–5.

Williams, Buzz. "The Wild and Scenic Chattooga River." *Chattooga Quarterly*, Spring 2004, 3–4.

Wilson, Donald H. "Chattooga!" *American Whitewater* 18, no. 3 (Autumn 1973): 113–17.

Wright, Frank. "Anchor of the Deep South." *AT Journeys: The Magazine of the Appalachian-Trail Conservancy* 1, no. 3 (November–December 2005): 24–28.

BOOKS AND ACADEMIC ARTICLES

Adkins, Leonard M. *Walking the Blue Ridge: A Guide to the Trails of the Blue Ridge Parkway*. 3rd ed. Chapel Hill: University of North Carolina Press, 2003.

Anderson, David G. *The Savannah River Chiefdoms: Political Change in the Late Prehistoric Southeast*. Tuscaloosa: University of Alabama Press, 1994.

Andrews, Thomas G. *Killing for Coal: America's Deadliest Labor War*. Cambridge: Harvard University Press, 2008.

Arsenault, Raymond. "The End of the Long Hot Summer: The Air Conditioner and Southern Culture." *Journal of Southern History* 50, no. 4 (November 1984): 597–628.

Atkins, Leah Rawls. *"Developed for the Service of Alabama": The Centennial History of the Alabama Power Company, 1906-2006*. Birmingham: Alabama Power Co., 2006.

Ayers, Edward L. *The Promise of the New South: Life after Reconstruction*. New York: Oxford University Press, 1992.

Bailes, Kendall E. *Environmental History: Critical Issues in Comparative Perspective.* Lanham, Md.: University Press of America and American Society for Environmental History, 1985.

Barnett, Cynthia. *Mirage: Florida and the Vanishing Water of the Eastern U.S.* Ann Arbor: University of Michigan Press, 2007.

Barrett, J. S. "History of Tapoco, North Carolina." In *Graham County Centennial, 1872–1972.* Robbinsville, N.C.: Graham County Centennial 1972, Inc., 1972.

Barry, John M. *Rising Tide: The Great Mississippi Flood of 1927 and How It Changed America.* New York: Simon and Schuster, 1997.

Bartlett, Richard A. *Troubled Waters: Champion International and the Pigeon River Controversy.* Knoxville: University of Tennessee Press, 1995.

Bartley, Numan V. *The New South, 1945–1980.* Baton Rouge: Louisiana State University Press, 1995.

Bartram, William. *The Travels of William Bartram.* Naturalist's ed. Edited by Francis Harper. Athens: University of Georgia Press, 1998.

Bayne, Coy. *Lake Murray: Legend and Leisure.* 3rd ed., rev. N.p.: Bayne Publishing Co., 1999.

Beatty, Bess. "Lowells of the South: Northern Influences on the Nineteenth-Century North Carolina Textile Industry." *Journal of Southern History* 53, no. 1 (February 1987): 37–62.

Billington, David P., and Donald C. Jackson. *Big Dams of the New Deal Era: A Confluence of Engineering and Politics.* Norman: University of Oklahoma Press, 2006.

Blackbourn, David. *The Conquest of Nature: Water, Landscape, and the Making of Modern Germany.* New York: Norton, 2006.

Blackford, Charles Minor. "The Shad—A National Problem." *Transactions of the American Fisheries Society* 46, no. 1 (December 1, 1916): 5–14.

Boyd, Brian. *The Chattooga Wild and Scenic River: A Guide to Boating, Hiking, and Camping in the Chattooga National Wild and Scenic River Corridor.* Conyers, Ga.: Ferncreek Press, 1990.

Brigham, Jay L. *Empowering the West: Electrical Politics before FDR.* Lawrence: University Press of Kansas, 1998.

Brinkley, Alan. *The End of Reform: New Deal Liberalism in Recession and War.* New York: Knopf, 1995.

Brooks, Karl Boyd. *Public Power, Private Dams: The Hells Canyon High Dam Controversy.* Seattle: University of Washington Press, 2006.

Brown, D. Clayton. *Electricity for Rural America: The Fight for the Rea.* Westport, Conn.: Greenwood Press, 1980.

Brown, Jonathan C. "Jersey Standard and the Politics of Latin American Oil Production, 1911–30." In *Latin American Oil Companies and the Politics of Energy,* edited by John D. Wirth, 1–42. Lincoln: University of Nebraska Press, 1985.

Brown, Margaret Lynn. *The Wild East: A Biography of the Great Smoky Mountains.* Gainesville: University Press of Florida, 2000.

Bullard, Robert D. *Dumping in Dixie: Race, Class, and Environmental Quality.* Boulder, Colo.: Westview Press, 1990.

Bullard, Robert, and Beverly Wright. *The Wrong Complexion for Protection: How the Government Response to Disasters Endangers African American Communities*. New York: New York University Press, 2012.

Callahan, North. *TVA: Bridge over Troubled Waters*. South Brunswick, N.J.: A. S. Barnes, 1980.

Carlton, David L. *Mill and Town in South Carolina, 1880–1920*. Baton Rouge: Louisiana State University Press, 1982.

Carlton, David L., and Peter A. Coclanis, eds. *Confronting Poverty in the Great Depression:* The Report on the Economic Conditions of the South *with Related Documents*. Boston: Bedford Books of St. Martin's Press, 1996.

Carney, Judith Ann. *Black Rice: The African Origins of Rice Cultivation in the Americas*. Cambridge: Harvard University Press, 2001.

Carr, Charles C. *ALCOA: An American Enterprise*. New York: Rinehart, 1952.

Carter, Dan. *The Politics of Rage: George Wallace, the Origins of the New Conservatism, and the Transformation of American Politics*. New York: Simon and Schuster, 1995.

Cashin, Edward J. *The Brightest Arm of the Savannah: The Augusta Canal, 1845–2000*. Augusta, Ga.: Augusta Canal Authority, 2002.

———. *The Story of Augusta*. Augusta, Ga.: Richmond County Board of Education, 1980.

Catesby, Mark, George Frederick Frick, and Joseph Ewan. *The Natural History of Carolina, Florida and the Bahama Islands, Containing Two Hundred and Twenty Figures of Birds, Beasts, Fishes, Serpents, Insects and Plants*. Savannah, Ga.: Beehive Press, 1974.

Chandler, William U. *The Myth of TVA: Conservation and Development in the Tennessee Valley, 1933–1983*. Cambridge, Mass.: Ballinger Pub. Co., 1984.

Christian-Smith, Juliet, and Peter H. Glick. *A Twenty-First Century US Water Policy*. New York: Oxford University Press, 2012.

Christie, Jean. *Morris Llewellyn Cooke, Progressive Engineer*. New York: Garland, 1983.

Cioc, Mark. *The Rhine: An Eco-Biography, 1815–2000*. Seattle: University of Washington Press, 2002.

"The Civilian Conservation Corps in Northeast Georgia." *Foxfire* 16, no. 4 (Winter 1982): 228–77.

Clark, Kathleen Ann. *Defining Moments: African American Commemoration and Political Culture in the South, 1863–1913*. Chapel Hill: University of North Carolina Press, 2005.

Clawson, Marion, and Carlton S. Van Doren. *Statistics on Outdoor Recreation*. Washington, D.C.: Resources for the Future, 1984.

Cobb, James C. "Beyond Planters and Industrialists: A New Perspective on the New South." *Journal of Southern History* 54, no. 1 (February 1988): 45–68.

———. *Industrialization and Southern Society, 1877–1984*. Lexington: University Press of Kentucky, 1984.

———. *The Selling of the South: The Southern Crusade for Industrial Development, 1936–1980*. Baton Rouge: Louisiana State University Press, 1982.

Cobb, James C., and Michael V. Namorato, eds. *The New Deal and the South*. Jackson: University Press of Mississippi, 1984.

Cobb, James C., and William Whitney Stueck. *Globalization and the American South.* Athens: University of Georgia Press, 2005.

Coclanis, Peter A. "Tracking the Economic Divergence of the North and the South." *Southern Cultures* 6, no. 4 (2000): 82–103.

Coleman, Charles M. *P.G. and E. of California: The Centennial Story of Pacific Gas and Electric Company, 1852–1952.* New York: McGraw-Hill, 1952.

Colten, Craig E. "Contesting Pollution in Dixie: The Case of Corney Creek." *Journal of Southern History* 72, no. 3 (August 2006): 605–34.

———. "Southern Pollution Permissiveness: Another Regional Myth?" *Southeastern Geographer* 48, no. 1 (May 2008): 75–96.

———. *An Unnatural Metropolis: Wresting New Orleans from Nature.* Baton Rouge: Louisiana State University Press, 2005.

Coulter, E. Merton. *Georgia Waters: Tallulah Falls, Madison Springs, Scull Shoals, and the Okefenokee Swamp.* Athens: Georgia Historical Quarterly, 1965.

———. *Old Petersburg and the Broad River Valley of Georgia; Their Rise and Decline.* Athens: University of Georgia Press, 1965.

Cowdrey, Albert E. *This Land, This South: An Environmental History.* Lexington: University Press of Kentucky, 1996.

Craige, Betty Jean. *Eugene Odum: Ecosystem Ecologist and Environmentalist.* Athens: University of Georgia Press, 2001.

Crist, James F. *They Electrified the South: The Story of the Southern Electric System.* N.p.: J. F. Crist, 1981.

Cronon, William. *Nature's Metropolis: Chicago and the Great West.* New York: Norton, 1991.

Crosby, Alfred W. *Children of the Sun: A History of Humanity's Unappeasable Appetite for Energy.* New York: Norton, 2006.

Daniel, Pete. *Breaking the Land: The Transformation of Cotton, Tobacco, and Rice Cultures since 1880.* Urbana: University of Illinois Press, 1985.

———. *Deep'n as It Come: The 1927 Mississippi River Flood.* New York: Oxford University Press, 1977.

———. *Lost Revolutions: The South in the 1950s.* Chapel Hill: University of North Carolina Press for Smithsonian National Museum of American History, Washington, D.C., 2000.

Davis, Donald E., Craig E. Colten, Megan Kate Nelson, Barbara L. Allen, and Mikko Saikku. *Southern United States: An Environmental History.* Santa Barbara, Calif.: ABC-CLIO, 2006.

Davis, Donald Edward. *Where There Are Mountains: An Environmental History of the Southern Appalachians.* Athens: University of Georgia Press, 2000.

Davis, Frederick R. "A Naturalist's Place: Archie Carr and the Nature of Florida." In *Paradise Lost? The Environmental History of Florida*, edited by Jack E. Davis and Raymond Arsenault, 72–91. Gainesville: University Press of Florida, 2005.

Davis, Jack E. *An Everglades Providence: Marjory Stoneman Douglas and the American Environmental Century.* Athens: University of Georgia Press, 2009.

de Sales Dundas, Francis. *The Calhoun Settlement, District of Abbeville, South Carolina.* 2nd ed. Staunton, Ga.: McClure, 1950.

De Vorsey, Louis. *The Georgia–South Carolina Boundary: A Problem in Historical Geography.* Athens: University of Georgia Press, 1982.

Dew, Charles B. *Ironmaker to the Confederacy: Joseph R. Anderson and the Tredegar Iron Works.* New Haven: Yale University Press, 1966.

Dewey, Scott H. "The Fickle Finger of Phosphate: Central Florida Air Pollution and the Failure of Environmental Policy, 1957–1970." *Journal of Southern History* 65, no. 3 (August 1999): 565–603.

Dilsaver, Larry M. *America's National Park System: The Critical Documents.* Lanham, Md.: Rowman and Littlefield, 1994.

Doran, William A. "Early Hydroelectric Power in Tennessee." *Tennessee Historical Quarterly* 27, no. 1 (1968): 72–82.

Downey, Tom. "Riparian Rights and Manufacturing in Antebellum South Carolina: William Gregg and the Origins of the 'Industrial Mind.'" *Journal of Southern History* 65, no. 1 (February 1999): 77–108.

Drake, Brian Allen. "The Skeptical Environmentalist: Barry Goldwater and the Environmental Management State." *Environmental History* 15, no. 4 (October 2010): 587–611.

Durden, Robert F. *The Dukes of Durham, 1865–1929.* Durham, N.C.: Duke University Press, 1975.

———. *Electrifying the Piedmont Carolinas: The Duke Power Company, 1904–1997.* Durham, N.C.: Carolina Academic Press, 2001.

Edgar, Walter B. *South Carolina: A History.* Columbia: University of South Carolina Press, 1998.

Eelman, Bruce W. *Entrepreneurs in the Southern Upcountry: Commercial Culture in Spartanburg, South Carolina, 1845–1880.* Athens: University of Georgia Press, 2008.

Ekbladh, David. *The Great American Mission: Modernization and the Construction of an American World Order.* Princeton: Princeton University Press, 2010.

Elrod, Martha, and Julie Groce. *Energizing Georgia: The History of Georgia Power, 1883–2004.* Macon, Ga.: Indigo Custom Publishing, 2004.

Evenden, Matthew D. *Fish versus Power: An Environmental History of the Fraser River.* New York: Cambridge University Press, 2004.

Fallows, James M., and Ralph Nader. *The Water Lords: Ralph Nader's Study Group Report on Industry and Environmental Crisis in Savannah, Georgia.* New York: Grossman, 1971.

Faulkner, William. *Big Woods: The Hunting Stories.* 1st Vintage international ed. New York: Vintage Books, 1994.

Fereres, Elias, David A. Goldhamer, and Larry R. Parsons. "Irrigation Water Management of Horticultural Crops." *HortScience* 38, no. 5 (August 2003): 1036–42.

Fiege, Mark. *Irrigated Eden: The Making of an Agricultural Landscape in the American West.* Seattle: University of Washington Press, 1999.

Fink, Gary M., and Hugh Davis Graham. *The Carter Presidency: Policy Choices in the Post–New Deal Era.* Lawrence: University Press of Kansas, 1998.

Fisher, Colin. "African Americans, Outdoor Recreation, and the 1919 Chicago Race Riot."

In *"To Love the Wind and the Rain": African Americans and Environmental History*, edited by Diane D. Glave and Mark Stoll, 63–76. Pittsburgh: University of Pittsburgh Press, 2006.

———. "Race and US Environmental History." In *A Companion to American Environmental History*, edited by Douglas Cazaux Sackman, 99–115. Chichester, West Sussex: Wiley-Blackwell, 2010.

Fisher, Stephen L. *Fighting Back in Appalachia: Traditions of Resistance and Change.* Philadelphia: Temple University Press, 1993.

Fishman, Charles. *The Big Thirst: The Secret Life and Turbulent Future of Water.* New York: Free Press, 2011.

Fite, Gilbert Courtland. *Cotton Fields No More: Southern Agriculture, 1865–1980.* Lexington: University Press of Kentucky, 1984.

Flynt, Wayne. *Poor but Proud: Alabama's Poor Whites.* Tuscaloosa: University of Alabama Press, 1989.

Frederickson, Kari. "Confronting the Garrison State: South Carolina in the Early Cold War Era." *Journal of Southern History* 72, no. 3 (May 2006): 349–78.

———. *The Dixiecrat Revolt and the End of the Solid South, 1932–1968.* Chapel Hill: University of North Carolina Press, 2001.

Frisch, Scott A., and Sean Q. Kelly. *Jimmy Carter and the Water Wars: Presidential Influence and the Politics of Pork.* Amherst, N.Y.: Cambria Press, 2008.

Funigiello, Philip J. *Toward a National Power Policy: The New Deal and the Electric Utility Industry, 1933–1941.* Pittsburgh: University of Pittsburgh Press, 1973.

Gaddy, L. L. *A Naturalist's Guide to the Southern Blue Ridge Front: Linville Gorge, North Carolina, to Tallulah Gorge, Georgia.* Columbia: University of South Carolina Press, 2000.

Gaston, Paul M. *The New South Creed: A Study in Southern Mythmaking.* New York: Knopf, 1970.

Georgia Power Company. *Brightening Peoples' Lives for More Than 100 Years: Georgia Power Company: A History in Pictures.* Atlanta: Georgia Power Co., 1998.

Giesen, James C. *Boll Weevil Blues: Cotton, Myth, and Power in the American South.* Chicago: University of Chicago Press, 2011.

Glennon, Robert Jerome. *Unquenchable: America's Water Crisis and What to Do about It.* Washington, D.C.: Island Press, 2009.

———. *Water Follies: Groundwater Pumping and the Fate of America's Fresh Waters.* Washington, D.C.: Island Press, 2002.

Goodell, Jeff. *Big Coal: The Dirty Secret behind America's Energy Future.* Boston: Houghton Mifflin, 2006.

Gottlieb, Robert. *Forcing the Spring: The Transformation of the American Environmental Movement.* Washington, D.C.: Island Press, 1993.

Grant, Chasity, Lori Lee, and Ashley Lesley. "Burton: The Town and Its People," *Foxfire* 25, no. 3 & 4 (Fall-Winter 1991): 181–93.

Grim, Valerie. "The High Cost of Water: African American Farmers and the Politics of Irrigation in the Rural South, 1980–2000." *Agricultural History* 76, no. 2 (Spring 2002): 338–53.

Hackney, Courtney Thomas, S. Marshall Adams, and William Haywood Martin. *Biodiversity of the Southeastern United States: Aquatic Communities*. New York: Wiley, 1992.

Hagen, Joel B. *An Entangled Bank: The Origins of Ecosystem Ecology*. New Brunswick, N.J.: Rutgers University Press, 1992.

Hains, John J. "Southeastern Lakes: Changing Impacts, Issues, Demands." *Lakeline*, Winter 2001/2002, 23–28.

Hall, Jacquelyn Dowd, Robert Korstad, and James Leloudis. "Cotton Mill People: Work, Community, and Protest in the Textile South, 1880–1940." *American Historical Review* 91, no. 2 (April 1986): 245–86.

Hall, Jacquelyn Dowd, James Leloudis, Robert Korstad, Mary Murphy, Lu Ann Jones, and Christopher B. Daly. *Like a Family: The Making of a Southern Cotton Mill World*. Chapel Hill: University of North Carolina Press, 1987.

Hargrove, Erwin C. *Prisoners of Myth: The Leadership of the Tennessee Valley Authority, 1933–1990*. Princeton: Princeton University Press, 1994.

Hargrove, Erwin C., Paul Keith Conkin, and Vanderbilt Institute for Public Policy Studies. *TVA: Fifty Years of Grass-Roots Bureaucracy*. Urbana: University of Illinois Press, 1983.

Harris, Joel Chandler, ed. *Life of Henry W. Grady Including His Writings and Speeches*. New York: Cassell Publishing Co., 1890.

Hart, T. Robert. "The Lowcountry Landscape: Politics, Preservation, and the Santee-Cooper Project." *Environmental History* 18, no. 1 (January 2013): 127–56.

Harvey, Mark W. T. *A Symbol of Wilderness: Echo Park and the American Conservation Movement*. Albuquerque: University of New Mexico Press, 1994.

Hayes, Jack I. *South Carolina and the New Deal*. Columbia: University of South Carolina Press, 2001.

Hayler, Nicole. *Sound Wormy: Memoir of Andrew Gennett, Lumberman*. Athens: University of Georgia Press, 2002.

Hays, Samuel P. *Conservation and the Gospel of Efficiency: The Progressive Conservation Movement, 1890–1920*. Cambridge: Harvard University Press, 1959.

———. *A History of Environmental Politics since 1945*. Pittsburgh: University of Pittsburgh Press, 2000.

Hays, Samuel P., and Barbara D. Hays. *Beauty, Health, and Permanence: Environmental Politics in the United States, 1955–1985*. New York: Cambridge University Press, 1987.

Herwiger, Celine, Richard Seager, and Edward Cook. "North American Droughts of the Mid to Late Nineteenth Century: A History, Simulation, and Implication for Mediaeval Drought." *The Holocene* 16, no. 2 (2006): 159–71.

Hirt, Paul W. *A Conspiracy of Optimism: Management of the National Forests since World War Two*. Lincoln: University of Nebraska Press, 1994.

Hodge, Clarence Lewis. *The Tennessee Valley Authority: A National Experiment in Regionalism*. New York: Russell and Russell, 1968.

Hubbard, Preston J. *Origins of the TVA: The Muscle Shoals Controversy, 1920–1932*. Nashville: Vanderbilt University Press, 1961.

Hudson, Charles M. *Knights of Spain, Warriors of the Sun: Hernando De Soto and the South's Ancient Chiefdoms*. Athens: University of Georgia Press, 1998.

Hudson, Charles M., Thomas J. Pluckhahn, and Robbie Franklyn Ethridge. *Light on the Path: The Anthropology and History of the Southeastern Indians.* Tuscaloosa: University of Alabama Press, 2006.

Hughes, Thomas P. *Networks of Power: Electrification in Western Society, 1880–1930.* Baltimore: Johns Hopkins University Press, 1983.

Humphreys, Margaret. *Malaria: Poverty, Race, and Public Health in the United States.* Baltimore: Johns Hopkins University Press, 2001.

Hundley, Norris, Jr. *The Great Thirst: Californians and Water—A History.* 1992. Rev. ed., Berkeley: University of California Press, 2001.

Hurley, Andrew. *Environmental Inequalities: Class, Race, and Industrial Pollution in Gary, Indiana, 1945–1980.* Chapel Hill: University of North Carolina Press, 1995.

Inscoe, John C. "Appalachian Otherness, Real and Perceived." In *The New Georgia Guide*, 165–203. Athens: University of Georgia Press, 1996.

Jackson, Harvey H., III. *Putting "Loafing Streams" to Work: The Building of Lay, Mitchell, Martin, and Jordan Dams, 1910–1929.* Tuscaloosa: University of Alabama Press, 1997.

———. *The Rise and Decline of the Redneck Riviera: An Insider's History of the Florida-Alabama Coast.* Athens: University of Georgia Press, 2012.

———. *Rivers of History: Life on the Coosa, Tallapoosa, Cahaba, and Alabama.* Tuscaloosa: University of Alabama Press, 1995.

Jacoby, Karl. *Crimes against Nature: Squatters, Poachers, Thieves, and the Hidden History of American Conservation.* Berkeley: University of California Press, 2001.

Jennings, Jesse D. "River Basin Surveys: Origins, Operations, and Results, 1945–1969." *American Antiquity* 50, no. 2 (April 1985): 281–96.

Jones, Christopher F. "A Landscape of Energy Abundance: Anthracite Coal Canals and the Roots of American Fossil Fuel Dependence, 1820–1860." *Environmental History* 15, no. 3 (July 2010): 449–84.

Judd, Richard W. *Common Lands, Common People: The Origins of Conservation in Northern New England.* Cambridge: Harvard University Press, 1997.

Kahrl, Andrew W. *The Land Was Ours: African American Beaches from Jim Crow to the Sunbelt South.* Cambridge: Harvard University Press, 2012.

———. "The 'Negro Park' Question: Land, Labor, and Leisure in Pitt County, North Carolina, 1920–1930." *Journal of Southern History* 79, no. 1 (February 2013): 113–42.

———. "The Political Work of Leisure: Class, Recreation, and African American Commemoration at Harpers Ferry, West Virginia, 1881–1931." *Journal of Social History* 42, no. 1 (2008): 57–77.

———. "'The Slightest Semblance of Unruliness': Steamboat Excursions, Pleasure Resorts, and the Emergence of Segregation Culture on the Potomac River." *Journal of American History* 94, no. 4 (March 2008): 1108–36.

Kapsch, Robert J. *Historic Canals and Waterways of South Carolina.* Columbia: University of South Carolina Press, 2010.

Kelman, Ari. *A River and Its City: The Nature of Landscape in New Orleans.* Berkeley: University of California Press, 2003.

Kindsvater, Carl Edward, Georgia Institute of Technology, Water Resources Center, and United States Study Commission: Southeast River Basins. *Organization and*

Methodology for River Basin Planning; Proceedings. Atlanta: Water Resources Center, Georgia Institute of Technology, 1964.

———. *Organization and Methodology for River Basin Planning; Proceedings*. Atlanta: Water Resources Center, Georgia Institute of Technology, 1967.

King, Judson. *The Conservation Fight, from Theodore Roosevelt to the Tennessee Valley Authority*. Washington, D.C.: Public Affairs Press, 1959.

Kirby, Jack Temple. *The Countercultural South*. Mercer University Lamar Memorial Lectures No. 38. Athens: University of Georgia Press, 1995.

———. *Poquosin: A Study of Rural Landscape and Society*. Chapel Hill: University of North Carolina Press, 1995.

———. *Rural Worlds Lost: The American South, 1920–1960*. Baton Rouge: Louisiana State University Press, 1987.

Klosky, Beth Ann. *"Six Miles That Changed the Course of the South": The Story of the Electric City, Anderson, South Carolina*. Anderson, S.C.: The Electric City Centennial Committee, in cooperation with the City of Anderson and Anderson Heritage, Inc., 1995.

Koeniger, A. Cash. "Climate and Southern Distinctiveness." *Journal of Southern History* 54, no. 1 (February 1988): 21–44.

Kohn, Augustus. *The Water Powers of South Carolina*. Charleston, S.C.: Walker, Evans, and Cogswell, 1911.

Koyle, Susan Lewis. *Genealogy Extracted from Forest Service Court Cases in Rabun County, Georgia*. Bowie, Md.: Heritage Books, 2001.

Kruse, Kevin M. *White Flight: Atlanta and the Making of Modern Conservatism*. Princeton: Princeton University Press, 2005.

LaFeber, Walter. *America, Russia, and the Cold War, 1945–2000*. Boston: McGraw-Hill, 2002.

Lander, Ernest McPherson. *Tales of Calhoun Falls*. Spartanburg, S.C.: Reprint Co., 1991.

Lane, John. *Chattooga: Descending into the Myth of Deliverance River*. Athens: University of Georgia Press, 2004.

Lakwete, Angela. *Inventing the Cotton Gin: Machine and Myth in Antebellum America*. Baltimore: Johns Hopkins University Press, 2003.

Lassiter, Matthew D. *The Silent Majority: Suburban Politics in the Sunbelt South*. Princeton: Princeton University Press, 2006.

Lassiter, Matthew D., and Joseph Crespino, eds. *The Myth of Southern Exceptionalism*. New York: Oxford University Press, 2010.

Lasswell, Harold D. "The Garrison State." *American Journal of Sociology* 46, no. 4 (January 1941): 455–69.

Leopold, Luna B. *A View of the River*. Cambridge: Harvard University Press, 1994.

Leopold, Luna B., and Thomas Maddock Jr. *The Flood Control Controversy: Big Dams, Little Dams, and Land Management*. New York: Ronald Press Co., 1954.

Leuchtenburg, William E. "Roosevelt, Norris and The 'Seven Little TVAs.'" *Journal of Politics* 14, no. 3 (1952): 418–41.

Lewis, W. David. *Sloss Furnaces and the Rise of the Birmingham District: An Industrial Epic*. Tuscaloosa: University of Alabama Press, 1994.

Logan, John H. *A History of the Upper Country of South Carolina from the Earliest Periods to the Close of the War of Independence*. Vol. 1. Columbia, S.C.: P. B. Glass and Charleston, S.C.: S. G. Courtenay & Co., 1859.

Maass, Arthur. *Muddy Waters: The Army Engineers and the Nation's Rivers*. Cambridge: Harvard University Press, 1951.

Manganiello, Christopher J. "Fish Tales and the Conservation State." *Southern Cultures* 20, no. 3 (Fall 2014): 43–62.

Marshall, Suzanne. *"Lord, We're Just Trying to Save Your Water": Environmental Activism and Dissent in the Appalachian South*. Gainesville: University Press of Florida, 2002.

Maunula, Marko. "Another Southern Paradox: The Arrival of Foreign Corporations: Change and Continuity in Spartanburg, South Carolina." In *Globalization and the American South*, edited by James C. Cobb and William Stueck, 164–84. Athens: University of Georgia Press, 2005.

McCraw, Thomas K. *TVA and the Power Fight, 1933–1939*. Philadelphia: Lippincott, 1971.

McCullough, David G. *The Johnstown Flood*. New York: Simon and Schuster, 1968.

McDonald, Michael J., and John Muldowny. *TVA and the Dispossessed: The Resettlement of Population in the Norris Dam Area*. Knoxville: University of Tennessee Press, 1982.

McDowall, Duncan. *The Light: Brazilian Traction, Light, and Power Company Limited, 1899–1945*. Toronto: University of Toronto Press, 1988.

McEvoy, Arthur F. *The Fisherman's Problem: Ecology and the Law in the California Fisheries, 1850–1980*. New York: Cambridge University Press, 1986.

McGirr, Lisa. *Suburban Warriors: The Origins of the New American Right*. Princeton: Princeton University Press, 2001.

McGurty, Eileen Maura. "From NIMBY to Civil Rights: The Origins of the Environmental Justice Movement." *Environmental History* 2, no. 3 (July 1997): 301–23.

McKay, Cuba S., and Archie McKay. *A Pictorial History of Rabun County*. Virginia Beach: Donning Co., 2003.

McMath, Robert Carroll, Ronald H. Bayor, James Edward Brittain, Lawrence Foster, August W. Giebelhaus, and Germaine M. Reed. *Engineering the New South: Georgia Tech, 1885–1985*. Athens: University of Georgia Press, 1985.

McPhee, John. *Encounters with the Archdruid*. New York: Farrar, Straus, and Giroux, 1971.

———. *The Founding Fish*. New York: Farrar, Straus and Giroux, 2002.

Mellinchamp, Josephine. *Senators from Georgia*. Huntsville, Ala.: Strode Publishers, 1976.

Melosi, Martin. *Precious Commodity: Providing Water for America's Cities*. Pittsburgh: University of Pittsburgh Press, 2011.

Milazzo, Paul Charles. *Unlikely Environmentalists: Congress and Clean Water, 1945–1972*. Lawrence: University Press of Kansas, 2006.

Mitchell, Broadus. *The Rise of Cotton Mills in the South*. New York: Da Capo Press, 1968.

Moore, John Robert. *The Economic Impact of TVA*. Knoxville: University of Tennessee Press, 1967.

Morgan, Arthur Ernest. *Dams and Other Disasters: A Century of the Army Corps of Engineers in Civil Works.* Boston: P. Sargent, 1971.

———. *The Making of the TVA.* Buffalo, N.Y.: Prometheus, 1974.

———. *The Miami Conservancy District.* New York: McGraw-Hill, 1951.

Morris, Christopher. *The Big Muddy: An Environmental History of the Mississippi and Its Peoples, from Hernando de Soto to Hurricane Katrina.* New York: Oxford University Press, 2012.

———. "A More Southern Environmental History." *Journal of Southern History* 75, no. 3 (August 2009): 581–98.

Muir, John. *A Thousand-Mile Walk to the Gulf.* Edited by William Frederic Badè. Boston: Houghton Mifflin, 1916.

Nelson, Megan Kate. *Trembling Earth: A Cultural History of the Okefenokee Swamp.* Athens: University of Georgia Press, 2005.

Newfont, Kathryn. *Blue Ridge Commons: Environmental Activism and Forest History in Western North Carolina.* Athens: University of Georgia Press, 2012.

———. "Grassroots Environmentalism: Origins of the Western North Carolina Alliance." *Appalachian Journal* 27, no. 1 (Fall 1999): 46–61.

Nixon, H. Clarence. "The Tennessee Valley: A Recreation Domain." In *Papers of the Institute of Research and Training in the Social Sciences*, 1–21. Nashville: Vanderbilt University Press, June 1945.

Noll, Steven, and David Tegeder. *Ditch of Dreams: The Cross Florida Barge Canal and the Struggle for Florida's Future.* Gainesville: University of Florida Press, 2009.

Nye, David E. *Consuming Power: A Social History of American Energies.* Cambridge: MIT Press, 1998; 3rd ed., 2001.

———. *Electrifying America: Social Meanings of a New Technology, 1880–1940.* Cambridge: MIT Press, 1990.

———. *When the Lights Went Out: A History of Blackouts in America.* Cambridge: MIT Press, 2010.

O'Connor, Cameron, and John Lazenby, eds. *First Descents: In Search of Wild Rivers.* Birmingham, Ala.: Menasha Ridge Press, 1989.

Odum, Eugene P. "Ecology and the Atomic Age." *Association of Southeastern Biologists Bulletin*, 4 no. 2 (1957): 27–29.

———. *Fundamentals of Ecology.* Philadelphia: Saunders, 1953.

Odum, Howard T. "Trophic Structure and Productivity of Silver Springs, Florida." *Ecological Monographs* 27, no. 1 (1957): 55–112.

Odum, Howard Washington, and Social Science Research Council (U.S.) Southern Regional Committee. *Southern Regions of the United States.* Chapel Hill: University of North Carolina Press, 1936.

O'Neill, Karen M. *Rivers by Design: State Power and the Origins of U.S. Flood Control.* Durham, N.C.: Duke University Press, 2006.

———. "Why the TVA Remains Unique: Interest Groups and the Defeat of New Deal River Planning." *Rural Sociology* 67, no. 2 (June 2002): 163–82.

Overton, Jim. "Taking on TVA." *Southern Exposure* 11, no. 1 (1983): 22–28.

Palmer, Tim. *Endangered Rivers and the Conservation Movement.* 2nd ed. Lanham, Md.: Rowman and Littlefield, 2004.

————. *The Wild and Scenic Rivers of America*. Washington, D.C.: Island Press, 1993.

Patrick, Ruth. *Rivers of the United States*. New York: J. Wiley, 1994.

Pederson, N., et al. "A Long-Term Perspective on a Modern Drought in the American Southeast." *Environmental Research Letters* 7 (2012): 1–9.

Peterson, Elmer T. *Big Dam Foolishness: The Problem of Modern Flood Control and Water Storage*. New York: Devin-Adair Co., 1954.

Phillips, Sarah T. *This Land, This Nation: Conservation, Rural America, and the New Deal*. New York: Cambridge University Press, 2007.

Phillips, William, and Augusta (Ga.) City Engineer. *Report of William Phillips, C.E., Upon the Topography and Hydrography in the Vicinity of Augusta, Ga., and the History of the Currents of the Savannah River in Times of Freshet. With Plates Accompanying*. Augusta, Ga.: J. M. Weigle & Co., 1892.

Pierce, Daniel S. *The Great Smokies: From Natural Habitat to National Park*. Knoxville: University of Tennessee Press, 2000.

Pierce, Henry J. *Looking Squarely at the Water Problem*. Seattle: n.p., 1915.

Pisani, Donald J. "Beyond the Hundredth Meridian: Nationalizing the History of Water in the United States." *Environmental History* 5, no. 4 (October 2000): 466–82.

————. *To Reclaim a Divided West: Water, Law, and Public Policy, 1848–1902*. Albuquerque: University of New Mexico Press, 1992.

————. *Water and American Government: The Reclamation Bureau, National Water Policy, and the West, 1902–1935*. Berkeley: University of California Press, 2002.

————. *Water, Land, and Law in the West: The Limits of Public Policy, 1850–1920*. Lawrence: University Press of Kansas, 1996.

Pratt, Joseph A. "The Ascent of Oil: The Transition from Coal to Oil in Early Twentieth-Century America." In *Energy Transitions: Long-Term Perspectives*, edited by Lewis J. Perelman, August W. Giebelhaus, and Michael D. Yokell, 9–34. Boulder, Colo.: American Association for the Advancement of Science and Westview Press, 1981.

————. "A Mixed Blessing: Energy, Economic Growth, and Houston's Environment." In *Energy Metropolis: An Environmental History of Houston and the Gulf Coast*, edited by Martin V. Melosi and Joseph A. Pratt, 21–51. Pittsburgh: University of Pittsburgh Press, 2007.

Purcell, Aaron D. "Struggle Within, Struggle Without: The Tepco Case and the Tennessee Valley Authority, 1936–1939." *Tennessee Historical Quarterly* 61, no. 3 (2002): 194–210.

Rash, Ron. *One Foot in Eden*. New York: Henry Holt, 2002.

Ray, Janisse. *Drifting into Darien: A Personal and Natural History of the Altamaha River*. Athens: University of Georgia Press, 2011.

Reel, Jerome V. *The High Seminary*. Vol. 1, *A History of the Clemson Agricultural College of South Carolina, 1889–1964*. Clemson: Clemson University Digital Press, 2011.

Reidy, Joseph P. *From Slavery to Agrarian Capitalism in the Cotton Plantation South: Central Georgia, 1800–1880*. Chapel Hill: University of North Carolina Press, 1992.

Reisner, Marc. *Cadillac Desert: The American West and Its Disappearing Water*. New York: Penguin, 1986; rev. and updated ed., 1993.

Reuss, Martin. "Andrew A. Humphreys and the Development of Hydraulic Engineering: Politics and Technology in the Army Corps of Engineers, 1850–1950." *Technology and Culture* 26, no. 1 (1985): 1–33.

———. "Coping with Uncertainty: Social Scientists, Engineers, and Federal Water Resources Planning." *Natural Resources Journal* 32 (Winter 1992): 101–35.

Richardson, Elmo R. *Dams, Parks and Politics: Resource Development and Preservation in the Truman-Eisenhower Era*. Lexington: University Press of Kentucky, 1973.

Riley, Jack. *Carolina Power and Light Company, 1908–1958: A Corporate Biography, Tracing the Origin and Development of Electric Service in Much of the Carolinas*. Raleigh: Edwards and Broughton, 1958.

Ring, Natalie J. *The Problem South: Region, Empire, and the New Liberal State, 1880–1930*. Athens: University of Georgia Press, 2012.

Ritchie, Andrew Jackson, ed. *Sketches of Rabun County History, 1819–1948*. Chelsea, Mich.: Rabun County, Georgia, Historical Society, 1995.

Robinson, Michael C. "The Relationship between the Army Corps of Engineers and the Environmental Community, 1920–1969." *Environmental Review* 13, no. 1 (Spring 1989): 1–41.

Rogers, J., K. Averyt, S. Clemmer, M. Davis, F. Flores-Lopez, P. Frumhoff, D. Kenney, J. Macknick, N. Madden, J. Meldrum, J. Overpeck, S. Sattler, E. Spanger-Siegfried, and D. Yates. *Water-Smart Power: Strengthening the U.S. Electricity System in a Warming World*. Cambridge, Mass.: Union of Concerned Scientists, July 2013.

Rome, Adam W. *The Bulldozer in the Countryside: Suburban Sprawl and the Rise of American Environmentalism*. New York: Cambridge University Press, 2001.

———. "'Give Earth a Chance': The Environmental Movement and the Sixties." *Journal of American History* 90, no. 2 (September 2003): 525–54.

Rymer, Russ. *American Beach: How "Progress" Robbed a Black Town—and Nation—of History, Wealth, and Power*. New York: Harper Perennial, Harper Collins, 1998.

Saikku, Mikko. *This Delta, This Land: An Environmental History of the Yazoo-Mississippi Floodplain*. Athens: University of Georgia Press, 2005.

Sassaman, Kenneth E. *People of the Shoals: Stallings Culture of the Savannah River Valley*. Gainesville: University Press of Florida, 2006.

Savage, Henry, and Lamar Dodd. *River of the Carolinas: The Santee*. New York: Rinehart, 1956.

Schaffer, Daniel. "Managing the Tennessee River: Principles, Practice, and Change." *Public Historian* 12, no. 2 (1990): 7–29.

Schulman, Bruce J. *From Cotton Belt to Sunbelt: Federal Policy, Economic Development, and the Transformation of the South, 1938–1980*. 1st ed., New York: Oxford University Press, 1991. 2nd ed., Durham, N.C.: Duke University Press, 1994.

Scott, James C. *Seeing Like a State: How Certain Schemes to Improve the Human Condition Have Failed*. New Haven: Yale University Press, 1998.

Seager, Richard, Alexandria Tzanova, and Jennifer Nakamura. "Drought in the Southeastern United States: Causes, Variability over the Last Millennium, and the Potential for Future Hydroclimate Change." *Journal of Climate* 22 (October 1, 2009): 5021–45.

Sellers, Charles Grier. *The Market Revolution: Jacksonian America, 1815–1846*. New York: Oxford University Press, 1991.

Sellers, Christopher. "Nature and Blackness in Suburban Passage." In *"To Love the Wind and the Rain": African Americans and Environmental History*, edited by Diane D. Glave and Mark Stoll, 93–119. Pittsburgh: University of Pittsburgh Press, 2006.

Selznick, Philip. *TVA and the Grass Roots: A Study in the Sociology of Formal Organization*. New York: Harper and Row, 1966.

Shallat, Todd A. *Structures in the Stream: Water, Science, and the Rise of the U.S. Army Corps of Engineers*. Austin: University of Texas Press, 1994.

Shaw, Ronald E. *Canals for a Nation: The Canal Era in the United States, 1790–1860*. Lexington: University Press of Kentucky, 1990.

Silver, Timothy. *Mount Mitchell and the Black Mountains: An Environmental History of the Highest Peaks in Eastern America*. Chapel Hill: University of North Carolina Press, 2003.

———. *A New Face on the Countryside: Indians, Colonists, and Slaves in South Atlantic Forests, 1500–1800*. New York: Cambridge University Press, 1990.

Simon, Bryant. *A Fabric of Defeat: The Politics of South Carolina Millhands, 1910–1948*. Chapel Hill: University of North Carolina Press, 1998.

Smith, Jason Scott. *Building New Deal Liberalism: The Political Economy of Public Works, 1933–1956*. New York: Cambridge University Press, 2006.

Smith, Marvin T., Robbie Franklyn Ethridge, and Charles M. Hudson. *The Transformation of the Southeastern Indians, 1540–1760*. Jackson: University Press of Mississippi, 2002.

Sorrells, Robert T. *Clemson Experimental Forest: Its First Fifty Years*. Clemson, S.C.: Clemson University, College of Forest and Recreation Resources, 1984.

Stahle, David W., Malcolm K. Cleaveland, Dennis B. Blanton, Matthew D. Therrell, and David A. Gay. "The Lost Colony and Jamestown Droughts." *Science* 280, no. 564 (April 24, 1998): 564–67.

Steinberg, Theodore. *Acts of God: The Unnatural History of Natural Disaster in America*. New York: Oxford University Press, 2006.

———. "Do-It-Yourself Deathscape: The Unnatural History of Natural Disaster in South Florida." *Environmental History* 2, no. 4 (October 1997): 414–38.

———. *Nature Incorporated: Industrialization and the Waters of New England*. New York: Cambridge University Press, 1991.

Stewart, Mart A. "From King Cane to King Cotton: Razing Cane in the Old South." *Environmental History* 12, no. 1 (January 2007): 59–79.

———. "If John Muir Had Been an Agrarian: American Environmental History West and South." *Environment and History* 11, no. 2 (May 2005): 139–62.

———. *"What Nature Suffers to Groe": Life, Labor, and Landscape on the Georgia Coast, 1680–1920*. Athens: University of Georgia Press, 1996.

Stine, Jeffrey K. "Environmental Policy during the Carter Presidency." In *The Carter Presidency: Policy Choices in the Post–New Deal Era*, edited by Gary M. Fink and Hugh Davis Graham, 179–201. Lawrence: University Press of Kansas, 1998.

———. *Mixing the Waters: Environment, Politics, and the Building of the Tennessee-Tombigbee Waterway*. Akron: University of Akron Press, 1993.

———. "United States Army Corps of Engineers." In *Government Agencies*, edited by Donald R. Whitnah, 513–16. Greenwood Encyclopedia of American Institutions. Westport, Conn.: Greenwood Press, 1983.

Stokes, Melvyn, and Stephen Conway, eds. *The Market Revolution in America: Social, Political, and Religious Expressions, 1800–1880*. Charlottesville: University Press of Virginia, 1996.

Stokes, Thomas Lunsford, and Lamar Dodd. *The Savannah*. New York: Rinehart, 1951.

Stoll, Steven. *Larding the Lean Earth: Soil and Society in Nineteenth-Century America*. New York: Hill and Wang, 2002.

Strand, Ginger Gail. *Inventing Niagara: Beauty, Power, and Lies*. New York: Simon and Schuster, 2008.

Stroud, Ellen. "Troubled Waters in Ecotopia: Environmental Racism in Portland, Oregon." *Radical History Review* 74 (Spring 1999): 65–95.

Sutter, Paul. *Driven Wild: How the Fight against Automobiles Launched the Modern Wilderness Movement*. Seattle: University of Washington Press, 2002.

———. "Nature's Agents or Agents of Empire? Entomological Workers and Environmental Change during the Construction of the Panama Canal." *Isis* 98 (2007): 724–54.

———. "What Gullies Mean: Georgia's 'Little Grand Canyon' and Southern Environmental History." *Journal of Southern History* 76, no. 3 (August 2010): 579–616.

Sutter, Paul, and Christopher J. Manganiello, eds. *Environmental History and the American South: A Reader*. Athens: University of Georgia Press, 2009.

Taft, Dub, and Sam Heys. *Big Bets: Decisions and Leaders That Shaped Southern Company*. Atlanta: Southern Co., 2011.

Taylor, Joseph E., III. *Making Salmon: An Environmental History of the Northwest Fisheries Crisis*. Seattle: University of Washington Press, 1999.

Taylor, Stephen Wallace. *The New South's New Frontier: A Social History of Economic Development in Southwestern North Carolina*. Gainesville: University Press of Florida, 2001.

Tindall, George Brown. *The Emergence of the New South, 1913–1945*. Baton Rouge: Louisiana State University Press, 1967.

Trimble, Stanley Wayne. *Man-Induced Soil Erosion on the Southern Piedmont, 1700–1970*. Ankeny, Iowa: Soil Conservation Society of America, 1974.

———. "Perspectives on the History of Soil Erosion Control in the Eastern United States." *Agricultural History* 59, no. 2 (April 1985): 162–80.

Tucker, Richard P., and Edmund Russell, eds. *Natural Enemy, Natural Ally: Toward an Environmental History of Warfare*. Corvallis: Oregon State University Press, 2004.

Tullos, Allen. *Habits of Industry: White Culture and the Transformation of the Carolina Piedmont*. Chapel Hill: University of North Carolina Press, 1989.

Turner, James M. "'The Specter of Environmentalism': Wilderness, Environmental Politics, and the Evolution of the New Right." *Journal of American History* 96, no. 1 (June 2009): 123–48.

Vance, Rupert B. *Human Geography of the South: A Study in Regional Resources and Human Adequacy*. Chapel Hill: University of North Carolina Press, 1932.

Waller, Robert A. "The Civilian Conservation Corps and the Emergence of South Carolina's State Park System, 1933–1942." *South Carolina Historical Magazine* 104, no. 2 (April 2003): 101–25.

Ware, Walter B. *Black Business in the New South: A Social History of the North Carolina Mutual Life Insurance Company*. Urbana: University of Illinois Press, 1973.

Warren, Louis S. *The Hunter's Game: Poachers and Conservationists in Twentieth-Century America*. New Haven: Yale University Press, 1997.

Watson, Harry L. "'The Common Rights of Mankind': Subsistence, Shad, and Commerce in the Early Republican South." *Journal of American History* 83, no. 1 (June 1996): 13–43.

Way, Albert G. *Conserving Longleaf: Herbert Stoddard and the Rise of Ecological Land Management*. Athens: University of Georgia Press, 2011.

Wengert, Norman. "The Antecedents of TVA: The Legislative History of Muscle Shoals." *Agricultural History* 26, no. 4 (October 1952): 141–47.

Weyeneth, Robert R. "The Architecture of Racial Segregation: The Challenges of Preserving the Problematical Past." *Public Historian* 27, no. 4 (2005): 11–44.

Wheeler, William Bruce, and Michael J. McDonald. *TVA and the Tellico Dam, 1936–1979: A Bureaucratic Crisis in Post-Industrial America*. Knoxville: University of Tennessee Press, 1986.

Whisnant, David E. *Modernizing the Mountaineer: People, Power, and Planning in Appalachia*. Rev. ed. Knoxville: University of Tennessee Press, 1994.

White, Michael C. *Historic Milling in Richmond County, Georgia*. Augusta, Ga.: Michael C. White, 1998.

———. *Waterways and Water Mills*. Warrenton, Ga.: C.S.R.A. Press, 1995.

White, Richard. *The Organic Machine: The Remaking of the Columbia River*. New York: Hill and Wang, 1995.

Whitnah, Donald R., ed. *Government Agencies*. Greenwood Encyclopedia of American Institutions. Westport, Conn.: Greenwood Press, 1983.

Wiener, Jonathan M. *Social Origins of the New South: Alabama, 1860–1885*. Baton Rouge: Louisiana State University Press, 1978.

Williams, James C. *Energy and the Making of Modern California*. Akron: University of Akron Press, 1997.

Willoughby, Lynn. *Flowing through Time: A History of the Lower Chattahoochee River*. Tuscaloosa: University of Alabama Press, 1999.

Wiltse, Jeff. *Contested Waters: A Social History of Swimming Pools in America*. Chapel Hill: University of North Carolina Press, 2007.

Wood, Betty. *Slavery in Colonial Georgia, 1730–1775*. Athens: University of Georgia Press, 1984.

Woodruff, Nan Elizabeth. *As Rare as Rain: Federal Relief in the Great Southern Drought of 1930–31*. Urbana: University of Illinois Press, 1985.

Woodward, C. Vann. *Origins of the New South, 1877–1913*. Baton Rouge: Louisiana State University Press, 1951. Reprinted in 1971.

Woodward, Doug. *Wherever Waters Flow: A Lifelong Love Affair with Wild Rivers*. Franklin, N.C.: Headwaters Publishing, 2006.

Worster, Donald. *Dust Bowl: The Southern Plains in the 1930s*. New York: Oxford University Press, 1979.

———. *A Passion for Nature: The Life of John Muir*. New York: Oxford University Press, 2008.

———. *Rivers of Empire: Water, Aridity, and the Growth of the American West*. New York: Pantheon, 1985.

———. *Under Western Skies: Nature and History in the American West*. New York: Oxford University Press, 1992.

———, ed. *The Ends of the Earth: Perspectives on Modern Environmental History*. New York: Cambridge University Press, 1988.

Wright, Gavin. *Old South, New South: Revolutions in the Southern Economy since the Civil War*. New York: Basic Books, 1986.

Wright, Wade H. *History of the Georgia Power Company, 1855–1956*. Atlanta: Georgia Power Co., 1957.

Wrigley, E. A. *Continuity, Chance, and Change: The Character of the Industrial Revolution in England*. New York: Cambridge University Press, 1988.

———. *Poverty, Progress, and Population*. New York: Cambridge University Press, 2004.

Yergin, Daniel. *The Prize: The Epic Quest for Oil, Money, and Power*. New York: Simon and Schuster, 1991.

———. *The Quest: Energy, Security, and the Remaking of the Modern World*. New York: Penguin, 2011.

Yoe, Charles E. *The Declining Role of the United States Army Corps of Engineers in the Development of the Nation's Water Resources*. Fort Collins: Colorado Water Resources Research Institute, Colorado State University, 1981.

Young, Terence. "'A Contradiction in Democratic Government': W. J. Trent, Jr., and the Struggle to Desegregate National Park Campgrounds." *Environmental History* 14, no. 4 (October 2009): 651–82.

THESES AND DISSERTATIONS

Askew, Dana Leigh. "Restoring the Dam Landscape: Removing Dams to Restore Rivers." M.A. thesis, University of Georgia, 2001.

Cox, Stephen Lewis. "The History of Negro State Parks in South Carolina, 1940–1965." M.A. thesis, University of South Carolina, 1992.

Lefkoff, Merle Schlesinger. "The Voluntary Citizens' Group as a Public Policy Alternative to the Political Party: A Case Study of the Georgia Conservancy." Ph.D. diss., Emory University, 1975.

McCallister, Andrew Beecher. "'A Source of Pleasure, Profit, and Pride': Tourism, Industrialization, and Conservation at Tallulah Falls, Georgia, 1820–1915." M.A. thesis, University of Georgia, 2002.

McFarland, Robert Ernest, Jr. "Of Time and the River: Economy, People, and the Environment in the Tennessee River Valley, 1500–1900." Ph.D. diss., University of Alabama, 1997.

Shapard, Robert P. "Building an Inland Sea: Clarks Hill Lake on the Upper Savannah and the Twentieth-Century Lives, Land, and River Hidden by Its Waters." M.A. thesis, North Carolina State University, 2009.

Shuler, Darren Anthony. "On Our Land: Progress, Destruction, and the Tennessee Valley Authority's Tellico Dam Project." M.A. thesis, University of Georgia, 2000.

UNPUBLISHED DOCUMENTS, PAMPHLETS, SPEECHES, AND PROCEEDINGS

Alabama Power Company. *Alabama Power Company, Golden Anniversary, December 4, 1956*. N.p.: The Company, 1956.

Arkwright, Preston S. *Threatened State Control of Water Powers: An Address before the Association of Edison Illuminating Companies, at White Sulphur Springs, West Virginia, October 11, 1922*.

Atkinson, Henry Morrell. *The Relation of Electric Power to Farm Progress; Georgia's Need, More Industries and Less Politics; an Address before the Eighteenth Annual Farmers' Week Conference at Athens, Georgia, January 28, 1925*. [Atlanta], 1925.

Augusta Canal Company, William Phillips, George R. Baldwin, and Augusta Manufacturing Co. *Special Report of the Engineer of the Augusta Canal to the Board of Managers: On the Matter in Controversy between the Augusta Canal Co. And the Augusta Manufacturing Co*. Augusta, Ga.: n.p., 1856.

Branch, Harllee. *Georgia and the Georgia Power Company: A Century of Free Enterprise!* New York: Newcomen Society in North America, 1957.

Georgia Council for the Preservation of Natural Areas. *Report of the First Year of Operation, 1967–69*. Decatur: n.p., n.d.

Georgia Power Company. *Georgia and the Georgia Power Company*. [Atlanta], 1950.

———. *Water Power Developments in North Georgia*. 3rd ed. N.p., 1924.

Georgia Water Use and Conservation Committee. *Water in Georgia, Submitted by the Georgia Water Use and Conservation Committee to the Governor, the General Assembly, and the People of Georgia*. Atlanta, 1955.

The Hartwell Project: A Request for an Appropriation. Hartwell Steering Committee, February 15, 1954. Pamphlet.

Herring, Harriet L., [J. Herman Johnson,] Rupert B. Vance, and T. J. Woofter Jr. *A Survey of the Catawba Valley: A Study Made by the Institute for Research in Social Science for the Tennessee Valley Authority*. 2 vols. Chapel Hill: Institute for Research in Social Justice at the University of North Carolina, 1935.

Johnson, A. Stephen. *Georgia Scenic Rivers Report*. Prepared for the Georgia Natural Areas Council, 1971.

Moore, Louis E. *Electricity: Its Story Simply Told, a Study of Its Development and Application to Present and Future Needs in Georgia*. Atlanta: Utilities Information Committee of Georgia, 1924. Pamphlet.

Nelson, Lynn. "'Harassed by the Floods and Storms of Nature': Remembering Private Hydro-Power and Rural Communities in Tennessee." Paper read at the American Society for Environmental History Conference, Tallahassee, Florida, February 2009.

Read, Granville M., Savannah River Plant (E. I. du Pont de Nemours & Company), and Rotary Club (Wilmington, Del.). *"The Savannah River Project": A Speech by Granville M. Read, Chief Engineer, E. I. Du Pont De Nemours & Company, before the Rotary Club, Wilmington, Delaware*. November 18, 1954.

Reid, Cecil L., Al G. Stanford, and Ed D. Sloan. *The Truth about "Hartwell."* Fredericksburg, Va.: January 7, 1952. Pamphlet.

South Carolina Electric and Gas. *Saluda Hydroelectric Project, FERC Project No. 516: Construction History, Exhibit C.* Prepared by Kleinschmidt Energy & Water Resources Consultants, December 2007.

———. *Stevens Creek Hydroelectric Project: Significant Historic and Archeological Resources.* N.p., n.d., 1999?, http://www.sceg.com/NR/rdonlyres/25DD5351-2826-478B-9691-BE26A3F1CEB3/0/StevensCreekReport.pdf. February 15, 2013.

Southern Rural Development Center and Farm Foundation. *Future Waves: Water Policy in the South, Proceedings of a Regional Conference, Ramada Inn Southwest Airport, Memphis, Tennessee, November 18–19, 1982.* SRDC Series Publication. Mississippi State: Southern Rural Development Center in cooperation with the Farm Foundation.

The Truth about the Clark's Hill Project. N.p.: Clark's Hill Authority of South Carolina, [1946?].

Index

and description, 80, 90, 94–99, 111,
128, 148; Georgia Power Co. surrenders
license for, 82, 99; opposition to, 84–85,
99–100, 113, 124–25, 147, 159; and
Hamburg, S.C., 87, 90; and big dam
consensus, 91; and source of name, 95,
113–14, 232 (n. 11); authorization for,
98; as "keystone," 99; and drought, 101,
112; and recreation planning, 101–8;
and real estate and removal for, 108–11,
137–38; and cultural surveys, 108–11;
construction costs of, 111, 119–20; as
"Georgia's new ocean," 112; and national
defense, 122; and water supply authorization, 135–37, 158; Savannah River
upstream of, 143, 145–56 passim, 161;
and public health, 153; and dissolved
oxygen, 156. *See also* Moody, Lester
Clayton, Ga., 18 (ill.), 19 (ill.), 189
Clean Water Act of 1972, 144, 195, 202
Clemson, S.C., 18 (ill.), 19 (ill.), 178
Clemson College. *See* Clemson University
Clemson University, 124–27, 137, 147, 177
Climate change, 195, 197; and National
Climate Assessment, 204
Coal: coal-fired steam plants, 2, 6, 13,
39–40, 118, 167, 196; rock coal, 6, 23,
46, 49–50, 65, 86, 121, 192; use of
during drought, 13, 64, 67, 176; rock
coal imported, 39, 41, 50, 147; and
Duke Energy, 49, 65, 126, 147, 150–51,
158; and Giant Power, 61; and Alabama
Power, 64; and Georgia Power, 64,
80–81, 93, 113, 176, 201; and Southern
Company, 194; and coal ash, 195–96
Coastal Plain physiographic province,
9, 12, 22, 24, 73; and natural water
features, 11; and water supply, 131,
199–200; and agriculture, 197
Cobb County, Ga., 2
Coca-Cola, 2
Coca-Cola Enterprises, 3
Cold War, 101, 121–22, 132
Colorado, 50, 170
Colorado River, 5, 10, 71, 111, 201
Colorado River Storage Project, 118
Columbia, S.C., 23, 40, 48 (ill.), 79
Columbia Cotton Mill, 40, 48 (ill.)
Columbia River, 10, 71, 126
Columbus, Ga., 23, 35, 37, 130–31, 200
Commonwealth and Southern Corpora-
tion, 59, 77, 84

Communism, 125–26
Conasauga River, 161
Confederate States of America, 35–36
Congaree River, 23
Congress: and water supply, 3, 135–36,
158, 195; and navigation, 14; and
multiple-purpose projects, 15, 132, 142;
and U.S. Army Corps of Engineers, 52;
and single-purpose projects, 52, 74–75,
85; and the Tennessee Valley Authority, 54–55, 78, 84, 91; and studies, 60,
76–77, 115; and Clarks Hill Dam and
Lake, 94–99, 113; and Hartwell Dam
and Lake, 118, 120, 121, 122, 123, 126;
and Trotters Shoals, 142, 161; and
environmental movement, 144, 155;
and Clean Water Act, 144–45, 170; and
Middleton Shoals, 147, 151; and civil
rights, 160, 171; and Flint River, 162;
and James "Jimmy" Earl Carter, 163;
and Chattooga River, 166, 179, 180, 181,
183
Conservation: as reduction in water
consumption, 2, 4, 92–93, 128, 202;
as storage of water, 15, 40, 129, 132,
142; New South water storage, 64, 68;
Progressive era, 53, 55, 61, 76–77; New
Deal, 85, 90, 95, 102, 163; as reduction
in energy consumption, 92
Conservationists, 132, 143–44; New South,
68; New Deal, 117
Conservatism, 17, 117, 158–60, 192
Cooke, Morris L., 61
Coosa River, 11, 196; and interbasin
transfers, 200
Coosawattee River, 65
Cotton, 5, 22, 26–29, 33–37, 73, 129, 198;
fields, 109; farmers, 149, 197, 200
Cotton Belt, 94, 117, 219
Council on Environmental Quality, 155
Countryside conservation, 15–16, 142,
144–45, 163–64, 192; defined, 144–45;
and Trotters Shoals, 154–55, 160–61,
173; and Chattooga River, 173–74,
179–80, 188
Craighead, Frank E., 170–73, 177, 180–81.
See also National Wild and Scenic
Rivers Act of 1968
Craighead, John C., 170–73, 177, 180–81.
See also National Wild and Scenic
Rivers Act of 1968
Cross Florida Barge Canal, 144

HARVARD UNIVERSITY

http://lib.harvard.edu

If the ~~item~~ is recalled, the borrower will
be notified of the ~~need for~~ an earlier return.

Thank you for helping us to preserve our collection!